	a	i	u	e	o
ky	キャ kya		キュ kyu		キョ kyo
sh	シャ sha		シュ shu	シェ she	ショ sho
ch	チャ cha		チュ chu	チェ che	チョ cho
ny	ニャ nya		ニュ nyu		ニョ nyo
hy	ヒャ hya		ヒュ hyu		ヒョ hyo
my	ミャ mya		ミュ myu		ミョ myo
ry	リャ rya		リュ ryu		リョ ryo
gy	ギャ gya		ギュ gyu		ギョ gyo
j	ジャ ja		ジュ ju	ジェ je	ジョ jo
by	ビャ bya		ビュ byu		ビョ byo
py	ピャ pya		ピュ pyu		ピョ pyo

	a	i	u	e	o
w		ウィ wi		ウェ we	ウォ wo
ts	ツァ tsa	ツィ tsi		ツェ tse	ツォ tso
t		ティ ti			
f	ファ fa	フィ fi	フュ fyu	フェ fe	フォ fo
d		ディ di	デュ dyu		
v	ヴァ va	ヴィ vi	ヴ vu	ヴェ ve	ヴォ vo

Katakana カタカナ

	a	*i*	*u*	*e*	*o*
	ア *a*	イ *i*	ウ *u*	エ *e*	オ *o*
k	カ *ka*	キ *ki*	ク *ku*	ケ *ke*	コ *ko*
s	サ *sa*	シ *shi*	ス *su*	セ *se*	ソ *so*
t	タ *ta*	チ *chi*	ツ *tsu*	テ *te*	ト *to*
n	ナ *na*	ニ *ni*	ヌ *nu*	ネ *ne*	ノ *no*
h	ハ *ha*	ヒ *hi*	フ *fu*	ヘ *he*	ホ *ho*
m	マ *ma*	ミ *mi*	ム *mu*	メ *me*	モ *mo*
y	ヤ *ya*		ユ *yu*		ヨ *yo*
r	ラ *ra*	リ *ri*	ル *ru*	レ *re*	ロ *ro*
w	ワ *wa*				ヲ *o*
	ン *n*				

g	ガ *ga*	ギ *gi*	グ *gu*	ゲ *ge*	ゴ *go*
z	ザ *za*	ジ *ji*	ズ *zu*	ゼ *ze*	ゾ *zo*
d	ダ *da*	ヂ *ji*	ヅ *zu*	デ *de*	ド *do*
b	バ *ba*	ビ *bi*	ブ *bu*	ベ *be*	ボ *bo*
p	パ *pa*	ピ *pi*	プ *pu*	ペ *pe*	ポ *po*

初級日本語

〔げんき〕

GENKI

SECOND EDITION

AN INTEGRATED COURSE IN
ELEMENTARY JAPANESE

げんき

〔第2版〕

II

Eri Banno　坂野永理

Yoko Ikeda　池田庸子

Yutaka Ohno　大野裕

Chikako Shinagawa　品川恭子

Kyoko Tokashiki　渡嘉敷恭子

The Japan Times

付属ディスクについて
付属のディスクには、MP3 形式のデジタル音声ファイルが収録されています。
コンピューターやデジタルオーディオ機器で再生してください。
CD プレーヤーでは再生できませんので、ご注意ください。

Note on the accompanying disk
The disk that comes with this book contains digital audio files in MP3 format.
The files can be played on computers or digital audio players, but not on CD players.

First edition: October 1999
Second edition: October 2011
9th printing: May 2013

JASRAC 出1110931-305
Illustrations: Noriko Udagawa and Reiko Maruyama
English translations and copyreading: 4M Associates, Inc., and Umes Corp.
Narrators: Miho Nagahori, Yumiko Muro, Tomoki Kusumi, Tsuyoshi Yokoyama,
          and Kit Pancoast Nagamura
Recordings: TBS Service, Inc.
Typesetting: guild
Cover art and editorial design: Nakayama Design Office
                    Gin-o Nakayama and Akihito Kaneko
Printing: Tosho Printing Co., Ltd.

Published by The Japan Times, Ltd.
5-4, Shibaura 4-chome, Minato-ku, Tokyo 108-0023, Japan
Phone: 03-3453-2013
Website: http://bookclub.japantimes.co.jp/
Genki-Online: http://genki.japantimes.co.jp/

ISBN978-4-7890-1443-4

Printed in Japan

はじめに

　本書は 1999 年に刊行された『初級日本語 げんき』の改訂版です。初版以来、多くの先生方や学習者の方々に使用していただき、増刷を重ねてきましたが、この度、改訂版を刊行することとなりました。

　『げんき』は 1999 年、日本語教師にとって「教えやすい」、学習者にとって「学びやすい」教科書を目指して、学習者のニーズ調査をもとに作成し、何度も試用しながら細部にわたる改訂を重ねた末に出版しました。もともと日本で日本語を学習する留学生を対象に作成した教材でしたが、その後、日本だけでなく海外でも広く使用されるようになりました。それに伴い、「もっと文化情報がほしい」「教科書に音声教材をつけてほしい」など、いろいろなご意見、ご要望が寄せられるようになりました。また、初版刊行から 10 年以上が経ち、語彙等にも改訂の必要が出てきていました。

　この改訂版では、『げんき』の特長である「教えやすさ」はそのままに、私たちの経験や皆様の声を反映させて、新しい内容の追加、改訂を行いました。改訂作業には 2 年の歳月を要しましたが、今までよりもさらに教えやすく学びやすい教材になったと自負しています。

　改訂版の作成にあたっては、『げんき』を使用してくださっている多くの先生方や学習者の方々の貴重なご意見が、大きな原動力となりました。心より感謝いたします。また、今や『げんき』のトレードマークになっているイラストを描いてくださった宇田川のり子さん、ジャパンタイムズの皆様、そしてだれよりも、初版作成時からずっと労を注いでくださったジャパンタイムズ出版局の関戸千明さんに、著者一同心より感謝いたします。

　この新しい『げんき』で、いっそう楽しく日本語を学んでいただけることを願っています。

2011 年 9 月　著者一同

Preface

This is a revised edition of the textbook *GENKI: An Integrated Course in Elementary Japanese*, which was published in 1999. Since it first came out, *GENKI* has become widely used by teachers and students of Japanese and has gone through numerous reprintings. Such wide acceptance led to the decision to publish this revised edition.

In 1999, our aim was to develop a textbook that teachers would find convenient and helpful, and one that students could easily use. We thus wrote the book based on a survey of students' needs and refined it through many test-teaching situations. Originally meant as a text for foreign students studying in Japan, *GENKI* gained popularity among those studying in other countries as well. As use increased, we began to hear from those who wanted "more information on culture" and "audio aids appended to the text." It's also been more than ten years since *GENKI* was originally published, and the passage of time has required revisions to vocabulary and expressions.

While retaining the ease-of-use quality for teachers, we have added new content and revisions that reflect our experiences and the voices of those who have used the text. The task of revision took two years to complete. We believe that this effort has resulted in a book that instructors and students will find even easier to use and learn from.

The opinions of the teachers and students who have used *GENKI* have been a major driving force in the preparation of this revised edition. We are truly grateful to those who have provided this input. The authors would also like to express their sincere appreciation to the following: Noriko Udagawa, our illustrator, whose work has become a *GENKI* trademark; the staff of The Japan Times; and particularly to Chiaki Sekido of the Publications Department of The Japan Times, who has worked tirelessly with us on this project since its inception.

It is our hope that students of the language will find additional pleasure in learning Japanese by using this new edition of *GENKI*.

The Authors
September 2011

初級日本語 [げんき] II

もくじ

会話・文法編
かい わ　ぶん ぽう へん

読み書き編
よみかきへん

巻末
かん まつ

本書について

Ⅰ 対象とねらい

　『初級日本語 げんき』は初めて日本語を学ぶ人のための教科書です。第Ⅰ巻・第Ⅱ巻の2冊、全23課で初級日本語の学習を修了します。大学生はもとより、高校生や社会人、日本語を独習しようとしている人も、効果的に日本語が習得できます。文法の説明などは英語で書いてあるので、英語がある程度わかることを前提としています。

　『初級日本語 げんき』は総合教材として、日本語の四技能（聞く・話す・読む・書く）を伸ばし、総合的な日本語の能力を高めていくことを目標としています。正確に文を作ることができても流暢さがなかったり、流暢ではあっても簡単なことしか言えないということがないように、言語の習得の目標とすべき「正確さ」「流暢さ」「複雑さ」がバランスよく高められるように配慮してあります。

Ⅱ 改訂版について

　今回の改訂版では、以下の点を中心に改訂を加えました。

1. Culture Noteの追加

　学習者が日本に関する知識を得られるように、「会話・文法編」の各課に「Culture Note」という項目を新しく設け、日本文化や生活についての情報を提供しました。

2. 音声をテキスト・ワークブックそれぞれに付属

　これまで別売としていた音声教材をMP3形式でテキストに付けるとともに、ワークブックで使用する「聞く練習」の音声はワークブックに付け、より使いやすくしました。また、テキスト「読み書き編」各課の読み教材も、今回新たに収録しました。

3. 語彙・表現の見直し

　語彙や表現を細かく見直し、「カセットテープ」「LL」などあまり使われなくなったものは削除して、より使用頻度の高いものを入れました。

4. 文法・練習・読み物の改訂

　「文法」では、各課で扱う文法項目に変更はありません。その中で、よりわかりやすくなるよう、細部にわたり加筆・修正しています。

　また、形容詞・名詞文の否定形「～くありません／～じゃありません」と「～なくちゃいけ

ません」の２つの表現は、日常の場面でより使用されている「〜くないです／〜じゃないです」「〜なければいけません／〜なきゃいけません」に変更しました。

「練習」は、各文法項目に対して十分な練習ができるように、会話形式などのコミュニカティブな練習をさらに増やしました。また、読み書き編の読み物についても、内容が古くなった部分には変更を加え、日本の現状に合わせました。

Ⅲ テキストの構成

テキストは大きく「会話・文法編」「読み書き編」「巻末」から構成されています。以下、順番に説明します。

A▶会話・文法編

「会話・文法編」では、基本的な文法を学び、語彙を増やしながら、「話すこと」「聞くこと」について学習します。「会話・文法編」の各課は以下の部分から構成されています。

●会話

「会話」は、日本に来た留学生とその友人・家族を中心に展開し、学習者が日常生活で経験しそうなさまざまな場面から成っています。会話文を通して、学習者は「あいづち」などを含めた自然なやりとりに触れ、会話の中で文と文がどのようにつながっていくか、どのような部分が省略されたりするかなどを学ぶことができます。「会話」には、その課で学ぶ新しい学習項目が多く含まれているため、課の初めに学習者がこれを読むと非常に難しいと感じるかもしれません。これらの項目は練習を通して定着が図られるので、初めは難しくてもあまり心配しないようにしてください。

また、「会話」は付属の音声教材（MP3形式）で聞くことができます。学習者には、音声教材を聞いて、発音やイントネーションなどに気をつけながら、くり返して言う練習をすることを勧めます。

●単語

「単語」には、その課の「会話」と「練習」に出てくる新しい単語がまとめてあります。この中で、「会話」に出てくる単語には＊印が付けてあります。第１課と第２課では機能別に単語を提示し、第３課からは品詞別に提示してあります。また、巻末には全課の単語を収録した「さくいん」があります。

「単語」の中の言葉はその後の課でもくり返し出てきますから、学習者は毎日少しずつ覚えるようにしたほうがいいでしょう。付属の音声教材には単語とその英語訳が入っていますか

ら、それを聞きながら覚えることもできます。第3課から、単語には漢字を併記してありますが、この漢字は覚える必要はありません。

なお、このテキストでは語のアクセント（拍の高低）を示していません。日本語のアクセントは地域差や個人差（世代間の差など）が激しい上に、語形変化や単語の連結などによる変化も複雑です。ですから、単語のアクセントにはあまり神経質になる必要はありません。

●文法

文法説明は、独習している人も容易に理解できるように、説明の平易さを心がけました。また、教室で学んでいる学習者はあらかじめ文法説明を読んでから授業に臨んでください。

後の「練習」で取りあげられている項目はすべて「文法」の中で説明してあります。練習はしないが説明が必要な文法や語彙については、「文法」の最後の「表現ノート」に随時まとめてあります。

●練習

「練習」は、各学習項目に関して基本練習から応用練習へと段階的に配列してあり、学習者がこれらの練習を順番にこなしていくことによって、無理なく日本語が習得できるように配慮してあります。

答えが一つに決められるような基本練習は付属の音声教材にも録音されており、[🔊] の印がついています。音声教材には解答も録音されていますから、学習者は各自で自習することが可能です。

また、「練習」の最後には「まとめの練習」があります。これは複数の学習項目を組み合わせた練習や「会話」を応用して別の会話を作る練習など、その課の仕上げとなる練習です。

●Culture Note

各課に「Culture Note」というコラムを設け、日本の文化や生活習慣などについて説明しています。「家族の呼び方」など言語に密接に関連した事項から、「日本の気候」など生活に密着した情報まで、幅広い分野が扱われています。学習者は、この説明を出発点にして、インターネットで情報収集をしたり、身近な日本人と話したりして、理解を深めていくことが期待されます。

●Useful Expressions

課の最後に必要に応じて、テーマごとに単語や表現を集めた「Useful Expressions」を設けてあります。ここには、第1課の「じかん・とし」のようにその課のトピックに関連した表現や、第10課の「駅で」のように場面ごとに使われる表現をまとめました。これらの単語も、巻末の「さくいん」に載せてあります。

B▶読み書き編

「読み書き編」では、日本語の文字を学び、文章を読んだり書いたりすることによって、読解力と書く力を伸ばします。第1課でひらがな、第2課でカタカナを学習した後、第3課以降で漢字を学習します。第3課以降の各課は、以下のような構成です。

●漢字表

漢字表には、その課で学ぶ新出漢字が掲載されています。各課で約15の漢字を学びますが、一度に覚えるには無理があるので、毎日少しずつ覚えていくようにしてください。漢字表は以下のようになっています。

① 漢字の通し番号
② 漢字　③ 漢字の読み方　⑤ この漢字を含んだ単語

017

| 本 | ▶ ほん
▷ もと

(book; basis) | 本 (ほん) book　　日本 (にほん) Japan
日本語 (にほんご) Japanese language
山本さん (やまもとさん) Mr./Ms. Yamamoto
(5) 一　十　オ　木　本 |

④ 漢字の意味　⑦ 筆順
⑥ 総画数

③に示された漢字の読み方で、▶は「音読み」、つまり昔の中国語の発音を輸入したものであることを示します。▷は「訓読み」、つまり日本語古来の読みです。音読みも訓読みも、単語の中で使われた時、音が変化する場合があります。(たとえば、「学」という漢字は「ガク」と読みますが、「学校」という単語の中では「ガッ」と読みます。) そのような派生的な読み方もこの部分に表記されています。

なお、漢字の中には多くの読み方を持っているものもありますが、漢字表には、初級レベルにふさわしい読みを中心に挙げています。

③と⑤で　　　の中に入っている読み方や単語は、その課で覚えるべきものです。一方、　　　以外のものは参考として挙げたもので、覚えなくてもかまいません。

それぞれの漢字は、ワークブックの読み書き編の中に練習シートがありますので、テキストの漢字表に示された筆順を見ながら何度も練習してください。

●練習

『げんきⅠ』には、漢字の練習、読解本文と内容についての質問、そして書く練習があります。漢字の練習は、漢字を分解してできる部品から漢字を再構築する問題や漢字から単語を作る問題など、さまざまな練習を通じて漢字に慣れていくことを目標としています。読解本文は、短

く、親しみやすいものを中心に構成しています。それまでに「会話・文法編」で学んだ文法や単語の知識が前提とされており、新出単語はその都度、単語表を掲載しています。練習の最後には、書く練習としての作文トピックが提示されています。

『げんきⅡ』には、読解本文と内容についての質問、そして書く練習があります。読解本文は、手紙、物語、エッセイ、広告など、さまざまな分野の日本語を取り上げています。その課までに学んだ単語や文法、漢字の知識が前提とされており、課を追うごとに、長さや難易度などが増していきます。新出単語も本文での出現順に掲載されています。練習の最後には、作文トピックが提示されています。

なお、今回の改訂版では、第Ⅰ巻・第Ⅱ巻とも、新たに読解本文も音声教材に収録しました。📢のついているものは、付属の音声教材（MP3形式）で聞くことができます。

C▶巻末

第Ⅰ巻・第Ⅱ巻それぞれの巻末に「さくいん」を準備しました。一つは和英さくいんで、各課の単語表や Useful Expressions に掲載されている単語を五十音順に再録しました（「Culture Note」の語彙は含みません）。単語に付された数字は、その単語が導入された課の番号を示しています。英和さくいんでは、各課の単語が訳語のアルファベット順に再録されています。今回の改訂版では、各動詞に [*ru*] [*u*] [irr.] の記号を表示して、どのグループに属する動詞かわかるようにしました。

その他に、全県名リスト付きの日本地図、および数字と助数詞の音の変化をまとめた表と動詞の活用表を掲載しました。

Ⅳ 表記と書体について

本文は基本的に、漢字仮名交じりで表記しています。漢字表記は、基本的に常用漢字表に従いましたが、常用漢字に含まれている漢字でも、初級の学習者には無縁であるようなものは、ひらがな表記にしてあります。

また、「会話・文法編」のみを学習することも可能なように、「会話・文法編」では漢字にはすべてふりがなが振ってあります。

ただし、「会話・文法編」冒頭の「あいさつ」と第1課、第2課は、学習者の負担を軽減し自習を容易にするため、ひらがな・カタカナ表記とし、ローマ字を併記しました。このローマ字併記はあくまでも補助的なものですから、最初から頼りすぎないように心がけてください。ひらがなは「読み書き編」の第1課で、カタカナは第2課で、それぞれ学習します。

なお、「読み書き編」では、漢字を第3課以降に学習していきますが、学習の定着が図れるよう、既習の漢字にはふりがなが振ってありません。

　本文の日本語は、ほとんどが「教科書体」の書体で組まれています。教科書体は手書き文字に近い書体ですから、学習者は自分が書く文字のモデルとすることができます。ただし、実際に印刷された日本語文では、さまざまな書体を見ることがあります。文字によっては、書体によってかなり形が異なります。特に離れた二つの線が筆づかいによって一つにつながる場合があるので、注意が必要です。

例：	教科書体	明朝体	ゴシック体	手書き文字
	さ	さ	**さ**	さ
	き	き	**き**	き
	り	り	**り**	り
	ら	ら	**ら**	ら
	こ	こ	**こ**	こ
	や	や	**や**	や

||| Introduction

 I Aim and purpose

GENKI: An Integrated Course in Elementary Japanese is a textbook for beginners in the study of the Japanese language. Students can complete the elementary-level study of Japanese in the 23 lessons of this text, which is divided into two volumes. The book is designed mainly for use in university courses, but is also effective for high school students and adults who are beginning to learn Japanese either at school or on their own. Hopefully, students will have at least a basic knowledge of English, because grammar explanations are given in English.

GENKI: An Integrated Course in Elementary Japanese is a comprehensive approach to developing the four basic language skills (listening, speaking, reading, and writing), which aims to cultivate overall Japanese-language ability. Emphasis has been placed on balancing accuracy, fluency, and complexity so that students using the material will not end up speaking accurately yet in a stilted manner, or fluently but employing only simple grammatical structures.

II Revised edition

The revised edition features changes in four major areas.

1. Addition of Culture Notes
Each lesson now contains a "Culture Note," which is designed to enhance students' knowledge of Japan through information on Japanese culture and daily life.

2. Audio material bundled with text and workbook
Audio aids, which had previously been sold separately, have now been added to the textbook and workbook in MP3 format. The addition of audio material for the workbook's "Listening Comprehension" exercises is especially convenient. We have also recorded the readings from the Reading and Writing section of the book.

3. Vocabulary and expressions
We rigorously reviewed the vocabulary and expressions to replace words, such as "cassette

tape" and "LL" that are no longer in common use, with words and phrases that students will encounter more frequently.

4. Grammar, practice and readings

While no changes were made to the grammatical topics introduced in each lesson, we supplemented the text and/or made the necessary corrections to make the material even easier to understand.

In the revised edition, we have replaced the negative forms of adjective and noun phrases *-ku arimasen/-ja arimasen* and *-nakucha ikemasen*, meaning "must," with the *-ku nai desu/ -ja nai desu* and *-nakereba ikemasen/-nakya ikemasen* forms, which are more commonly used in everyday life.

We also increased communicative practice material—mainly dialogues—so that students would be given sufficient opportunity to practice the grammar that they learn. Moreover, we have updated the readings in the Reading and Writing section to make them more relevant to the Japan of today.

Ⅲ   Structure of the textbook

This textbook basically consists of three sections: Conversation and Grammar, Reading and Writing, and the Appendix. A detailed explanation of each part follows.

A ▶ Conversation and Grammar

The Conversation and Grammar section aims at improving students' speaking and listening abilities by having them learn basic grammar and by increasing their vocabulary. The Conversation and Grammar section of each lesson is organized as follows:

● Dialogue

The dialogues revolve around the lives of foreign students living in Japan and their friends and families, presenting various scenes that students are likely to face in their daily lives. By practicing natural expressions and *aizuchi* (responses that make conversations go smoothly), students are able to understand how sentences are connected and how some phrases are shortened in daily conversation. Because the Dialogue section of each lesson covers a lot of new grammar and vocabulary, students may feel it is too difficult to understand at first. Don't be overly concerned, however, because the grammar and vocabulary will gradually take root with practice.

Students can listen to dialogues on the accompanying audio aids (in MP3 format). Students are encouraged to practice regularly by listening to the audio and carefully noting pronunciation and intonation.

● Vocabulary

The Vocabulary section presents all the new words encountered in both the Dialogue and Practice sections of each lesson. Words that appear in the Dialogue are marked with an asterisk (*). Words are listed according to their function in Lessons 1 and 2, and by parts of speech in Lesson 3 and all subsequent lessons. In addition, all words presented in the text are also found in the Index at the end of each volume.

Words found in the Vocabulary section of each lesson appear frequently in subsequent lessons, thus encouraging students to learn little by little each day. The new words, along with their English translations, also appear in the audio material, which enables students to absorb through listening. Starting with Lesson 3, the Vocabulary section also gives the kanji rendering, but students are not required to memorize the kanji orthography.

This textbook does not indicate a word's accents. The accent of a Japanese word varies considerably, depending on region, the speaker's age (including the generation gap between speakers), the word's inflections, and its connection with other words in the sentence. Therefore, there is no need to be overly concerned about accent, but try to imitate as closely as possible the intonation heard on the accompanying audio aids.

● Grammar

Easy-to-understand grammar explanations are provided so that even those studying on their own can easily follow. Students at school should read the explanations before each class.

All grammar items covered in the lesson's Practice section are explained in the Grammar section. Grammar and vocabulary that require explanation but are not practiced are summarized in the Expression Notes section at the end of each Grammar section.

● Practice

For each grammar point covered, Practice sections provide drills that advance in stages from basic practice to application. The intent is to enable students to gain a grasp of Japanese naturally by completing the drills in the order presented.

Basic exercises that call for a single predetermined answer are marked with a 🔊 and recorded with their answers on the audio aids, thus allowing students to practice and learn on their own.

The last part of the Practice section contains Review Exercises that help summarize what has been learned. For example, some exercises combine various topics covered in the lesson, while others require students to create dialogues by applying what was learned in the Dialogue section.

● Culture Note

We have integrated a Culture Note section into each lesson, where we explain aspects of the culture and everyday life of Japan. These notes cover a wide variety of topics, ranging from matters closely linked to language, such as kinship terms, to information deeply ingrained in daily life, such as the Japanese climate. Our hope is that these comments will serve as a springboard for students to deepen their understanding of Japanese culture even further by taking steps of their own, such as by gathering information from the Internet or by discussing the topics with their Japanese friends.

● Useful Expressions

When necessary, we include sections on Useful Expressions at the end of the lessons in order to present supplementary vocabulary and phrases. These sections list expressions that are related to the lesson's topic (as in "Time and Age" in Lesson 1) or to particular situations (as in "At the Station" in Lesson 10). The vocabulary introduced in Useful Expressions is also listed in the index of each volume.

B ▶ Reading and Writing

The Reading and Writing section aims to foster comprehension and writing ability through the study of Japanese characters and through practice in both reading and writing. After learning *hiragana* in Lesson 1 and *katakana* in Lesson 2, students begin studying kanji in Lesson 3. Each lesson after Lesson 3 is organized as follows:

● Kanji list

The list contains the new kanji introduced in each lesson. Students are exposed to about 15 new characters in each lesson. Since it is probably not feasible to learn all of these at once, we encourage students to tackle a few each day. We have formatted each kanji list as follows.

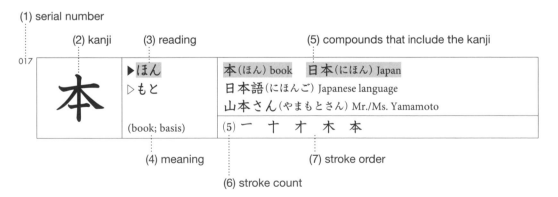

The ▶ mark appearing next to readings in item (3) indicates the *on-yomi*, or the reading of the character that was imported from China. The ▷ mark indicates the *kun-yomi*, or the native Japanese reading. The sound of *on-yomi* and *kun-yomi* may change when the kanji is used in certain words. For example, the ordinary pronunciation of 学 is *gaku*, but this becomes *gak* when the kanji is used in the word 学校 (*gakkoo*). Such derivative readings are also included in the readings section.

Although some kanji have many readings, we include principally those readings that are appropriate for an elementary level course.

Readings and words that are shaded should be memorized. The others are for reference, so students don't need to memorize them. The Reading and Writing section of the workbook includes practice sheets for the kanji learned in each lesson. Students should practice writing the kanji repeatedly, following the stroke order shown on the kanji list in the textbook.

● Practice

GENKI I consists of kanji practice, readings for comprehension, questions about the content of the readings, and writing practice. Kanji practice is aimed at getting students accustomed to kanji through practice in various forms, such as reconstructing kanji from their component parts or making new words by combining kanji. Readings for comprehension are generally short and deal with subjects familiar to the students. They assume knowledge of the vocabulary and grammar that the student has learned in the Conversation and Grammar section. New words that appear in the readings are listed. At the end of each Practice section, we suggest topics for students to write on.

GENKI II contains readings for comprehension, questions about the content of the readings, and writing practice. The readings introduce Japanese as it is used in a variety of areas, ranging from letters and fables to essays and advertisements. They assume knowledge of the vocabulary and grammar that the student has encountered in the lesson so far, and with each lesson the readings become longer and more difficult. New words in the readings are listed in the order in which they appear. At the end of each Practice section, we suggest topics for students to write on.

We provide recordings of these readings in both Volumes I and II of the revised edition. These are denoted by a ⏴⏵ mark. Students can listen to them through the accompanying audio aids (in MP3 format).

C ▶ Appendix

The Appendix of Volumes I and II contains an Index. The Japanese-English Index, in *hiragana* order, lists words and expressions from the Vocabulary and Useful Expression sections of each lesson (the index does not contain the vocabulary used in Culture Notes). The number next to a word indicates the lesson in which the word was introduced. In the English-Japanese Index, English equivalents to Japanese words are arranged in alphabetical order. In both indexes of this revised edition, verbs are indicated with [*ru*] [*u*] [irr.], to show which verb group they belong to.

Also included in the Appendix are a map of Japan with the names of all the prefectures, a table of changes in the sounds of numbers and counters, and a table of verb conjugations.

Ⅳ Orthography and font

The basic text is written in kanji and *hiragana*. In the case of kanji, we follow the official Joyo Kanji list. However, *hiragana* is used instead when the Joyo Kanji equivalent is deemed unnecessary for beginning students of Japanese.

The pronunciation of every kanji in the Conversation and Grammar section is indicated in *hiragana* so that this section can be studied alone. To lessen the burden on the students and allow them to study on their own, however, the "Greetings" unit and Lessons 1 and 2 are written in *hiragana* and *katakana*, alongside which the same statement is presented in romanization. The romanizations are purely for supplemental purposes and students should avoid relying on them too much. Students study *hiragana* and *katakana* in Lessons 1 and 2, respectively, of the Reading and Writing section.

Students begin studying kanji in Lesson 3 of the Reading and Writing section. To encourage students to maintain a firm grasp of the kanji they have learned, the Reading and Writing section does not provide *hiragana* readings for kanji that have already been introduced.

The Japanese in the basic text is set mainly in the Textbook font, which resembles handwriting and serves as a good model for students. Students will encounter a variety of fonts used for Japanese materials, however, and should be aware that the shape of some characters differs considerably, depending on the font used. Note especially that in certain fonts two separate strokes may merge into a single stroke because they mimic the characters produced by a writing brush.

Example:	Textbook font	Mincho font	Gothic font	Handwriting
	さ	さ	さ	さ
	き	き	き	き
	り	り	り	り
	ら	ら	ら	ら
	こ	こ	こ	こ
	や	や	や	や

会話・文法編
かい　わ　ぶん　ぽう　へん
Conversation and Grammar Section

第13課 | L E S S O N ⋯⋯⋯⋯ 13
アルバイト探し Looking for a Part-time Job
さが

会 話 Dialogue
かい わ

Ⅰ John calls the restaurant Little Asia. 🔊 K13-01/02

1 店 長： はい、「リトル・アジア」です。
てん ちょう

2 ジョン： 私、ジョン・ワンと申します。アルバイト募集の広告を見たんですが。
わたくし　　　　　　　　もう　　　　　　　　ぼ しゅう こうこく み

3 店 長： そうですか。じゃあ、会って、話しましょうか。今日店に来られますか。
てん ちょう　　　　　　　　　　　　あ　　　はな　　　　　　きょうみせ こ

4 ジョン： 今日はちょっと行けないんですが、あしたなら行けると思います。
きょう い　　　　　　　　　　　　　　　い　　　　おも

5 店 長： そうですか。今日はだめですか。じゃあ、あしたの一時ごろはどうですか。
てん ちょう　　　　　　きょう　　　　　　　　　　　　　　いちじ

6 ジョン： 一時ですね。わかりました。
いちじ

Ⅱ At the restaurant. 🔊 K13-03/04

1 店 長： ワンさんはどうしてこのアルバイトに興味があるんですか。
てん ちょう　　　　　　　　　　　　　　　　　きょう み

2 ジョン： おもしろそうですから。いろいろな人に会えるし、日本語も使えるし。
ひと あ　　　　　にほんご つか

3 店 長： レストランで働いたことがありますか。
てん ちょう　　　　　はたら

4 ジョン： はい。ウエイターならしたことがあります。

5 店 長： あしたから始められますか。
てん ちょう　　　　はじ

6 ジョン： はい。よろしくお願いします。
ねが

7 店 長： がんばってください。
てん ちょう

Ⅲ Professor Yamashita comes to Little Asia. 🔊 K13-05/06

1 ジョン： いらっしゃいませ。あ、山下先生。
やましたせんせい

2 山下先生： ジョンさん。ここでアルバイトをしているんですか。
やましたせんせい

3 ジョン： ええ。一週間に三日働いています。
いっしゅうかん みっか はたら

4 山下先生： そうですか。どれがおいしいですか。
やましたせんせい

5 ジョン：　　　このカレーが一番人気がありますよ。
　　　　　　　　　いちばんにん き
6 山下先生：　　おいしそうですね。じゃあ、食べてみます。
　　やましたせんせい　　　　　　　　　　　　　　　た

 I

Manager: Yes, this is Little Asia.

John: My name is John Wang. I saw your classified ad.

Manager: I see. Well, shall we meet and have a talk? Can you come to the store today?

John: I cannot come today, but if it's tomorrow, I think I can come.

Manager: I see. Today is no good . . . All right. How about one o'clock tomorrow?

John: One o'clock. Okay, I've got it.

II

Manager: Mr. Wang, why are you interested in this job?

John: It seems interesting. I can meet various people; I can also use Japanese . . .

Manager: Have you worked at a restaurant before?

John: Yes. As a waiter, I have.

Manager: Can you start tomorrow?

John: Yes. I'll do my best.

Manager: Good luck.

III

John: Welcome. Oh, Professor Yamashita.

Prof. Yamashita: John, do you work here?

John: Yes. I work three days a week.

Prof. Yamashita: I see. Which one is good?

John: This curry is the most popular one.

Prof. Yamashita: It looks good. Well, I will try this one.

単語
たん　　ご

 K13-07

V o c a b u l a r y

N o u n s

* ウエイター		waiter
おたく	お宅	(someone's) house/home
おとな	大人	adult
がいこくご	外国語	foreign language
がっき	楽器	musical instrument
からて	空手	karate
* カレー		curry
きもの	着物	kimono; Japanese traditional dress
* こうこく	広告	advertisement
こうちゃ	紅茶	tea (black tea)
ことば	言葉	language
ゴルフ		golf
セーター		sweater
ぞう	象	elephant
バイオリン		violin
バイク		motorcycle
ぶっか	物価	(consumer) prices
ぶんぽう	文法	grammar
べんごし	弁護士	lawyer
* ぼしゅう	募集	recruitment
* みせ	店	shop; store
やくざ		*yakuza*; gangster
やくそく	約束	promise; appointment
レポート		(term) paper
* わたくし	私	I (formal)

い - a d j e c t i v e s

うれしい		glad
かなしい	悲しい	sad
からい	辛い	hot and spicy; salty
きびしい	厳しい	strict
すごい		incredible; awesome
ちかい	近い	close; near

* Words that appear in the dialogue

な-adjectives

* いろいろ（な）		various; different kinds of
しあわせ（な）	幸せ	happy (lasting happiness)
* だめ（な）		no good

U-verbs

あむ	編む	to knit（〜を）
かす	貸す	to lend; to rent
		(*person* に *thing* を)
* がんばる	頑張る	to do one's best; to try hard
なく	泣く	to cry
みがく	磨く	to brush (teeth); to polish（〜を）
やくそくをまもる	約束を守る	to keep a promise

Irregular Verb

かんどうする	感動する	to be moved/touched (by . . .)
		（〜に）

Adverbs and Other Expressions

いらっしゃいます		(someone honorable) is present/ home
〜かい	〜回	. . . times
〜キロ		. . . kilometers; . . . kilograms
じつは	実は	as a matter of fact, . . .
ぜんぶ	全部	all
* 〜ともうします	〜と申します	my name is . . .

Numbers (used to count days)

いちにち	一日	one day
ふつか	二日	two days
* みっか	三日	three days
よっか	四日	four days
いつか	五日	five days
むいか	六日	six days
なのか	七日	seven days
ようか	八日	eight days
ここのか	九日	nine days
とおか	十日	ten days

文法 G r a m m a r
ぶん ぽう

1　Potential Verbs

We use the potential verb to say that someone "can," or "has the ability to," do something, or that something is "possible."

We make potential verbs using the rules listed below:

> *ru*-verbs: Drop the final -*ru* and add -*rareru*.
> 　見る (*mi-ru*)　→　見られる (*mi-rareru*)
> 　み　　　　　　　　み
> *u*-verbs: Drop the final -*u* and add -*eru*.
>
> | | | | | | |
> |---|---|---|---|---|---|
> | 行く (*ik-u*) | → | 行ける (*ik-eru*) | 待つ | → | 待てる |
> | 話す | → | 話せる | 読む | → | 読める |
> | 買う | → | 買える | 死ぬ | → | 死ねる |
> | 泳ぐ | → | 泳げる | 取る | → | 取れる |
> | 遊ぶ | → | 遊べる | | | |
>
> irregular verbs:
> 　くる　　　　　→　　　　こられる　　　　　する　→　　できる

You may note that the potential forms of *ru*-verbs are considerably longer than those of the *u*-verbs, which happen to end in the *hiragana* る. (Compare 見られる and 取れる in the above list.) There actually are shorter, alternative potential forms of *ru*-verbs and the irregular verb くる, which are made by adding the suffix -*reru*, instead of -*rareru*. These *ra*-less forms are gaining popularity especially among young speakers, but are considered slightly substandard.

			potential forms	*ra*-less potential forms
ru-verbs:	出る	→	出られる	出れる
	見る	→	見られる	見れる
irregular verb:	くる	→	こられる	これる

Potential verbs themselves conjugate as regular *ru*-verbs.

私は日本語が話せます。
わたし　にほんご　はな
I can speak Japanese.

私は<u>泳げないんです</u>。
(The truth is) I cannot swim.

雨が降ったので、海に<u>行けませんでした</u>。
We could not go to the beach, because it rained.

The table below summarizes the conjugation pattern of potential verbs.[1]

	short forms		long forms	
	affirmative	negative	affirmative	negative
present	見られる	見られない	見られます	見られません
past	見られた	見られなかった	見られました	見られませんでした
te-form	見られて			

Those verbs that take the particle を can take either を or が when they have been made into the potential. できる, the potential counterpart of the verb する, is somewhat special, and takes が almost all the time. All particles other than を remain the same when the verb is turned into the potential.

verbs with を：
　　漢字<u>を</u>読む　→　漢字<u>が</u>読める　or　漢字<u>を</u>読める
する—できる：
　　仕事<u>を</u>する　→　仕事<u>が</u>できる　（仕事<u>を</u>できる is considered substandard.）
verbs with particles other than を：
　　山に登る　→　山に登れる　（No particle change involved.）

2　〜し

To give the reason for something, we can use the conjunction から.

(reason) から、(situation)。

---

[1] You can also express the idea of "can do" using a more complex construction: verb dictionary form ＋ ことができる. This construction is found mostly in the written language. The negative version of the sentence will be dictionary form ＋ ことができない.

　メアリーさんはギターを弾くことができます。　　（Compare: ギターが弾けます）
　Mary can play the guitar.
　このアパートでは犬や猫を飼うことができません。（Compare: 犬や猫が飼えません）
　You cannot keep dogs and cats in this apartment.

Q：どうしてパーティーに来ないんですか。

Why aren't you coming to the party?

A：あした試験があるから、今日は勉強しなきゃいけないんです。

I have to study today, because there will be an exam tomorrow.

When you want to mention not just one but two (or more) reasons, you can use し in place of から. し usually follows a predicate in the short form.

> (reason₁) し、(reason₂) し、(situation)。

日本語はおもしろい<u>し</u>、先生はいい<u>し</u>、私は日本語の授業が大好きです。

I really like my Japanese class, because Japanese language is interesting, and our teacher is good.

友だちが遊びに来た<u>し</u>、彼と電話で話した<u>し</u>、きのうはとてもいい日でした。

Yesterday was a great day—a friend came by, and I talked with my boyfriend on the phone.

Q：国に帰りたいですか。

Do you want to go back home?

A：いいえ、日本の生活は楽しい<u>し</u>、いい友だちがいる<u>し</u>、帰りたくないです。

No. Life here in Japan is good, and I have good friends here. So I don't want to go back.

You can use just one し clause, implying that it is not the only reason for the situation.

物価が安い<u>し</u>、この町の生活は楽です。

Life in this city is an easygoing one. Things are inexpensive, for one thing.

Sometimes the し clauses follow the description of the situation explained.

山下先生はいい先生です。教えるのが上手だ<u>し</u>、親切だ<u>し</u>。

Professor Yamashita is a great teacher. He is good at teaching, and he is kind.

Note that し follows the short forms.[2] In present tense sentences, this means that だ appears with な-adjectives and nouns, but not with い-adjectives.

い-adjectives:	おもしろい<u>し</u>
な-adjectives:	好きだ<u>し</u>
noun ＋です:	学生だ<u>し</u>

3   ～そうです (It looks like . . .)

We add そうです to い- and な-adjective bases to say that something "seemingly" has those properties.[3] When we say ～そうです, we are guessing what something is like on the basis of our impressions.

To form ～そうです sentences with い-adjectives, you drop the final い; with な-adjectives, you just drop な. The only exception is with the い-adjective いい, which will be changed to よさ before そう.

このりんごはおいしそうです。　　　　*This apple looks delicious.*

あしたは天気がよさそうです。　　　　*It looks like the weather will be fine tomorrow.*

メアリーさんは元気そうでした。　　　*It looked like Mary was fine.*

い -adjectives:	おいしい	→	おいしそうです
(exception)	いい	→	よさそうです
な -adjectives:	元気(な)	→	元気そうです

You can use そうです with negative adjectives too. The negative ending ない is changed to なさ before そう.[4]

この本は難しくなさそうです。
This book does not look difficult.

ともこさんはテニスが上手じゃなさそうです。
It does not look like Tomoko is good at tennis.

---

[2] In the very polite speech style, し can also follow the long forms, just like another reason connective から, which may follow long forms (as we learned in Lesson 6) as well as short forms (see Lesson 9).

私は来年も日本語を勉強します。日本が好きですし、日本語はおもしろいですし。
I will study Japanese next year, too. I like Japan, and what is more, the Japanese language is interesting.

[3] You can also use そうです with a verb stem to describe your impression or guess.

このセーターは家で洗えそうです。 (With 洗える, the potential form of 洗う.)
It looks like this sweater is washable at home.

The impression you express may be an event about to happen.

雨が降りそうです。　*It looks like it will rain.*

[4] You can also put the negative on そうです instead of an adjective and say:

この本は難しそうじゃないです。
ともこさんはテニスが上手そうじゃないです。

You can use the adjective ＋ そう combination to qualify a noun. そう is a な-adjective, thus we say そうな before a noun.

暖かそうなセーターを着ています。
She is wearing a warm-looking sweater.

In many そうです sentences, the guesswork is done on the basis of visual impressions. It is wrong, however, to assume that そう is linked only to the visual medium. We use そうです when we lack conclusive evidence. (For example, we say an apple is おいしそう before we have had the chance to taste it. Once we have tasted it, we say おいしい.) With an adjective for which visual evidence is crucial, such as きれいな, we do not use そう and say that something is きれいそうです, if it looks pretty; we already have enough evidence to conclude that it is pretty.

4 ～てみる

You can use the *te*-form of a verb plus the helping verb みる to express the idea of "doing something tentatively," or "trying something." You are not sure what the outcome of your action will be, but do it and see what effect it might have.

漢字がわからなかったので、日本人の友だちに聞いてみました。
I did not know the kanji, so I tried asking a Japanese friend of mine.

友だちがあの店のケーキはおいしいと言っていましたから、今度食べてみます。
My friends say that the cake at the shop is good. I will have a piece one of these days (and see if it really lives up to its reputation).

みる comes from the verb 見る, and conjugates as a regular *ru*-verb. Unlike the main verb 見る, however, ～てみる is always written in *hiragana*.

5 なら

A statement of the form "noun A なら predicate X" says that the predicate X *applies only to A* and is not more generally valid. The main ideas of a なら sentence, in other words, are contrast (as in Situation 1) and limitation (as in Situation 2).

Situation 1

Q：ブラジルに行ったことがありますか。
　　Have you ever been to Brazil?

A：チリなら行ったことがありますが、ブラジルは行ったことがありません。[5]
　　I've been to Chile, but never to Brazil.

Situation 2

Q：日本語がわかりますか。
　　Do you understand Japanese?

A：ひらがなならわかります。
　　If it is (written) in hiragana, yes.

なら introduces a sentence that says something "positive" about the item that is contrasted. In the first situation above, なら puts Chile in a positive light, and in contrast with Brazil, which the question was originally about. In the second situation, a smaller part, namely *hiragana*, is brought up and contrasted with a larger area, namely, the language as a whole.

6　一週間に三回

You can describe the frequency of events over a period of time by using the following framework.

(period) に　(frequency)	(frequency) *per* (period)

私は一週間に三回髪を洗います。　　　　　*I shampoo three times a week.*

私は一か月に一回家族に電話をかけます。　*I call my family once a month.*

父は一年に二回旅行します。　　　　　　　*My father goes on a trip twice a year.*

---

[5] You can optionally keep the particle に before なら in this example. Particles such as に, で, and から may, but do not have to, intervene between the noun and なら, while は, が, and を never go with なら.

表現ノート········1
ひょう げん

ギターを弾く▶Playing musical instruments requires different verbs.
　　ひ

For stringed and keyboard instruments:

ギターを<u>弾く</u> 　　　　ひ	*to play the guitar*
ピアノを<u>弾く</u> 　　　　ひ	*to play the piano*

For wind instruments:

サックスを<u>吹く</u> 　　　　　ふ	*to play the saxophone*

For percussion instruments:

ドラムを<u>たたく</u>	*to play the drum*

Referring to musical instruments in general, やる and できる (for potential) are usually used.

何か楽器が<u>できますか</u>。 なに　がっき	*Can you play any instruments?*
何か楽器を<u>やりますか</u>。 なに　がっき	*Do you play any instruments?*

上手に▶Both い-adjectives and な-adjectives can modify verbs as adverbs. With
じょう ず
い-adjectives, the final い is dropped and く is added. With な-adjectives, に is added.

ロバートさんは料理が上手です。 　　　　　　りょうり　じょうず	*Robert is good at cooking.*
ロバートさんは上手に料理ができます。 　　　　　じょうず　りょうり	*Robert cooks well.*
日本語のクラスは楽しいです。 にほんご　　　　たの	*The Japanese class is fun.*
毎日日本語を楽しく勉強しています。 まいにちにほんご　たの　べんきょう	*I enjoy studying Japanese every day.*

練習 P r a c t i c e

れん しゅう

① 一キロ泳げます

いち およ

A. Change the verbs into the potential forms. 📢 K13-08

Example: たべる → たべられる

1. はなす　3. いく　5. くる　7. やめる　9. のむ　11. およぐ　13. あむ
2. する　　4. ねる　6. みる　8. かりる　10. まつ　12. はたらく

B. Describe the things that Mary can do. 📢 K13-09

Example: メアリーさんは一キロ泳げます。
いち およ

Ex.

1 km

(1) Japanese song

(2)

(3)

(4)

(5)

(6) in Japanese

(7)

(8) sweater

(9) in Japanese

(10) early in the morning

(11) hot bath

C. Pair Work—Ask if your partner can do the above.

Example:　　Ａ：一キロ泳げますか。
　　　　　　Ｂ：はい、泳げます。／いいえ、泳げません。

D. Pair Work—You meet a person on a blind date. To get to know them, ask if they can do the following things and take notes. Add your own questions. After asking the questions, decide if you want to have a date again with them.

Questions	Your partner's information	
speak foreign languages?	Yes / No	(what language?)
drive a car?	Yes / No	(good?)
cook?	Yes / No	(what dish?)
play tennis?	Yes / No	(good?)

E. Pair Work—Ask if your partner could do the following things when they were children. Expand your conversation.

Example:　　泳ぐ
　　　→　　Ａ：子供の時、泳げましたか。
　　　　　　Ｂ：はい、泳げました。
　　　　　　Ａ：どのぐらい泳げましたか。
　　　　　　Ｂ：100 メートルぐらいです。
　　　　　　Ａ：すごいですね。今も 100 メートル泳げますか。
　　　　　　Ｂ：たぶん泳げると思います。

1. 自転車に乗る
2. からい料理を食べる
3. サッカーをする
4. ピアノを弾く
5. 外国語を話す
6. 夜一人でトイレに行く

F.　Answer the questions using the potential verb in the negative.  K13-10

Example:　Q：着物を買いましたか。 (too expensive)
　　　　　　A：いいえ、高すぎて買えませんでした。

1. スリランカ (Sri Lanka) のカレーを食べましたか。 (too spicy)
2. 宿題をしましたか。 (too difficult)
3. 温泉に入りましたか。 (too hot)
4. きのう出かけましたか。 (too busy)
5. 漢字を全部覚えましたか。 (too many)
6. 海で泳ぎましたか。 (too cold)

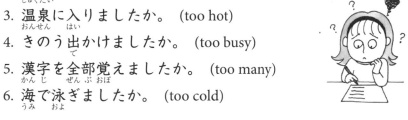

G.　Group Activity—"What Is It?" Game
The class will be divided into two or more groups. The instructor will show the name of a place to the representative of each group. The rest of the group members ask their group representative whether one can do certain things there and guess what place it is. The representative can answer the questions only with はい or いいえ. The first group that gets the correct answer gets a point. Change representatives.

Example:

|図　書　館|
|としょかん|

Sample Questions:　　　　　　　　　Answers:
そこで食べられますか。　→　いいえ。
本が読めますか。　　　　→　はい。
図書館ですか。　　　　　→　そうです。

(Ⅱ) 物価が高いし、人がたくさんいるし

A.　Answer the questions using ～し～し. Examine the ideas in the cues and decide whether you want to answer in the affirmative or in the negative.  K13-11

Example:　Q：日本に住みたいですか。
　　　　　　A：(物価が高いです。人がたくさんいます。)
　　　　　　　→　物価が高いし、人がたくさんいるし、住みたくないです。

1. 今週は忙しいですか。
   （試験があります。宿題がたくさんあります。）

2. 新しいアパートはいいですか。
   （会社に近いです。静かです。）

3. 経済の授業を取りますか。
   （先生は厳しいです。長いレポートを書かなきゃいけません。）

4. 旅行は楽しかったですか。
   （食べ物がおいしくなかったです。言葉がわかりませんでした。）

5. 今晩、パーティーに行きますか。
   （かぜをひいています。きのうもパーティーに行きました。）

6. 日本語の新聞が読めますか。
   （漢字が読めません。文法がわかりません。）

7. 一人で旅行ができますか。
   （日本語が話せます。もう大人です。）

8. 田中さんが好きですか。
   （うそをつきます。約束を守りません。）

B. Answer the following questions and add reasons for your answer.

   Example: Q：日本の生活は楽しいですか。
             A：はい、楽しいです。友だちがたくさんいるし、みんなは親切だし。

1. このごろ忙しいですか。
2. 今、幸せですか。
3. 来学期も日本語の授業を取りますか。
4. 日本に住みたいですか。
5. 日本語の授業は大変ですか。

Ⅲ おいしそうです

A. Describe the following pictures using 〜そう. 🔊 K13-12

Example:　このすしはおいしそうです。

Ex. すし

delicious

(1) ケーキ

sweet

(2) カレー

spicy

(3) 服
<small>ふく</small>

old

(4) 先生
<small>せんせい</small>

strict

(5) 時計
<small>とけい</small>

new

(6) やくざ

scary

(7) 男の人
<small>おとこ　ひと</small>

lonely

(8) 女の人
<small>おんな　ひと</small>

glad

(9) おじいさん

energetic

(10) おばあさん

mean

(11) 女の人
<small>おんな　ひと</small>

kind

(12) 弁護士
<small>べんごし</small>

smart

(13) 学生
<small>がくせい</small>

sleepy

(14) セーター

warm

(15) 子供
<small>こども</small>

sad

B. Look at the pictures in A and make sentences as in the example. K13-13

Example:　すし　→　おいしそうなすしです。

C. Pair Work—Talk about the picture taken at a party using 〜そう.

Example:　Ａ：おいしそうな料理ですね。
　　　　　Ｂ：そうですね。

　　　　　Ａ：この人はうれしそうですね。
　　　　　Ｂ：そうですね。

D. Pair Work—Comment on your partner's belongings using 〜そうな.

Example:　Ａ：おもしろそうな本ですね。
　　　　　Ｂ：そうですか。実はつまらないんですよ。

E. Pair Work—B acts out the following situations and A makes a guess. Continue
    the conversation like the example below.

Example:　　おなかが痛い
　　　　→　　A：おなかが痛そうですね。
　　　　　　　　　どうしたんですか。
　　　　　　　B：食べすぎたんです。
　　　　　　　A：そうですか。
　　　　　　　　　薬を飲んだほうがいいですよ。

1. うれしい　　　2. 悲しい　　　3. 眠い　　　4. 忙しい

Ⅳ 着てみます

A. Respond to the following sentences using 〜てみる.  K13-14

Example:　　A：この服はすてきですよ。
　　　　　　　B：じゃあ、着てみます。

1. 経済の授業はおもしろかったですよ。
2. あの映画を見て泣きました。
3. この本は感動しました。
4. このケーキはおいしいですよ。
5. 東京はおもしろかったですよ。
6. このCDはよかったですよ。
7. この辞書は便利でしたよ。

B. Pair Work—You are at a shopping center. Ask store attendants whether you
    can try out the following, using appropriate verbs.

Example:

Customer: すみません。使ってみてもいいですか。
Store attendant: どうぞ、使ってみてください。

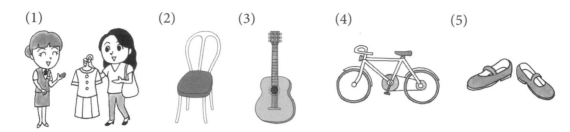

(1)　　　　　　(2)　　　(3)　　　　(4)　　　　　　(5)

C. Talk about what you want to try in the following places.

Example:

インド (India)

→　A：インドに行ったことがありますか。

　　B：いいえ。ありません。でも、行ってみたいです。

　　A：そうですか。インドで何がしたいですか。

　　B：インドでぞうに乗ったり、ヨガ (Yoga) を習ったりしてみたいです。

1. ケニア (Kenya)　　　3. タイ (Thailand)　　　5. チベット (Tibet)

2. 東京　　　　　　　　4. ブラジル (Brazil)　　　6. Your own

Ⓥ 紅茶なら飲みました

A. Answer the questions as in the example. 🔊 K13-15

Example:　　Q：メアリーさんはけさ、コーヒーを飲みましたか。

　　　　　　A：(◯ tea　　✕ coffee)

　　　　　　→　紅茶なら飲みましたが、コーヒーは飲みませんでした。

1. メアリーさんはバイクに乗れますか。　　　　　　(◯ bicycle　　✕ motorbike)

2. メアリーさんはニュージーランドに行ったことがありますか。

　　　　　　　　　　　　　　　　　　　　　　　(◯ Australia　　✕ New Zealand)

3. メアリーさんはゴルフをしますか。　　　　　(◯ tennis　　✕ golf)

4. けんさんは日本の経済に興味がありますか。　(◯ history　　✕ economics)

5. けんさんは彼女がいますか。　　　　　　　　(◯ friend　　✕ girlfriend)

6. けんさんは土曜日に出かけられますか。　　　(◯ Sunday　　✕ Saturday)

B. Answer the following questions. Use 〜なら whenever possible.

Example:　　Q：スポーツをよく見ますか。

　　　　　　　A：ええ、野球なら見ます。／いいえ、見ません。

1. 外国語ができますか。
2. アルバイトをしたことがありますか。
3. 日本の料理が作れますか。
4. 有名人に会ったことがありますか。
5. 楽器ができますか。
6. お金が貸せますか。

Ⅵ 一日に二回食べます

A. Look at the following pictures and make sentences as in the example. 🔊K13-16

Example：　一日に二回食べます。

Ex. twice a day

(1) three times a day

(2) seven hours a day

(3) three hours a day

(4) once a week

(5) twice a week

(6) three days a week   (7) five days a week   (8) once a month

part-time job   school

B. Pair Work—Look at the pictures in A and ask your partner the questions using the patterns below.

$$
\left\{
\begin{array}{l}
一日_{いちにち} \\
一週間_{いっしゅうかん} \\
一か月_{いっ　げつ}
\end{array}
\right\}
に
\left\{
\begin{array}{l}
何回_{なんかい} \\
何時間_{なんじかん} \\
何日_{なんにち}
\end{array}
\right\}
～ますか
$$

Example:

Ａ：Ｂさんは一日に何回食べますか。
　　　　　いちにち　なんかい　た

Ｂ：そうですね。たいてい一日に二回食べます。朝ご飯は食べません。
　　　　　　　　　　　　いちにち　にかい　た　　　あさ　はん　た

C. Class Activity—Ask two people how often they do the following things. Add your own questions.

Example:　床屋／美容院に行く
　　　　　とこや　びよういん　い
　　→　Ａ：Ｂさんはよく床屋／美容院に行きますか。
　　　　　　　　　　　　　とこや　びよういん　い
　　　　Ｂ：一か月に一回ぐらい行きます。
　　　　　　いっ　げつ　いっかい　い

Questions	(　　　　　　)さん	(　　　　　　)さん
スーパーに行く		
料理する		
運動する		
ゲームをする		

Ⅶ まとめの練習
れんしゅう

A. Answer the following questions.

1. 子供の時に何ができましたか。何ができませんでしたか。
   こども　とき　なに　　　　　　　　　　　　　　なに
2. 百円で何が買えますか。
   ひゃくえん　なに　か
3. どこに行ってみたいですか。どうしてですか。
   い
4. 子供の時、何がしてみたかったですか。
   こども　とき　なに
5. 今、何がしてみたいですか。
   いま　なに
6. 一日に何時間ぐらい勉強しますか。
   いちにち　なんじかん　　　　　べんきょう
7. 一週間に何回レストランに行きますか。
   いっしゅうかん　なんかい　　　　　　　い
8. 一か月にいくらぐらい使いますか。
   いっ　げつ　　　　　　　　　つか

B. Pair Work—Talk about part-time jobs.

1. アルバイトをしたことがありますか。
2. いつしましたか。
3. どんなアルバイトでしたか。
4. 一週間に何日働きましたか。
   いっしゅうかん　なんにちはたら
5. 一時間にいくらもらいましたか。
   いちじかん
6. どんなアルバイトがしてみたいですか。どうしてですか。

C. Role Play—One of you is the manager of one of the following organizations, and the other is the student who is looking for a job.

(a) Call the organization and make an appointment for a job interview, as in Dialogue Ⅰ.

(b) Then, discuss experiences and qualifications, etc., as in Dialogue Ⅱ.

小山日本語学校　　　アジア・トラベル　　　山本屋デパート
こやまにほんごがっこう　　　　　　　　　　　　　　やまもとや

げんきスポーツクラブ　　　ハロー子供英語学校
　　　　　　　　　　　　　　　　こどもえいごがっこう

Culture Note

年号と干支 Names of Years
ねん ごう　え と

年号
ねんごう

Japanese people use two systems of reference for years. One is the Gregorian calendar year, and the other is 年号, Japanese imperial eras that, since the Meiji era, have coincided with ねんごう the emperors' tenures. Under the 年号 system, the year 2000, for instance, was 平成12年, the ねんごう へいせい ねん 12th year of the Heisei era (Emperor Akihito's tenure).

The four most recent 年号 are: 明治 (1868–1912), 大正 (1912–1926), 昭和 (1926–1989), and ねんごう めいじ たいしょう しょうわ 平成 (1989–). Japanese people remember Meiji as the era of modernization, Taisho as the へいせい time the movement toward democracy was born, Showa as a period of war and economic growth, and Heisei as an era marked by recession and big earthquakes.

干支
え と

Japanese people associate their birth years with the 12 animals in the East Asian zodiac, which is referred to as 干支 and 十二支. The table below lists the animals in the zodiac, and え と じゅうに し the years they are associated with. People born in 2000, for example, are 辰年生まれ. たつどし う

Eto	Animal		Years of birth		
子　ne =nezumi	rat		1984	1996	2008
丑　ushi	ox		1985	1997	2009
寅　tora	tiger		1986	1998	2010
卯　u =usagi	rabbit		1987	1999	2011
辰　tatsu	dragon		1988	2000	2012
巳　mi =hebi	snake		1989	2001	2013
午　uma	horse		1990	2002	2014
未　hitsuji	sheep		1991	2003	2015
申　saru	monkey		1992	2004	2016
酉　tori	chicken		1993	2005	2017
戌　inu	dog		1994	2006	2018
亥　i =inoshishi	boar		1995	2007	2019

Useful Expressions

銀行で
ぎんこう

At the Bank

Useful Vocabulary

口座 —————————— account
こうざ

手数料 ————————— commission
てすうりょう

キャッシュカード —— bank card

通帳 —————————— passbook
つうちょう

預金 —————————— savings
よきん

百円玉 ————————— 100-yen coin
ひゃくえんだま

金額 —————————— amount
きんがく

暗証番号 ———————— personal identification number
あんしょうばんごう

Useful Expressions

口座を開きたいんですが。————— I would like to open an account.
こうざ ひら

口座を閉じたいんですが。————— I would like to close an account.
こうざ と

ドルを円にかえてください。———— Please change dollars into yen.
えん

口座にお金を振り込みたいんですが。——— I would like to deposit money
こうざ かね ふ こ into the account.

一万円札を千円札十枚に両替できますか。— Can you change a 10,000-yen
いちまんえんさつ せんえんさつじゅうまい りょうがえ bill into ten 1,000-yen bills?

お金をおろします。————————— I will withdraw money.
かね

ATM

① deposit
② withdrawal
③ passbook update
④ bank transfer
⑤ credit card
⑥ balance inquiry

第14課 | L E S S O N ·················14
バレンタインデー Valentine's Day

会話 D i a l o g u e
かい わ

Ⓘ A month before Valentine's Day. 📢 K14-01/02

1 メアリー： バレンタインのプレゼントは何がいいと思いますか。
なに おも
2 みちこ： そうですね。たけしさんはいつも同じセーターを着ているから、
おな き
3 セーターをあげたらどうですか。
4 メアリー： それはいいかもしれませんね。

Ⓘ On Valentine's Day. 📢 K14-03/04

1 メアリー： たけしくん、はい、これ。
2 たけし： えっ、ぼくに？ どうもありがとう。開けてもいい？
あ
3 メアリー： うん。
4 たけし： わあ、いいね、このセーター。こんなのがほしかったんだ。
5 メアリーが編んだの？
あ
6 メアリー： うん、小さいかもしれないから着てみて。
ちい き
7 たけし： ちょうどいいよ。ありがとう。

Ⅲ The next day. 🔊 K14-05/06

1 ジョン：　暖かそうなセーターですね。
2 たけし：　これ、メアリーがくれたんです。
3 ジョン：　よく似合っていますよ。ぼくも彼女がほしいなあ。ロバートさんは
4 　　　　　チョコレートを十個ももらったんですよ。
5 たけし：　へえ、すごいですね。ジョンさんは？
6 ジョン：　ぼくは一個しかもらえませんでした。大家さんから。さびしいなあ。
7 たけし：　でも、ロバートさんはホワイトデーが大変ですよ。
8 ジョン：　ホワイトデー？
9 たけし：　ええ、男の人は三月十四日にお返しをしなきゃいけないんですよ。

Ⅰ

Mary: What do you think is good for a Valentine's present?

Michiko: Well, Takeshi always wears the same sweater, so why don't you give him a sweater?

Mary: That might be a good idea.

Ⅱ

Mary: Takeshi, this is for you.

Takeshi: For me? Thank you. May I open it?

Mary: Yes.

Takeshi: Wow, this is a nice sweater! I've wanted one like this. Did you knit it, Mary?

Mary: Yes. It may be small, so please try it on.

Takeshi: It fits perfectly. Thank you.

Ⅲ

John: Your sweater looks warm.

Takeshi: Mary gave me this.

John: It looks good on you. I want a girlfriend, too. You know, Robert got as many as ten chocolates.

Takeshi: Hah, that's incredible. How about you, John?

John: I only got one. From my landlady. How sad.

Takeshi: But Robert will probably have a tough day on White Day.

John: White Day?

Takeshi: Yes, boys have to return the favor on March 14th.

単語
たん　ご
V o c a b u l a r y

 K14-07

N o u n s

あに	兄	(my) older brother
* おおやさん	大家さん	landlord; landlady
* おかえし	お返し	return (as a token of gratitude)
おくさん	奥さん	(your/his) wife
おじさん		uncle; middle-aged man
おばさん		aunt; middle-aged woman
グラス		tumbler; glass
クリスマス		Christmas
ごしゅじん	ご主人	(your/her) husband
さら	皿	plate; dish
じかん	時間	time
チケット		ticket
* チョコレート		chocolate
トレーナー		sweat shirt
ぬいぐるみ		stuffed animal (e.g., teddy bear)
ネクタイ		necktie
* バレンタインデー		St. Valentine's Day
ビデオカメラ		camcorder
ふうふ	夫婦	married couple; husband and wife
* ホワイトデー		"White Day" (yet another gift-giving day)
マフラー		winter scarf
まんが	漫画	comic book
マンション		multistory apartment building; condominium
みかん		mandarin orange
みなさん	皆さん	everyone; all of you
ゆびわ	指輪	ring
ラジオ		radio
りょうしん	両親	parents
りれきしょ	履歴書	résumé

✳ Words that appear in the dialogue

い-adjective

* ほしい	欲しい	to want（*thing* が）

な-adjective

けち（な）		stingy; cheap

U-verbs

おくる	送る	to send（*person* に *thing* を）
* にあう	似合う	to look good（on somebody）（*thing* が）

Ru-verbs

あきらめる		to give up（〜を）
* あげる		to give (to others)（*person* に *thing* を）
* くれる		to give (me)（*person* に *thing* を）
できる		to come into existence; to be made（〜が）

Irregular Verbs

そうだんする	相談する	to consult（*person* に）
プロポーズする		to propose marriage（*person* に）

Adverbs and Other Expressions

* おなじ	同じ	same
* 〜くん	〜君	Mr./Ms. . . . (casual)
* こんな〜		. . . like this; this kind of . . .
〜たち		[makes a noun plural]
わたしたち	私たち	we
* ちょうど		exactly
どうしたらいい		what should one do
よく		well

Counters

* 〜こ	〜個	[generic counter for smaller items]
〜さつ	〜冊	[counter for bound volumes]
〜だい	〜台	[counter for equipment]
〜ひき	〜匹	[counter for smaller animals]
〜ほん	〜本	[counter for long objects]

文 法 G r a m m a r
ぶん ぽう

1 ほしい

ほしい means "(I) want (something)." It is an い-adjective and conjugates as such. The object of desire is usually followed by the particle が. In negative sentences, the particle は is also used.

いい漢字の辞書がほしいです。
かん じ　じ しょ
I want a good kanji dictionary.

子供の時、ゴジラのおもちゃがほしかったです。
こ ども　とき
When I was young, I wanted a toy Godzilla.

お金はあまりほしくないです。
かね
I don't have much desire for money.

| （私は）Xが　ほしい | *I want X.* |
| わたし | |

ほしい is similar to たい (I want to do . . .), which we studied in Lesson 11, in that its use is primarily limited to the first person, the speaker. These words are called "private predicates," and they refer to the inner sensations which are known only to the person feeling them. Everyone else needs to rely on observations and guesses when they want to claim that "person X wants such and such." Japanese grammar, ever demanding that everything be stated in explicit terms, therefore calls for an extra device for sentences with private predicates as applied to the second or third person.[1]

You can quote the people who say they are feeling these sensations.

ロバートさんはパソコンがほしいと言っています。
い
Robert says he wants a computer.

You can make clear that you are only making a guess.

---

[1] Among the words we have learned so far, かなしい (sad), うれしい (glad), and いたい (painful) are private predicates. The observations we make about ほしい below apply to these words as well.

きょうこさんはクラシックの C D がほしくないでしょう。
シーディー
Probably Kyoko does not want a CD of classical music.

Or you can use the special construction which says that you are making an observation of a person feeling a private-predicate sensation. In Lesson 11, we learned the verb たがる, which replaces たい.

ともこさんは英語を習いたがっています。
えいご　なら
(I understand that) Tomoko wants to study English.

ほしい too has a special verb counterpart, ほしがる. It conjugates as an *u*-verb and is usually used in the form ほしがっている, to describe an observation that the speaker currently thinks holds true. Unlike ほしい, the particle after the object of desire is を.

トムさんは友だちをほしがっています。
とも
(I understand that) Tom wants a friend.

2 　～かもしれません

We have already learned the expression でしょう in Lesson 12, with which we can say that a given state of affairs is probable or likely. The new sentence-final expression かもしれません, and its short form counterpart かもしれない, are much like でしょう, and mean that something is a "possibility." You can use かもしれません when you are not sure what is really the case but are willing to make a guess.

かもしれません is placed after the short forms of predicates, in the affirmative and in the negative, in the present as well as the past tense.

あしたは雨が降るかもしれません。
あめ　ふ
It may rain tomorrow.

田中さんより、鈴木さんのほうが背が高いかもしれません。
たなか　すずき　せ　たか
Suzuki is perhaps taller than Tanaka.

あしたは天気がよくないかもしれません。
てんき
The weather may not be good tomorrow.

トムさんは、子供の時、いじわるだったかもしれません。
こども　とき
Tom may have been a bully when he was a kid.

Just like でしょう, かもしれません goes directly after a noun or a な-adjective in the present tense affirmative sentences. In other words, だ is dropped in these sentences.

トムさんはカナダ人だ。
Tom is a Canadian.

→ トムさんはカナダ人かもしれません。
Tom might be a Canadian.

山下先生は犬がきらいだ。
Professor Yamashita is not fond of dogs.

→ 山下先生は犬がきらいかもしれません。
It is possible that Professor Yamashita is not fond of dogs.

> Present tense, affirmative
> verbs: 行く
> い-adjectives: 寒い
> な-adjectives: 元気
> noun ＋です： 学生
> ｝かもしれません

3　あげる/くれる/もらう

Japanese has two verbs for giving. The choice between the pair depends on the direction of the transaction. Imagine a set of concentric spheres of relative psychological distances, with me at the center, you next to me, and all the others on the edge. When a thing moves *away* from the center, the transaction is described in terms of the verb あげる. When a thing moves *toward* the center, the verb we use is くれる.

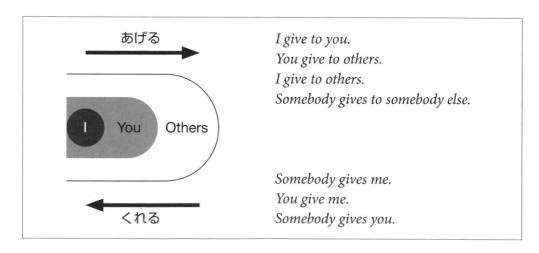

あげる
I give to you.
You give to others.
I give to others.
Somebody gives to somebody else.

I　You　Others

Somebody gives me.
You give me.
Somebody gives you.
くれる

With both あげる and くれる, the giver is the subject of the sentence, and is accompanied by the particle は or が. The recipient is accompanied by the particle に.

私はその女の人に花をあげます。
I will give the woman flowers.

その女の人は男の人に時計をあげました。[2]
The woman gave the man a watch.

両親が（私に）新しい車をくれるかもしれません。
My parents may give me a new car.

(giver) は / が　(recipient) に $\left\{\begin{array}{l}\text{あげる}\\\text{くれる}\end{array}\right\}$	(giver) *gives to* (recipient)

Transactions that are described with the verb くれる can also be described in terms of "receiving" or もらう. With もらう, it is the recipient that is the subject of the sentence, with は or が, and the giver is accompanied by the particle に or から.

私は　姉に／姉から　古い辞書をもらいました。
I received an old dictionary from my big sister.

(recipient) は / が　(giver) に / から　もらう[3]	(recipient) *receives from* (giver)

Compare the above もらう sentence with the くれる version below, noting the particle switch.

姉が私に古い辞書をくれました。
My big sister gave me an old dictionary.

---

[2] When a transaction takes place between two people other than yourself, as in this example, the verb to use is normally あげる. くれる is possible only in limited contexts in which you think you yourself have benefited because somebody very close to you has received something. It should be relatively easy for you to identify yourself with a member of your immediate family or a very good friend, for example.
　　大統領が妹に手紙をくれました。　　*The President gave my little sister a letter.*

[3] もらう is like くれる and implies that you identify yourself more closely with the recipient than with the giver. Thus it is wrong to use もらう if *you* receive from *me*, for example. (It is one indication that nobody can be detached from their ego.)
　　× （あなたは）私から手紙をもらいましたか。　　*Did you receive a letter from me?*
You can use もらう for third-party transactions if you can assume the perspective of the recipient.
　　妹は大統領に手紙をもらいました。　　*My little sister received a letter from the President.*

4   ～たらどうですか

たらどうですか after a verb conveys advice or recommendation. The initial た in たらどうですか stands for the same ending as in the past tense short form of a verb in the affirmative. In casual speech, たらどうですか may be shortened to たらどう or たら.

もっと勉強<ruby>勉強<rt>べんきょう</rt></ruby>したらどうですか。
Why don't you study harder?

薬<ruby>薬<rt>くすり</rt></ruby>を飲<ruby>飲<rt>の</rt></ruby>んだらどうですか。
How about taking some medicine?

たらどうですか may sometimes have a critical tone, criticizing the person for not having performed the activity already. It is, therefore, safer not to use it unless you have been tapped for consultation.

Also, the pattern is not to be used for extending invitations. If, for example, you want to tell your friend to come visit, you do not want to use たらどうですか, but should use ませんか.

うちに来<ruby>来<rt>き</rt></ruby>ませんか。   Compare: × うちに来<ruby>来<rt>き</rt></ruby>たらどうですか。
Why don't you come to my place?

5   number ＋ も / number ＋ しか ＋ negative

Let us recall the basic structure for expressing numbers in Japanese.

$$\text{noun} \left\{ \begin{array}{c} が \\ を \end{array} \right\} + \text{number}$$

私<ruby>私<rt>わたし</rt></ruby>のうちには<u>猫<ruby>猫<rt>ねこ</rt></ruby>が</u> <u>三匹<ruby>三匹<rt>さんびき</rt></ruby></u>います。
There are three cats in our house.

<u>かさを</u> <u>三本<ruby>三本<rt>さんぼん</rt></ruby></u>買<ruby>買<rt>か</rt></ruby>いました。
We bought three umbrellas.

You can add も to the number word, when you want to say "as many as."

私<ruby>私<rt>わたし</rt></ruby>の母<ruby>母<rt>はは</rt></ruby>は猫<ruby>猫<rt>ねこ</rt></ruby>を<u>三匹<ruby>三匹<rt>さんびき</rt></ruby>も</u>飼<ruby>飼<rt>か</rt></ruby>っています。
My mother owns three, count them, three cats.

きのうのパーティーには<ruby>学生<rt>がくせい</rt></ruby>が<ruby>二十人<rt>にじゅうにん</rt></ruby>も<ruby>来<rt>き</rt></ruby>ました。

As many as twenty students showed up at the party yesterday.

You can add しか to the number word, *and* turn the predicate into the negative when you want to say "as few as" or "only."

<ruby>私<rt>わたし</rt></ruby>は<ruby>日本語<rt>にほんご</rt></ruby>の<ruby>辞書<rt>じしょ</rt></ruby>を<ruby>一冊<rt>いっさつ</rt></ruby>しか<ruby>持<rt>も</rt></ruby>っていません。

I have only one Japanese dictionary.

この<ruby>会社<rt>かいしゃ</rt></ruby>にはパソコンが<ruby>二台<rt>にだい</rt></ruby>しかありません。

There are only two computers in this company.

表現ノート……2
ひょう げん

Expression Notes 2

The use of short forms in casual speech▶The dialogues in this lesson contain many examples of short forms as they are used in informal, casual spoken Japanese. Let us examine some of the lines from the Dialogue section.

<ruby>開<rt>あ</rt></ruby>けてもいい？　This is a question that simply asks for a yes or a no. These types of questions hardly ever have the question particle か at the end. The rising intonation alone marks them as questions.

わあ and へえ　You say わあ when you find something exciting. It is like the English "wow!" We saw this interjection of enthusiasm in Lesson 5. You say へえ when you hear something amusing, hard to believe, or mildly surprising: "Oh, is that right?"

こんなのがほしかったんだ。　んだ is the explanation modality, the short form counterpart of んです. Female speakers have the choice between the gender-neutral んだ and the more feminine の in closing an explanation sentence.

メアリーが<ruby>編<rt>あ</rt></ruby>んだの？　Many question sentences in casual spoken Japanese end in の, which is the short form counterpart of the explanation modality んです. As are questions ending in んですか, most の questions are fishing for detailed explanations as a response. They are gender-neutral.

<ruby>着<rt>き</rt></ruby>てみて。　The *te*-form of a verb is used as a request. More politely, you of course would want to say 〜てください.

なあ▶なあ at the end of a sentence, after a short form predicate, indicates exclamation of admiration, frustration, or some such strong emotion. なあ is mostly used when you are talking to yourself.

日本語の先生はやさしいなあ。	*Wow, isn't my Japanese professor nice!*
いい教科書だなあ。	*Whoa, this is a great textbook!*
おなかがすいたなあ。	*Gee, am I hungry!*
あの人はけちだなあ。	*Darn, isn't that guy cheap!*

できる▶できる has a number of different meanings depending on the context.

"can do/be good at/do well"

日本語ができます。	*I am capable in Japanese.*
彼はスキーができません。	*He can't ski.*
テストであまりできませんでした。	*I didn't do well on the exam.*

"be completed/finished"

晩ご飯ができましたよ。	*Dinner is ready.*
宿題はできましたか。	*Is your homework done yet?*

"appear/come into existence/be made"

新しい店ができました。	*A new store has opened.*
友だちがたくさんできました。	*I have made many friends.*

練習 Practice
<small>れん しゅう</small>

ⓘ 本がほしいです
<small>ほん</small>

A. Items marked with ○ are what you want, and items marked with × are what you do not want. Make sentences using ほしい. K14-08

Example:

本がほしいです。
<small>ほん</small>
マフラーがほしくないです。

Ex. ○ ×

(1) ○   (2) ×   (3) ×   (4) ○   (5) ×

B. Items marked with ○ are what you wanted when you were a child, and items marked with × are what you did not want. Make sentences using ほしい.

 K14-09

Example:

子供の時、本がほしかったです。
<small>こ ども と き ほん</small>
子供の時、マフラーがほしくなかったです。
<small>こ ども と き</small>

Ex. ○ ×

(1) ○   (2) ×   (3) ×   (4) ○   (5) ×

C. Pair Work—Ask if your partner wants/wanted the items above.

Example:　A：子供の時、本がほしかったですか。
　　　　　　　こども　とき　ほん
　　　　　　B：いいえ、ほしくなかったです。

D. Pair Work—Ask your partner which of the two items in the list they want more of and why.

Example：　車／パソコン
　　　　　くるま
　　　→　A：車とパソコンと、どちらがほしいですか。
　　　　　　くるま
　　　　　B：車よりパソコンのほうがほしいです。
　　　　　　くるま
　　　　　A：どうしてですか。
　　　　　B：車が運転できませんから。
　　　　　　くるま　うんてん

1. コンサートのチケット／映画のＤＶＤ
　　　　　　　　　　　　　えい が　　ディープイディー
2. 小さい家／大きいマンション
　ちい　いえ　おお
3. 彼(彼女)／いい友だち
　かれ かのじょ　　とも
4. 猫／犬
　ねこ　いぬ
5. 時間／お金
　じかん　かね

E. Class Activity—Ask four people when their birthdays are and what they want on their birthdays.

名前 なまえ	誕生日はいつですか たんじょう ぴ	何がほしいですか なに

Based on the findings, make a short dialogue by filling in the underlined parts.

Example:

A：もうすぐ、　＿メアリー＿　さんの誕生日ですよ。
　　　　　　　　　　　　　　たんじょうび

B：そうですか。じゃ、何かプレゼントを買いましょうか。
　　　　　　　　　　　　なに　　　　　　　　　　　　か
　　何がいいと思いますか。
　　なに　　　　おも

A：そうですね。　＿キティちゃん（Hello Kitty）のぬいぐるみ＿　はどうですか。
　　　＿メアリー＿　さんは＿ぬいぐるみ＿がほしいと言っていましたから。
　　　　　　　　　　　　　　　　　　　　　　　　　　　　　　　　い
　　　　　　　　　　　　　　　　（をほしがっています。）

B：いいですね。そうしましょう。

Ⅱ 女の人は学生かもしれません
　　　おんな　ひと　がくせい

A. Look at the picture and change the sentences using ～かもしれません. 🔊 K14-10

Example:

女の人は学生です。（maybe）　　→　女の人は学生かもしれません。
おんな　ひと　がくせい　　　　　　　　おんな　ひと　がくせい

女の人は学生です。（maybe not）　→　女の人は学生じゃないかもしれません。
おんな　ひと　がくせい　　　　　　　　　おんな　ひと　がくせい

1. 女の人は会社員です。（maybe）
　　おんな　ひと　かいしゃいん

2. 男の人は先生です。（maybe not）
　　おとこ　ひと　せんせい

3. 女の人はテニスが上手です。（maybe）
　　おんな　ひと　　　　　じょうず

4. 男の人は背が低いです。（maybe not）
　　おとこ　ひと　せ　ひく

5. 今、寒いです。（maybe not）
　　いま　さむ

6. 女の人は今日テニスをします。（maybe）
　　おんな　ひと　きょう

7. 男の人と女の人は、今、駅にいます。（maybe not）
　　おとこ　ひと　おんな　ひと　いま　えき

8. 男の人は結婚しています。（maybe）
　　おとこ　ひと　けっこん

9. 男の人と女の人は夫婦です。（maybe not）
　　おとこ　ひと　おんな　ひと　ふうふ

10. 女の人は男の人に興味があります。（maybe）
　　　おんな　ひと　おとこ　ひと　きょうみ

11. 女の人はきのうテニスをしました。（maybe）
　　　おんな　ひと

B. Complete the following sentences.

1. あしたの天気_{てんき}は＿＿＿＿＿＿＿＿＿＿＿＿＿＿＿かもしれません。

2. 今週_{こんしゅう}の週末_{しゅうまつ}、私_{わたし}は＿＿＿＿＿＿＿＿＿＿＿＿かもしれません。

3. 私_{わたし}たちの日本語_{にほんご}の先生_{せんせい}は＿＿＿＿＿＿＿＿＿＿＿かもしれません。

4. 私_{わたし}のとなりの人_{ひと}は、きのう＿＿＿＿＿＿＿＿＿＿＿かもしれません。

5. 今学期_{こんがっき}の後_{あと}、私_{わたし}は＿＿＿＿＿＿＿＿＿＿＿＿＿かもしれません。

C. Pair Work—Ask your partner what they think they will be doing in ten years.

Example:　日本語を勉強しRemoteしていますか。
　　　　→　Ａ：十年後、日本語を勉強していますか。
　　　　　　Ｂ：日本語を勉強しているかもしれません。／
　　　　　　　　たぶん、日本語を勉強していると思います。

1. どこに住_すんでいますか。　　　　　5. 仕事_{しごと}は何_{なん}ですか。

2. 結婚_{けっこん}していますか。　　　　　　6. お金持_{かねも}ちですか。

3. 奥_{おく}さん／ご主人_{しゅじん}はどんな人_{ひと}ですか。　7. 週末_{しゅうまつ}よく何_{なに}をしますか。

4. 子供_{こども}がいますか。

D. Pair Work—Make a dialogue with your partner by filling out the blanks as in the example.

Example:　Ａ：今度_{こんど}の週末_{しゅうまつ}、<u>うちに来_こない</u>？
　　　　　　Ｂ：今度_{こんど}の週末_{しゅうまつ}はちょっと……。
　　　　　　　　<u>アルバイトがある</u>かもしれないから。
　　　　　　Ａ：そうか。じゃあ、また今度_{こんど}。

Ａ：今度_{こんど}の週末_{しゅうまつ}、＿＿＿＿＿＿＿＿＿ない？
Ｂ：今度_{こんど}の週末_{しゅうまつ}はちょっと……。
　　＿＿＿＿＿＿＿＿＿かもしれないから。
Ａ：そうか。じゃあ、また今度_{こんど}。

⒳きょうこさんはディエゴさんにトレーナーをあげました

A. You have just come back from a trip. Look at the picture and tell what you will give to the following people. [🔊] K14-11

Example: 父<small>ちち</small>にお酒<small>さけ</small>をあげます。

B. Pair Work—Ask what your partner would give the following people on their birthdays. When you answer, give reasons, too.

Example: A：お父<small>とう</small>さんの誕生日<small>たんじょうび</small>に何<small>なに</small>をあげるつもりですか。
B：料理<small>りょうり</small>の本<small>ほん</small>をあげるつもりです。父<small>ちち</small>は料理<small>りょうり</small>をするのが好<small>す</small>きですから。

1. お母<small>かあ</small>さん
2. おばさん
3. おじさん

4. 友<small>とも</small>だち
5. 兄弟<small>きょうだい</small>
6. 彼<small>かれ</small>／彼女<small>かのじょ</small>

C. Look at the pictures and make sentences using くれる／もらう. 🔊 K14-12

Example: 彼女がマフラーをくれました。／彼女にマフラーをもらいました。
かのじょ かのじょ

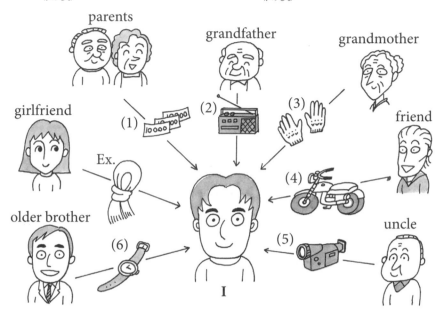

D. Describe who gave what to whom using あげる／くれる／もらう. 🔊 K14-13

Example: きょうこさんはディエゴさんにトレーナーをあげました。
きょうこさんはディエゴさんにトレーナーをもらいました。

E. Pair Work—One student looks at picture A below, and the other looks at picture B on p. 71. Ask and answer questions to find out who gave what to whom in order to complete the picture below.

Example:　A：たけしさんはメアリーさんに何をあげましたか。

　　　　　　メアリーさんはたけしさんに何をもらいましたか。

　　　　　B：花をあげました／もらいました。

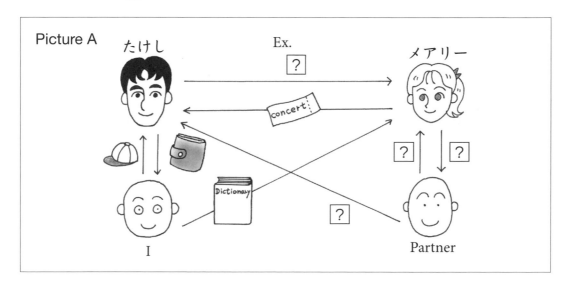

F. Answer the following questions.

1. 去年の誕生日に何をもらいましたか。

2. 家族の誕生日に何をあげましたか。

3. 友だちの誕生日に何をあげたいですか。

4. バレンタインデーに何かあげたことがありますか。何をあげましたか。

5. バレンタインデーに何かもらったことがありますか。何をもらいましたか。

6. あなたの国ではお正月に何かあげますか。だれがだれにあげますか。

7. 一番うれしかったプレゼントは何ですか。だれにもらいましたか。

8. 一番うれしくなかったプレゼントは何ですか。だれにもらいましたか。

Ⅳ 家に帰ったらどうですか
いえ　かえ

A. Give advice to the people below. 🔊 K14-14

Example:　メアリー／check newspaper　→　新聞を見たらどうですか。
しんぶん　み

メアリー

日本で仕事がしたいんです。
にほん　しごと

Ex. check newspaper
1. consult with the teacher
2. send résumé to companies

ジョン

彼女がほしいです。
かのじょ
でも、できないんです。

3. go to a party
4. join a club（サークルに入る）
はい
5. give up

けん

彼女と結婚したいんです。
かのじょ　けっこん

6. propose marriage
7. give her a ring
8. meet her parents

B. Pair Work—Give your partner some suggestions on the following comments using 〜たらどうですか.

Example:　A：頭が痛いんです。
あたま　いた
　　　　　　B：じゃあ、家に帰ったらどうですか。
いえ　かえ

1. おいしいケーキが食べたいんです。
た
2. 安いカメラがほしいんです。
やす
3. ちょっと太ったんです。
ふと
4. このごろ疲れているんです。
つか
5. 勉強が大きらいなんです。
べんきょう　だい

6. よく寝られないんです。
ね
7. 友だちができないんです。
とも
8. お金がないんです。
かね
9. 彼／彼女がけちで、何も
かれ　かのじょ　なに
　　くれないんです。

C. Group Work—You have a problem. Ask your classmates for advice.

Example:　A：日本人の友だちがほしいんですが、できないんです。
　　　　　　　どうしたらいいですか。

　　　　　　B：そうですか。じゃあ、サークルに入ったらどうですか。

　　　　　　A：うーん。忙しいから、サークルはちょっと……。

　　　　　　C：じゃあ、日本語の先生に相談したらどうですか。

　　　　　　A：わかりました。そうします。ありがとうございます。

Ⓥ 四時間も勉強しました

A. Describe the picture using counters. 🔊 K14-15

Example:　fish　→　魚が五匹います。

1. cat
2. flower
3. necktie
4. book
5. radio
6. DVD
7. magazine
8. pencil
9. glass
10. plate

B. Describe the following pictures using ～も or ～しか. 🔊 K14-16

Example:　勉強しました

　　　　　→　メアリーさんは四時間も勉強しました。
　　　　　　　ジョンさんは三十分しか勉強しませんでした。

Ex.　勉強しました

4 hours

30 minutes

	(1) 食べました	(2) 読みました	(3) 持っています	(4) 飲みました	(5) 寝ます
メアリー	🍔	📖	💿 50	🍾🍾🍾	🕚 11 hours
ジョン	🍔🍔🍔🍔	📚 6	💿💿	🍾	🕔 5 hours

C. Pair Work—Ask your partner the following questions. Respond to the answers using 〜しか or 〜も when appropriate.

Example:　まんがを何冊持っていますか。

→　A：まんがを何冊持っていますか。

　　　B：一冊持っています。

　　　A：えっ、一冊しか持っていないんですか。

　　　B：ええ、興味がありませんから。

→　A：まんがを何冊持っていますか。

　　　B：百冊ぐらい持っています。

　　　A：えっ、百冊も持っているんですか。

　　　B：日本のまんがが大好きですから。

1. 今いくら持っていますか。
2. きのう何時間勉強しましたか。
3. 一か月に映画を何本ぐらい見ますか。
4. 今学期、授業をいくつ取っていますか。
5. 今学期、授業を何回サボりましたか。
6. 将来、子供が何人ほしいですか。
7. セーターを何枚持っていますか。

Ⅵ まとめの練習
れんしゅう

A. Choose one of the special days celebrated in your country and talk about it.

Example: みなさんの国には「先生の日」がありますか。私の国では、五月
くに　　　　　せんせい　ひ　　　　　　　　　　わたし　くに　　　　　　　　　ごがつ
十五日は「先生の日」です。学生は先生に花やカードをあげます。
じゅうごにち　せんせい　ひ　　　　　　　がくせい　せんせい　はな

B. Class Activity—Show and Tell
Bring something that you have received from someone and talk about it.

Example: これは指輪です。誕生日に母がくれました。将来、私の子供にあ
ゆびわ　　　　たんじょうび　はは　　　　　　　しょうらい　わたし　こども
げたいです。

C. Role Play—Using actual items, engage in short conversations about giving and receiving things. Use Dialogue I as a model.

Pair Work Ⅲ E.

(→ p. 67)

Example: A：たけしさんはメアリーさんに何をあげましたか。
なに
メアリーさんはたけしさんに何をもらいましたか。
なに
B：花をあげました／もらいました。
はな

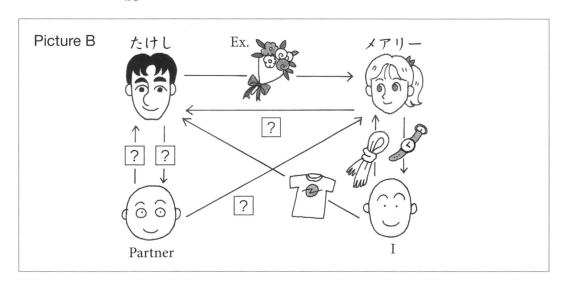

Culture Note

日本の年中行事 Annual Events in Japan
　にほん　　ねんちゅうぎょうじ

節分 (Bean-throwing Festival)──二月三日
せつぶん　　　　　　　　　　　　　　　　　　　にがつみっか

節分 is a festival held on February 3, one day before the start of
せつぶん
spring, according to the old Japanese lunar calendar. People hold

a ceremony called 豆まき (bean-throwing) at shrines, temples,
　　　　　　　　まめ

and their homes to chase away evil spirits at the start of spring.

ひな祭り (Doll Festival/Girls' Day)──三月三日
　　まつ　　　　　　　　　　　　　　　　　さんがつみっか

On the day of ひな祭り, families with young daughters display ひな
　　　　　　　　　まつ

人形 (hina dolls) inside the home to express their wish for their girls'
にんぎょう
health and happiness. The dolls represent the emperor, empress,

attendants, and musicians in traditional court dress of the Heian

period (794–1185).

こどもの日 (Children's Day/Boys' Day)──五月五日
　　　　ひ　　　　　　　　　　　　　　　　　　　　ごがついつか

This festival was originally for boys but was renamed for both

sexes since the aforementioned Girls' Day is not a public holiday.

Families with young sons wish for the healthy growth and hap-

piness of their boys by flying 鯉のぼり (carp streamers) and dis-
　　　　　　　　　　　　　　　こい
playing decorations of samurai helmets and armor. Both carp and

armor are symbols of strength and success.

七夕 (Tanabata Festival)──七月七日
たなばた　　　　　　　　　　　　　　しちがつ なのか

七夕 is based on a Chinese legend in which 彦星 (the star Altair) and
たなばた　　　　　　　　　　　　　　　　　　　　　ひこぼし

織姫 (the star Vega) are two lovers who are separated by the Milky
おりひめ

Way and can meet over it only once a year on this day (see 読み書き
　　　　　　　　　　　　　　　　　　　　　　　　　　よ　か
編, Lesson 12). People write their wishes on 短冊 (paper strips) and
へん　　　　　　　　　　　　　　　　　　　　たんざく

hang them on bamboo branches.

お盆 (Obon Festival)──八月十五日ごろ
　ぼん　　　　　　　　　　　　　はちがつじゅうごにち

お盆 is a Buddhist event held on three days around August 15
　ぼん
(or July 15 in some regions). Many people believe that the spirits

of deceased ancestors come home during this period. Around

お盆, outdoor dance events called 盆踊り (Bon Dance) are held,
　ぼん　　　　　　　　　　　　　ぼんおど
and many take summer vacations to return to their hometown to

see their family.

Useful Expressions

数え方
かぞ かた

C o u n t e r s

	こ（個） small items	さつ（冊） bound volumes	ひき（匹） small animals	ほん（本） long objects	だい（台） equipment	まい（枚） flat objects
1	いっこ	いっさつ	いっぴき	いっぽん	いちだい	いちまい
2	にこ	にさつ	にひき	にほん	にだい	にまい
3	さんこ	さんさつ	さんびき	さんぼん	さんだい	さんまい
4	よんこ	よんさつ	よんひき	よんほん	よんだい	よんまい
5	ごこ	ごさつ	ごひき	ごほん	ごだい	ごまい
6	ろっこ	ろくさつ	ろっぴき	ろっぽん	ろくだい	ろくまい
7	ななこ	ななさつ	ななひき	ななほん	ななだい	ななまい
8	はっこ	はっさつ	はっぴき	はっぽん	はちだい	はちまい
9	きゅうこ	きゅうさつ	きゅうひき	きゅうほん	きゅうだい	きゅうまい
10	じゅっこ じっこ	じゅっさつ じっさつ	じゅっぴき じっぴき	じゅっぽん じっぽん	じゅうだい	じゅうまい
How many	なんこ／ いくつ	なんさつ	なんびき	なんぼん	なんだい	なんまい
Ex.	candy tomato eraser	book magazine dictionary	cat dog snake	pencil umbrella movie bottle	computer TV car bicycle	paper plate T-shirt

Notes:

1. The pronunciation of numbers 1, 6, 8, and 10 changes before the counters こ, さつ, ひき, and ほん, except for ろくさつ.

2. The initial sound of the counters ひき and ほん changes to ぴき and ぽん after numbers 1, 6, 8, and 10, and to びき and ぼん after number 3 and なん, respectively.

第15課 | L E S S O N ⋯⋯⋯⋯⋯ 15

長野旅行 A Trip to Nagano
なが の りょ こう

会 話 D i a l o g u e
かい わ

(I) Before the vacation. 🔊 K15-01/02

1 メアリー： たけしくん、今度の休み、予定ある？
こん ど やす よ てい

2 たけし： ううん。別に。どうして？
べつ

3 メアリー： みちこさんの長野のうちに行こうと思ってるんだけど、一緒に行か
なが の い おも いっしょ い

4 ない？

5 たけし： いいの？

6 メアリー： うん。みちこさんが、「たけしくんも誘って」と言ってたから。
さそ い

7 たけし： じゃあ、行く。電車の時間、調べておくよ。
い てんしゃ じ かん しら

8 メアリー： ありがとう。じゃあ、私、みちこさんに電話しておく。
わたし でん わ

(II) At Nagano Station. 🔊 K15-03/04

1 たけし： 早く着いたから、ちょっと観光しない？
はや つ かんこう

2 メアリー： うん。どこに行く？
い

3 たけし： 善光寺はどう？ 有名なお寺だよ。
ぜんこう じ ゆうめい てら

4 メアリー： そうだね。昼ご飯は何にする？
ひる はん なん

5 たけし： 長野はそばがおいしいから、
なが の

6 そばを食べようよ。
た

(III) At the Travel Information Office. 🔊 K15-05/06

1 たけし： すみません、善光寺に行くバスはどれですか。
ぜんこう じ い

2 案内所の人： 善光寺なら、十一番のバスですよ。
あんないじょ ひと ぜんこう じ じゅういちばん

3 たけし： ありがとうございます。この地図、もらってもいいですか。
ち ず

4 案内所の人： ええ、どうぞ。それから、これ、美術館の割引券ですが、よかった
あんないじょ ひと び じゅつかん わりびきけん

5 らどうぞ。

6 メアリー： これ、東山魁夷の絵がある美術館ですね。あした行く予定なんです。
7 どうもありがとう。
8 案内所の人： 気をつけて。

「白馬の森 (Forest with a White Horse)」
東山魁夷 /1972 年
長野県信濃美術館 東山魁夷館蔵

I

Mary: Takeshi, do you have any plans for the holiday?

Takeshi: Not really. Why?

Mary: I am thinking of going to Michiko's home in Nagano. Do you want to go?

Takeshi: Is it okay?

Mary: Yes, Michiko told me to invite you.

Takeshi: Then, I will go. I will check the train schedule.

Mary: Thanks. I will call Michiko.

II

Takeshi: Since we got here early, do you want to do a little sightseeing?

Mary: Yes. Where shall we go?

Takeshi: How about Zenkoji Temple? It's a famous temple.

Mary: Sounds good. What shall we eat for lunch?

Takeshi: *Soba* noodles in Nagano are delicious, so let's eat *soba*.

III

Takeshi: Excuse me, which bus goes to Zenkoji Temple?

Information agent: For Zenkoji, it's bus number 11.

Takeshi: Thank you very much. Can I have this map?

Information agent: Yes. And these are discount tickets for the museum. Please take them, if you like.

Mary: This is the museum that has paintings of Higashiyama Kaii, isn't it? We are planning to go tomorrow. Thank you.

Information agent: Have a safe trip.

単語
たん　　ご

 K15-07

V o c a b u l a r y

N o u n s

インターネット		Internet
* え	絵	painting; picture; drawing
えいがかん	映画館	movie theater
がいこくじん	外国人	foreigner
かぐ	家具	furniture
クラブ		night club
けいけん	経験	experience
けっこんしき	結婚式	wedding
じしん	地震	earthquake
しめきり	締め切り	deadline
ジャケット		jacket
しゅうかん	習慣	custom
ぜいきん	税金	tax
そつぎょうしき	卒業式	graduation ceremony
* そば		*soba*; Japanese buckwheat noodle
* ちず	地図	map
でんち	電池	battery
にわ	庭	garden
はっぴょう	発表	presentation
ばんぐみ	番組	broadcast program
プール		swimming pool
ペット		pet
ほけん	保険	insurance
* よてい	予定	schedule; plan
りょかん	旅館	Japanese inn
* わりびきけん	割引券	discount coupon

い - a d j e c t i v e

ひろい	広い	spacious; wide

U - v e r b s

うる	売る	to sell（～を）
おろす	下ろす	to withdraw (money)（～を）

* Words that appear in the dialogue

かく	描く	to draw; to paint（〜を）
さがす	探す	to look for（〜を）
* さそう	誘う	to invite（〜を）
しゃべる		to chat
つきあう	付き合う	(1) to date (someone)（*person* と）
		(2) to keep company（*purpose* に）
* つく	着く	to arrive（*place* に）
ほけんにはいる	保険に入る	to buy insurance

Ru-verbs

* きをつける	気をつける	to be cautious/careful（〜に）
* しらべる	調べる	to look into (a matter)（*matter* を）
みえる	見える	to be visible（〜が）

Irregular Verbs

* かんこうする	観光する	to do sightseeing
* する		to decide on (an item)（*item* に）
そつぎょうする	卒業する	to graduate (from . . .)（*school* を）
よやくする	予約する	to reserve（〜を）

Adverbs and Other Expressions

いちにちじゅう	一日中	all day long
* 〜けど		. . . , but; . . . , so
さいきん	最近	recently
* 〜ばん	〜番	number . . .
〜め	〜目	-th
もういちど	もう一度	one more time

文法 G r a m m a r

1 Volitional Form

The volitional form of a verb is a less formal, more casual equivalent of ましょう. You can use it to suggest a plan to a close friend, for example.

---

ru-verbs: Drop the final *-ru* and add *-yoo*.

食べる (*tabe-ru*)　→　食べよう (*tabe-yoo*)

u-verbs: Drop the final *-u* and add *-oo*.

行く (*ik-u*)	→	行こう (*ik-oo*)	待つ	→	待とう
話す	→	話そう	読む	→	読もう
買う	→	買おう	死ぬ	→	死のう
泳ぐ	→	泳ごう	取る	→	取ろう
遊ぶ	→	遊ぼう			

irregular verbs:

くる	→	こよう
する	→	しよう

あしたは授業がないから、今晩、どこかに食べに行こう。
We don't have any classes tomorrow. Let's go some place for dinner tonight.

結婚しようよ。
Hey, let's get married!

You can use the volitional plus the question particle か to ask for an opinion in your offer or suggestion.

手伝おうか。
Shall I lend you a hand?

友だちがおもしろいと言っていたから、この映画を見ようか。
Shall we see this film? My friends say it is good.

今度、いつ会おうか。
When shall we meet again?

2　Volitional Form ＋ と思っています

We use the volitional form ＋ と思っています to talk about our determinations.

毎日三時間日本語を勉強しようと思っています。
I've decided to/I'm going to study Japanese for three hours every day.

You can also use the volitional ＋ と思います, which suggests that the decision to perform the activity is being made *on the spot* at the time of speaking. と思っています, in contrast, tends to suggest that you have *already decided* to do something.

Situation 1

Q：一万円あげましょう。何に使いますか。
I will give you 10,000 yen. What will you use it for?

A：漢字の辞書を買おうと思います。
I will buy a kanji dictionary. (decision made on the spot)

Situation 2

Q：両親から一万円もらったんですか。何に使うんですか。
You got 10,000 yen from your parents? What are you going to use it for?

A：漢字の辞書を買おうと思っています。
I am going to buy a kanji dictionary. (decision already made)

Note that verbs in volitional forms and verbs in the present tense convey different ideas when they are used with と思います or と思っています. When you use volitionals, you are talking about your intention. When you use the present tense, you are talking about your prediction.

日本の会社で働こうと思います。
I will/intend to work for a Japanese company.

日本の会社で働くと思います。
I think they/I will be working for a Japanese company.

3　～ておく

The *te*-form of a verb plus the helping verb おく describes an action performed *in preparation for something*. ておく is often shortened to とく in speech.

あした試験があるので、今晩勉強しておきます。
Since there will be an exam tomorrow, I will study (for it) tonight.

友だちが来るから、部屋を掃除しておかなきゃいけません。
I have to clean the room, because my friends are coming.

ホテルを予約しとくね。
I will make a hotel reservation in advance.

4　Using Sentences to Qualify Nouns

In the phrase おもしろい本, the い-adjective おもしろい qualifies the noun 本 and tells us what kind of book it is. You can also use sentences to qualify nouns. The sentences that are used as qualifiers of nouns are shown in the boxes below.

1.	きのう買った	本	the book	that I bought yesterday
2.	彼がくれた	本	the book	my boyfriend gave me
3.	つくえの上にある	本	the book	that is on the table
4.	日本で買えない	本	the book	that you can't buy in Japan

Qualifier sentences in these examples tell us what kind of book we are talking about, just like adjectives. The verbs used in such qualifier sentences are in their short forms, either in the present (as in examples 3 and 4) or the past tense (1 and 2), and either in the affirmative (1-3) or in the negative (4). When the subject of the verb—that is to say, the person performing the activity—appears inside a qualifier sentence, as in example 2 above, it is accompanied by the particle が, and not は.

You can use a noun with a qualifier sentence just like any other noun. In other words, a "qualifier sentence + noun" combination is just like one big noun phrase. You can put it anywhere in a sentence that has a noun.

これは 去年の誕生日に彼女がくれた 本です。　　　（cf. これは本です。）

This is a book that my girlfriend gave me on my birthday last year.

父が 村上春樹が書いた 本をくれました。　　　（cf. 父が本をくれました。）

My father gave me a book that Haruki Murakami wrote.

私が一番感動した 映画は「生きる」です。　　　（cf. 映画は「生きる」です。）

The movie I was touched by the most is "To Live."

Culture Note

日本の宿 Japanese Accommodations

There are different types of accommodations in Japan, such as ホテル (hotels), 旅館 (Japanese-style inns), 民宿 (Japanese-style guest houses), and ペンション (Western-style guest houses).

ホテル in Japan offer western-style facilities similar to those found in Europe and the United States. There are also inexpensive hotels called "ビジネスホテル," which have only small rooms but suffice for those who just need a good night's rest.

写真提供：芝パークホテル

旅館, which offer Japanese-style rooms with a 畳 floor, are the best choice if you wish to experience the uniqueness of Japan—the architecture, lifestyle, traditions, and culture. Guests change into a 浴衣 (Japanese cotton robe) and sleep on a 布団 mattress. Most 旅館 have gender-separated communal baths, which are sometimes fed by an 温泉 (hot spring). Some even have a smaller bath that can be reserved for private use. The accommodation fee is charged per person for each night, and includes dinner and breakfast. Usually both meals are Japanese style and feature regional and seasonal specialties.

Your cheaper options are 民宿 and ペンション. These are usually owned and run by a family, and offer a homelike atmosphere. The overnight charge includes two meals. In 民宿, guests are expected to lay out their bedding (布団) at night. ペンション are furnished with beds.

表現ノート………3
ひょう げん

The use of short forms in casual speech ▶ Let us examine some more examples of short forms used in informal, casual spoken Japanese in the Dialogue.

今度の休み、予定ある？　The verb ある calls for the particle が, as in 予定が
こんど やす よてい よてい
ある. The particles は, が, and を are frequently dropped in casual speech. Note also that this sentence is a yes/no question, and the particle か is dropped. (The question particle か is retained in special cases only, such as the pattern "the volitional + か (*Shall we . . . ?*)")

思ってるんだけど。　思ってる is the contraction of 思っている, where the
おも おも おも
vowel い of the helping verb いる is dropped. Such contractions do occur in the long form (です and ます) speech patterns, too, but are more frequent in casual speech with short forms.

言ってたから。　言ってた is the contraction of 言っていた, and another ex-
い い い
ample of the vowel い in the helping verb ている dropping out.

有名なお寺だよ。　だ is systematically dropped at the end of a sentence, but it
ゆうめい てら
is retained when followed by よ or ね.

> A：今日、何曜日？
> きょう なんようび
> B：水曜日。／水曜日だよ。
> すいようび すいようび

While sentences ending with だよ are quite common in the casual speech of women today, until very recently, women were "supposed to" drop だ when they end a sentence with よ.

〜けど and 〜が ▶ You can use けど and が not only in the sense of "but" (contrasting two situations), but also to present the background to what you are about to say. In the Dialogue, 一緒に行かない？ alone would be too abrupt, and
いっしょ い
Takeshi would wonder what Mary is talking about. Mary could have used two separate sentences, as in みちこさんの長野のうちに行こうと思ってるんだ。
ながの い おも
一緒に行かない？ By inserting けど, Mary indicates that she still has something
いっしょ い
to say at the end of the first sentence.

Short present ＋ 予定です ▶ You can add 予定です to a verb in the present tense
よてい よてい
short form when you want to say that something is scheduled to take place.

私は今度の週末に韓国に行く予定です。
I am scheduled to go to Korea this coming weekend.
私の兄は九月に結婚する予定です。
My big brother is scheduled to get married this September.

You can also use 予定です with verbs in the negative.

あしたは学校に来ない予定です。
I am not planning to come to school tomorrow.

見える/見られる ▶ 見える is different from 見られる, the regular potential form of 見る. 見える means "something or someone is spontaneously visible"; 見られる, on the other hand, means that the subject of the sentence can see something or someone actively rather than passively.

部屋の窓から海が見えます。
I can see the ocean from the window of the room.
どこであの映画が見られますか。
Where can I see that movie?

The difference between 聞こえる and 聞ける is the same. 聞こえる means "something is spontaneously audible." On the other hand, 聞ける, the potential form of 聞く, means that the subject of the sentence can hear the sound actively.

けさ、鳥の声が聞こえました。
This morning, I heard the voices of the birds.
インターネットで日本のラジオ番組が聞けます。
We can listen to Japanese radio programs on the Internet.

〜目 ▶ The suffix 目 turns a number into a reference to a position in a series, like *first*, *second*, *third*, and *fourth*.

	first	second	third
〜人目	一人目 (first person)	二人目 (second person)	三人目 (third person)
〜枚目	一枚目 (first sheet)	二枚目 (second sheet)	三枚目 (third sheet)
〜年目	一年目 (first year)	二年目 (second year)	三年目 (third year)
〜日目	一日目 (first day)	二日目 (second day)	三日目 (third day)

練習 Practice
れん　しゅう

Ⅰ コーヒーを飲もうか
の

A. Change the verbs into the volitional forms.  K15-08

Example:　いく　→　いこう

1. たべる
2. さそう
3. かりる

4. よむ
5. くる
6. まつ

7. はいる
8. いそぐ
9. はなす

10. みる
11. かく
12. よやくする

B. Pair Work—Suggest your plans to your partner using informal speech. K15-09

Example:　Ａ：喫茶店でコーヒーを飲もう（か）。
きっ さ てん　　　　　　　　の
　　　　　　Ｂ：うん、そうしよう。／うーん、ちょっと……。

Ex.

drink coffee at a coffee shop

(1)

read magazines in the library

(2)

see a movie in town

(3)

take pictures at school

(4)

swim in a pool

(5)

buy hamburgers at
McDonald's

(6)

dance at a club

(7)

climb a mountain in Nagano

(8)

have a barbecue at a park

C. Pair Work—You and your partner are going on a trip together for four days. Decide (1) where you are going, and (2) what you are going to do each day. Use the volitional forms as in the example.

Example:　A：どこに行こうか。

　　　　　B：九州に行こう。

　　　　　A：うん。じゃあ、九州で何をしようか。

　　　　　B：いい温泉があるから、温泉に入ろう。

1. どこに行きますか。　_____

2. 何をしますか。　　　一日目_____

　　　　　　　　　　　二日目_____

　　　　　　　　　　　三日目_____

　　　　　　　　　　　四日目_____

D. Let's sing the song 幸せなら手をたたこう.

♪　幸せなら<u>手をたたこう</u>　　　幸せなら<u>手をたたこう</u>

　幸せなら態度で示そうよ　　ほら、みんなで<u>手をたたこう</u>

　　　　　＊手をたたく (clap your hands)　態度 (attitude)　示す (show)

What do you suggest doing when you are happy?

Change the underlined parts into other verbs using the volitional forms.

Example:　握手をする (shake hands)　→　握手をしよう

　　　　　ウインクする (wink)　　　→　ウインクしよう

Ⅱ 運動しようと思っています

A. Describe what each person is planning to do. 🔊 K15-10

Example: メアリー (have various experiences in Japan)

→ メアリーさんは日本でいろいろな経験をしようと思っています。

1. きょうこ (do physical exercise)
2. 山下先生 (quit smoking)
3. ともこ (go on a diet)
4. ジョン (get up early in the morning)
5. ロバート (practice Japanese all day)
6. たけし (eat more vegetables)
7. スー (make lots of Japanese friends)
8. けん (look for a job)

B. Ask three classmates what they are going to do this weekend and fill in the chart.

Example: A：週末何をしようと思っていますか。
B：キャンプをしようと思っています。
A：いいですね。だれと行くんですか。
B：けんさんと行こうと思っています。

名前	何を	どこで	だれと

C. Pair Work—Practice the following dialogue with your partner. Then substitute the boxed part with the other occasions listed below and complete the rest of the underlined parts accordingly.

Dialogue:

A：もうすぐ、 二十一歳の誕生日 ですね。
にじゅういっさい　たんじょうび

B：ええ、 うちでパーティーをしよう と思っています。
　　　　　　　　　　　　　　　　　おも

A：そうですか。それは、 いいですね。

冬休み ふゆやす	夏休み なつやす	試験 しけん	レポートの締め切り し　き
卒業式 そつぎょうしき	お正月 しょうがつ	先生の結婚式 せんせい　けっこんしき	日本語のクラスの発表 にほんご　　　　　　　はっぴょう

Ⅲ お金を借りておきます
　　かね　か

A. A famous prophet said that there will be a big earthquake next week. Tell what the people below will do in advance. 🔊 K15-11

来週、大きい地震があります。
らいしゅう　おお　　じしん

Example:　みちこ（電池を買う）　→　みちこさんは電池を買っておきます。
　　　　　　　　　てんち　か　　　　　　　　　　　　てんち　か

1. メアリー　　　　　　　（水と食べ物を買う）
　　　　　　　　　　　　　みず　た　もの　か
2. スー　　　　　　　　　（お金をおろす）
　　　　　　　　　　　　　かね
3. ロバート　　　　　　　（お金を借りる）
　　　　　　　　　　　　　かね　か
4. 山下先生　　　　　　　（うちを売る）
　　やましたせんせい　　　　　う
5. たけしのお母さん　　　（保険に入る）
　　　　　　　かあ　　　　ほけん　はい
6. ともこ　　　　　　　　（大きい家具を捨てる）
　　　　　　　　　　　　　おお　かぐ　す
7. たけし　　　　　　　　（たくさん食べる）
　　　　　　　　　　　　　　　　　た

B. What do you need to do to prepare for the following situations? Make as many sentences as possible using 〜おく.

Example: 週末、旅行します。
しゅうまつ　りょこう

> インターネットで旅館を予約しておきます。
> りょかん　　よやく
> 地図で調べておきます。
> ちず　しら
> ビデオカメラを借りておきます。
> か

1. 来週ハワイに行きます。
らいしゅう　　　　　い

2. 両親が来ます。
りょうしん　き

3. デートをします。

4. パーティーをします。

C. Pair Work—Talk with your partner about what you would need to do in preparation for the following events.

Example: 土曜日にパーティーをする
どようび
→ A：土曜日にパーティーをしようか。
どようび
B：いいね。じゃ、食べ物や飲み物を買っておかなきゃいけな
た　もの　の　もの　か
いね。
A：そうだね。それから、部屋を掃除しておいたほうがいいよ。
へや　そうじ
B：じゃあ、私／ぼくは部屋を掃除しておく。
わたし　　　　へや　そうじ
A：じゃあ、私／ぼくは飲み物を買っておく。
わたし　　　　の　もの　か

1. 今度の休みに旅行する
こんど　やす　りょこう

2. 週末にキャンプをする
しゅうまつ

3. Your own

Ⅳ 韓国に住んでいる友だち
かんこく　す　　　　とも

A. Look at the pictures and make noun phrases, as in the example. 🔊 K15-12

Example: a friend who lives in Korea → 韓国に住んでいる友だち
かんこく　す　　　　とも

(1) a friend who can speak Spanish

(2) a watch I got from my girlfriend

(3) a friend who went to China last year

(4) a bag I use every day

(5) a coffee shop I sometimes go to

(6) a temple I saw last week

(7) a T-shirt I bought in Hawaii

(8) the house I live in now

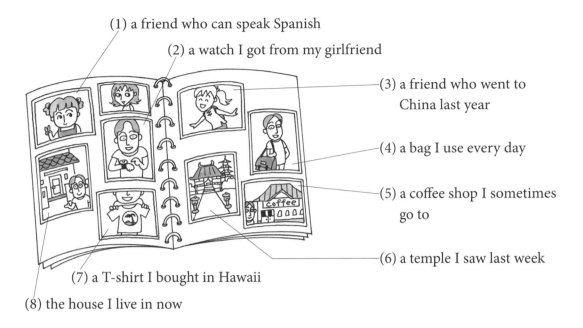

B. You are a collector of items associated with world-famous figures. Show your collection to your guest. 🔊 K15-13

Example: これはブルース・リーが使ったヌンチャクです。

Ex.

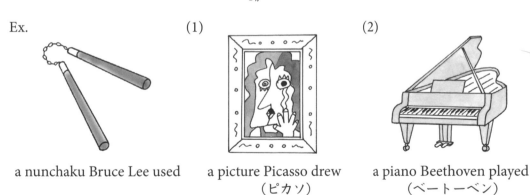

a nunchaku Bruce Lee used

(1) a picture Picasso drew
（ピカソ）

(2) a piano Beethoven played
（ベートーベン）

(3) a jacket Michael Jackson wore
（マイケル・ジャクソン）

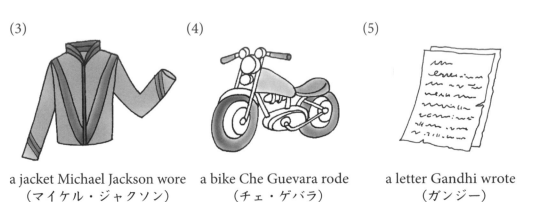

(4) a bike Che Guevara rode
（チェ・ゲバラ）

(5) a letter Gandhi wrote
（ガンジー）

(6)    (7)    (8)

a movie Kurosawa made   a telephone Bell made   a cap Mao Tse-tung wore
　　　　　　　　　　　　　　　　（ベル）　　　　　　　　　　（毛沢東）
　　　　　　　　　　　　　　　　　　　　　　　　　　　　　　もうたくとう

C. Talk about something you have, as in the example.

Example:　　A：これは父にもらった時計です。
　　　　　　　　　　ちち　　　　　　　　とけい
　　　　　　　B：いい時計ですね。
　　　　　　　　　　とけい

D. Make the following two sentences into one sentence. The underlined words will be modified. 🔊 K15-14

Example:　　コーヒーを飲んでみました。
　　　　　　　　　　　の
　　　　　　　　└──（田中さんにもらいました）
　　　　　　　　　　　　　たなか
　　　→　田中さんにもらったコーヒーを飲んでみました。
　　　　　　たなか　　　　　　　　　　　　　　の

1. 料理はおいしくないです。
　　りょうり
　　└──（妹が作りました）
　　　　　いもうと　つく

2. 旅館に泊まりたいです。
　　りょかん　と
　　└──（温泉があります）
　　　　　おんせん

3. 人と結婚したくないです。
　　ひと　けっこん
　　└──（料理ができません）
　　　　　りょうり

4. 学生を知っていますか。
　　がくせい　し
　　└──（アメリカで勉強したことがあります）
　　　　　　　　　べんきょう

5. 外国人を探しています。
　　がいこくじん　さが
　　└──（日本の習慣についてよく知っています）
　　　　　にほん　しゅうかん　　　　　　し

6. 人にもう一度会いたいです。
　　ひと
　　↑——（去年の夏に会いました）
　　　　きょねん　なつ　あ

7. 人とルームメートになりたくないです。
　　ひと
　　↑——（よくしゃべります）

E. Pair Work—Ask your partner the following questions. Later, report your findings to the class, as in the example.

Example:　What did you buy lately?
　　　→　Ａ：最近何を買いましたか。
　　　　　　さいきんなに　か
　　　　　Ｂ：辞書です。
　　　　　　　じしょ
　　　　　Ａ：Ｂさんが最近買った物は辞書です。
　　　　　　　　　　さいきんか　もの　じしょ

1. What movie did you see recently?

2. What gift have you received lately?

3. Which celebrity do you want to meet?

4. What country have you been to?

5. What kind of music did you listen to when you were in high school?

6. Where did you have your first date?

F. Pair Work—Ask which of the three alternatives your partner likes the most.

Example:　Ａ：どの ＤＶＤ が見たいですか。
　　　　　　　　　ディーブイディー　み
　　　　　　Ｂ：友だちがくれた ＤＶＤ が見たいです。
　　　　　　　　とも　　　　　　ディーブイディー　み

(a)　　　　　　　　　　(b)　　　　　　　　　　(c)

my friend gave me

I borrowed yesterday

good-looking men appear

1. どのレストランに行きましょうか。

(a)

we went last week to

(b)

our friend is working
part-time at

(c)

we have never been to

2. どの人と付き合いたいですか。

(a)

graduated from
the University of Tokyo

(b)

has a Porsche（ポルシェ）

(c)

can play the piano

3. どんな町に住みたいですか。

(a)

there are movie theaters

(b)

there are nice restaurants

(c)

tax is not high

4. どんな家に住みたいですか。

(a)

there is a swimming pool

(b)

garden is spacious

(c)

with an ocean view
（海が見える）

5. ルームメイトを探しています。どの人がいいですか。

(a)   (b)   (c)

likes cooking   doesn't smoke   has pets

Ⓥ まとめの練習

A. Pair Work—Guessing Game

Write down what you do often in Column I. Write down what you think your partner does often in Column II. Ask each other to find out if you have guessed right. If you have guessed your partner's answers correctly, you score a point. You win the game if you have scored higher than your partner.

Example:　　A：よく食べる物は、ハンバーガーですか。
　　　　　　B：はい、そうです。／いいえ、私がよく食べる物は、そばです。

	I. I do often:	II. I think my partner does often:	Was I correct?
よく食べる物			
よく行く所			
よく作る料理			
よく聞く音楽			
よく見るテレビ番組			
よく読む雑誌			
よくするスポーツ			

B. Class Activity—Find someone who . . .

1. 来週、発表があります。
   らいしゅう　　はっぴょう
   _____さん

2. 保険に入っていません。
   ほ けん　はい
   _____さん

3. 旅館に泊まったことがあります。
   りょかん　と
   _____さん

4. 週末、一日中寝ます。
   しゅうまつ　いちにちじゅう ね
   _____さん

5. 週末、大学に行かなきゃいけません。
   しゅうまつ　だいがく　い
   _____さん

6. 来年も日本語を勉強しようと思っています。
   らいねん　に ほん ご　べんきょう　　おも
   _____さん

7. 彼／彼女を探しています。
   かれ　かのじょ　さが
   _____さん

Later, report to the class, as in the example.

Example:　来週、発表がある人は_____さんです。
　　　　　　らいしゅう　はっぴょう　　　ひと

C. Tell the class about your New Year's resolution (新年の抱負).
　　　　　　　　　　　　　　　　　　　　　　　　　　　　しんねん　ほう ふ

Example:　去年は遊びすぎたから、今年は、もっと勉強しようと思っています。
　　　　　　きょねん　あそ　　　　　　　ことし　　　　べんきょう　　　　　おも
　　　　　　それから、外国語を習いたいです。
　　　　　　　　　　　　がいこく ご　なら

D. Pair Work—Suppose you and your partner have just arrived at your travel destination. (You choose the place.) Using Dialogue Ⅱ as a model, decide to do something together with your partner. Use the informal speech.

Useful Expressions
ホテルで

At the Hotel

Useful Vocabulary

〜泊 ────────── . . . nights （何泊／一泊／二泊／三泊／四泊……）
（はく）　　　　　　　　　　　　　　（なんぱく　いっぱく　にはく　さんぱく　よんぱく）

〜付 ────────── with . . .
（つき）

食事付 ────────── with meals
（しょくじつき）

一泊二食付 ────────── one night with two meals
（いっぱくにしょくつき）

チェックイン（する）────────── checking in

チェックアウト（する）────────── checking out

シングル ────────── single room

ダブル────────── double room　　　　フロント────── receptionist; front desk

ツイン────────── twin room　　　　禁煙ルーム────── non-smoking room
　　　　　　　　　　　　　　　　　　（きんえん）

〜名 ────────── . . . person(s)　　　喫煙ルーム────── smoking room
（めい）　　　　　　　　　　　　　　（きつえん）

Useful Expressions

クレジットカードで払えますか。──────── Can I pay by credit card?
　　　　　　　　（はら）

二時まで荷物を預かってくれませんか。── Could you keep my luggage
（にじ）　　（にもつ）（あず）　　　　　　　until 2 o'clock?

*　　　　　　*　　　　　　*

旅館の予約
（りょかん）（よやく）

A：一泊いくらですか。　　　　　　　*How much is it for one night?*
　　（いっぱく）

B：何名様ですか。　　　　　　　　　*How many people?*
　（なんめいさま）

A：三名です。　　　　　　　　　　　*Three.*
　（さんめい）

B：一泊二食付でお一人様、一万二千円です。*For one night with two meals, 12,000 yen.*
　（いっぱくにしょくつき）（ひとりさま）（いちまんにせんえん）

A：じゃあ、予約お願いします。　　　*Well, I would like to make a reservation.*
　　　　　（よやく）（ねが）

B：何日から何泊のご予約ですか。　　*How many nights, starting from what day?*
　（なんにち）（なんぱく）（よやく）

A：来週の金曜日から三泊です。　　　*Three nights from next Friday.*
　（らいしゅう）（きんようび）（さんぱく）

B：はい。かしこまりました。お客様の　　*All right. Your name and*
　　　　　　　　　　　　　　（きゃくさま）

　　お名前とお電話番号をお願いします。　*phone number, please.*
　　（なまえ）（でんわばんごう）（ねが）

第16課 | L E S S O N ············16

忘れ物 Lost and Found
わす もの

会話 D i a l o g u e
かい わ

Ⅰ At Professor Yamashita's Office. 🔊 K16-01/02

1 ジョン： 失礼します。先生、今日授業に来られなくてすみませんでした。
しつれい せんせい きょう じゅぎょう こ

2 山下先生： どうしたんですか。
やましたせんせい

3 ジョン： 実は、朝寝坊して、電車に乗り遅れたんです。すみません。
じつ あさねぼう てんしゃ の おく

4 山下先生： もう三回目ですよ。目覚まし時計を買ったらどうですか。
やましたせんせい さんかいめ めざ どけい か

5 ジョン： はい。あの、先生、宿題をあしたまで待っていただけませんか。
せんせい しゅくだい ま

6 宿題を入れたファイルがないんです。
しゅくだい い

7 山下先生： 困りましたね。見つかるといいですね。
やましたせんせい こま み

Ⅱ At the station. 🔊 K16-03/04

1 ジョン： すみません。ファイルをなくしたんですが。

2 駅員： どんなファイルですか。
えき いん

3 ジョン： 青くてこのぐらいの大きさです。電車を降りる時、忘れたと思うんで
あお おお てんしゃ お とき わす おも

4 すが。

5 駅員： ええと……ちょっと待ってください。電話して聞いてみます。
えき いん ま てんわ き

Ⅲ At school the next day. 🔊 K16-05/06

1 山下先生：　ジョンさん、ファイルはありましたか。
　やましたせんせい

2 ジョン：　　はい、駅員さんが探してくれたんです。
　　　　　　　　えきいん　　さが

3 山下先生：　よかったですね。
　やましたせんせい

4 ジョン：　　これ、宿題です。遅くなってすみませんでした。
　　　　　　　　しゅくだい　おそ

5 山下先生：　いいえ。よくできていますね。
　やましたせんせい

6 ジョン：　　ええ、駅員さんに手伝ってもらいましたから。
　　　　　　　　えきいん　て つだ

Ⅰ

John: Excuse me. Professor Yamashita, I am sorry that I couldn't come to the class today.

Prof. Yamashita: What happened?

John: Well, I got up late and I missed the train. I am sorry.

Prof. Yamashita: This is the third time. Why don't you buy an alarm clock?

John: Yes . . . um, Professor Yamashita, as for the homework, could you please wait till tomorrow? I cannot find the file I put my homework in.

Prof. Yamashita: That's a problem. I hope you will find it.

Ⅱ

John: Excuse me, I have lost my file.

Station attendant: What is the file like?

John: It's blue and about this size. I think I left it when I got off the train.

Station attendant: Please wait for a minute. I will call and ask.

Ⅲ

Prof. Yamashita: John, did you find the file?

John: Yes, a station attendant found it for me.

Prof. Yamashita: Good.

John: This is the homework. I am sorry it is late.

Prof. Yamashita: That's okay. It's well done.

John: Yes, because the station attendant helped me.

単語
<ruby>単<rt>たん</rt></ruby> <ruby>語<rt>ご</rt></ruby>

 K16-07

Vocabulary

Nouns

* えきいん（さん）	駅員	station attendant
* おおきさ	大きさ	size
おや	親	parent
きまつしけん	期末試験	final examination
けんきゅう	研究	research
ごみ		garbage
さとう	砂糖	sugar
しょうがくきん	奨学金	scholarship
しんせき	親せき	relatives
すいせんじょう	推薦状	letter of recommendation
だいがくいん	大学院	graduate school
たいふう	台風	typhoon
ひ	日	day
* ファイル		file; portfolio
みち	道	way; road; directions
* めざましどけい	目覚まし時計	alarm clock

い-adjective

きたない	汚い	dirty

U-verbs

おこす	起こす	to wake (someone) up （〜を）
おごる		to treat (someone) to a meal （person に meal を）
おちこむ	落ち込む	to get depressed
* こまる	困る	to have difficulty
だす	出す	to take (something) out; to hand in (something) （〜を）
つれていく	連れていく	to take (someone) to (a place) （person を place に）
なおす	直す	to correct; to fix （〜を）
みちにまよう	道に迷う	to become lost; to lose one's way
* みつかる	見つかる	to be found （〜が）

* Words that appear in the dialogue

むかえにいく	迎えに行く	to go to pick up (*place* まで/に *person* を)
やくす	訳す	to translate（*source* を *target* に）
わらう	笑う	to laugh

Ru-verbs

アイロンをかける		to iron (clothes)（〜に）
あつめる	集める	to collect（〜を）
* いれる	入れる	to put (something) in (*thing* を *place* に)
* のりおくれる	乗り遅れる	to miss (a train, bus, etc.)（〜に）
みせる	見せる	to show（〜を）

Irregular Verbs

* あさねぼうする	朝寝坊する	to oversleep
あんないする	案内する	to show (someone) around (*place* を)
せつめいする	説明する	to explain
むかえにくる	迎えに来る	to come to pick up (*place* まで/に *person* を)

Adverbs and Other Expressions

* ええと		well . . . ; let me see . . .
きょうじゅうに	今日中に	by the end of today
このあいだ	この間	the other day
* このぐらい		about this much（＝これぐらい /このくらい/これくらい）
ごめん		I'm sorry. (casual)
これから		from now on
* しつれいします	失礼します	Excuse me.; Sorry to interrupt you.
じぶんで	自分で	(do something) by oneself
じゅぎょうちゅうに	授業中に	in class; during the class
ほかの		other

文法 Grammar
ぶん ぽう

1 〜てあげる/くれる/もらう

We learned in Lesson 14 that the verbs あげる, くれる, and もらう describe transactions of things. Here we will learn the use of these words as helping verbs. When these verbs follow the *te*-form of a verb, they describe the giving and receiving of services.

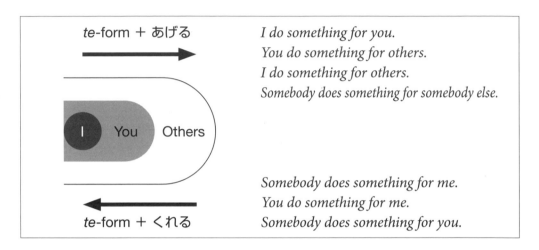

We use the *te*-form + あげる when we do something for the sake of others, or somebody does something for somebody else. The addition of the helping verb あげる does not change the basic meaning of the sentences, but puts focus on the fact that the actions were performed "on demand" or "as a favor."[1]

> 私は妹にお金を貸して<u>あげました</u>。
> わたし いもうと かね か
>
> *I (generously) lent my sister money (to help her out of her destitute conditions).*
>
> cf. 私は妹にお金を貸しました。 [an objective statement]
> わたし いもうと かね か

---

[1] Note that in あげる sentences the nouns referring to the beneficiaries are accompanied by whatever particle the main verb calls for. 貸す goes with the particle に, while 連れていく goes with を. These particles are retained
か つ
in the あげる sentences.

When you want to add the idea of "doing somebody a favor" to a verb which does not have the place for the beneficiary, you can use 〜のために.

> 私は<u>ともこさんのために</u>買い物に行きました。　cf. 私は買い物に行きました。
> わたし か もの い わたし か もの い
>
> *I went shopping for Tomoko.*

きょうこさんはトムさんを駅<ruby>駅<rt>えき</rt></ruby>に連れていって<u>あげました</u>。

Kyoko (kindly) took Tom to the station (because he would be lost if left all by himself).

cf. きょうこさんはトムさんを駅<ruby>駅<rt>えき</rt></ruby>に連れていきました。[an objective statement]

We use くれる when somebody does something for us.[2]

友<ruby>友<rt>とも</rt></ruby>だちが宿題<ruby>宿題<rt>しゅくだい</rt></ruby>を手伝<ruby>手伝<rt>てつだ</rt></ruby>って<u>くれます</u>。

A friend helps me with my homework (for which I am grateful).

親<ruby>親<rt>しん</rt></ruby>せきがクッキーを送<ruby>送<rt>おく</rt></ruby>って<u>くれました</u>。

A relative sent me cookies. (I should be so lucky.)

We use the *te*-form + もらう to say that we get, persuade, or arrange for, somebody to do something for us. In other words, we "receive" somebody's favor. The person performing the action for us is accompanied by the particle に.[3]

私<ruby>私<rt>わたし</rt></ruby>は友<ruby>友<rt>とも</rt></ruby>だち<u>に</u>宿題<ruby>宿題<rt>しゅくだい</rt></ruby>を手伝<ruby>手伝<rt>てつだ</rt></ruby>って<u>もらいました</u>。

I got a friend of mine to help me with my homework.

Compare the last sentence with the くれる version below. They describe more or less the same event, but the subjects are different. In もらう sentences, the subject is the beneficiary. In くれる sentences, the subject is the benefactor.

友<ruby>友<rt>とも</rt></ruby>だちが宿題<ruby>宿題<rt>しゅくだい</rt></ruby>を手伝<ruby>手伝<rt>てつだ</rt></ruby>って<u>くれました</u>。

A friend of mine helped me with my homework.

---

[2] The beneficiary is almost always understood to be the speaker in くれる sentences. Therefore it usually does not figure grammatically. If you have to explicitly state who received the benefit, you can follow the same strategies employed in あげる sentences. That is, if the main verb has the place for the person receiving the benefit, keep the particle that goes with it. The verb 連れていく calls for を, while 教える calls for に, for example.

きょうこさんが私<ruby>私<rt>わたし</rt></ruby>を駅<ruby>駅<rt>えき</rt></ruby>に連れていって<ruby>連れていって<rt>つ</rt></ruby>くれました。　(Compare: 私<ruby>私<rt>わたし</rt></ruby>を駅<ruby>駅<rt>えき</rt></ruby>に連れていく)
Kyoko took me to the station.

たけしさんが私<ruby>私<rt>わたし</rt></ruby>に漢字<ruby>漢字<rt>かんじ</rt></ruby>を教<ruby>教<rt>おし</rt></ruby>えてくれました。　　　(Compare: 私<ruby>私<rt>わたし</rt></ruby>に漢字<ruby>漢字<rt>かんじ</rt></ruby>を教<ruby>教<rt>おし</rt></ruby>える)
Takeshi taught me that kanji.

If the main verb does not have the place for the person, use 〜のために. 掃除する is one such verb.

けんさんが私<ruby>私<rt>わたし</rt></ruby>のために部屋<ruby>部屋<rt>へや</rt></ruby>を掃除<ruby>掃除<rt>そうじ</rt></ruby>してくれました。
Ken cleaned the room for me.

[3] Sometimes, a もらう sentence simply acknowledges a person's goodwill in doing something for us. For example, you can say the following, even if you had not actively asked for any assistance. (The sentence is of course okay with the "get somebody to do" reading.)

私<ruby>私<rt>わたし</rt></ruby>は知<ruby>知<rt>し</rt></ruby>らない人<ruby>人<rt>ひと</rt></ruby>に漢字<ruby>漢字<rt>かんじ</rt></ruby>を読<ruby>読<rt>よ</rt></ruby>んでもらいました。
I am glad that a stranger read the kanji for me.

2　〜ていただけませんか

We will learn three new ways to make a request. They differ in the degrees of politeness shown to the person you are asking.

〜て	いただけませんか	(polite)
	くれませんか	
	くれない？	(casual)

We use the *te*-form of a verb ＋ いただけませんか to make a polite request.[4] This is more appropriate than ください when you request a favor from a nonpeer or from a stranger.

ちょっと手伝っていただけませんか。
Would you lend me a hand?

The *te*-form ＋ くれませんか is a request which is roughly equal in the degree of politeness to ください. くれませんか of course comes from the verb くれる. This is probably the form most appropriate in the host-family context.

ちょっと待ってくれませんか。
Will you wait for a second?

You can use the *te*-form ＋ くれない, or the *te*-form by itself, to ask for a favor in a very casual way. This is good for speaking with members of your peer group.

それ取ってくれない？　or　それ取って。
Pick that thing up (and pass it to me), will you?

---

[4] いただけませんか comes from いただける, the potential verb, which in turn comes from いただく, "to receive (something or a favor) from somebody higher up." We also have くださいませんか, which comes from the verb くださる, "somebody higher up gives me (something or a favor)." ください is historically a truncation of くださいませんか.

　　The variants of the いただけませんか pattern are listed in what is felt by most native speakers to be the order of decreasing politeness. In addition to these, each verb can be used in the affirmative as well as in the negative.

　　〜ていただけませんか　　（いただける, the potential verb for いただく）
　　〜てくださいませんか　　（くださる）
　　〜てもらえませんか　　　（もらえる, the potential verb for もらう）
　　〜てくれませんか　　　　（くれる）
　　〜てもらえない？　　　　（もらえる, in the short form）
　　〜てくれない？　　　　　（くれる, in the short form）

3   〜といい

You can use the present tense short form + といいですね (polite)/といいね (casual) to say that you hope something nice happens. When you say といいですね or といいね, you are wishing for the good luck of somebody other than yourself.

いいアルバイトが見つかるといいですね。
I hope you find a good part-time job.

雨が降らないといいね。
I hope it doesn't rain.

To say what you hope for, for your own good, you can use といいんですが (polite) or といいんだけど (casual). These endings show the speaker's attitude is more tentative and make the sentence sound more modest.[5]

試験がやさしいといいんですが。
I am hoping that the exam is easy.

八時の電車に乗れるといいんだけど。
I hope I can catch the eight o'clock train.

(short, present) と	いいですね / いいね。	I hope . . . (for you/them)
	いいんですが / いいんだけど。	I hope . . . (for myself)

Note that all these といい sentences mean that you are hoping that something nice *happens*. This means that these patterns cannot be used in cases where you hope to do something nice, which is under your control. In such cases, you can usually turn the verb into the potential form.

大学に行けるといいんですが。   Compare: ✕ 大学に行くといいんですが。
I am hoping to go to college. = I am hoping that I can go to college.

---

[5] If I hope that *you* do something *for me*, that is, if I want to make an indirect request, we use てくれる before といいんですが, as in:

スーさんが来てくれるといいんですが。   *Sue, I hope you will come.*

4 ～時
とき

We use the word 時 to describe *when* something happens or happened.
とき

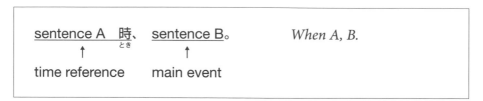

The sentence A always ends with a short form, either in the present tense or the past tense. You can decide which tense to use in A by doing a simple thought experiment. Place yourself at the time the main event B takes place, and imagine how you would describe the event in A. If A is current or yet to happen, use the present tense in A. If A has already taken place, use the past tense.[6]

The present tense in A If, at the time the main event B takes place, A is current or is still "in the future," use the present tense in A.

チベットに行く時、ビザを取ります。
い　　とき　　　　と
I will get the visa issued when I go to Tibet.

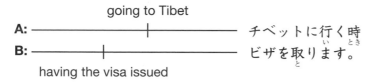

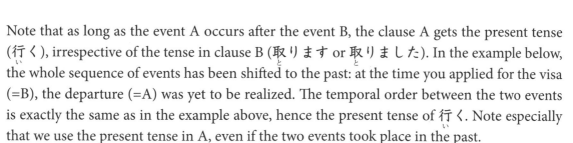

Note that as long as the event A occurs after the event B, the clause A gets the present tense (行く), irrespective of the tense in clause B (取ります or 取りました). In the example below, い　　　　　　　　　　　　　　　　　と　　　　　　と the whole sequence of events has been shifted to the past: at the time you applied for the visa (=B), the departure (=A) was yet to be realized. The temporal order between the two events is exactly the same as in the example above, hence the present tense of 行く. Note especially い that we use the present tense in A, even if the two events took place in the past.

チベットに行く時、ビザを取りました。
い　　とき　　　　と
I had the visa issued when I was going to go to Tibet.

---

[6] The grammar of the 時 temporal clauses in reality has more twists and quirks than are shown here, but this とき should be a good enough start.

Observe more examples of this tense combination.

寝る時、コンタクトを取ります。

I take out the contact lenses when I go to sleep.

(You take out the lenses [=B], and then go to bed [=A].)

出かける時、ドアにかぎをかけました。

I locked the door when I went out.

(You locked the door [=B], and then went out [=A].)

Clause A also gets the present tense, when the state of A holds when the event B takes place.[7]

さびしい時、友だちに電話します。

I call up friends when I am lonely.

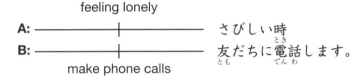

Note that な-adjectives get な, and nouns get の before 時.

寒い時、頭が痛くなります。

I get a headache when it is cold.

---

[7] If A is a verbal idea (action) and describes an ongoing event during which B takes or took place, the verb in A is in the ている form. In the example below, the phone call event (=B) occurs in the middle of TV viewing (=A).

テレビを見ている時、友だちから電話がありました。

A phone call came when I was watching TV.

Note in this connection that it is wrong to use the following sentence pattern, because 行っている does not describe an ongoing event but is a description of the result of "going," that is, *being* in a faraway place after going (see Lesson 7).

×沖縄に行っている時、飛行機に乗りました。

I went by plane when I was going to Okinawa.

元気な時、公園を走ります。
I jog in the park when I feel fit.

犬が病気の時、病院に連れていきました。
I took the dog to a vet when it was sick.

The past tense in A If, at the time of the main event B, A is already "in the past," use the past tense in A. Note that we use the past tense even when the two events are yet to take place; it is the order of the two that matters. In the example below, you will have already arrived in China (=A) at the time you buy tea (=B).

中国に行った時、ウーロン茶を買います。
I will buy oolong tea when I go to China.

中国に行った時、ウーロン茶を買いました。
I bought oolong tea when I went to China.

中国に来ました

```
                going to China
A: ─────────────┼─────────────    中国に行った時
B: ─────────────────┼─────────    ウーロン茶を買います／買いました。
                buying oolong tea
```

疲れた時、ゆっくりお風呂に入ります。
I take a long bath when I have gotten tired.

(You get tired [=A], and then take a bath [=B].)

宿題を忘れた時、泣いてしまいました。
I cried when I had forgotten to bring the homework.

(You found out about the homework [=A] and then cried [=B].)

5 ～てすみませんでした

You use the *te*-form of a verb to describe the things you have done that you want to apologize for.

汚い言葉を使って、すみませんでした。
I am sorry for using foul language.

デートの約束を忘れて、ごめん。
Sorry that I stood you up.

When you want to apologize for something you have failed to do, you use 〜なくて, the short, negative *te*-form of a verb. (To derive the form, first turn the verb into the short, negative 〜ない, and then replace the last い with くて.)

宿題を持ってこなくて、すみませんでした。
I am sorry for not bringing in the homework.

もっと早く言わなくて、ごめん。
Sorry that I did not tell you earlier

表現ノート………4

Expression Notes 4

このぐらいの大きさです ▸ You can turn an い-adjective into a noun by replacing the last い with さ. Thus from 大きい you can get 大きさ (size). Similarly, やさしさ (kindness), さびしさ (loneliness), and so forth. Some な-adjectives too can be turned into nouns by replacing な with さ, as in 便利さ (convenience).

おごる ▸ おごる is mainly used among friends. ごちそうする is a polite alternative for おごる. Use ごちそうする instead when the person who will treat, or treated, you to a meal is a superior, such as a teacher or a business associate. ごちそうする refers to "invite for a meal" as well as "pay for a meal."

佐藤さんが昼ご飯をごちそうしてくれました。
Mr. Sato treated me to lunch.

週末友だちを呼んで晩ご飯をごちそうしました。
I invited friends for dinner this weekend.

練習 P r a c t i c e
れん しゅう

① 紹介してあげます
しょう かい

A. Your friend is sick, and you did the following for your friend. Describe them with 〜てあげる. 🔊 K16-08

Example:　cook dinner　→　晩ご飯を作ってあげました。
　　　　　　　　　　　　　　　ばん はん　つく

1. help with his homework
2. correct his paper
3. buy flowers
4. take him to the hospital
5. do laundry
6. clean his room
7. lend him your notebook
8. send an e-mail to his teacher
9. go to a bank and withdraw money
10. do dishes

B. Pair Work—Your partner needs help. Tell what you would do for your partner in each situation using 〜てあげる.

Example:　A：友だちがいなくてさびしいんです。
　　　　　　　　　とも
　　　　　　　B：そうですか。私の友だちを紹介してあげましょうか。
　　　　　　　　　　　　　　わたし　とも　　　しょうかい
　　　　　　　A：ありがとうございます。

1. 天ぷらが食べたいけど、作れないんです。
　 てん　　た　　　　　つく
2. 海に行きたいけど、車がないんです。
　 うみ　い　　　　　くるま
3. 今日中に宿題をしなきゃいけないんです。
　 きょう じゅう　しゅくだい
4. お金がないので、昼ご飯が食べられないんです。
　 かね　　　　　　ひる　はん　た
5. 部屋が汚いんです。
　 へ　や　きたな
6. バスに乗り遅れたんです。
　 　　の　おく
7. 美術館に行きたいけど、道がわからないんです。
　 び じゅつかん　い　　　　　みち

C. The following are what your host mother, your friend, and a stranger did for you. Describe them with 〜てくれる and 〜てもらう. K16-09

Example:　お母さんがご飯を作ってくれました。
　　　　　お母さんにご飯を作ってもらいました。

お母さん

| Ex. ご飯を作る |
| 1. 部屋を掃除する |
| 2. 洗濯する |
| 3. アイロンをかける |
| 4. 迎えに来る |

友だち

| 5. コーヒーをおごる |
| 6. 京都に連れていく |
| 7. セーターを編む |
| 8. 家族の写真を見せる |

知らない人

| 9. 案内する |
| 10. 道を教える |
| 11. 荷物を持つ |
| 12. 百円貸す |

D. Describe what the following people did for you using 〜てくれる／〜てもらう.

1. 母／父
2. 兄弟
3. 親せき
4. 友だち
5. 同じクラスの人

E. You visited a Japanese family last weekend. Describe what they did for you and what you did for them using 〜てくれる／〜てあげる／〜てもらう. 🔊 K16-10

お父さん　　　　　お母さん　　　　　ゆみ

Example:　お母さんが晩ご飯を作ってくれました。
　　　　　お母さんに晩ご飯を作ってもらいました。

F. *Omiai* Game—You are at an *Omiai* Party. Ask three people if they are willing to do the following after they get married. Add your own question. After the interview, tell the class who you want to see again and why.

> *Omiai* (お見合い) is a meeting between potential mates for an arranged marriage.
> み あ

Example: do laundry

→ 　Ａ：洗濯してくれますか。
　　　せんたく

　　Ｂ：ええ、もちろんしてあげます。／

　　　いいえ、自分でしてください。
　　　　　　じ ぶん

(After the interview.)

→ 　私はたけしさんと付き合いたいです。たけしさんは日本料理
　　わたし　　　　　　　　　　つ あ　　　　　　　　　　　　　　に ほんりょう り
　　を作ってくれますから。
　　　つく

	name (　　　　　　)	name (　　　　　　)	name (　　　　　　)
cook			
clean the house			
wake me up			
do dishes			
take out the garbage			
buy present			
iron			

G. Answer the following questions.

1. 今度の母の日／父の日に何をしてあげようと思いますか。
　こん ど　はは ひ　ちち ひ　なに　　　　　　　　　　おも
2. 子供の時、家族は何をしてくれましたか。
　こ ども　とき　か ぞく　なに
3. 彼／彼女に何をしてもらいたいですか。
　かれ　かのじょ　なに
4. 家族に何をしてもらいたいですか。
　か ぞく　なに
5. 友だちが落ち込んでいます。何をしてあげますか。
　とも　　　お こ　　　　　　　なに
6. 病気の時、友だちに何をしてもらいたいですか。
　びょう き　とき　とも　　　なに

ⓘ ゆっくり話していただけませんか

A. Ask these people the following favors, as in the example. 🔊 K16-11

Example:　ゆっくり話す

→ （友だち）ゆっくり話してくれない？

（ホストファミリーのお母さん）ゆっくり話してくれませんか。

（先生）ゆっくり話していただけませんか。

 友だち

 ホストファミリーのお母さん

 先生

1. ノートを貸す
2. 本を返す
3. 友だちを紹介する
4. 今晩電話する

5. 六時に起こす
6. 駅に迎えに来る
7. お弁当を作る
8. 宿題を手伝う

9. 文法を説明する
10. 推薦状を書く
11. 英語に訳す
12. 作文を直す

B. Pair Work—Practice request sentences in the following situations, altering the level of speech (〜くれない／くれませんか／いただけませんか) depending on whom you are asking. Expand the conversation.

Example:　You want to go somewhere. (to your boyfriend/girlfriend)

→ 　Ａ：ドライブに連れていってくれない？

Ｂ：いいよ。どこに行きたい？

Ａ：海に行きたい。

1. You are broke. (to your host mother)
2. You need one more day to finish the homework. (to your teacher)
3. You are expecting a guest, and you need help around the house. (to your child)
4. You love your host father's tempura. (to your host father)
5. You want to meet more people. (to your friend)
6. You want to have the letter that you wrote corrected. (to your boss)

Ⅲ よくなるといいですね

A. Read each person's situation, and express what you hope for him/her. 🔊 K16-12

Example:

> かぜをひいたんです。

You get well soon.

→ 早くよくなるといいですね。
　はや

ロバート

> あしたから旅行に行くんです。
> 　　　　りょこう　い

1. It is good weather.
2. It is not cold.
3. It is fun.

スー

> 日本の大学院に行きたいんです。
> にほん　だいがくいん　い

4. You can get into a graduate school.
5. You can get a scholarship.
6. You can do good research.

ジョン

> 宿題を忘れたんです。
> しゅくだい　わす

7. Your teacher does not collect the homework.
8. Your teacher does not come to class.
9. A typhoon comes and there is no class today.

B. You are in the following situations. Explain your situation and say what you hope for.

Example:　You want to live in Japan.

→ 日本に住みたいんです。仕事が見つかるといいんですが。
　にほん　す　　　　　　しごと　み

1. You have a test tomorrow.
2. You are going to climb a mountain tomorrow.
3. You want to get married.
4. You will begin a homestay next week.
5. You will study abroad.

C. Pair Work—One of you is in the following situations. Make a short dialogue for each situation expressing what you hope for.

Example:　　B is going to Disneyland this weekend.

→　A：どうしたの。<u>うれしそうだね。</u>

　　B：<u>週末、ディズニーランドに行くんだ。</u>
　　　　　しゅうまつ

　　A：そう。<u>天気がいいと</u>いいね。(I hope for you.)
　　　　　　　てんき

　　B：うん。<u>ミッキーと写真が撮れる</u>といいんだけど。
　　　　　　　　　しゃしん　と
　　　　　　　　　　　　　　　　　　　　　(I hope for myself.)

1. B is going to go skiing this weekend.
2. B has a final exam tomorrow.
3. B is going to meet someone on a date tonight.

4. B lost his/her wallet.
5. B has caught a cold.
6. Your own

Ⅳ かぜをひいた時、病院に行きます
　　　　　とき　びょういん　い

A. Describe each situation using 〜時. K16-13
　　　　　　　　　　　　　　とき

Example:

→　食べすぎた時、
　　た　　　　とき
　　薬を飲みます。
　　くすり　の

→　コーヒーを飲む時、
　　　　　　　の　とき
　　砂糖を入れます。
　　さとう　い

(1)

眠いです。
ねむ

(2)

わかりません。

(3)

日本語で手紙を書きました。
にほんご　てがみ　か

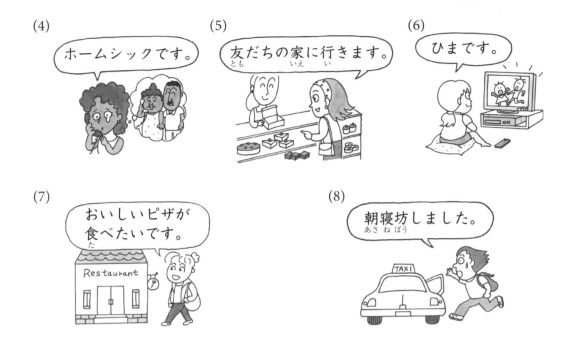

(4) ホームシックです。

(5) 友だちの家に行きます。

(6) ひまです。

(7) おいしいピザが食べたいです。

(8) 朝寝坊しました。

B. Connect the sentences using 〜時. Pay attention to the tense before 時. 🔊 K16-14

Example: 道に迷う／親切そうな人に道を聞く

→ 道に迷った時、親切そうな人に道を聞きます。

1. 友だちが来る／私の町を案内する
2. さびしい／友だちに電話をする
3. 電車に乗る／切符を買う
4. 写真を撮る／「チーズ」と言う
5. ひまだ／料理をする
6. ディズニーランドに行く／ミッキー・マウスのぬいぐるみを買った
7. ホームシックだ／泣く
8. かぜをひく／病院に行く

C. Pair Work—Ask each other the following questions. Answer them with 〜時.

Example: A：どんな時薬を飲みますか。
B：頭が痛い時、薬を飲みます。

1. どんな時学校をサボりますか。
2. どんな時親に電話しますか。
3. どんな時うれしくなりますか。
4. どんな時緊張しますか。
5. どんな時泣きましたか。
6. どんな時感動しましたか。

D. Complete the following sentences.

1. _____時、笑ってはいけません。
　　　　　　　　　　　　　　　　　　　　　　　（とき）（わら）

2. _____時、パーティーをしましょう。
　　　　　　　　　　　　　　　　　　　　　　　（とき）

3. _____時、友だちに相談します。
　　　　　　　　　　　　　　　　　　　　　　　（とき）（とも）（そうだん）

4. さびしい時、_____。
　　　　　　（とき）

5. 初めて日本語を習った時、_____。
　　（はじ）（にほんご）（なら）（とき）

6. 友だちが_____時、_____てあげます。
　　（とも）　　　　　　　　　　　　（とき）

7. ペットが死んだ時、_____。
　　　　　　　（し）（とき）

(v) 来られなくてすみませんでした
　　　（こ）

A. Make sentences apologizing for the following things using 〜てすみませんでした／
　〜てごめん. 🔊 K16-15

Example: 授業に来られない　→　授業に来られなくてすみませんでした。
　　　　　（じゅぎょう）（こ）　　　　　（じゅぎょう）（こ）
　　　　　遅くなる　　　　　　→　遅くなってごめん。
　　　　　（おそ）　　　　　　　　　　（おそ）

(to your professor)

1. 授業中に話す
　（じゅぎょうちゅう）（はな）
2. 授業中に寝る
　（じゅぎょうちゅう）（ね）
3. 遅刻する
　（ちこく）
4. 教科書を持ってこない
　（きょうかしょ）（も）

(to your friend)

5. 夜遅く電話する
　（よるおそ）（でんわ）
6. 約束を守らない
　（やくそく）（まも）
7. パーティーに行かない
　（い）
8. 迎えに行けない
　（むか）（い）

B. Make sentences to apologize for the following things and add excuses. Use
　〜てすみませんでした or 〜てごめん depending on whom you are talking to.

Example: You came late to the class. (to your professor)

　　→　A：先生、遅くなってすみませんでした。
　　　　　（せんせい）（おそ）
　　　　B：どうしたんですか。
　　　　A：朝寝坊したんです。
　　　　　（あさねぼう）
　　　　B：そうですか。これから気をつけてくださいね。
　　　　　　　　　　　　　　（き）

1. You couldn't come to the class. (to your professor)

2. You woke your roommate up. (to your roommate)

3. You forgot your friend's birthday. (to your friend)

4. You laughed at your friend. (to your friend)

5. You told a lie. (to your friend)

6. You lost the book that you borrowed from your host father. (to your host father)

Ⅵ まとめの練習

A. Talk about a good experience you had recently.

Example:　この間、一人で京都にお寺を見に行った時、道に迷ったんです。その時、女の人に道を聞きました。その人はとても親切で、お寺に連れていってくれました。そして、その人はほかのお寺も案内してくれました。とてもうれしかったです。

B. Role Play—Make a skit based on the following situations.

1. You were absent from class yesterday. Apologize to your teacher and explain why you were absent.

2. You forgot your date. Apologize to him/her. Then tell him/her that you are too busy to have a date this week, and ask him/her to wait till next week.

Culture Note

贈り物の習慣　Gift-giving in Japan

Gift-giving is an important part of Japanese culture, and takes place on various occasions. For example, in July (in some areas, August) and December, people give presents to their bosses, colleagues, and relatives to express their gratitude. These gifts are called お中元 and お歳暮, respectively. Japanese department stores offer a wide variety of お中元/お歳暮 items during the season. The most common gifts are liquor, sweets, coffee, tea, and various daily necessities, including soap and detergent. On average, the gifts cost somewhere between 3,000–5,000 yen.

　Another type of gift is お土産 (souvenirs). When Japanese people travel, they purchase local food products or small items to give to their friends, family, and co-workers.

　When visiting someone's house, Japanese people often take 手土産 (lit., hand souvenir), such as sweets or fruits. If you are invited to a Japanese home, it is a good idea to take some 手土産 with you.

お中元 items at a department store

第17課 | L E S S O N ················ 17
ぐちとうわさ話 Grumble and Gossip

会話 D i a l o g u e

Ⅰ Sue and Takeshi have just run into each other at the station. 🔊 K17-01/02

1 スー： たけしさん、久しぶりですね。旅行会社に就職したそうですね。おめ
2 でとうございます。

3 たけし： ありがとうございます。

4 スー： もう仕事に慣れましたか。

5 たけし： ええ。でも学生の時に比べてすごく忙しくなりました。自分の時間が
6 ぜんぜんないんです。

7 スー： 大変ですね。私の友だちの会社は休みが多くて、残業をしなくてもい
8 いそうですよ。

9 たけし： うらやましいですよ。ぼくの会社は休みも少ないし、給料も安いし、
10 最低です。

11 スー： 会社に入る前にどうしてもっと調べなかったんですか。

12 たけし： 旅行会社に入ったら、旅行ができると思ったんです。

Ⅱ Ken and Sue have arranged to meet at the coffee shop. 🔊 K17-03/04

1 スー： けさ、駅でたけしさんに会ったよ。

2 けん： たけしさんが卒業してからぜんぜん会ってないけど、元気だった？

3 スー： ずいぶん疲れているみたい。毎晩四、五時間しか寝ていないそうだよ。

4 けん： やっぱりサラリーマンは大変だなあ。

5 スー： それに、忙しすぎてメアリーとデートする時間もないって。

6 けん： そうか。ぼくだったら、仕事より彼女を選ぶけど。あの二人、大丈夫か
7 なあ。

Ⓘ

Sue: Takeshi, long time no see. I've heard you got a job at a travel agency. Congratulations!

Takeshi: Thank you.

Sue: Have you gotten used to the job yet?

Takeshi: Yes. But compared to my college days, I have become very busy. I don't have any time for myself.

Sue: That's tough. At my friend's company, there are many holidays, and they don't have to work overtime, I heard.

Takeshi: I'm envious. At my company, there are few holidays and the salary is low . . . It can't get worse.

Sue: Why didn't you check more before you entered the company?

Takeshi: I thought that I could travel around when I got in a travel agency.

ⒾⒾ

Sue: I happened to meet Takeshi at the station this morning.

Ken: I haven't seen him since he graduated. How was he?

Sue: He looked very tired. He said he sleeps only four or five hours every night.

Ken: Company employees in Japan have a hard time, after all.

Sue: Besides that, he said he doesn't have time to go out with Mary.

Ken: I see. If I were him, I would choose the girlfriend over the job. I hope they'll be okay.

単語
たん　ご

 K17-05

Ｖｏｃａｂｕｌａｒｙ

Ｎ ｏ ｕ ｎ ｓ

おきゃくさん	お客さん	guest; visitor; client; customer
おとこ	男	man
おゆ	お湯	hot water
おんな	女	woman
かぎ		lock; key
かじ	火事	fire
かみ	紙	paper
* きゅうりょう	給料	salary
コンタクト		contact lenses
* さいてい	最低	the lowest; the worst
* サラリーマン		salaryman; company employee
* ざんぎょう	残業	overtime work
しゅしょう	首相	prime minister
ショッピングモール		shopping mall
スプーン		spoon
たからくじ	宝くじ	lottery
ちがい	違い	difference
どうぶつえん	動物園	zoo
ニュース		news
パンダ		panda
ヒーター		heater
ひげ		beard
ひみつ	秘密	secret
ブーツ		boots
りょう	寮	dormitory
* りょこうがいしゃ	旅行会社	travel agency

い - ａ ｄ ｊ ｅ ｃ ｔ ｉ ｖ ｅ ｓ

あぶない	危ない	dangerous
* うらやましい		envious
* すくない	少ない	a little; a few
つよい	強い	strong

＊ Words that appear in the dialogue

U-verbs

* えらぶ	選ぶ	to choose; to select （〜を）
おゆをわかす	お湯を沸かす	to boil water
かみをとかす	髪をとかす	to comb one's hair
こむ	込む	to get crowded （〜が）
たからくじにあたる	宝くじに当たる	to win a lottery
ぬぐ	脱ぐ	to take off (clothes) （〜を）
ひげをそる		to shave one's beard

Ru-verbs

いれる		to make tea, coffee, etc. （〜を）
うまれる	生まれる	to be born （〜が）
かぎをかける		to lock （〜に）
たりる	足りる	to be sufficient; to be enough （〜が）
* なれる	慣れる	to get used to . . . （〜に）

Irregular Verbs

おいのりする	お祈りする	to pray （〜に）
けしょうする	化粧する	to put makeup on
* しゅうしょくする	就職する	to get a full-time job (at . . .) (*company* に)
する		to wear small items (necktie, watch, etc.) （〜を）
りこんする	離婚する	to get a divorce

Adverbs and Other Expressions

* おめでとうございます		Congratulations!
* 〜かな（あ）		I wonder . . . (casual)
* じぶん	自分	oneself
* ずいぶん		very
* そうか		I see. (casual)
* それに		moreover, . . .
たとえば	例えば	for example
* 〜にくらべて	〜に比べて	compared with . . .
〜によると		according to . . .
* まえ	前	before . . .
* やっぱり		after all

文法 Grammar
ぶん ぽう

1 〜そうです (I hear)

In Lesson 13, we discussed the sentence-final expression そうです, which means "seemingly." Here we will study another sentence-final そうです, which presents a "hearsay report." The two そうです differ not only in their semantics, but also in the forms of predicates they are attached to.

You can add the そうです of a report to a sentence ending in the short form.[1]

<table>
<tr><td>If you heard someone say:</td><td></td><td>You can report it as:</td></tr>
<tr><td>「日本語の授業は楽しいです。」
に ほん ご じゅぎょう たの
"Our Japanese class is fun."</td><td>→</td><td>日本語の授業は楽しい<u>そうです</u>。
に ほん ご じゅぎょう たの
I have heard that their Japanese class is fun.</td></tr>
<tr><td>「先生はとても親切です。」
せんせい しんせつ
"Our professor is very kind."</td><td>→</td><td>先生はとても親切だ<u>そうです</u>。
せんせい しんせつ
I have heard that their professor is very kind.</td></tr>
<tr><td>「今日は授業がありませんでした。」
きょう じゅぎょう
"We did not have a class today."</td><td>→</td><td>その日は授業がなかった<u>そうです</u>。
ひ じゅぎょう
I've heard that they didn't have a class that day.</td></tr>
</table>

When we use そうです, the reported speech retains the tense and the polarity of the original utterance. We simply turn the predicates into their short forms. (Thus です after a な-adjective or a noun changes to だ, while です after an い-adjective is left out.) Compare the paradigms of the two そうです.

			I hear that . . .	It looks like . . .
verbs:	話す はな	→	話すそうです はな	—[2]
い-adjectives:	さびしい	→	さびしいそうです	さびしそうです
な-adjectives:	好きだ す	→	好きだそうです す	好きそうです す
noun ＋です :	学生だ がくせい	→	学生だそうです がくせい	—

You can also use そうです to report on things that you have come to know via people, printed matter or a broadcast. To specify the information source, you can preface a sentence with

[1] The そうです of report is robustly invariant. The only forms commonly used are そうです and the more casual そうだ. We do not use the negative そうじゃないです, and the past tense version そうでした.

[2] See the footnote on そうです in Lesson 13.

the phrase 〜によると, as in トムさんによると (according to Tom), 新聞によると (according to the newspaper report), and 天気予報によると (according to the weather forecast).

天気予報によると、台風が来るそうです。
According to the weather forecast, a typhoon is approaching.

2　〜って

In informal speech, you can add って at the end of a sentence, instead of そうです, to quote what you have heard. って is the informal variant of the quotation particle と and follows the short forms in much the same way as と言っていました and そうです.[3]

Thus, when your friend Mary says,

「今日は忙しいです。あした、試験があるんです。」

you can report it as:

メアリーさん、今日は忙しいって。あした、試験があるんだって。
Mary says she's busy today. She says she has an exam tomorrow.

You can also use って in place of the quotation particle と before verbs like 言う.

あきらさんは何て言ってた？[4]	*What did Akira say?*
チョコレートを食べすぎたって言ってた。	*He said he ate too much chocolate.*

3　〜たら

たら is one of the several words in Japanese that refer to conditional (*if*) dependence.[5] When we say "A たら B," we mean that "B is valid, contingent on the fulfillment of A." That is to say, the event, action, or situation in B is realized if and when the condition A is met.

日本に行ったら、着物を買います。
I will buy kimono if and when I go to Japan.

---

[3] って and と can also follow the long forms, and indeed sentence final particles like か, ね, and よ, if your intent is to quote verbatim, preserving the style and tone of the original utterance.

[4] って changes to て after ん.

[5] We learned one use of this word in Lesson 14: たらどうですか used in recommending an activity to the listener. たらどうですか literally translates as "how is it if."

The initial た in たら comes from the short form past tense endings of predicates.

			affirmative	negative
verbs:	読む	→	読んだら	読まなかったら
い-adjectives:	やさしい	→	やさしかったら	やさしくなかったら
な-adjectives:	静かだ	→	静かだったら	静かじゃなかったら
noun ＋です:	休みだ	→	休みだったら	休みじゃなかったら

Sometimes, the clause before たら describes a *possible* condition and the clause after it the consequence which *then* follows. Whether or not the condition is actually met is largely an open issue with this set of sentences. It may be fairly likely, as in the first example, or very unlikely, as in the last.

天気がよかっ<u>たら</u>、散歩に行きます。
We will go for a walk, if the weather is fine.

山下先生に会っ<u>たら</u>、そのことを聞こうと思います。
I will ask about it, if I see Professor Yamashita.

日本人だっ<u>たら</u>、この言葉を知っているでしょう。
If somebody is a Japanese person, then they will probably know this word.

宝くじに当たっ<u>たら</u>、アムネスティにお金を送ります。
I would send money to Amnesty International, if I should win the lottery.

Note that when you say "A たら B," you cannot express a sequence of events in which B occurs before A; B can only take place at the time A comes true or later. You cannot therefore use たら to describe an "if" sentence like the following. ("B" = this weekend, which comes before "A" = next week.)

× <u>来週試験があったら</u>、<u>今度の週末</u>は勉強したほうがいいですよ。
It will be better for you to study this weekend, if you have an exam next week.

Sometimes, the たら clause describes a very *probable* condition, and the second clause describes the event that will take place *as soon as* the situation is realized. With this type of sentence, たら simply arranges future events and activities in a temporal sequence.

今晩、うちに帰っ<u>たら</u>、電話します。
I will call you when I get home tonight.

宿題が終わっ<u>たら</u>、遊びに行きましょう。
Let's go out and have some fun once we are done with the homework.

Note that the very same sentences could be interpreted in this way or in the way shown earlier. The difference lies not in the sentences themselves, but in the different ways the real world could possibly be. If you expect to be home tonight in all likelihood, the first sentence here describes what you will do *when* you get home. If, on the other hand, you are not certain whether you will be home tonight, the same たら sentence describes what you will do *if* you get home.[6]

Finally, the たら clause can describe a condition that is unreal and contrary to fact. With this type sentence, you express a purely hypothetical condition and its probable result.

私が猫だっ<u>たら</u>、一日中寝ているでしょう。
If I were a cat, I would be asleep all day long.

お金があっ<u>たら</u>、車を買うんですけど。
If I had money, I would buy a car.

4 〜なくてもいいです

To describe what you *do not need to* do, take a negative sentence in the short form, drop the final い of ない, and add くてもいいです. なくて is the negative *te*-form, which we studied in the last lesson.[7]

靴を脱がなくてもいいです。
You do not need to take off your shoes.

プレゼントは高くなくてもいいです。
The present does not need to be anything expensive.

〜ない → 〜なくてもいいです *does not need to . . .*

---

[6] Throughout the uses of the たら conditional clauses discussed here, one thing remains constant: A たら B can only describe a conditional dependency that holds *naturally* between A and B. You cannot describe with たら an "if" dependency of the "B even if A" type, where B holds *in spite of* A.
　　× あなたが結婚したかっ<u>たら</u>、私は結婚しません。
　　　I will not marry you even if you want to.
[7] You can omit も in なくてもいい and say なくていい, which makes it slightly more casual.

5   ～みたいです

みたいです follows a noun and expresses the idea that something or somebody *resembles* the thing or the person described by the noun. The resemblance noted is usually in terms of external characteristics, but not necessarily so.[8]

私の父はカーネルおじさんみたいです。
My dad looks/acts like Colonel Sanders, the KFC founder.

(*Has a portly figure? Has a white goatee? Stands on the street 24/7?*)

あの人はゴリラみたいです。
That person over there is like a gorilla.

(*Sturdily built? Thumps his chest often? Good at climbing trees?*)

みたいです can also follow a verb[9] and expresses the idea that something "appears to be the case." It can follow the short form of the present tense and the past tense, both in the affirmative and in the negative.

雨が降ったみたいです。
It looks like it has rained.

あの人はおなかがすいているみたいです。
It looks like that person is hungry.

あの人はきのうの夜寝なかったみたいです。
It looks like that person did not sleep last night.

先生はあした学校に来ないみたいです。
It looks like the professor is not coming to school tomorrow.

> verb ＋ みたいです   *It looks like . . .*

---

[8] You can use みたいです about yourself, when you are not clear about the situation you are in.
財布を忘れたみたいです。
It looks like I have left my wallet at home.

[9] みたいです can in fact follow adjectives too, but it is far more common to use そうです with adjectives. See Lesson 13 for the adjective base ＋ そうです construction.

6 〜前に/〜てから

You can use the present tense short form and 前に to describe the event *before* which something happens.

| verb A (short present) ＋ 前に　verb B | *B before A.* |

国に帰る前に、もう一度東京に行きます。
I will go to Tokyo one more time before I go back home.

日本に来る前に、一学期日本語を勉強しました。
I studied Japanese for one semester before I came to Japan.

The verb that precedes 前に is always in the present tense, whether the tense of the overall sentence is in the present tense (as in the first example above) or in the past tense (as in the second).

To describe an event after which another thing happens, you can use the *te*-form of a verb ＋ から.[10]

| verb A ＋ てから　verb B | *A, and then B. / B after A.* |

勉強してから、友だちに手紙を書きました。
I studied and then wrote letters to my friends.

けんさんが来てから、食べましょう。
Why don't we (start) eat(ing) after Ken has arrived.

---

[10] An "A てから B" sentence can also describe the state of B that has held true *since* the event A.
猫が死んでから、とてもさびしいです。
I have been feeling very lonely since my cat died.

Culture Note

日本人のジェスチャー Japanese Gestures
に　ほん　じん

We use language to communicate with people. However, we send and receive more messages through nonverbal communication than we do with words. Nonverbal communication includes gestures, facial expressions, eye contact, posture, touching, and even the way you dress.

The use of gestures varies around the world. Here are some examples of gestures that Japanese people use.

Come here.

Sorry.

I, me

No good.

Not me. / I don't understand.

I don't know.

練習 Practice
れん しゅう

① 宝くじを買ったそうです
たから か

A. Listen to Sue's story and report it using 〜そうです. 🔊 K17-06

Example: きのう宝くじを買いました。 → きのう宝くじを買ったそうです。
たから か たから か

1. きのうは暖かかったです。
あたた
2. きのう京都に行って、友だちに会いました。
きょうと い とも あ
3. 友だちは大学院の学生です。
とも だいがくいん がくせい
4. 友だちは元気でした。
とも げんき
5. 友だちと映画を見に行きました。
とも えいが み い
6. 映画館は込んでいました。
えいがかん こ
7. 映画はあまりおもしろくなかったです。
えいが
8. その後、一緒に買い物をしました。
あと いっしょ か もの
9. 何も買いませんでした。
なに か
10. きのうはぜんぜん英語を話しませんでした。
えいご はな

B. Pair Work—You have heard the following news. Tell your partner and discuss it.

Example: 長野で大きい地震がありました。
なが の おお じしん
→ A：ニュースによると、長野で大きい地震があったそうですよ。
なが の おお じしん
B：そうなんですか。死んだ人がいるんですか。
し ひと

1. 山下先生の家で火事がありました。
やましたせんせい いえ かじ
2. 動物園でパンダの赤ちゃんが生まれました。
どうぶつえん あか う
3. 首相がやめました。
しゅしょう
4. ショッピングモールができます。

5. Your own

C. Pair Work—One person chooses one of the following topics and talks about it. The other takes notes about what the person says and reports it to the class using 〜そうです.

1. 先週の週末
   せんしゅう　しゅうまつ
2. 家族
   か ぞく
3. 休みの予定
   やす　　よ てい

Ⅱ 今週は忙しいって
こんしゅう　いそが

A. Report on what Mary and Robert said using 〜って. K17-07

Example:　メアリー／ I am busy this week.

→　Q：メアリーさんは何て言ってた？
　　　　　　　なん い
　A：今週は忙しいって。
　　　こんしゅう　いそが

メアリー

Ex. I am busy this week.
1. I have to study tonight.
2. Tom and Kyoko are dating.
3. I slept only three hours last night.

ロバート

4. Mr. Sato got divorced.
5. I quit a part-time job.
6. I have to go back to England in June.
7. Japan is not dangerous.

B. Pair Work—First practice the following dialogue with your partner. Then change the underlined parts and make another dialogue with your partner.

Dialogue:　A：知ってる？ ジョンさん、宝くじに当たったって。
　　　　　　　　し　　　　　　　　　　たから　　　あ
　　　　　　B：えっ、そうなの？
　　　　　　A：うん、百万円もらえるって。
　　　　　　　　　　ひゃくまんえん
　　　　　　B：いいなぁ。

```
A：知ってる？ ＿＿＿＿＿＿＿＿＿＿＿＿＿＿＿＿＿＿って。
　　し
B：えっ、そうなの？
A：うん、＿＿＿＿＿＿＿＿＿＿＿＿＿＿＿＿＿＿＿＿＿って。
B：＿＿＿＿＿＿＿＿＿＿＿＿＿＿＿。
```

Ⅲ お金があったら、うれしいです
　　かね

A. Make sentences with ～たら、うれしいです using the cues. 🔊 K17-08

Example: お金がある → お金があったら、うれしいです。
　　　　　かね　　　　　　　　かね

1. 友だちがたくさんできる
　　とも
2. 成績がいい
　　せいせき
3. 日本に行ける
　　にほん　い
4. 学校が休みだ
　　がっこう　やす
5. 宿題がない
　　しゅくだい

6. プレゼントをもらう
7. 物価が安い
　　ぶっか　やす
8. いい天気だ
　　てんき
9. 弁護士になれる
　　べんごし
10. 先生がやさしい
　　せんせい

B. Change the cues 1 through 8 into たら clauses, choose the appropriate phrases to follow them from a through i, and make sentences. 🔊 K17-09

Example: 卒業したら、旅行会社に就職するつもりです。
　　　　　そつぎょう　　りょこうがいしゃ　しゅうしょく

Ex. 卒業する　　　　　　　　・
　　そつぎょう
1. 太る　　　　　　　　　　・
　　ふと
2. 動物園に行く　　　　　　・
　　どうぶつえん　い
3. 宿題が終わらない　　　　・
　　しゅくだい　お
4. 寒い　　　　　　　　　　・
　　さむ
5. カメラが高くない　　　　・
　　　　　　たか
6. 友だちが病気だ　　　　　・
　　とも　　びょうき
7. 部屋がきれいじゃない・
　　へや
8. お客さんが来る　　　　　・
　　きゃく　く

・a. 掃除します。
　　そうじ
・b. どこにも行けません。
　　　　　　い
・c. 買おうと思っています。
　　か　　　おも
・d. 旅行会社に就職するつもりです。
　　りょこうがいしゃ　しゅうしょく
・e. ダイエットをしなきゃいけません。
・f. 薬を買ってきてあげます。
　　くすり　か
・g. パンダが見られます。
　　　　　　み
・h. お茶をいれてください。
　　　ちゃ
・i. ヒーターをつけたほうがいいですよ。

C. Pair Work—Ask what your partner would do in the following situations, using 〜たら.

Example:　 ０点を取る　 →　 Ａ：０点を取ったら、どうしますか。
　　　　　　　　　　　　　　　 Ｂ：０点を取ったら、日本語の勉強をやめます。

1. 卒業する
2. お金がない
3. 日本語が上手になる
4. 男／女だ
5. 先生だ
6. 彼／彼女がほかの人と付き合う
7. 宝くじに当たる
8. 買い物の時、お金が足りない

Ⅳ 勉強しなくてもいいです

A. John doesn't have to do the following things. Make sentences using 〜なくてもいい. 🔊 K17-10

Example:　 need not study　 →　 ジョンさんは勉強しなくてもいいです。

On Saturday:

1. need not memorize vocabulary
2. need not practice kanji
3. need not speak Japanese
4. need not get up early in the morning
5. need not go to school

At his homestay:

6. need not wash dishes
7. need not do laundry
8. need not cook
9. need not clean his own room
10. need not come home early

B. Pair Work—Tell your partner what you have to do this week and ask if he/she has to do it. You may choose from the following.

Example: write a paper

→ 　A：今週、レポートを書かなきゃいけません。Bさんは？
　　　　B：私は書かなくてもいいです。
　　　　A：いいですね。

memorize new kanji	go to the hospital
do homework	go shopping
return books to the library	pay the rent（家賃）
read a book	buy a present
cut classes	work part-time
go on a diet	practice (something)
make a reservation	withdraw money

C. Pair Work—You and your friend are doing research on companies. Student A has looked into SOMY and Student B has looked into Bamasonic (B's memo is on p. 138). The things you must do are checked. Look at the memo and exchange the information using 〜なきゃいけませんか. After getting all the information, discuss which company would be better.

Example: A：バマソニックでは土曜日に働かなきゃいけませんか。
　　　　　　B：いいえ、働かなくてもいいです。ソミーはどうですか。

Student A

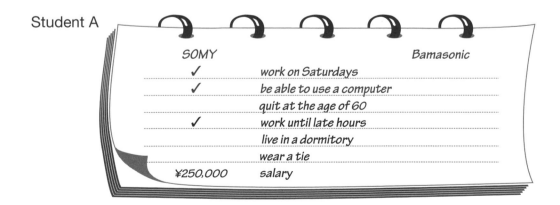

SOMY		Bamasonic
✓	work on Saturdays	
✓	be able to use a computer	
	quit at the age of 60	
✓	work until late hours	
	live in a dormitory	
	wear a tie	
¥250,000	salary	

Ⓥ スーパーマンみたいですね

A. Describe what the following things/people are like with 〜みたいですね. 🔊 K17-11

Example:　私の友だちです。すごく強いんです。
　　　　→　スーパーマンみたいですね。

Ex.

スーパーマン

(1) のり (seaweed) です。

紙

(2) 耳かき (earpick) です。

スプーン

(3) イタリアです。

ブーツ

(4) 男です。

女

(5) パンダです。

ぬいぐるみ

(6) 私の友だちです。
　　よく寝るんです。

猫

(7) 私の友だちです。
　　秘密がたくさん
　　あるんです。

バットマン

(8) 私の友だちです。
　　とてもかっこいい
　　んです。

マイケル・ジャクソン

B. Describe the following pictures with a verb ＋ みたいです.

Example:　出かけるみたいです。
　　　　　　て

Ex.　　　　　　(1)　　　　　　(2)　　　　　　(3)

(4)　　　　　　(5)　　　　　　(6)　　　　　　(7)

C. Pair Work—Ask your partner the following questions about the picture. When you answer, use 〜みたいです.

Example:　Ａ：この人は男の人ですか。
　　　　　　　　ひと　おとこ　ひと
　　　　　　Ｂ：ええ、男の人みたいです。／
　　　　　　　　　　おとこ　ひと
　　　　　　　　いいえ、男の人じゃないみたいです。
　　　　　　　　　　　　　おとこ　ひと

1. この人は学生ですか。
　　　ひと　がくせい
2. この人は結婚していますか。
　　　ひと　けっこん
3. 今日は休みですか。
　　きょう　やす
4. 今、雨が降っていますか。
　　いま　あめ　ふ
5. この人はテニスをしますか。
　　　ひと
6. たばこを吸いますか。
　　　　　　す
7. よく掃除しますか。
　　　　そうじ
8. 料理ができますか。
　　りょうり
9. ギターが弾けますか。
　　　　　ひ
10. 今、何をしていますか。
　　いま　なに

D. Pair Work—Make a dialogue, as in the example.

Example: It seems like you (=B) caught a cold.

   →   A：どうしたの？

          B：<u>かぜをひいたみたい。</u>

          A：<u>そう。早くよくなるといいね。お大事に。</u>

          B：<u>ありがとう。</u>

1. It seems like you lost your wallet.

2. You cannot find your homework. It seems like you forgot your homework at home.

3. You are driving a car. It seems like you got lost.

4. You like (one of your classmates) very much. But it looks like he/she is dating someone.

Ⅵ 電話をかけてから、友だちの家に行きます

A. Look at the following pictures and make sentences using 〜てから. 🔊 K17-12

Example: 電話をかけてから、友だちの家に行きます。

Ex.　　　　　　　　　　　　　　　　　　(1)

(2)　　　　　　　　　　　　　　　　　(3)

(4)　　　　　　　　　　　　　　　　(5)

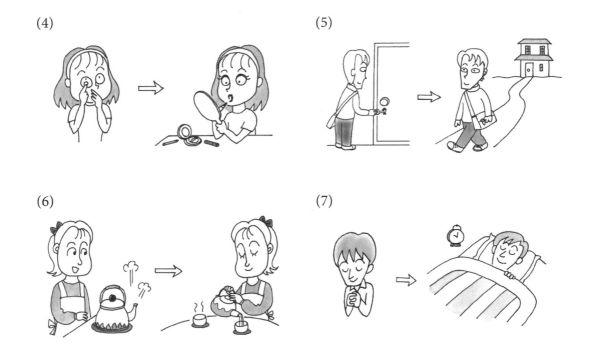

(6)　　　　　　　　　　　　　　　　(7)

B.　Look at the pictures above and make sentences using 〜前に. 🔊 K17-13
　　　　　　　　　　　　　　　　　　　　　　　　　まえ

　　Example:　友だちの家に行く前に、電話をかけます。
　　　　　　　　とも　　　いえ　い　まえ　　　てんわ

C.　Pair Work—Ask your partner the following questions.

　　1.　学校に来る前に、何をしますか。
　　　　がっこう　く　まえ　　なに
　　2.　就職する前に、何をしなければいけませんか。
　　　　しゅうしょく　まえ　　なに
　　3.　結婚する前に、何がしたいですか。
　　　　けっこん　　まえ　　なに
　　4.　きのううちへ帰ってから、何をしましたか。
　　　　　　　　　　かえ　　　　なに
　　5.　今日授業が終わってから、何をするつもりですか。
　　　　きょう じゅぎょう　お　　　　　なに

Ⅶ まとめの練習
れんしゅう

A. Gossip about people (e.g., a celebrity/your teacher/your classmate) by using 〜そうです／〜って. You can make up your own story.

B. Talk about the things you have to or don't have to do in Japan, comparing them to similar situations in your country.

Example: 日本とアメリカの間にはいろいろな違いがあります。たとえば、
にほん　　　　　　　　あいだ　　　　　　　　　　　ちが
日本ではうちの中で靴を脱がなければいけません。でも、アメリカ
にほん　　　　なか　くつ　ぬ
では脱がなくてもいいです。
ぬ

Pair Work Ⅳ C.
(→ p. 133)

Example: A：バマソニックでは土曜日に働かなきゃいけませんか。
どようび　はたら
B：いいえ、働かなくてもいいです。ソミーはどうですか。
はたら

Student B

Bamasonic		SOMY
	work on Saturdays	
	be able to use a computer	
	quit at the age of 60	
✓	work until late hours	
✓	live in a dormitory	
✓	wear a tie	
¥220,000	salary	

Useful Expressions

床屋／美容院で
とこ　や　び　よう　いん

At the Barber/Beauty Salon

Useful Expressions

カット（パーマ）お願いします。
ねが

—— I would like to have a hair cut (permanent).

あまり短くしないでください。
みじか

—— Please don't make it too short.

そらないでください。

—— Please don't shave.

３センチぐらい切ってください。 —— Please cut off about 3 centimeters.
き

後ろをそろえてください。 —— Please cut the back all the same length.
うし

赤にそめてください。 —— Please dye my hair red.
あか

ボブ・マーリーみたいな髪形にしたいんですが。
かみがた

—— I want my hair to be like Bob Marley's. (showing the picture)

Useful Vocabulary

シャンプー	shampoo	切る き	to cut
カット	cut	そる	to shave
ブロー	blow-dry	刈る か	to crop
パーマ	permanent	そめる	to dye
セット	set	そろえる	to make hair even; to trim
髪形 かみがた	hair style	パーマをかける	to have one's hair permed
もみあげ	sideburns		

分け目　前髪
わ　め　まえがみ

横
よこ

後ろ
うし

第18課｜L E S S O N ⋯⋯⋯ 18
ジョンさんのアルバイト John's Part-time Job

会話 かい わ D i a l o g u e

Ⅰ At Little Asia restaurant. 🔊 K18-01/02

1 店　長： ジョン、今日は森田くん、かぜで来られないそうだ。夕方になると忙
2 　　　　 しくなるから、頼むよ。

3 ジョン： はい。がんばります。

4 店　長： まず、冷蔵庫に野菜が入っているから、出しておいて。それから、外
5 　　　　 の電気はついている？

6 ジョン： いいえ、ついていません。つけましょうか。

7 店　長： うん。そこのスイッチを押すとつくよ。

8 ジョン： はい。

Ⅱ A customer calls John. 🔊 K18-03/04

1 客： すみません。しょうゆを落とし
2 　　　 ちゃったんです。ごめんなさい。

3 ジョン： いえ、大丈夫です。あっ、スカー
4 　　　　 トが汚れてしまいましたね。

5 客： 本当だ。どうしよう。

6 ジョン： 今すぐ、タオルを持ってきます。

Ⅲ After closing time. 🔊 K18-05/06

1 店　長： 今日はジョンのおかげで、助かったよ。

2 ジョン： いいえ。でも本当に忙しかったですね。

3 店　長： あしたは学校があるんだろう。アルバイトをしながら学校に行くのは
4 　　　　 大変だね。

5 ジョン： ええ、時々、遅刻しちゃうんですよ。

6 店　長： ぼくも学生の時はよく授業をサボったよ。もっと勉強すればよかった

7 　　　　　 なあ。後はぼくが片付けるから。

8 ジョン： じゃあ、お先に失礼します。お疲れさまでした。

9 店　長： お疲れさま。

Ⅰ

Manager: John, I heard Mr. Morita has a cold and is not able to come today. In the evening it will get busy, so I am counting on you.

John: Sure, I will do my best.

Manager: First of all, vegetables are in the refrigerator, so take them out. Then, is the outside light on?

John: No, it isn't. Shall I turn it on?

Manager: Yes. If you press the button there, the light will be on.

John: Yes.

Ⅱ

Customer: Excuse me. I have dropped the soy sauce. I am sorry.

John: Please don't worry. Oh, your skirt has become dirty, hasn't it?

Customer: Oh, no! What should I do?

John: I will bring a towel right away.

Ⅲ

Manager: You were so helpful today.

John: Don't mention it. But, it was such a busy day.

Manager: You have school tomorrow, right? It is tough to go to school working part-time, isn't it?

John: Yes. I am late for classes sometimes.

Manager: When I was a student, I often cut classes, too. I should have studied more. Well, I will tidy up the rest then.

John: Excuse me for leaving early. Good-bye.

Manager: Thank you. Bye.

単語
たん ご

 K18-07

Vocabulary

Nouns

* あと	後	the rest
エアコン		air conditioner
カーテン		curtain
クッション		cushion
シャンプー		shampoo
* しょうゆ	しょう油	soy sauce
* スイッチ		switch
スープ		soup
* スカート		skirt
* そと	外	outside
ソファ		sofa
* タオル		towel
にっき	日記	diary
バナナ		banana
ポップコーン		popcorn
むし	虫	insect
やちん	家賃	rent
* ゆうがた	夕方	evening
るすばんでんわ	留守番電話	answering machine
* れいぞうこ	冷蔵庫	refrigerator
ろうそく		candle

い-adjectives

あかるい	明るい	bright
きぶんがわるい	気分が悪い	to feel sick
くらい	暗い	dark
はずかしい	恥ずかしい	embarrassing; to feel embarrassed

U-verbs

あく	開く	(something) opens（〜が）
あやまる	謝る	to apologize（*person* に）
* おす	押す	to press; to push（〜を）

* Words that appear in the dialogue

* おとす	落とす	to drop (something)（〜を）
おゆがわく	お湯が沸く	water boils
ころぶ	転ぶ	to fall down
こわす	壊す	to break (something)（〜を）
さく	咲く	to bloom（〜が）
しまる	閉まる	(something) closes（〜が）
* たすかる	助かる	to be saved; to be helped
* たのむ	頼む	to ask (a favor)（*person* に〜を）
* つく		(something) turns on（〜が）
よごす	汚す	to make dirty（〜を）

Ru-verbs

おちる	落ちる	(something) drops（〜が）
* かたづける	片付ける	to tidy up（〜を）
かんがえる	考える	to think (about); to consider
きえる	消える	(something) goes off（〜が）
こわれる	壊れる	(something) breaks（〜が）
* よごれる	汚れる	to become dirty（〜が）

Irregular Verb

ちゅうもんする	注文する	to place an order（〜を）

Adverbs and Other Expressions

* いますぐ	今すぐ	right away
* おかげで		thanks to ...（〜の）
* おさきにしつれいします	お先に失礼します	See you. (lit., I'm leaving ahead of you.)
* おつかれさま（でした）	お疲れ様（でした）	You must be tired after working so hard. (ritualistic expression)
* 〜（ん）だろう		short form of 〜（ん）でしょう
* どうしよう		What should I/we do?
* ほんとうに	本当に	really
* まず		first of all
〜までに		by (time/date)

文法 G r a m m a r
ぶん ぽう

1 Transitivity Pairs

Some verbs describe situations in which human beings act on things. For example, I *open* the door, you *turn on* the TV, and they *break* the computer. Such verbs are called "transitive verbs." Some other verbs describe changes that things or people undergo. For example, the door *opens*, the TV *goes on*, and the computer *breaks down*. These latter verbs are called "intransitive verbs."

While most verbs are loners and do not have a counterpart of the opposite transitivity, some important verbs come in pairs.

Transitive		Intransitive	
開ける	*open something*	開く	*something opens*
閉める	*close something*	閉まる	*something closes*
入れる	*put something in*	入る	*something goes inside*
出す	*take something out*	出る	*something goes out*
つける	*turn something on*	つく	*something goes on*
消す	*turn something off;*	消える	*something goes off*
	extinguish something		
壊す	*break something*	壊れる	*something breaks*
汚す	*make something dirty*	汚れる	*something becomes dirty*
落とす	*drop something*	落ちる	*something drops*
沸かす	*boil water*	沸く	*water boils*

Transitive verbs call for both the subject (agent) and the object (the thing that is worked on). Intransitive verbs call only for the subject (the thing or the person that goes through the change).

たけしさんが電気をつけました。
てん き
Takeshi turned the light on.

電気がつきました。
てん き
The light went on.

たけしさんがお湯を沸かしました。
ゆ　　わ
Takeshi boiled the water.

お湯が沸きました。
ゆ　わ
The water boiled.

Transitive verbs describe activities, while intransitive verbs describe changes. They behave differently when they are followed by the helping verb ている. Let us first recall that activity verbs (話す, for example) ＋ ている refer to actions in progress, while change verbs (結婚する, for example) ＋ ている refer to the states resulting from the change, as we learned in Lesson 7.

スーさんは今、電話でお母さんと話しています。　(activity, action in progress)
Sue is talking on the phone with her mother right now.

山下先生は結婚しています。　(change, result state)
Professor Yamashita is married.

Similarly, when followed by ている, transitive verbs refer to actions in progress, while intransitive verbs refer to states that hold after the change takes place.

ロバートさんは窓を開けています。
Robert is opening the windows.

ドアが開いています。
Doors are open. / There's an open door.

ともこさんは電気を消しています。
Tomoko is turning the light off.

テレビは消えています。
The TV set is off.

ゴジラが町を壊しています。
There goes Godzilla, destroying the city.

このパソコンは壊れています。
This computer is broken.

2　〜てしまう

The *te*-form of a verb ＋ しまう has two meanings, which at first might appear rather incongruous. In the first instance, しまう indicates that one "carries out with determination" a plan described by the verb. It typically involves bringing something to a culmination point. You, in other words, do something completely, or finish doing something, or have something done.

本を読んでしまいました。
I read the book completely. / I finished reading the book.

The second meaning of しまう is "lack of premeditation or control over how things turn out." This often comes with *the sense of regret*; something regrettable happens, or you do something which you did not intend to.[1]

電車の中にかばんを忘れてしまいました。
I inadvertently left my bag on the train.

宿題を忘れたので、先生は怒ってしまいました。
To my horror and sorrow, my professor got angry, because I had forgotten my homework.

Both nuanced meanings focus on the discrepancy between what we intend and what the world is like when it is left on its own. A しまう sentence may be ambiguous between the two meanings. How a given しまう sentence should be interpreted depends on the assumptions the speaker has when uttering it. For example, the "finished reading" sentence above can be read as meaning "regrettably" just as easily if you read the book although you had not planned to, or knowing that it was wrong but unable to resist the temptation.

In speech, 〜てしまう and 〜でしまう are often contracted to 〜ちゃう and 〜じゃう, respectively.

宿題をなくしちゃった。
I lost my homework!

食べてしまいました	→	食べちゃいました
食べてしまった	→	食べちゃった
飲んでしまいました	→	飲んじゃいました
飲んでしまった	→	飲んじゃった

3 〜と

The present tense short form of a predicate ＋ と means *whenever* the situation described by the predicate holds, another thing happens. In most と sentences, the first clause describes the cause, and the second the effect.

---

[1] Since しまう goes with the verbal *te*-form, which is affirmative, it only gives us sentences meaning that something regrettable does or did happen. In other words, we cannot express negated ideas with しまう such as "regrettably, x did not take place" or "unfortunately, I did not do x."

私はその人と話すと元気になる。
Whenever I talk with that person, I feel uplifted.

道が込んでいると時間がかかる。
Whenever the streets are crowded, it takes longer to get there.

<u>clause A</u> 　と　 <u>clause B</u>。　　*Whenever A happens, B happens too.*
(short, present)

Sometimes, a と sentence describes a cause-effect relationship between specific events.

メアリーさんが国に帰るとさびしくなります。
If Mary goes back home, we will be sad and lonely.

While the clause that comes before と is always in the present tense, the second clause can be in the present or in the past tense.

私は子供の時、冬になるとかぜをひきました。
When I was young, whenever winter arrived, I caught a cold.

The event described by the second clause must follow the event described in the first half of the sentence. Thus it is wrong to say:

✕ 私はその人と話すと喫茶店に行きます。
Whenever I talk with that person, we go to a coffee shop.

If you want an adjective idea in the second clause, it is usually expressed as a change. It is very common therefore to find in the second clause an い-adjective base ＋ くなる, and a な-adjective base ＋ になる (see Lesson 10 for adjective ＋ なる).

秋になると木が赤くなります。
Whenever fall arrives, trees turn red.

夜になると町が静かになります。
Whenever night comes, the town becomes quiet.

4 〜ながら

You can connect two verbs with ながら to say that the two actions are performed at the same time. ながら follows a verb stem. The second verb, which goes after ながら, can be in any form.

私はいつも音楽を聞きながら日本語を勉強します。
I always study Japanese while listening to music.

たけしさんは歌を歌いながら洗濯をしています。
Takeshi is doing laundry singing a song.

アルバイトをしながら学校に行くのは大変です。
It is not easy to go to school working part-time.

Note that the two verbs that flank ながら must be two actions performed by the same person. ながら, in other words, cannot describe an action performed while another person does something.

5 〜ばよかったです

ばよかったです means *I wish I had done* or *I should have done* something. You can use it to describe an alternative course of action you, to your great regret, did not take.

あの時、「愛している」と言えばよかったです。
I wish I had told her that I loved her.

彼女と別れなければよかったです。
I should not have broken up with her.

All verbs can regularly be turned into a ばよかったです sentence with no exception or irregularity. You form the ば-form on the basis of the present tense short forms.

Verbs in the affirmative: Drop the final *-u* and add *-eba*.

食べる (*tabe-ru*)	→	食べれば (*tabe-r-eba*)
行く (*ik-u*)	→	行けば (*ik-eba*)
待つ	→	待てば
買う	→	買えば
する	→	すれば
くる	→	くれば

Verbs in the negative: Drop the final い and add ければ.

食べない	→	食べなければ
行かない	→	行かなければ
待たない	→	待たなければ
買わない	→	買わなければ
しない	→	しなければ
こない	→	こなければ

We will learn about the ば-forms used in broader contexts in Lesson 22.

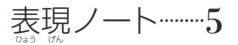

表現ノート………5   Expression Notes 5

おかげ▶Nounのおかげ（で）is used to express gratitude to something or some-one when things turn out as desired.

友だちが書いてくれた地図のおかげで道に迷わなかった。
Thanks to the map my friend drew, I didn't get lost.

先生：卒業おめでとう。　　　*Congratulations on your graduation.*
学生：先生のおかげです。　　*I owe it to you, Professor.*

The expression　おかげさまで (lit., Thanks to you) is the proper response when asked 元気ですか.

A：元気ですか。　　　　　　*How are you?*
B：ええ、おかげさまで。　　*I'm fine, thanks to you.*

おかげさまで is also used to show appreciation for the addressee's help/support/concern.

A：仕事に慣れましたか。
　　Have you gotten used to the job?
B：ええ、おかげさまで、だいぶ慣れました。
　　Yes, I have gotten used to it mostly. Thank you for your concern.

練習 P r a c t i c e
れん しゅう

① 窓が開いています
まど あ

A. Describe the pictures using transitive and intransitive verbs.  K18-08

Example:　(a) ドアを開けます。　(b) ドアが開きます。
あ あ

8.

(a)

(b)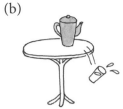

9.

(a)

(b)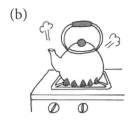

B. Answer the following questions.

1. 寝る時、窓を閉めますか。
   <ruby>寝<rt>ね</rt></ruby>　<ruby>時<rt>とき</rt></ruby>　<ruby>窓<rt>まど</rt></ruby>　<ruby>閉<rt>し</rt></ruby>

2. 寝る時、電気／エアコンを消しますか。
   <ruby>寝<rt>ね</rt></ruby>　<ruby>時<rt>とき</rt></ruby>　<ruby>電気<rt>でんき</rt></ruby>　<ruby>消<rt>け</rt></ruby>

3. 朝、窓を開けますか。
   <ruby>朝<rt>あさ</rt></ruby>　<ruby>窓<rt>まど</rt></ruby>　<ruby>開<rt>あ</rt></ruby>

4. けさ、かばんの中に何を入れましたか。
   <ruby>中<rt>なか</rt></ruby>　<ruby>何<rt>なに</rt></ruby>　<ruby>入<rt>い</rt></ruby>

5. 今日、宿題を出しましたか。
   <ruby>今日<rt>きょう</rt></ruby>　<ruby>宿題<rt>しゅくだい</rt></ruby>　<ruby>出<rt>だ</rt></ruby>

6. 最近、何か壊しましたか／落としましたか。
   <ruby>最近<rt>さいきん</rt></ruby>　<ruby>何<rt>なに</rt></ruby>　<ruby>壊<rt>こわ</rt></ruby>　<ruby>落<rt>お</rt></ruby>

7. 最近、何か汚しましたか。
   <ruby>最近<rt>さいきん</rt></ruby>　<ruby>何<rt>なに</rt></ruby>　<ruby>汚<rt>よご</rt></ruby>

8. よくお湯を沸かしますか。
   <ruby>湯<rt>ゆ</rt></ruby>　<ruby>沸<rt>わ</rt></ruby>

C. Describe the condition using 〜ている. 🔊 K18-09

Example:　窓が開いています。
　　　　　<ruby>窓<rt>まど</rt></ruby>　<ruby>開<rt>あ</rt></ruby>

Ex.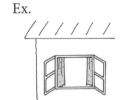

(1)

(2)

(3)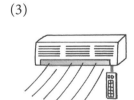

(4)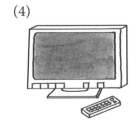

(5)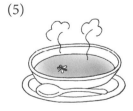

(6)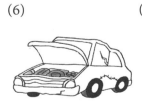

(7)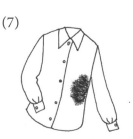

(8)　　　　　　　　(9)

D. Pair Work—One person looks at picture A below and the other looks at picture B (p. 162). The two pictures look similar but are not identical. Find out the difference by asking each other questions.

Example:　A：冷蔵庫にりんごが入っていますか。
　　　　　　 B：はい。一つ入っています。

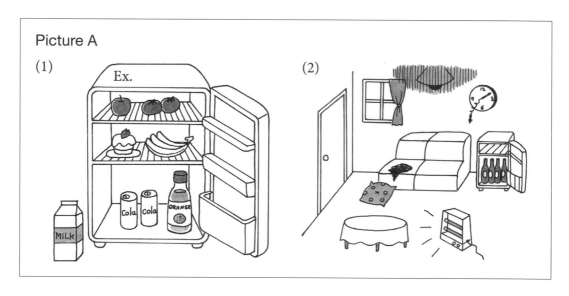

E. Pair Work—You and your partner are working part-time at Little Asia. The manager is sick, and you need to take care of the restaurant for the day. Look at the picture and discuss what needs to be done to open the place for business.

Example:　A：エアコンがついていませんね。
　　　　　　 B：そうですね。じゃ、私がつけますよ。
　　　　　　 A：すみません。お願いします。

Ⅱ 昼ご飯を食べてしまいました
（ひる はん た）

A. You finished doing the following things. Express what you did with 〜てしまう.

🔊 K18-10

Example:　finished eating lunch　→　もう昼ご飯を食べてしまいました。
　　　　　　　　　　　　　　　　　　　　（ひる はん た）

1. finished doing homework
2. finished writing a paper
3. finished reading a book
4. finished tidying up the room
5. finished doing the laundry
6. finished seeing a movie

B. The following things happened and you regret them. Express them with 〜てしまう. 🔊 K18-11

Example:　お金があまりないんですが、(bought a lot)
　　　　　　　（かね）

　　　　　　→　お金があまりないんですが、たくさん買ってしまいました。
　　　　　　　　　（かね）　　　　　　　　　　　　　　　（か）

1. 友だちにパソコンを借りたんですが、(broke it)
　（とも）　　　　　　　　（か）
2. 給料をもらったんですが、(spent all)
　（きゅうりょう）
3. 急いでいたので、(fell down)
　（いそ）
4. きのう寒かったので、(caught a cold)
　　　　（さむ）
5. きのうあまり寝なかったので、(slept in class)
　　　　　　　（ね）
6. ゆみさんが好きだったんですが、(Yumi got married)
　　　　　　　（す）
7. 今日までに家賃を払わなきゃいけなかったんですが、(forgot it)
　（きょう）　（やちん）（はら）
8. 朝寝坊したので、(missed a train)
　（あさ ね ぼう）

C. You stayed at your friend's apartment while he/she was away. Now your friend is back; make an apology using 〜ちゃう／じゃう for what you have done in the apartment.

Example:　　A：ごめん。

　　　　　　B：どうしたの？

　　　　　　A：実は冷蔵庫の食べ物を全部食べちゃった。
　　　　　　　　　れいぞうこ　　た　もの　　ぜんぶ　た

　　　　　　B：えっ！

D. Pair Work—You did the following things. Explain the situations to your partner in informal speech. Continue the conversation.

Example: You borrowed a camera from your friend but broke it.

→ A：友だちからカメラを借りたんだけど、壊しちゃった。

B：えっ。今すぐ謝ったほうがいいよ。

A：そうだね。そうするよ。

1. You borrowed a book from your friend but lost it.

2. You received a scholarship but you bought a car with that money.

3. You told a lie to your friend.

4. You had a fight with your boyfriend/girlfriend.

5. You didn't want to go to class, so you cut class.

6. You overslept and came late for class.

（Ⅲ）春になると暖かくなります

A. Change the cues in 1 through 6 into と clauses and choose the correct phrase on the right to complete each sentence. 🔊 K18-12

Example: 秋になると涼しくなります。

Ex. 秋になります ・
1. 電気をつけます ・
2. お酒を飲みすぎます ・
3. 日本語を話しません ・
4. 家族から手紙が来ません・
5. 暗い所で本を読みます ・
6. 春になります ・

・a. 日本語が上手になりません。
・b. 目が疲れます。
・c. 明るくなります。
・d. 花が咲きます。
・e. 涼しくなります。
・f. 悲しくなります。
・g. 気分が悪くなります。

B. Pair Work—Give advice to your partner who has the following problems using
〜と.

Example: A：車の運転が下手なんです。
         くるま うんてん へた
         B：練習すると上手になりますよ。
         れんしゅう   じょう ず

1. A：疲れているんです。
   つか
   B：＿＿＿＿＿＿＿＿＿＿＿＿＿＿＿と元気になりますよ。
                              げん き
2. A：友だちがいないんです。
   とも
   B：＿＿＿＿＿＿＿＿＿＿＿＿＿＿＿と友だちができますよ。
                              とも
3. A：かぜをひいたんです。
   B：＿＿＿＿＿＿＿＿＿＿＿＿＿＿＿とよくなりますよ。
4. A：太りたいんです。
   ふと
   B：＿＿＿＿＿＿＿＿＿＿＿＿＿＿＿と太りますよ。
                              ふと
5. A：寝られないんです。
   ね
   B：＿＿＿＿＿＿＿＿＿＿＿＿＿＿＿と寝られますよ。
                              ね

C. Pair Work—Talk with your partner using the cues below. Expand your conversation.

Example: ＿＿＿＿＿＿＿＿と顔が赤くなる
                      かお あか
   → A：私は、恥ずかしいと顔が赤くなるんです。
        わたし は   かお あか
      B：そうですか。ぼくは、お酒を飲むと顔が赤くなるんです。
                              さけ の かお あか
      A：どれぐらい飲むと顔が赤くなるんですか。
              の   かお あか

1. ＿＿＿＿＿＿＿＿＿＿と気分が悪くなる
                    き ぶん わる
2. ＿＿＿＿＿＿＿＿＿＿とうれしくなる
3. ＿＿＿＿＿＿＿＿＿＿と悲しくなる
                    かな
4. ＿＿＿＿＿＿＿＿＿＿と元気になる
                    げん き
5. ＿＿＿＿＿＿＿＿＿＿と疲れる
                    つか
6. ＿＿＿＿＿＿＿＿＿＿と緊張する
                    きんちょう
7. ＿＿＿＿＿＿＿＿＿＿と踊りたくなる
                    おど

Ⅳ テレビを見ながら勉強します

A. The pictures below show what Michiko does. Describe them using 〜ながら.

K18-13

Example: テレビを見ながら勉強します。／勉強しながらテレビを見ます。

B. Pair Work—Ask your partner the following questions.

1. ご飯を食べながら、何をしますか。
2. 何をしながら、勉強しますか。
3. シャワーを浴びながら、何をしますか。
4. 音楽を聞きながら、何をしますか。
5. 何をしながら、考えますか。

C. Class Activity—Let's play charades. The teacher gives a sentence card to each student. One of the students mimes the sentence. All other students guess what the person is doing and raise their hands when they recognize the action. The person that gets the most points is the winner.

Example: 歩きながら、アイスクリームを食べています。

D. Talk about the following, using 〜ながら.

1. two things you often do at the same time when you are busy

Example: 忙しい時、食べながら勉強します。

2. two things it is better not to do at the same time

Example: 歩きながらメールをしないほうがいいです。

3. two things you like to do at the same time

Example: 音楽を聞きながら運転するのが好きです。

4. two things you cannot do at the same time

Example: 自転車に乗りながらそばを食べられません。

Ⓥ もっと勉強すればよかったです

A. Change the following verbs into ば-forms. 📢 K18-14

Example: いく → いけば

1. よむ   4. はなす   7. あそぶ   10. たべない   13. しない
2. くる   5. する   8. おきる   11. きかない
3. みる   6. つかう   9. こない   12. つかわない

B. The following pictures are what happened to you as a result of action you took or didn't take (marked with ×). Express your regret using 〜ばよかったです.

📢 K18-15

Example: かさを持ってくればよかったです。

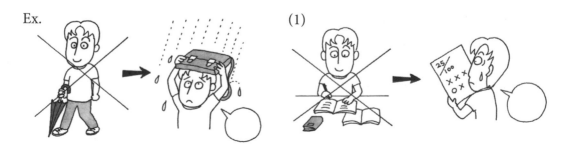

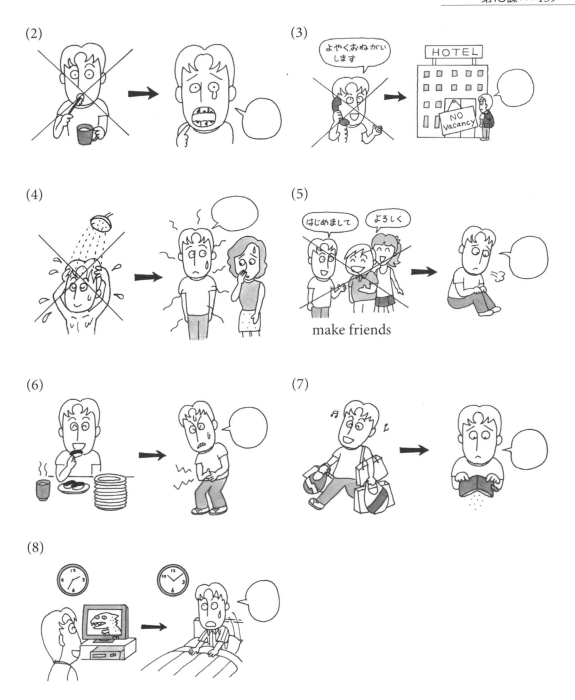

C. Pair Work—You are unhappy. Explain your situation and express your regret using 〜ばよかった. Then, expand the conversation.

Example: You didn't do well on your test.

→　Ａ：テストがよくなかったんです。

　　　もっと勉強すればよかったです。

Ｂ：どれぐらい勉強したんですか。

Ａ：テストの前に30分ぐらい。

Ｂ：それは少なすぎますよ。

1. You were late for class.

2. You went to a restaurant but it was closed for a holiday.

3. You went on a trip but you didn't bring a camera.

4. Your college life is boring.

5. You ordered a hamburger but it didn't taste good.

6. You ate too much and you are not feeling well.

7. You have just started a job. You have too much work.

8. You broke up with your boyfriend/girlfriend. You can't help thinking about them.

D. Pair Work—Express your regret using 〜ばよかった, then expand the conversation.

Example: きのう

→　Ａ：きのう、買い物しなければよかった。

Ｂ：どうして？

Ａ：買いすぎて、お金がなくなっちゃったんだ。

Ｂ：そう。じゃ、お金、貸そうか？

1. 先週
   せんしゅう

2. 子供の時
   こども　とき

3. 高校の時
   こうこう　とき

4. Your own

Ⅵ まとめの練習
れんしゅう

A. Pair Work—Tell each other a story of a failure or a sad experience, which happened contrary to your wishes.

Example:　A：けさ、起きられなくて、授業に遅れてしまったんです。
お　　　　じゅぎょう　おく
　　　　　B：きのう何時に寝たんですか。
なんじ　ね
　　　　　A：二時です。
にじ
　　　　　B：もっと早く寝ればよかったですね。
はや　ね

B. Pair Work—Ask your partner the following questions.

1. あしたまでに何をしなければいけませんか。
なに
2. レポートの宿題がありますか。いつまでに出さなければいけませんか。
しゅくだい　　　　　　　　　　　　だ
3. 卒業までに何をしようと思っていますか。
そつぎょう　なに　　　　　おも
4. 大学の食堂は何時から何時まで開いていますか。
だいがく　しょくどう　なんじ　　　なんじ　あ
5. 図書館は何曜日に閉まっていますか。
としょかん　なんようび　し
6. あなたの冷蔵庫の中に何が入っていますか。
れいぞうこ　なか　なに　はい
7. お酒を飲みすぎるとどうなりますか。
さけ　の

C. You are an owner of a restaurant. Look at the picture I-E (p. 153) and tell your employee what they should do. Use Dialogue I as a model.

Pair Work (I) D.

(→ p. 152)

Example:　A：冷蔵庫にりんごが入っていますか。
　　　　　　　　れいぞうこ　　　　　　　　　はい
　　　　　　B：はい。一つ入っています。
　　　　　　　　　　ひと　はい

Picture B

(1)　　　　　　　　　　　　　　　　　　　(2)

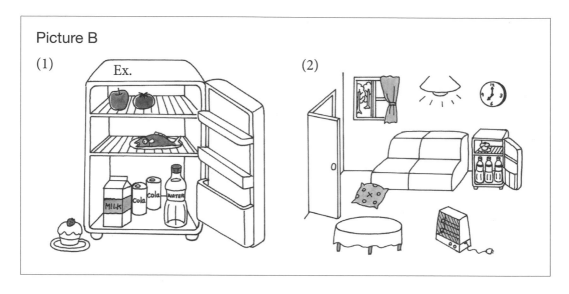

Culture Note

すし Sushi

Sushi is probably the best-known Japanese dish. Some of you might think all sushi is made with raw fish, but actually quite a few types are made with cooked items. There are also some vegetarian choices, such as かっぱ巻き (cucumber roll) and いなりずし (a pouch of fried tofu filled with sushi rice). Rice for sushi is vinegared rice, and sushi is generally dipped in しょうゆ (soy sauce) before being eaten.

すしの種類 (Types of sushi)

にぎりずし

Pressed sushi rice topped with a piece of fish/shellfish, roe, etc., and seasoned with わさび (green horseradish).

Popular sushi toppings		
まぐろ tuna	とろ fatty tuna	えび shrimp
いか squid	あなご saltwater eel	うなぎ freshwater eel
たこ octopus	はまち yellowtail	あじ Spanish mackerel
うに sea urchin	いくら salmon roe	たい snapper

巻きずし

Rice with various ingredients inserted, rolled up in Japanese seaweed. In most 巻きずし, the のり (seaweed) is on the outside, but in some the rice is placed on the outside.

手巻きずし

Very similar to 巻きずし except that it is rolled into a cone shape by hand. It is easy to make at home. Everyone picks their favorite ingredients to make their own hand-rolled sushi.

ちらしずし

Various ingredients scattered artfully over a bed of sushi rice in a box.

回転ずし (Conveyor belt sushi)

回転ずし is sushi served at a restaurant where the plates are placed on a rotating conveyor belt that moves past every seat. Customers pick the items they want. Items of the same price are placed on the same type of plate, so the bill is based on the number and type of plates taken. Conveyor belt sushi is rather inexpensive compared to traditional sushi restaurants.

第19課 | L E S S O N ·······19

出迎え <small>で　むか</small> Meeting the Boss

会話 <small>かい　わ</small> Dialogue

Ⅰ Takeshi came to the airport to pick up the department manager who went to America on business.  K19-01/02

1 たけし：　　　部長、出張お疲れさまでした。
<small>ぶ ちょう　しゅっちょう　つか</small>

2 部　長：　　木村くん、迎えに来てくれてありがとう。本当はシアトルを一時に
<small>ぶ　ちょう　　き む ら　　むか　　き　　　　　　　　　　ほんとう　　　　　　　　　いち じ</small>

3 　　　　　　　出るはずだったんだけど、遅れちゃってね。
<small>て　　　　　　　　　　おく</small>

4 たけし：　　　じゃあ、お疲れになったでしょう。
<small>つか</small>

5 部　長：　　大丈夫だけど、ちょっとおなかがすいてるんだ。
<small>ぶ ちょう　だいじょうぶ</small>

6 たけし：　　　じゃあ、何か召し上がってから、お帰りになりますか。
<small>なに　め　あ　　　　　　　　かえ</small>

7 部　長：　　うん。そうしようか。
<small>ぶ ちょう</small>

Ⅱ At a restaurant.  K19-03/04

1 ウエートレス：いらっしゃいませ。何名様ですか。
<small>なんめいさま</small>

2 たけし：　　　　二人です。
<small>ふたり</small>

3 ウエートレス：おたばこをお吸いになりますか。
<small>す</small>

4 部　長：　　　いいえ。
<small>ぶ ちょう</small>

5 ウエートレス：こちらへどうぞ。お決まりになりましたらお呼びください。
<small>き　　　　　　　　　　　　よ</small>

Ⅲ In front of the department manager's house. 🔊 K19-05/06

1 部長：　　　　うちまで送ってくれてありがとう。

2 たけし：　　　いいえ。今日はごちそうしてくださってありがとうございました。

3 部長：　　　　ゆっくり話ができてよかったよ。ちょっとうちに寄らない？

4 たけし：　　　いえ、もう遅いし、奥様もお休みになっているでしょうから。

5 部長：　　　　この時間ならまだ起きているはずだよ。

6 たけし：　　　でも、今日は遠慮しておきます。奥様によろしくお伝えください。

Ⅰ

Takeshi: Boss, welcome back. You must be tired after the business trip.

Department manager: Thank you for coming here to pick me up, Mr. Kimura. Originally, I was
supposed to leave Seattle at one o'clock, but it ran late.

Takeshi: You must be tired then.

Department manager: No, I am fine, but I am a little hungry.

Takeshi: Then would you like to eat something and go home?

Department manager: That sounds good to me.

Ⅱ

Waitress: Welcome. How many?

Takeshi: Two.

Waitress: Do you smoke?

Department manager: No.

Waitress: This way, please. When you decide, please call me.

Ⅲ

Department manager: Thank you for giving me a ride home.

Takeshi: Not at all. Thank you very much for paying for the dinner.

Department manager: It was nice to have a good talk with you. Would you like to drop by my
house?

Takeshi: It's okay. It's late, and your wife is probably sleeping.

Department manager: No. She must still be awake around this time.

Takeshi: But I'd rather not today. Please give her my best regards.

単語
たん　ご

 K19-07

V o c a b u l a r y

N o u n s

* おくさま	奥様	(your/his) wife (polite)
おこさん	お子さん	(your/their) child (polite)
おれい	お礼	expression of gratitude
けいご	敬語	honorific language
* こちら		this way (polite)
* しゅっちょう	出張	business trip
しゅるい	種類	a kind; a sort
せいかく	性格	personality
ちゅうがくせい	中学生	junior high school student
どちら		where (polite)
なまけもの	怠け者	lazy person
なやみ	悩み	worry
はずかしがりや	恥ずかしがり屋	shy person
* はなし	話	chat; talk
* ぶちょう	部長	department manager
ぶんか	文化	culture
まちがい	間違い	mistake

い - a d j e c t i v e

なかがいい	仲がいい	be on good/close terms; to get along well

な - a d j e c t i v e

まじめ（な）		serious; sober; diligent

U - v e r b s

いらっしゃる		honorific expression for いく, くる, and いる
* おくる	送る	to walk/drive (someone) (person を place まで)
おこる	怒る	to get angry
おっしゃる		honorific expression for いう
* おやすみになる	お休みになる	honorific expression for ねる
* きまる	決まる	to be decided （〜が）
くださる	下さる	honorific expression for くれる

* Words that appear in the dialogue

ごらんになる	ご覧になる	honorific expression for みる
しりあう	知り合う	to get acquainted with（〜と）
〜ていらっしゃる		honorific expression for 〜ている
なさる		honorific expression for する
ひっこす	引っ越す	to move (to another place to live)（〜に）
* めしあがる	召し上がる	honorific expression for たべる and のむ
* よぶ	呼ぶ	to call (one's name)（〜を）; to invite (*person* を *event* に)
* よる	寄る	to stop by（〜に）

Ru-verbs

* おくれる	遅れる	to become late（〜に）
かける		to sit down (*seat* に)
はれる	晴れる	to become sunny
もてる		to be popular (in terms of romantic interest)（*people* に）

Irregular Verbs

* えんりょする	遠慮する	to hold back for the time being; to refrain from
* ごちそうする		to treat/invite (someone) to a meal (*person* に *meal* を)
しょうたいする	招待する	to invite someone (to an event/a place) (*person* を *event/place* に)
ちゅういする	注意する	to watch out; to give warning
* はなしをする	話をする	to have a talk

Adverbs and Other Expressions

おととい		the day before yesterday
それで		then; therefore
なぜ		why（＝どうして）
* ほんとうは	本当は	in fact; originally
まいあさ	毎朝	every morning
* まだ		still
* 〜めいさま	〜名様	party of . . . people
ようこそ		Welcome.
* よろしくおつたえ ください	よろしくお伝 えください	Please give my best regards (to . . .).（〜に）

文法 G r a m m a r
ぶん ぽう

1 Honorific Verbs

We use special verbs to describe the actions of people whom you respect. These special verbs are called honorific verbs, because they bestow honor on, or exalt, the person performing the activities.

	honorific verbs	irregular conjugations
いる 行く 来る	いらっしゃる	いらっしゃ<u>い</u>ます
見る	ご<u>覧</u>になる	
言う	おっしゃる	おっしゃ<u>い</u>ます
する	なさる	なさ<u>い</u>ます
食べる 飲む	召し上がる	
くれる	くださる	ください<u>い</u>ます
寝る	お休みになる	
～ている	～ていらっしゃる	～ていらっしゃ<u>い</u>ます

All the honorific verbs listed above are *u*-verbs, but some of them have irregular conjugations. The long forms of いらっしゃる, おっしゃる, なさる, くださる, and ～ていらっしゃる end with います, instead of the expected ります.

When we use an honorific verb instead of a normal verb, we will have sentences which mean that somebody graciously does something. (Thus we never use these verbs to describe our own actions.) We use them when we talk about what is done by (1) somebody higher up in the social hierarchy, or (2) somebody whom you do not know very well, especially when addressing them directly.

先生は今日学校に<u>いらっしゃいません</u>。　cf. 行きません／来ません／いません
せんせい　きょう がっこう
The professor will (graciously) not go to/come to/be at the school.　(three-way ambiguous)

何を<u>召し上がります</u>か。　　　　　cf. 食べますか／飲みますか
なに　め　あ
What will you (graciously) eat/drink?

田中さんのお母さんがこの本を<u>くださいました</u>。　　　cf. <u>くれました</u>

Ms. Tanaka's mother (graciously) gave me this book.

先生は自分で料理<u>なさる</u>そうです。　　　cf. 料理<u>する</u>そうです

I hear that the professor (graciously) cooks for himself.

心配<u>なさらない</u>でください。　　　cf. 心配<u>しない</u>でください

Please don't (graciously) worry.

先生はテレビを<u>ご覧になって</u>います。　　　cf. <u>見て</u>います

The professor is (graciously) watching TV.

For the activities for which we lack special honorific verbs, we add the respect factor as follows:

(1) Using ていらっしゃいます instead of ています, if the sentence has the helping verb ている.

先生は電話で話し<u>ていらっしゃいます</u>。　　　（< 話し<u>ています</u>）

The professor is (graciously) talking on the phone.

先生は疲れ<u>ていらっしゃる</u>みたいです。　　　（< 疲れ<u>ている</u>みたいです）

It appears that the professor is (graciously) tired.

(2) Flanking a verb stem with お and になる, in most other cases.[1]

お ＋ verb stem ＋ になる

先生はもう<u>お帰りになりました</u>。　　　（< <u>帰りました</u>）

The professor has already (graciously) gone home.

---

[1] As the examples show, you can turn most combinations of a verb and a post-predicate expression into the honorific style by simply turning the verb into the honorific form. Post-predicate expressions, such as ことが あります and ください, remain unchanged. This rule also applies to expressions like てもいい and てはいけ ない, and to the potential verbs. It is, however, not considered in good taste to talk about what an "honorable" person can or cannot do, and may or must not do.

　ている is exceptional in being a post-predicate that regularly undergoes the honorific style shift. Special honorific verbs generally take priority over ていらっしゃる, as seen in the <u>ご覧になって</u>います example above, but forms like <u>見</u>ていらっしゃいます are also considered acceptable.

この雑誌をお読みになったことがありますか。　（＜読んだことがありますか）
Have you ever (graciously) read this magazine?

どうぞお使いになってください。　　　　　　（＜使ってください）
Please (graciously) use it.

2　Giving Respectful Advice

You may hear the form "お ＋ verb stem ＋ ください" in public address announcements and in the speech of store attendants.

切符をお取りください。　　　　（＜取る）
Please take a ticket.

説明をお読みください。　　　　（＜読む）
Please read the instruction.

Although such sentences end with ください, it is better to consider that they are (courteously phrased) commands, rather than requests. When somebody tells you お〜ください, you are being encouraged to perform the actions *for your own good*. Thus if I want somebody to pass the salt *for me* it is wrong to say:

× 塩をお取りください。
Please take the salt (and pass it to me).

You should say instead:　塩を取っていただけませんか。

With most する compound verbs, for example, the prefix ご is used instead of お. Note also the examples with special honorific verbs below.

ご注意ください。　　　　　　　（＜注意する）
Please watch out.

ご覧ください。　　　　　　　　（＜ご覧になる ＜見る）
Please look.

お召し上がりください。　　　　（＜召し上がる ＜食べる）
Please help yourself.

お休みください。　　　　　　　（＜お休みになる ＜寝る）
Please have a good rest.

3　～てくれてありがとう

When you want to express gratitude to someone and if you want to refer specifically to the action you are grateful for in doing so, you can use the *te*-form ＋ くれてありがとう.[2]

| verb *te*-form ＋ くれてありがとう | *Thank you for doing . . .* |

手伝ってくれてありがとう。
て つだ
Thank you for helping me out.

If you are thanking someone who needs to be talked to with the honorific language, such as when you and the person are not close or when the person ranks higher than you in any of the social hierarchies, you should say "*te*-form ＋ くださってありがとうございました."

推薦状を書いてくださってありがとうございました。
すいせんじょう　　か
Thank you for writing a letter of recommendation for me.

4　～てよかったです

Te-form ＋ よかった means "I'm glad that such and such is/was the case." If you want to mention something in the negative in the part before よかった, you can use the negative *te*-form なくて.

| ～てよかったです | *I am glad that . . .* |

日本語を勉強してよかったです。
に ほん ご　　べんきょう
I'm glad that I have studied Japanese.

メアリーさんが元気になってよかったです。
げん き
I'm glad that Mary got well.

きのうのパーティーに行かなくてよかったです。
い
I'm glad that I did not go to the party yesterday.

---

[2] You can use this pattern to say "thank you for being such-and-such a person," by using でいる instead of です.
　　いい友だちでいてくれてありがとう。　　*Thank you for being a good friend.*
　　　とも

5 ～はずです

You can say something is "supposed to be the case," by adding はずです to a sentence ending in the short form.

| ～はずです | *It is supposed to be the case . . .* |

今日は日曜日だから、銀行は閉まっているはずです。
きょう　にちようび　　　　　ぎんこう　し
Banks must be closed, because today is a Sunday.

きのうメアリーさんはどこにも行かなかったはずです。[3]
い
I believe that Mary did not go anywhere yesterday.

A はずです sentence is a statement about what you believe is true or likely, though you lack conclusive evidence. It is used when situations surrounding the case and/or our common sense point naturally to such a belief. はずです cannot be used in a situation in which you are "supposed" to do something because of duty, responsibility, or law.

You can turn はずです into the past tense to describe something that was supposed to have been the case but which actually turned out otherwise. The part that precedes はずでした is in the present tense.

先週電話をもらうはずでしたが、電話がありませんでした。
せんしゅうでん わ　　　　　　　　　　　　　でん わ
I was supposed to receive a phone call last week, but I did not.

You can use はずです with adjectives and nouns as well as with verbs.

い-adjectives:	おもしろいはずです
な-adjectives:	元気なはずです
	げん き
nouns:	日本人のはずです
	に ほんじん

---

[3] You see in this example that verbs in the negative can come before はずです. You may also hear another type of negative, はずがありません and はずがない, which means that something is inconceivable.

あの人がうそをつくはずがありません。
ひと
I cannot imagine that the person would tell a lie.

表現ノート……6
ひょう げん

Expression Notes 6

Honorific forms of nouns and adjectives▶Some nouns and adjectives are made into honorific forms by adding the prefixes お or ご. お is usually used with words that originated in Japanese and ご with words borrowed from Chinese.

お〜： お名前　お仕事　お好き　お元気　おたばこ　お忙しい
　　　　なまえ　　しごと　　す　　げんき　　　　　　　いそが
ご〜： ご両親　ご兄弟　ご病気　ご主人　ご親切
　　　　りょうしん　きょうだい　びょうき　しゅじん　しんせつ

Some other words are replaced by special vocabulary items.

家　　→　お宅　　　　　　　　　どこ　　　　→　どちら
いえ　　　　たく
子供　→　お子さん　　　　　　　どうですか　→　いかがですか
こども　　　こ
だれ　→　どなた／どちら様
　　　　　　　　　　　　さま

These words and expressions cannot be used when you refer to yourself, your family, or the group you belong to.

A：ご両親はお元気ですか。　　　　　*How are your parents?*
　　りょうしん　げんき
B：はい。おかげさまで元気です。　　*Thanks to you, they are fine.*
　　　　　　　　　　　　げんき
　　（×お元気です）
　　　　　げんき

たら in polite speech▶We learned that the conditional たら is based on the past tense short forms. In honorific speech, たら also follows the long form.

お決まりになり<u>ましたら</u>お呼びください。　　cf.決まっ<u>たら</u>呼んで
　き　　　　　　　　　　　　　よ　　　　　　　　き　　　　　　　ください。
Please let us know when you are ready to order.

それで/そして/それから▶These "and" words are used in different meanings.

それで　"and therefore" (to introduce the consequence of what comes before it)

　電車が来ませんでした。それで、遅刻しました。
　てんしゃ　き　　　　　　　　　　ちこく
　Trains didn't come. Therefore, I was late for class.

そして　"and last but not least" (to say something remarkable)

　スーさんは韓国語と英語が話せます。そして、日本語も話せます。
　　　　　　かんこくご　えいご　はな　　　　　　にほんご　はな
　Sue speaks Korean and English. And believe it or not, Japanese too.

それから　"and then" (to add an item that comes later in time or in the order of importance)

　京都と奈良に行きました。それから、大阪にも行きました。
　きょうと　なら　い　　　　　　　　おおさか　い
　I went to Kyoto and Nara. And then I also went to Osaka.

練習 Practice

① コーヒーを召し上がります

A. Change the following verbs into honorific expressions.

(a) Special honorific verbs 🔊 K19-08

Example: 行く → いらっしゃる

1. 食べる
2. 言う
3. いる
4. する
5. 寝る
6. 来る
7. 見る
8. 飲む
9. 住んでいる
10. 読んでいる
11. くれる

(b) お〜になる 🔊 K19-09

Example: 歌う → お歌いになる

1. わかる
2. 調べる
3. 読む
4. 聞く
5. 座る
6. 立つ
7. 乗る
8. 入る
9. 待つ

B. Describe what Professor Yamashita does in a day using honorific expressions.

🔊 K19-10

Example: 山下先生はコーヒーを召し上がります。

Ex.
(1)
(2)
(3)

(4)
(5)
(6)
(7)

(8) (9) (10)

C. Change the following questions into honorific expressions. K19-11

Example: よく写真を撮りますか。 → よく写真をお撮りになりますか。
　　　　　　　しゃしん　と　　　　　　　　　　　しゃしん　と

1. お名前は何と言いますか。
　　なまえ　なん　い

2. どちらに住んでいますか。
　　　　す

3. どんな音楽をよく聞きますか。
　　　　おんがく　　き

4. 車を持っていますか。
　　くるま　も

5. ご兄弟／お子さんがいますか。
　　きょうだい　こ

6. 週末、よく何をしますか。
　　しゅうまつ　なに

7. 週末、どちらへよく行きますか。
　　しゅうまつ　　　　い

8. きのう何を食べましたか。
　　　　なに　た

9. 外国に行ったことがありますか。
　　がいこく　い

10. どんな外国語を話しますか。
　　　　がいこくご　はな

11. 最近、映画を見ましたか。
　　さいきん　えいが　み

12. 毎日、何時ごろ寝ますか。
　　まいにち　なんじ　ね

13. 日本の歌を知っていますか。
　　にほん　うた　し

14. ペットを飼っていますか。
　　　　か

15. どんなスポーツをしますか。

16. お酒を飲みますか。
　　さけ　の

17. 結婚していますか。
　　けっこん

18. 有名人に会ったことがありますか。
　　ゆうめいじん　あ

19. なぜ日本語を勉強しているんですか。
　　にほんご　べんきょう

D. Pair Work—Ask your partner the questions above made with honorific expressions. Make sure that you don't use honorific forms when you answer.

E. Role Play—Act the role of a reporter or a celebrity whom you like.

Reporter: Ask questions using honorific expressions.
Celebrity: Answer the questions.

Ⅱ お待ちください

Match the following expressions with the pictures. Put answers in the (   ). 📶 K19-12

(1) (　　)

(2) (　　)

(3) (　　)

(4) (　　)

(5) (　　)

(6) (　　)

(7) (　　)

(8) (　　)

(9) (　　)

a. お待ちください。

b. ご覧ください。

c. お入りください。

d. ご注意ください。

e. お召し上がりください。

f. おかけください。

g. お使いください。

h. お書きください。

i. おたばこはご遠慮ください。

Ⅲ 悩みを聞いてくれてありがとう

A. Express your appreciation to the following people using 〜てくれてありがとう／
〜てくださってありがとうございました. K19-13

Example:　悩みを聞く

  to your friend　→　悩みを聞いてくれてありがとう。

  to your teacher　→　悩みを聞いてくださってありがとうございました。

Your friend

1. ノートを見せる
2. うちまで送る
3. 宿題を手伝う
4. 部屋を片付ける
5. 昼ご飯をおごる

Your teacher

6. 推薦状を書く
7. 宿題の間違いを直す
8. パーティーに招待する
9. 日本の文化を教える
10. 辞書を貸す

B. Role Play—In pairs, act the role of the following, expressing your appreciation
to each other as much as possible.

Example:　Husband and Wife

→　Husband:　いつもおいしい料理を作ってくれてありがとう。

    Wife:　いつも犬を散歩に連れていってくれてありがとう。

    （掃除する／服を買う／毎朝駅まで送る, etc.）

1. Husband and Wife

2. Boss and Secretary

3. Roommates

4. Boyfriend and Girlfriend

C. Tell the class who you want to express your gratitude to, and what you want to say to them, as in the example.

Example: 私はホストファミリーのお母さんにお礼が言いたいです。お母さんは毎朝起こしてくれました。おかげで日本語の授業に遅刻しませんでした。「毎朝起こしてくれてありがとう」と言いたいです。

Ⅳ 日本に留学してよかったです

A. Express that you are glad you did/didn't do the things below using 〜てよかった.

🔊 K19-14

Example: 日本に留学する → 日本に留学してよかったです。

1. 財布が見つかる
2. 敬語を習う
3. 日本語の勉強をやめない
4. 友だちに手伝ってもらう
5. 授業をサボらない
6. この大学を選ぶ
7. 授業に遅れない
8. 早くレポートを書いてしまう
9. いろいろな人と知り合える
10. 新しいアパートに引っ越す

B. Pair Work—Talk about the things you are glad you have done/you haven't done. Expand the conversation as in the example.

Example: おととい

→ A：おととい、秋葉原でゲームを買いました。秋葉原に行ってよかったです。

B：どうしてですか。

A：ほかの店より安いし、いろいろな種類のゲームがあるし。

B：いくらぐらいでしたか。

1. きのう
2. 先週
3. 去年
4. 大学に入ってから
5. 子供の時

Ⓥ 頭<small>あたま</small>がいいはずです

A. Read the information about Mr. Ishida and Ms. Sato and answer the questions using 〜はず. 🔊 K19-15

Example:　Q：石田さんは頭<small>あたま</small>がいいですか。

　　　　　A：ええ。東京大学<small>とうきょうだいがく</small>を卒業<small>そつぎょう</small>したから、頭<small>あたま</small>がいいはずです。

石田さん<small>いしだ</small>

graduated from the University of Tokyo

works for a computer company

lives in a big house

vegetarian（ベジタリアン）

good personality

佐藤さん<small>さとう</small>

diligent student

studied in China for one year

tennis circle member

lives alone

1. 石田<small>いしだ</small>さんはコンピューターが使<small>つか</small>えますか。
2. 石田<small>いしだ</small>さんはお金持<small>かねも</small>ちですか。
3. 石田<small>いしだ</small>さんは肉<small>にく</small>を食<small>た</small>べますか。
4. 石田<small>いしだ</small>さんは女<small>おんな</small>の人<small>ひと</small>にもてますか。
5. 佐藤<small>さとう</small>さんはよく授業<small>じゅぎょう</small>をサボりますか。
6. 佐藤<small>さとう</small>さんは中国語<small>ちゅうごくご</small>が話<small>はな</small>せますか。
7. 佐藤<small>さとう</small>さんはテニスが上手<small>じょうず</small>ですか。
8. 佐藤<small>さとう</small>さんは自分<small>じぶん</small>で洗濯<small>せんたく</small>や掃除<small>そうじ</small>をしますか。

B. Complete the sentences using 〜はず.

1. きょうこさんは性格がいいから、＿＿＿＿＿＿＿＿＿＿＿＿＿＿＿＿＿＿。
2. たくやくんはまだ中学生だから、＿＿＿＿＿＿＿＿＿＿＿＿＿＿＿＿＿＿。
3. けんさんは怠け者だから、＿＿＿＿＿＿＿＿＿＿＿＿＿＿＿＿＿＿。
4. みちこさんは恥ずかしがり屋だから、＿＿＿＿＿＿＿＿＿＿＿＿＿＿＿＿。
5. たけしさんとメアリーさんは仲がいいから、＿＿＿＿＿＿＿＿＿＿＿＿＿。
6. スーさんはまじめだから、＿＿＿＿＿＿＿＿＿＿＿＿＿＿＿＿＿＿。

C. The following are things you expected to happen but didn't. Make sentences as in the example.

Example:　友だちがパーティーに来る
　　　　　→　友だちがパーティーに来るはずでしたが、来られませんでした。

1. きのうは晴れる
2. きのうまでにレポートが終わる
3. 友だちに会える
4. 友だちがおごってくれる
5. 飛行機は二時に着く
6. 先週引っ越す
7. 今年卒業できる

D. Takeshi went to Nara with Mary, but things turned out differently from what he had expected. Talk about what he had expected and what really happened, using 〜はず. 🔊 K19-16

Example:　　　What he had expected

his father would lend his car

What happened

his father left early in the morning to play golf using his car

→　お父さんが車を貸してくれるはずでしたが、朝早く車でゴルフに行ってしまいました。

What he had expected	What happened
1. they would get on the 10 o'clock bus	they missed the bus
2. it would become sunny according to the weather forecast	it rained
3. it would take only one hour to Nara	it took as long as three hours
4. they would go to a nice restaurant	they lost their way
5. the date would be fun	Mary got angry

E. Pair Work—Using the cues in D, make dialogues as in the example.

Example:　　A：お父さんが車を貸してくれるはずだったんだけど、
　　　　　　　朝早く車でゴルフに行っちゃったんだ。
　　　　　　B：そうなんだ。それで、どうしたの？
　　　　　　A：車がないから、タクシーで行ったんだ。

Then create your own dialogue below.

A：＿＿＿＿＿＿＿＿＿＿＿＿＿＿＿＿＿はずだったんだけど、

　＿＿＿＿＿＿＿＿＿＿＿＿＿＿＿＿＿ちゃったんだ。

B：そうなんだ。それで、どうしたの？

A：＿＿＿＿＿＿＿＿＿＿＿＿＿＿＿＿＿＿＿＿

B：＿＿＿＿＿＿＿＿＿＿＿＿＿＿＿＿＿＿＿＿

Ⅵ まとめの練習

A. Class Activity—Using honorific expressions, ask questions and find someone who . . .

1. plays golf　　　　　　　＿＿＿＿＿＿＿＿＿＿＿

2. writes lots of letters　　＿＿＿＿＿＿＿＿＿＿＿

3. often buys a lottery ticket　＿＿＿＿＿＿＿＿＿＿＿

4. has an older brother　　＿＿＿＿＿＿＿＿＿＿＿

5. has been to Okinawa　　＿＿＿＿＿＿＿＿＿＿＿

6. watches TV every day   _____

7. drinks coffee every day   _____

8. comes to school by bicycle _____

B. A Japanese official from a sister city has come to your city. You came to the airport to pick him/her up. Using honorific expressions, ask questions in order to get to know the official.

Example: カルガリーにようこそ。カナダは初めていらっしゃいましたか。
〔はじ〕

C. Role Play—Make a skit based on the following situations.

1. This is your last day in Japan. You had a great time because of your host family. Express your appreciation to the host family.

2. Japanese language was hard for you. You thought about quitting it many times during the semester, but you could make it because of your teacher's help. Visit your teacher's office and express your appreciatioin to the teacher.

Culture Note

訪問のしかた Visiting Someone's House
ほう もん

Here are some examples of expressions used when you visit someone's house.

1.

   The guest arrives at the entrance of the house.

   Guest: ごめんください。
   Hello, is anyone home?

2.

   The host comes to the entrance.

   Host: よくいらっしゃいました。どうぞ、おあがりください。
   Welcome. Please come in.

   The guest goes inside.

   Guest: おじゃまします。*
   I am sorry to intrude on you.

   *At the entrance, take off your shoes and place them neatly together facing the doorway.

3.

   The guest gives a gift.

   Guest: これ、気に入っていただけるといいんですが。
   き　い
   Here, I hope you will like this.

   Host: どうもすみません。
   Thank you very much.

4.

   The guest senses that the host is going to serve tea.

   Guest: どうぞ、おかまいなく。すぐ失礼しますから。
   しつれい
   Please don't bother. I will excuse myself soon.

5.

   The guest leaves the house.

   Guest: おじゃましました。*
   I've intruded on you.

   Host: また、いらっしゃってください。
   Please come again.

*おじゃまします is used only when you visit someone's residence; when visiting a professor's office, for example, use 失礼します instead. Likewise、おじゃましました is used when leaving someone's house, while 失礼しました is
しつれい   しつれい
used when leaving a professor's office.

第20課 | L E S S O N 20
メアリーさんの買い物 Mary's Shopping
かもの

会話 D i a l o g u e
かいわ

Ⅰ At an electric appliance store. 🔊 K20-01/02

1 メアリー： すみません。この間この電子辞書を買ったんですが、音が聞こえな
あいだ　　　てんしじしょ　か　　　　　　　　　　おと　き
2 いんです。

3 店　員： 少々、お待ちください。今、係の者を呼んで参ります。
てんいん　　しょうしょう　ま　　　　　いま　かかり もの　よ　　まい

4 田　中： お待たせいたしました。田中と申します。電子辞書を見せていただ
たなか　　　　　　　　　　　　　　　たなか　もう　　　てんしじしょ　み

5 けますか。……壊れているみたいですね。失礼いたしました。よろ
こわ　　　　　　　　　　　　しつれい

6 しかったら、交換いたしますが。
こうかん

7 メアリー： じゃあ、お願いします。
ねが

8 ＊　　　　　　　　　＊　　　　　　　　　＊

9 田　中： 申し訳ございません。今、同じ物がございませんので、二、三週間
たなか　もう　わけ　　　　　　　　いま　おな　もの　　　　　　　　　　に　さんしゅうかん

10 待っていただけませんか。
ま

11 メアリー： それは、ちょっと……。もうすぐ国に帰るので、できれば返品した
くに　かえ　　　　　　　　　へんぴん

12 いんですが。

13 田　中： かしこまりました。まことに申し訳ございませんでした。
たなか　　　　　　　　　　　　　　　　もう　わけ

Ⅱ On a street. 🔊 K20-03/04

1 メアリー： すみません。にしき屋という店はどこにあるか教えていただけま
や　　　　　みせ　　　　　　　おし

2 せんか。地図があるんですけど、わかりにくいんです。
ちず

3 おじいさん： 扇子の店ですね。次の角を左に曲がったら見えますよ。扇子を買
せんす　みせ　　　　　つぎ　かど　ひだり　ま　　　　　み　　　　　せんす　か

4 いに行くんですか。
い

5 メアリー： ええ。おみやげに扇子を買おうと思っているんです。
せんす　か　　　おも

6 おじいさん： いいおみやげになりますよ。おや、雨ですね。かさを持っていま
あめ　　　　　　　　　　も

7 すか。

8 メアリー：　　　いいえ。急いでいたから、かさを持たないで、来ちゃったんです。

9 おじいさん：　　じゃあ、一緒に店まで行きましょう。

10 メアリー：　　　どうもすみません。荷物が重そうですね。お持ちします。

11 おじいさん：　　ありがとう。

Ⅰ

Mary: Excuse me. I bought this electronic dictionary the other day, but I can't hear anything.

Shop assistant: Please wait a moment. I will call the person in charge.

Tanaka: I'm sorry to have kept you waiting. My name is Tanaka. Could I see your electronic dictionary? . . . It seems to be broken. I am sorry. If you like, we will exchange it.

Mary: Please.

            *   *   *

Tanaka: I am very sorry. We don't have the same one, so could you wait for a couple of weeks?

Mary: Well . . . I am going home soon. If possible, I want to return it.

Tanaka: Certainly. I am really sorry.

Ⅱ

Mary: Excuse me. Could you please tell me where Nishikiya is? I have a map, but I can't make it out.

Old man: It is a fan store, isn't it? You can see it when you turn left at the next corner. Are you going to buy fans?

Mary: Yes. I'm thinking of buying fans as a souvenir.

Old man: It is a good souvenir. Oh, it's raining. Do you have an umbrella?

Mary: No. I was in a hurry, so I left without an umbrella.

Old man: Then let's go to the store together.

Mary: Thank you so much. Your bag looks heavy. I'll carry it.

Old man: Thank you.

単語
たん　　ご

Vocabulary

Nouns

あちら		that way (polite)
アニメ		animation
うちゅうじん	宇宙人	space alien
* おと	音	sound
おにぎり		rice ball
* かかりのもの	係の者	our person in charge
* かど	角	corner
くうこう	空港	airport
じ	字	letter; character
してん	支店	branch office
しゅみ	趣味	hobby; pastime
しょうせつ	小説	novel
しんごう	信号	traffic light
スニーカー		sneakers
* せんす	扇子	fan
つき	月	moon
* でんしじしょ	電子辞書	electronic dictionary
ドイツ		Germany
ハイヒール		high heels
* 〜や	〜屋	. . . shop

い-adjectives

* おもい	重い	heavy; serious (illness)
かるい	軽い	light

U-verbs

* いたす	致す	extra-modest expression for する
いただく	頂く	extra-modest expression for たべる and のむ
* いただく	頂く	humble expression for もらう
うかがう	伺う	to humbly visit; to humbly ask
おる		extra-modest expression for いる
* ござる		extra-modest expression for ある

* Words that appear in the dialogue

〜ておる		extra-modest expression for 〜ている
〜でござる		extra-modest expression for です
* まいる	参る	extra-modest expression for いく and くる
* まがる	曲がる	to turn (right/left) (*corner* を *direction* に)
* もうす	申す	extra-modest expression for いう
もどる	戻る	to return; to come back （〜に）

Ru-verbs

* きこえる	聞こえる	to be audible （〜が）
さしあげる	差し上げる	humble expression for あげる
つたえる	伝える	to convey (message)
* またせる	待たせる	to keep (someone) waiting （〜を）

Irregular Verbs

* こうかんする	交換する	to exchange （X と Y を）
せいかつする	生活する	to lead a life
* へんぴんする	返品する	to return (merchandise) （〜を）

Adverbs and Other Expressions

* おや？		Oh!
〜かい	〜階	. . . th floor
* かしこまりました		Certainly.
さあ		I am not sure, . . .
* しつれいしました	失礼しました	I'm very sorry.
* しょうしょう	少々	a few seconds
それでは		if that is the case, . . .
* できれば		if possible
* まことに	誠に	really (very polite)
また		again
〜みたいな X		X such as . . .
* もうしわけありません	申し訳ありません	You have my apologies.
* よろしかったら		if it is okay (polite)

文法 Grammar
ぶん ぽう

1 Extra-modest Expressions

In the last lesson, we learned the special expressions to be used when we want to show respect to another person. Here we will learn to *talk modestly of our own actions*. We use the verbs below when we want to sound modest and respectful in our speech, to show an extra amount of deference to the listener. These verbs are almost always used in long forms, because the purpose of using them is to be polite to the person you are talking to. Having one of these verbs is like ending a sentence with words like *sir* or *ma'am*.

extra-modest expressions		
いる	おります	（おる）
行く / 来る	参ります	（参る）
言う	申します	（申す）
する	いたします	（いたす）
食べる / 飲む	いただきます	（いただく）
ある	ございます	（ござる）
〜ている	〜ております	（〜ておる）
〜です	〜でございます	（〜でござる）

You can use these verbs instead of the normal ones on very formal occasions, for example, when you introduce yourself at a job interview. (They are typically used with the more stilted first-person word 私, rather than the normal 私.)
わたくし　　　　　　　　　　　　　　　　　　　　　　　　わたし

私は来年も日本に<u>おります</u>。　　　　cf. います
わたくし らいねん　にほん
I will be in Japan next year, too, sir/ma'am.

私は今年の六月に大学を卒業<u>いたしました</u>。　　cf. 卒業しました
わたくし ことし　ろくがつ　だいがく　そつぎょう　　　　　　　　　　そつぎょう
I graduated from college this June, sir/ma'am.

私は一年間日本語を勉強<u>しております</u>。　　cf. 勉強しています
わたくし いちねんかん にほんご　べんきょう　　　　　　　　　　　べんきょう
I have been studying Japanese for a year.

私は日本の文化に興味が<u>ございます</u>。　　cf. あります
わたくし にほん　ぶんか　きょうみ
I am interested in the Japanese culture.

You can also use these expressions to talk modestly about your own family or about the company you work for. Extra-modest expressions are frequently used by people in business when they talk to customers. Thus you hear many extra-modest sentences like the examples below, in public address announcements (as in the first example), and in the speech of shop clerks (as in the second).

電車が<u>参ります</u>。　　　　　　　　cf. 来ます
でんしゃ　まい　　　　　　　　　　　　　き
A train is pulling in.

お手洗いは二階で<u>ございます</u>。　　cf. です
て あら　　に かい
The bathroom is on the second floor.

ございます and でございます are very stylized and you rarely hear them outside formal business-related situations.

Because the effect of the extra-modest expressions is to put the subject in a modest light, you cannot use them to describe the actions performed by the person you are talking to or by somebody who is not in your group. Therefore, it is wrong to say:

× 先生はあした学校に参りますか。
　せんせい　　　　がっこう　まい
Are you coming to school tomorrow, Professor?

2　Humble Expressions

When you do something out of respect for somebody, you can sometimes describe your action using a verb in the humble pattern "お + verb stem + する." (Not all verbs are used this way, so you may want to use only the ones you have actually heard used.) You can speak of "humbly" meeting, lending to, or borrowing from someone, for example.

> お + stem + する　　　*I (humbly) do . . .*

私はきのう<u>先生</u>に<u>お会い</u>しました。
わたし　　　　せんせい　　あ
I (humbly) met my professor yesterday.

私は<u>先生</u>に本を<u>お貸し</u>するつもりです。
わたし　せんせい　ほん　　か
I intend to (humbly) lend my professor a book.

私は<u>先生</u>に辞書を<u>お借り</u>しました。
わたし　　せんせい　じ しょ　　か
I borrowed a dictionary from my professor (and feel very obliged).

する compound verbs do not follow this pattern. Instead they simply have the prefix ご or お, such as ご紹介する, ご案内する, ご説明する, and お電話する.

もらう and あげる have special replacement verbs:

もらう	→ いただく	私は先生にこの本をいただきました。 *I (humbly) received this book from my professor.*
		私は先生に漢字を教えていただきました。 *I (humbly) had my professor teach me kanji.*
あげる	→ さしあげる[1]	私は先生に花をさしあげます。 *I will (humbly) give my professor flowers.*

うかがう is a verb with which you can portray yourself as humble in the actions of visiting and asking questions:

私は先生のお宅にうかがいました。
I (humbly) visited my professor's house.

私は先生にテストについてうかがいました。
I (humbly) asked my professor about the exam.

The subjects in the above examples are all "I," and "I" humbly performs these actions in deference to the person that is underlined.[2] The difference between this pattern and the extra-modest expressions that we studied earlier lies here: the extra-modest expressions show respect to the listeners you are talking to, while the humble pattern shows respect to someone

---

[1] We do not endorse the use of さしあげる with the *te*-form of a verb in the sense of "humbly doing something for somebody," because many people object to this type of sentence. They argue that the idea that you are doing a service for somebody is ultimately an insolent belief and that trying to talk humbly about it is a rather unconvincing facade. Such speakers prefer instead to use the "お ＋ stem ＋ する" pattern.

Instead of: 私は先生に地図を見せてさしあげました。
Use: 私は先生に地図をお見せしました。　　　*I (humbly) showed a map to my professor.*

[2] You can also talk about one of "your people," such as a member of your family or another worker at the company you work for, humbly performing an action in deference to somebody outside the group.

私の父はお客さんにお茶をおいれしました。
My father (humbly) served the guest tea.
私の母は大統領に手紙をいただきました。
My mother (humbly) received a letter from the President.

that appears in the event you are describing. This of course does not preclude the possibility of you humbly performing an action for the person you are talking to.[3] For example,

（私はあなたを）駅までお送りします。　*I will (humbly) walk you to the station.*

Let us summarize the three types of "respect language" we have learned in the last two lessons. The up arrow and the down arrow indicate the person whose profile is raised or lowered, respectively, by the use of the respect element in the sentence.

1. **Honorific expressions** exalt the subject of the sentence.
   先生が↑ いらっしゃいました／お帰りになりました。
   My professor has (graciously) arrived/left.

2. **Extra-modest expressions** talk modestly of what you do.
   私は↓ メアリー・ハートと申します。 (person listening to you ↑)
   My name is Mary Hart.

3. **Humble expressions** demote the subject and raise the profile of another person.
   私は↓ 先生に↑ 本をお返ししました。
   I (humbly) returned the book to my professor.

3　〜ないで

If you do something without doing something else, the missed action can be mentioned as 〜ない (the short negative present) plus で. Note that the present tense form 〜ない is used for both the present and past actions.

verb ＋ ないで	*without doing x*

きのうの夜は、寝ないで、勉強しました。
Last night, I studied without getting any sleep.

辞書を使わないで、新聞を読みます。
I read a newspaper without using dictionaries.

---

[3] Sometimes we can use a humble expression to describe a situation where we do something for the person we are talking to, meaning "for you," "instead of you," and "saving you trouble."
テレビをおつけしましょう。　*Let me (humbly) turn on the TV (for you).*

4 Questions within Larger Sentences

You can include a question as a part of a longer sentence and express ideas such as "I don't know when the test is" and "I don't remember whether Mary came to the party."

Quoted question clauses are shown in the boxes in the examples below. Quoted questions are in short forms. Note (1) that the clause ends with the question particle か when it contains a question word like だれ and なに, as in the first two examples, and (2) that it ends with かどうか when it does not contain such a question word, as in the third example.[4]

山下先生は きのう何を食べたか 覚えていません。
やましたせんせい　　　　　なに　た　　　　　　おぼ
Professor Yamashita does not remember what he ate yesterday.

メアリーさんがどこに住んでいるか 知っていますか。
　　　　　　　　　　　す　　　　　　　　　し
Do you know where Mary lives?

週末、 旅行に行くかどうか 決めましょう。
しゅうまつ　りょこう　い　　　　　　　き
Let's decide whether we will go on a trip this weekend.

Question-word question か	わかりません, 知っています, etc.
Yes/no question かどうか	し

The present tense short form だ which is used with a な-adjective or a noun at the end of the clause is usually dropped.[5]

だれが一番上手だ か わかりません。
　　　いちばんじょう ず
I do not know who is the best.

あの人が学生だ かどうか わかりません。
　　ひと　がくせい
I do not know if that person is a student.

---

[4] Many people use か instead of かどうか in their speech for questions of this second type as well.

[5] Explanatory んです sentences can also be quoted. When a んですか question is quoted, だ (the short form counterpart of です) is dropped, and ん is changed to の.

Direct question: どうしてメアリーさんは来なかったんですか。

Quoted question: どうしてメアリーさんが来なかったのかわかりません。

We often use the particle が on the subject within a quoted sentence where は is expected. Thus corresponding to the direct question たけしさんは何を食べましたか, we say:

私はたけしさんが何を食べたか知っています。
I know what Takeshi ate.

5 　name という item

When you want to talk about a person or a thing that goes by a certain name, but if you believe the person you are talking to is not familiar with it, you can use the following pattern.

(name) という (item)　　　(item) *called* "(name)"

ポチという犬（を飼っていました。）　　　*(I used to have) a dog called "Pochi."*

「花」という歌（を知っていますか。）　　　*(Do you know) a song called "Hana"?*

6 　〜やすい／〜にくい

You can describe something that is "easy-to-do" by adding the adjective-forming suffix やすい to a verb stem. A verb stem ＋ やすい conjugates like an い-adjective.[6]

使う　　→　　使いやすい　　この電子辞書は使いやすいです。
　　　　　　　　　　　　　　　This electronic dictionary is easy to use.

読む　　→　　読みやすい　　この本は読みやすかったです。
　　　　　　　　　　　　　　　This book was easy to read.

If something is "hard-to-do," you can use another い-adjective-forming suffix にくい with a verb stem.

食べる　　→　　食べにくい　　骨が多いので、魚は食べにくいです。
　　　　　　　　　　　　　　　Fish are hard to eat, because they have many bones.

---

[6] Note that やすい as a separate word means "cheap" and not "easy." "Easy" is やさしい.

Sometimes, the subject of a ～やすい／にくい sentence is a place (where it is easy/difficult to do something in), a tool (easy/difficult to do something with), and so forth.

この町はとても住みやすいです。
This town is quite livable.

このグラスは飲みにくいです。
This glass is hard to drink from.

～やすい and ～にくい tend to focus on the psychological ease or difficulty of doing something when you use them with verbs describing actions. It is therefore odd to use やすい or にくい when the difficulty is defined in terms of a physical or statistical *success rate*. Thus compare:

漢字は覚えにくい。
Kanji is hard to memorize.　（＝ I have kanji anxieties）

漢字を覚えるのは難しい。
It is hard to memorize kanji.　（＝ too complicated, too many）

この雑誌は買いにくい。
It is embarrassing to buy this magazine.　（＝ you are unwilling）

この雑誌を買うのは難しい。
This magazine is hard to buy.　（＝ small circulation; hard to come by）

練習 Practice
れん しゅう

(1) 田中と申します
た なか もう

A. Change the following words into extra-modest expressions. 🔊 K20-06

Example: 行く → 参ります
い まい

1. 食べる　2. 言う　3. 来る　4. する　5. いる　6. ある　7. 飲む　8. あちらだ
た い く の

B. Match the following sentences with the pictures. Put answers in the (　).

🔊 K20-07

(1)

(　　)

(2)

(　　)

(3)

(　　)

(4)

(　　)

(5)

(　　)

(6)

(　　)

a. 上に参ります。次は七階でございます。
　うえ まい　　つぎ　ななかい
b. 電車が参ります。
　でんしゃ まい
c. 田中と申します。よろしくお願いいたします。
　たなか もう　　　　　　ねが
d. 父は今出かけております。
　ちち いま で
e. いただきます。
f. お手洗いはあちらにございます。
　て あら

✳ Ⓒ Pair Work—You are at a very formal reception and have just met your partner for the first time. Ask each other the following questions using honorific expressions. When you answer, use extra-modest expressions. 📢 K20-08

1. お名前は何と言いますか。
2. いつ日本に来ましたか。
3. どちらに住んでいますか。
4. ビールをよく飲みますか。
5. お姉さんがいますか。
6. 何かスポーツをしますか。
7. 毎日どのぐらい日本語を勉強しますか。
8. 毎日何時ごろ晩ご飯を食べますか。
9. 先週の週末はどこかへ行きましたか。
10. 日本文学に興味がありますか。

(handwritten annotations) yes/no の質問 なさる or お勉強しますか。 おありになりますか。 or おありですか。

D. Below on the left is Mr. Brown's speech of self-introduction at an informal party. Rephrase the speech for a very formal reception by filling in the blanks with extra-modest expressions. 📢 K20-09

ビル・ブラウンと言います。
トマス銀行から来ました。
横浜支店に勤めています。
どうぞよろしくお願いします。

ビル・ブラウンと＿＿＿＿＿＿。
トマス銀行から＿＿＿＿＿＿。
横浜支店に勤めて＿＿＿＿＿＿。
どうぞよろしくお願い＿＿＿＿＿＿。

Now make your own formal speech supposing you were representing a company.

E. Pair Work—Telephone Conversation
Smith calls Yamada's house. Change the undelined parts and practice the dialogue with your partner. K20-10

山　田：　はい、<u>山田</u>でございます。
スミス：　<u>スミス</u>と申しますが、<u>ようこ</u>さんはいらっしゃいますか。
山　田：　今、ちょっと出かけておりますが……。
スミス：　そうですか。じゃあ、<u>スミスから電話があった</u>と伝えていただけませんか。
山　田：　<u>スミス</u>さんですね。わかりました。
スミス：　失礼します。

Ⅱ　お持ちします

A. Change the verbs into humble expressions. K20-11

Example:　会う　→　お会いする

1. 借りる　　3. 送る　　5. 取る　　7. 読む　　9. もらう
2. 返す　　　4. 持つ　　6. 話す　　8. 貸す　　10. あげる

B. Look at the pictures and politely offer your help. K20-12

Example:　お持ちしましょうか。

Ex.

(1)
取れない

(2)

(3)
駅まで
行くんです

(4)
書けない

(5)
一緒に
撮ろうよ

(6)

(7)

C. Pair Work—One of you is a boss. The other is a subordinate. The boss asks the subordinate to do various things. The subordinate responds using humble expressions.

Example: Boss's situation: You want to take a taxi. Ask your subordinate to call a taxi.

→ Ａ：タクシーに乗りたいんだけど、呼んでくれない？

Ｂ：はい、お呼びします。

Boss's situations:

1. Your bag is very heavy. Ask your subordinate to carry it.

2. You are thirsty. Ask your subordinate to make some tea.

3. You want to go home. Ask your subordinate to give you a ride.

4. You are going to move to a new house next week. Ask your subordinate to help you.

5. You want to borrow your subordinate's book. Ask him/her to lend you the book.

6. You want to know Tanaka-san's telephone number. Ask your subordinate to look up the number.

7. You want to eat rice balls. Ask your subordinate to make some.

8. You want to have your subordinate's watch. Ask him/her to give it to you.

D. Change the underlined parts into honorific, humble, or extra-modest expressions.

1. たけし：部長、何か飲みますか。

部長：うん。

たけし：じゃあ、お茶をいれますね。

2. たけし：部長、もうこの本を<u>読みましたか。</u>

　　部　長：うん、<u>読んだ</u>よ。

　　たけし：じゃあ、<u>借りて</u>もいいですか。

　　　　　　来週、<u>返します。</u>

3. たけし：部長、荷物が重そうですね。<u>持ちます。</u>

　　部　長：ありがとう。

　　たけし：どちらに<u>行く</u>んですか。

　　部　長：駅まで<u>行く</u>んだ。

　　たけし：じゃあ、車で<u>送ります。</u>

4. たけし：アジアトラベルの木村と<u>言います。</u>

　　　　　　山田部長に<u>会いたい</u>んですが。

　　受　付：<u>すみません。</u>山田は今、出張で

　　　＊　　東京に行って<u>います。</u>→行ってあります。

　　たけし：そうですか。いつ<u>戻ります</u>か。

　　受　付：あしたの夕方に戻ると思います。

　　たけし：そうですか。それでは、また

　　　　　　あしたうかがいます。

b/c using "in-group" in talking outside party.

Ⅲ ひげをそらないで、大学に行きました

A. Describe the pictures using ～ないで. K20-13

Example:　　たけしさんはひげをそらないで、大学に行きました。

Ex.

1. たけしさんは大学に行きました。

(a)　　　　　　(b)　　　　　　(c)

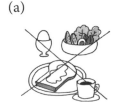

2. メアリーさんは寝ました。

   (a)   (b)   (c)

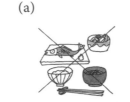   

3. ジョンさんは出かけました。

   (a)   (b)   (c)

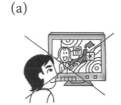   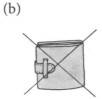   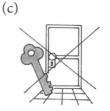

B. Complete the following sentences.

1. ＿＿＿＿＿＿＿＿＿＿＿＿＿ないで、空港に行ってしまいました。

2. ＿＿＿＿＿＿＿＿＿＿＿ないで、ジーンズを買ってしまいました。

3. ＿＿＿＿＿＿＿＿＿＿＿ないで、部長のお宅にうかがってしまいました。

4. 忙しかったので、＿＿＿＿＿＿＿＿＿＿＿＿ないで、寝ました。

5. お金がないので、＿＿＿＿＿＿＿＿＿＿＿＿ないで、生活しています。

6. 宿題は難しかったけど、＿＿＿＿＿＿＿＿＿＿＿ないで、やりました。

Ⅳ アメリカ人かどうかわかりません

A. You have been involved in a car accident and have lost all your memory. (For some reason you can speak Japanese.) You are at the hospital and your doctor will ask you the questions below. Answer them using ～か(どうか)わかりません. 🔊 K20-14

Example:　Q：あなたはアメリカ人ですか。
　　　　　　A：さあ、アメリカ人かどうかわかりません。

1. あなたは日本人ですか。　　　3. 結婚していますか。

2. 学生ですか。　　　　　　　　4. 子供がいますか。

5. 外国語が話せますか。
   がいこくご　はな

6. 名前は何ですか。
   なまえ　なん

7. 何歳ですか。
   なんさい

8. 仕事は何をしていますか。
   しごと　なに

9. どこに住んでいますか。
   す

10. 今日何を食べましたか。
    きょうなに　た

11. きのう何をしましたか。
    なに

12. どうやってここに来ましたか。
    き

B. You are interested in Hayashi, a friend of your friend. Ask your friend about Hayashi. 🔊 K20-15

Example:　　Do you know if Hayashi likes tennis?

　　　　　→　はやしさんはテニスが好きかどうか知っていますか。
　　　　　　　　　　　　　　　　　　　す　　　　　　し

Do you know . . .

1. if Hayashi is good at singing
2. if Hayashi can speak German
3. if Hayashi is interested in politics
4. where Hayashi lives
5. what kind of music Hayashi likes
6. what Hayashi will do this weekend
7. what time Hayashi goes to bed
8. what Hayashi's hobby is

C. Pair Work—Using the questions in B, ask questions about your classmates or your teacher. When you talk about your teacher, use honorific expressions.

Example:　　where the teacher lives

　　　　　→　Ａ：先生がどちらに住んでいらっしゃるか知っていますか。
　　　　　　　　　　せんせい　　　　　す　　　　　　　　　　し
　　　　　　　Ｂ：はい。駅の近くに住んでいらっしゃいますよ。
　　　　　　　　　　　えき　ちか　す
　　　　　　　or さあ、私も先生がどこに住んでいらっしゃるか知りません。
　　　　　　　　　　　わたし　せんせい　　　　す　　　　　　　　し

D. Pair Work—Ask your partner the following questions.

Example:　　Ａ：先週の土曜日に何をしましたか。
　　　　　　　　せんしゅう　どようび　なに
　　　　　　　Ｂ：さあ、何をしたか覚えていません。／映画を見に行きました。
　　　　　　　　　　　なに　　　おぼ　　　　　　　えいが　み　い

1. 一年後も日本語を勉強していますか。
   いちねんご　にほんご　べんきょう

2. 五年後、何をしていますか。
   ごねんご　なに

3. きのうの夜、夢を見ましたか。どんな夢を見ましたか。
   よる　ゆめ　み　　　　　　　ゆめ　み

4. メアリーさんとたけしさんは結婚しますか。
   けっこん

5. 宇宙人がいると思いますか。
   うちゅうじん　　　おも

6. 将来、人が月に住めると思いますか。
   しょうらい　ひと　つき　す　　　おも

Ⓥ ローソンというコンビニ

A. Describe the pictures using ～という. 🔊 K20-16

Example: ローソンというコンビニ

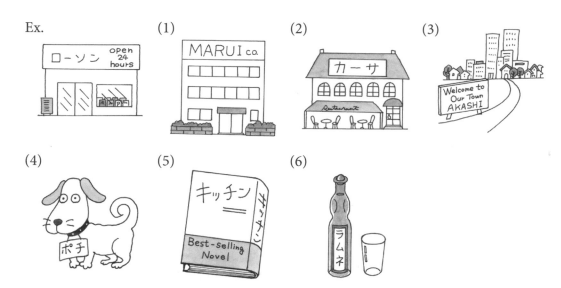

B. Pair Work—Talk about the following topics, using ～という as in the example.

Example: movie

→ Ａ：「となりのトトロ」という映画を知っていますか。

Ｂ：いいえ、どんな映画ですか。

Ａ：日本のアニメで、二人の女の子がトトロに会う話です。
日本語もやさしいし、絵もきれいだし、おもしろいですよ。

Ｂ：そうですか。見てみたいです。ＤＶＤを持っていますか。

1. person　　　　　4. shop　　　　　7. others

2. restaurant　　　5. movie

3. book　　　　　　6. singer

C. Tell your classmates about your favorite places or people.

Example: 私の町にはハリーズというレストランがあります。ピザがとても
おいしくて、よく友だちと食べに行きます。……

Ⅵ 覚えやすいです
おぼ

A.　Make sentences using やすい and にくい.  K20-17

Example:　　川という漢字は覚えやすいですが、髪という漢字は覚えにくいです。
かわ　　　かんじ　　おぼ　　　　　　　　　かみ　　　かんじ　　おぼ

Ex. 覚える
おぼ

川という漢字　　髪という漢字
かわ　　　かんじ　　かみ　　　かんじ

(1) 食べる
た

ハンバーガー　　魚
さかな

(2) 歩く
ある

ハイヒール　　スニーカー

(3) 持つ
も

メアリーさんの　　たけしさんの
かばん　　　　　かばん

(4) わかる

スーさんの話　　けんさんの話
はなし　　　　　　はなし

(5) 使う
つか

大きい辞書　　小さい辞書
おお　　じしょ　　ちい　　じしょ

(6) 運転する
うんてん

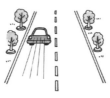

せまい道　　広い道
みち　　　ひろ　みち

(7) 読む
よ

お元気
ですか？

お元気
ですか？

スーさんの字　　ロバートさんの字
じ　　　　　　　　じ

B. Class Activity—Show something to the class. Introduce it and talk about it using 〜やすい／にくい.

Example:

これは誕生日に母にもらったかばんです。軽くて、とても持ちやすいです。
これは漢字の辞書です。字が小さくて、ちょっと見にくいです。

C. Pair Work—Ask your partner the following questions and expand the conversation.

Example:　　どんな人が話しやすいと思いますか。
→　Ａ：どんな人が話しやすいと思いますか。
Ｂ：そうですね。スーさんみたいな人が話しやすいです。
Ａ：どうしてですか。
Ｂ：スーさんはやさしいし、話を聞いてくれるし。
Ａさんはどんな人が話しやすいと思いますか。

1. どんな車が運転しやすいと思いますか。
2. どんな町が住みやすいと思いますか。
3. どんな会社が働きにくいと思いますか。

Ⅶ まとめの練習

A. Pair Work—One of you looks at picture A (p. 205) and the other looks at picture B (p. 206). Ask each other questions about how to get to the following places from "HERE" on the map. When you are asked, answer the question as in the example.

Example:　　店「にしきや」
→　Ａ：にしきやという店はどこにあるか教えていただけませんか。
Ｂ：三つ目の信号を右に曲がったら左に見えますよ。

Picture A

You want to go to the following places:

1. スーパー「サンコー」
2. ホテル「ふじた」
3. 喫茶店「ベルン」
4. 映画館「きたのシネマ」
5. レストラン「たけ」
6. 花屋「ひまわり」

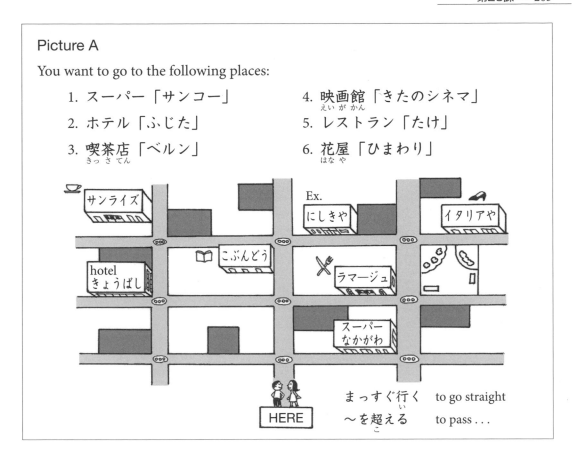

B. Class Activity—Suppose you are at a very formal party. Walk around the reception hall (classroom) and make acquaintance with VIPs (classmates). Ask questions and fill in the table below. Add your own questions.

	VIP 1	VIP 2	VIP 3
name?			
live where?			
do what for a living?			
play what sport?			
drink what?			
have brothers & sisters?			

C. Role Play—One of you is working at a shop, and the other is a customer. Using Dialogue I as a model, make conversations about the following situations.

1. The customer bought a shirt for his/her father, but it was too small for him. The customer wants to exchange it for a bigger one.

2. The customer bought a jacket, but it doesn't look good on him. The customer wants to return it.

Pair Work Ⅶ A.

(→ p. 204)

Example: 店「にしきや」
　　　　みせ

　→　A：にしきやという店はどこにあるか教えていただけませんか。

　　　B：三つ目の信号を右に曲がったら左に見えますよ。
　　　　みっ　め　しんごう　みぎ　ま　　　　ひだり　み

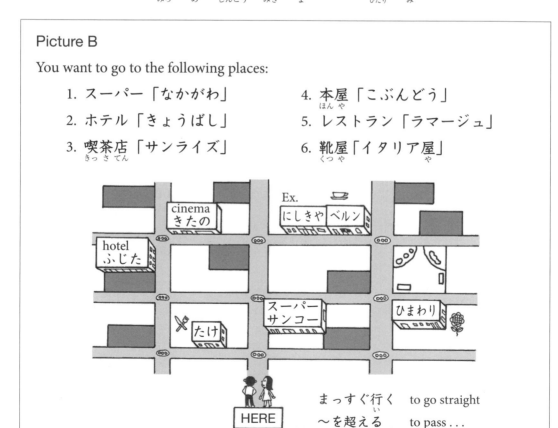

Picture B

You want to go to the following places:

1. スーパー「なかがわ」　　　4. 本屋「こぶんどう」
　　　　　　　　　　　　　　　　　ほん や

2. ホテル「きょうばし」　　　5. レストラン「ラマージュ」

3. 喫茶店「サンライズ」　　　6. 靴屋「イタリア屋」
　きっ さ てん　　　　　　　　　　くつ や　　　　や

まっすぐ行く　to go straight
　　　　い
〜を超える　to pass . . .
　　こ

日本のポップカルチャー Japanese Pop Culture
にほん

Some of you may have grown up watching セーラームーン (Sailor Moon), collecting ポケモンカード (Pokemon trading cards), or playing ドラゴンクエスト (Dragon Quest). Japanese pop culture—manga, anime, video games, music, fashion, and more—is attracting attention worldwide. Here is a quick introduction to some forms of this culture.

秋葉原 (Akihabara)
あきはばら

Located in central Tokyo, Akihabara has long been known as a major shopping area for electronic appliances and computer goods. Recently, it has also gained a reputation as a hangout for オタク*, featuring many shops that offer old and new video games, rare manga, anime character figures, and other pop-culture merchandise.

*オタク: People with a passionate, or even obsessive, interest in anime, manga, computers, etc.

まんが (Manga)

Manga, or Japanese comics, are not just for children—many titles are targeted at grownups as well. They deal with a broad range of subjects, covering basically everything found in films and literature. They also form an important part of the Japanese publishing industry;『ワンピース』(*One Piece*), for example, has sold over 230 million volumes as of 2011.

©尾田栄一郎／集英社

アニメ (Anime)

Like manga, anime (Japanese animation) has developed distinctive styles of character design, story-telling, and other features of animation. Countless anime TV shows and films have been produced since 1963, the year when Osamu Tezuka created the first animated Japanese TV show,『鉄腕アトム』(*Astro Boy*).
てつわん

©手塚プロダクション・虫プロダクション

ビジュアル系 (Visual-*kei*)
けい

Visual-*kei* (lit., visual style) is a sub-genre of Japanese rock characterized mostly by the appearance of its performers, particularly their heavy make-up, distinctive hair styles, and ornate costumes.

©ソニー・ミュージックレコーズ

第21課 L E S S O N 21
どろぼう Burglar

会 話 Dialogue
かい わ

Ⅰ John runs into his landlord's house. 🔊 K21-01/02

1 ジョン： 大家さん、大変です。どろぼうに入られました。
　　　　　おおや　　　たいへん　　　　　　　　　　　　はい

2 大　家： えっ。何かとられたんですか。
　おお　や　　　　　なに

3 ジョン： パソコンと……バイトでためたお金もないです。
　　　　　　　　　　　　　　　　　　　　　かね

4 大　家： とにかく、警察に連絡したほうがいいですよ。
　おお　や　　　　　　けいさつ　れんらく

Ⅱ A police officer comes to John's apartment. 🔊 K21-03/04

1 警　察： かぎはかけてあったんですか。
　けい　さつ

2 ジョン： さあ……きのうの夜は飲んで帰ったから、かぎをかけたかどうかよく
　　　　　　　　　　　　よる　の　　かえ

3 　　　　 覚えていないんです。
　　　　　おぼ

4 警　察： じゃあ、何時ごろ帰ったか覚えていますか。
　けい　さつ　　　　　　なんじ　　かえ　　おぼ

5 ジョン： 終電だったから……たぶん、一時半ごろです。
　　　　　しゅうでん　　　　　　　　　　　いちじはん

6 警　察： どろぼうは、その後入ったんですね。
　けい　さつ　　　　　　　　あとはい

7 ジョン： ええ。朝、部屋がめちゃくちゃだっ
　　　　　　　　あさ　へや

8 　　　　 たので、びっくりしたんです。

9 警　察： 寝ている間にどろぼうに入られて、
　けい　さつ　ね　　　あいだ　　　　　　はい

10 　　　　 気がつかなかったんですか。
　　　　　き

11 ジョン： すみません。

Ⅲ A few days later. 🔊 K21-05/06

1 大家： ジョンさん、留守の間に警察から電話がありましたよ。犯人が捕まっ
　　　　　（おおや）　　　　　　　（るす）　（あいだ）（けいさつ）　　　（でんわ）　　　　　　　　　　（はんにん）（つか）
2 　　　　 たので、警察に来てほしいそうです。
　　　　　　　　　　（けいさつ）（き）
3 ジョン： ありがとうございます。よかった。
4 大家： それから、かぎを新しくしましたから、どうぞ。本当に大変でしたね。
　　　　　（おおや）　　　　　　　　（あたら）　　　　　　　　　　　　　　（ほんとう）　（たいへん）
5 ジョン： ええ。でも、そのおかげで、いいこともありました。みんないろいろ
6 　　　　 な物をくれたり、おごってくれたりしたんです。
　　　　　　（もの）
7 大家： ジョンさんは、いい友だちがたくさんいて、幸せですね。
　　　　　（おおや）　　　　　　　　　　（とも）　　　　　　　　　（しあわ）

Ⅰ

John: Ms. "Landlady"! I am in trouble. I had my room broken into.

Landlady: Oh! Has something been taken?

John: My computer and . . . the money that I've saved from the part-time job has gone.

Landlady: Anyway, you should call the police.

Ⅱ

Police: Was the door locked?

John: Let me think . . . I don't remember whether I locked it or not since I drank (alcohol) and went home last night.

Police: Well, do you remember about what time you returned home?

John: I took the last train, so maybe around one-thirty.

Police: The burglar broke in after that, right?

John: Yes. I was surprised that the room was such a mess in the morning.

Police: Your room was broken into while you were sleeping, and you didn't notice it?

John: I am afraid not . . .

Ⅲ

Landlady: John, there was a phone call when you were out. They said that they want you to come to the police station because the burglar has been arrested.

John: Thank you. I am glad.

Landlady: Oh, I changed the lock. Here's the key. You really had a hard time, didn't you?

John: Yes, but because of that, many good things have happened to me as well. Everyone gave me various things and treated me to meals, and so on.

Landlady: John, you are lucky because you have many good friends.

単語
V o c a b u l a r y

 K21-07

N o u n s

あかちゃん	赤ちゃん	baby
か	蚊	mosquito
かいぎ	会議	business meeting; conference
ガソリン		gasoline
かんきょう	環境	environment
＊ けいさつ	警察	police; police station
こうじょう	工場	factory
＊ こと	事	things; matters
＊ しゅうでん	終電	last train
じゅんび	準備	preparation
スピーチ		speech
せいふ	政府	government
ちかん		sexual offender; pervert
どうりょう	同僚	colleague
＊ どろぼう	泥棒	thief; burglar
＊ バイト		abbreviation of アルバイト
＊ はんにん	犯人	criminal
ポスター		poster
むかし	昔	old days; past
もんく	文句	complaint
＊ るす	留守	absence; not at home

い - a d j e c t i v e s

とおい	遠い	far (away)
ひどい		awful

な - a d j e c t i v e s

あんぜん（な）	安全	safe
たいせつ（な）	大切	precious; valuable
＊ めちゃくちゃ（な）		messy; disorganized

U - v e r b s

おく	置く	to put; to lay; to place
		(*place* に *object* を)

＊ Words that appear in the dialogue

* きがつく	気が付く	to notice（〜に）
ける		to kick（〜を）
さす	刺す	to bite（〜を）
さわる	触る	to touch（〜に/を）
* つかまる	捕まる	to be arrested; to be caught（〜が）
つつむ	包む	to wrap; to cover（〜を）
なぐる	殴る	to strike; to hit; to punch（〜を）
ぬすむ	盗む	to steal; to rob（〜を）
はる	貼る	to post; to stick（*place* に *object* を）
ふむ	踏む	to step on（〜を）
ふる		to turn down (somebody); to reject; to jilt（〜を）
もんくをいう	文句を言う	to complain
やく	焼く	to bake; to burn; to grill（〜を）
やる		to give (to pets, plants, younger siblings, etc.)（〜を）

Ru-verbs

いじめる		to bully（〜を）
きがえる	着替える	to change clothes
* ためる		to save money（〜を）
つづける	続ける	to continue（〜を）
ほめる		to praise; to say nice things（〜を）
まちがえる	間違える	to make a mistake（〜を）
みつける	見つける	to find（〜を）

Irregular Verbs

ばかにする		to insult; to make a fool of . . .（〜を）
* びっくりする		to be surprised（〜に）
ひるねをする	昼寝をする	to take a nap
* れんらくする	連絡する	to contact（*person*に）

Adverbs and Other Expressions

* 〜あいだに	〜間に	while . . .
* ころ		time of . . . ; when . . .
すこし	少し	a little
* とにかく		anyhow; anyway

文法 G r a m m a r

ぶん　ぽう

1 Passive Sentences

When you are inconvenienced by something somebody else has done, you can express your dissatisfaction using the passive sentence. Suppose, for example, that you were bothered by your friend's unauthorized use of your car. Compare (a) the objective description of the event and (b) the passive version, which makes clear how you feel about it:

(a)	友だちが 車を 使いました。	*A friend of mine used my car.*
(b)	私は 友だちに 車を 使われました。	*I had my car used by a friend of mine (and I am mad/sad about it).*

As you can see from the above example, the basic makeup of a passive sentence is like the following examples.

> 私は　　　　友だちに　　車を使われました。
> (victim) は　(villain) に　　(evil act)
> *I had my car used by a friend.*
>
> The "victim" is affected by an event. Marked with the particle は or が.
> The "villain" performs an action which causes the suffering. Marked with に.
> The "evil act" is described with the passive form of a verb.

Let us first examine what the passive form of a verb looks like.

> *ru*-verbs: Drop the final *-ru* and add *-rare-ru*.
>
> 食べる　→　食べられる
>
> *u*-verbs: Drop the final *-u* and add *-are-ru*.
>
> | | | | | | |
> |---|---|---|---|---|---|
> | 行く | → | 行かれる | 話す | → | 話される |
> | 待つ | → | 待たれる | 死ぬ | → | 死なれる |
> | 読む | → | 読まれる | 取る | → | 取られる |
> | 泳ぐ | → | 泳がれる | 遊ぶ | → | 遊ばれる |
> | 買う | → | 買われる[1] | | | |
>
> irregular verbs:
>
> くる　→　こられる
> する　→　される

You may have noticed that the passive forms of *ru*-verbs and the irregular くる is the same as the potential verbs (see Lesson 13), but the passive form of an *u*-verb looks different from the potential verb: for the verb 読む, the passive is 読まれる, while the potential is 読める.

Passive forms of verbs themselves conjugate as regular *ru*-verbs.

読まれる				
	short forms		long forms	
	affirmative	negative	affirmative	negative
present	読まれる	読まれない	読まれます	読まれません
past	読まれた	読まれなかった	読まれました	読まれませんでした
te-form	読まれて			

Let us now turn to the ways in which these forms are used in sentences. In most passive sentences, the "victim" has been unfavorably affected by the "villain's" act. They may be unfavorably affected in various ways, such as being angry, embarrassed, sad, and hurt.[2]

私は となりの人に たばこを吸われました。
I was annoyed with the person sitting next to me for smoking.

たけしさんは メアリーさんに よく笑われます。
Takeshi is often laughed at by Mary.

山下先生は だれかに パスワードを盗まれたそうです。
I hear that Professor Yamashita had his password stolen by someone.

Compare the inadvertent/unfavorable focus of a passive sentence with the intended/favorable focus of a てもらう sentence (see Lesson 16).

---

[1] With the verbs that end with the *hiragana* う, we see a "*w*" intervening, just as in the negative short forms.

[2] Since the passive only applies to a verb, you cannot express your suffering from an adjectival situation. Thus you can say 私は雨に降られました (I was annoyed by the fact that it rained/I was rained on), because 降る is a verb, but you cannot use the passive to say something like "I was annoyed by the fact that the weather was bad," because 悪い (bad) is an adjective. You cannot express your suffering from somebody *failing* to do something either, because you cannot add the passive suffix to an already negated verb. Therefore you cannot use the passive to say things like "Professor Yamashita was annoyed because students did not come to his class."

私は 友だちに 日記を 読まれました。
I was annoyed with a friend of mine for reading my diary.

私は 友だちに 手紙を 読んでもらいました。
I had a friend of mine read the letter for me.

Finally, we note that some passive sentences are not perceptibly unfavorable.

私は その人に デートに 誘われました。
I was asked out by that person for a date.

私は 兄に 友だちに 紹介されました。
I was introduced by my big brother to a friend of his.

私は 友だちに パーティーに 呼ばれました。
I was invited by a friend to a party.

その人は みんなに 尊敬されています。
That person is looked up to by most everyone.

When someone says these, they probably do not mean that they were inconvenienced by how things have turned out. There are relatively few verbs that come out neutral in their meaning when they are turned into the passive form.[3]

2　〜てある

You can use the *te*-form of a verb + the helping verb ある to characterize a situation that *has been brought about on purpose* by somebody who remains unnamed in the sentence.

---

[3] There is another type of passive sentence, with non-human subjects, which naturally lacks the implication that the inanimate, nonsentient subjects are inconvenienced. The passive sentences of this type are found more commonly in the written language than in the spoken language. The type of passive sentences we learn in this lesson is called "affective passive," while the other type presented in this footnote is called "direct passive."

ここに公園が作られます。　　　　　　A park will be built here.
この絵はピカソによってかかれました。　The picture was drawn by Picasso.
南アフリカでワールドカップが開かれました。　The World Cup was held in South Africa.

As you can see in the second example above, the human agent of the actions in such sentences is followed by によって instead of に.

寒いので、ヒーターがつけてあります。
_{さむ}

The heater is on, because it is cold.

(= *The heater was turned on and has been kept that way.*)

テーブルの上に本が置いてあります。
_{うえ} _{ほん} _お

A book is on the table.

(= *The book was put on the table and it has remained there ever since.*)

You can say 〜てあります if somebody, possibly yourself, performed an action on purpose earlier, which can be described in terms of 〜ておきました ("do something by way of preparation," see Lesson 15), and if the result of that action can still be observed at this moment. Note that 〜てあります describes a current state, hence the present tense.

レストランの予約がしてあります。　is the result of　予約をしておきました。
_{よやく} _{よやく}

A restaurant reservation has been made.　　　　　　　*(I) made a reservation in advance.*

パンが買ってあります。　　　　　is the result of　パンを買っておきました。
_か _か

Bread has been bought (and is ready).　　　　　*(I) bought bread (for future use).*

As you can see from the above examples, てある normally assigns the particle が (or は) to the noun, which is usually marked with を. てある almost exclusively goes with a transitive verb.

Compare also てある sentences with ている sentences that describe current states. ている goes with intransitive verbs, in contrast with てある.

窓が閉めてあります。　　　　　(閉める = transitive)
_{まど} _し _し

The window has been kept closed.

窓が閉まっています。　　　　　(閉まる = intransitive)
_{まど} _し _し

The window is closed.

These sentences describe the same situation: the window is closed. The two sentences, however, differ in their connotations. With the transitive てある sentence, the current state of the window is the result of a human action; somebody closed it and kept it that way. With the intransitive ている sentence, there is no such clear implication of human intervention. The window is closed, but this may or may not be the result of somebody closing it.

3 ～間に
あいだ

You can use the pattern "A 間に B" when the event B takes place *in the middle of* another event A. Most often, the containing event A is described with the continuous ている. The verb A is in the present tense, even when the clause A describes a situation in the past.

お風呂に入っている間に電話がありました。
ふろ　はい　　　　　あいだ　てんわ
There was a phone call while I was taking a bath.

きのうの夜、寝ている間に地震がありました。
よる　ね　　　あいだ　じしん
There was an earthquake while I was asleep last night.

両親が日本にいる間に京都に連れていきたいです。
りょうしん　にほん　　　あいだ　きょうと　つ
I want to take my parents to Kyoto while they are in Japan.

A（ている）間に B	*B takes place, while A.*
あいだ	

The "A" above can be a noun as well:

留守の間に友だちが来ました。
るす　あいだ　とも　　き
A friend came while I was out.

The event B must be of short duration and properly contained within the bounds of activity A. If B extends *throughout* the time when A occurs, we use 間 instead of 間に.
あいだ　　　　　　　　　　　　　あいだ

ルームメートがメールを書いている間、私は本を読んで待ちました。
か　　　　あいだ　わたし　ほん　よ　　ま
I waited, reading a book, while my roommate was writing an e-mail.

4 adjective ＋ する

We learned in Lesson 10 how to say "become," as in 寒くなる (become cold/colder) and 上手になる (become good/better at doing X). Here we learn to use adjectives together with the irregular verb する, which in combination with adjectives means "to make."
さむ
じょう
ず

冷たい	→ 冷たくする	*to make something cold / colder*
つめ	つめ	
簡単な	→ 簡単にする	*to make something simple / simpler*
かんたん	かんたん	

この間の試験は難しすぎたので、次の試験はやさしくしてください。
Please make the next exam easier, because the last one was too difficult.

みんなで世界をよくしましょう。　（よく ← いい, irregular adjective）
Let's join our forces and make the world a better place.

部屋をきれいにしました。
I made the room clean.

髪をボブ・マーリーみたいにしたいです。
I want to make my hair like Bob Marley's.

Note also the following idiomatic use of this pattern:

静かにする　　make it quiet　　→　　keep quiet　　　静かにしてください。
Please be quiet!

5　〜てほしい

When you want somebody to do something, you can describe your wish by using the *te*-form of a verb and the adjective ほしい. The person the wish is directed to is marked with the particle に.

私は　病気の友だちに　元気になってほしいです。
I want my sick friend to get well.

私は　ルームメートに　宿題を手伝ってほしかったです。
I wanted my roommate to help me with my homework.

（私は）　person　に　　verb *te*-form　ほしい　　　　*I want* (person) *to do* . . .

When you want to say you don't want them to do something, you can negate ほしい and say 〜てほしくないです or negate the verb and say 〜ないでほしいです.

私は　お父さんに　昔の話をしてほしくないです。
I don't want my father to talk about the good old times.

私は　ホストファミリーに　英語で話さないでほしいです。
I don't want my host family to speak in English.

Let us now summarize the three words for "want":[4]

たい　　　　(Lesson 11)　| verb stem ＋ たい　　　　*I want to do ...* |

私はベトナムに行きたいです。　　　*I want to go to Vietnam.*

ほしい　　　(Lesson 14)　| noun が　ほしい　　　　*I want something.* |

私はいい辞書がほしいです。　　　*I want a good dictionary.*

てほしい　(this lesson)　| verb *te*-form ＋ ほしい　　*I want somebody to do ...* |

私は弟に電話をしてほしいです。　*I want my little brother to call me.*

表現ノート………7
（ひょうげん）

Expression Notes 7

バイトでためたお金もないです▶ないです is the alternative negative form of the verb ある. The standard negative form of ある is ありません, while the sub-standard alternative form is built up of the short form negative ない plus the politeness marker です.

More generally, you may hear the long form alternative negative verbs made up of short form negative plus です.

	standard	alternative
present	見えません	見えないです
past	見えませんでした	見えなかったです

---

[4] These are all private predicates, and used only for the speaker's wishes. When you want to describe the emotions of people other than the speaker, the predicate needs to be changed as in the examples below (see Lessons 11 and 14 for details).

先生は　学生に　たくさん勉強してほしいと言っています。
Our professors say they want their students to study a lot.

先生は　学生に　たくさん勉強してほしがっています。
Our professors (are acting in a way that suggests that they) want their students to study a lot.

練習 P r a c t i c e

① どろぼうにかばんをとられました

A. Change the following verbs into the passive forms. 🔊 K21-08

Example: 飲む　→　飲まれる

1. 食べる	5. 捨てる	9. うそをつく	13. 立つ
2. やめる	6. 壊す	10. 連れていく	14. 来る
3. なくす	7. 見る	11. ばかにする	15. 怒る
4. する	8. 笑う	12. たばこを吸う	

B. Describe the pictures with the passive forms. 🔊 K21-09

Example:　たけしさんは どろぼうに かばんをとられました。

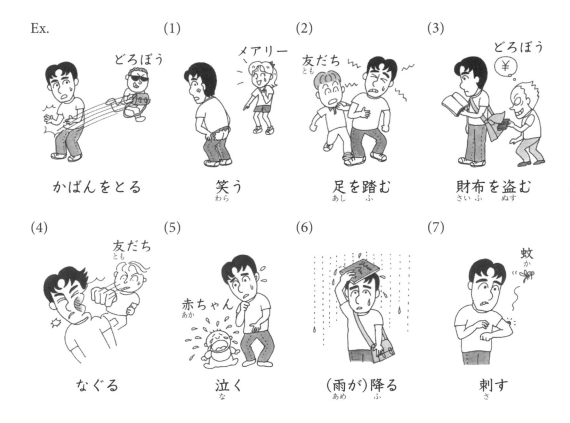

Ex.
かばんをとる

(1)
笑う

(2)
足を踏む

(3)
財布を盗む

(4)
なぐる

(5)
泣く

(6)
(雨が)降る

(7)
刺す

(8) 友だち　いじめる

(9) おじさん　怒る

(10) きょうこ　ふる

(11) ちかん　さわる

C. Pair Work—Make questions using the passive forms and ask your partner the questions.

Example:　友だちが笑う

　　　→　Ａ：友だちに笑われたことがありますか。

　　　　　Ｂ：ええ、あります。この間、「かわいい」と「こわい」を
　　　　　　　間違えたんです。

1. 友だちがばかにする
2. 友だちが（あなたの）大切な物をなくす
3. 先生が怒る
4. ちかんがさわる

5. だれかがなぐる
6. だれかが財布を盗む
7. きらいな人がデートに誘う
8. 彼／彼女がふる

D. Pair Work—Your partner looks upset. Ask what the problem is. When you answer, use the passive form. Expand the conversation.

Example:　A stranger punched you.

　　　→　Ａ：どうしたんですか。

　　　　　Ｂ：知らない人になぐられたんです。

　　　　　Ａ：それはひどいですね。警察に行ったほうがいいですよ。

　　　　　Ｂ：大丈夫です。なぐられた後、私もその人をけりましたから。

1. Your roommate made the room dirty.
2. A burglar broke into your house.
3. A customer complained.

4. A colleague read your e-mail.
5. Your friends make fun of you all the time.
6. (They) are bullying your child at school.

Ⅱ 写真が置いてあります
しゃしん お

A. Describe the pictures with 〜てある. 🔊 K21-10

Example: 家族の写真が置いてあります。
か ぞく しゃしん お

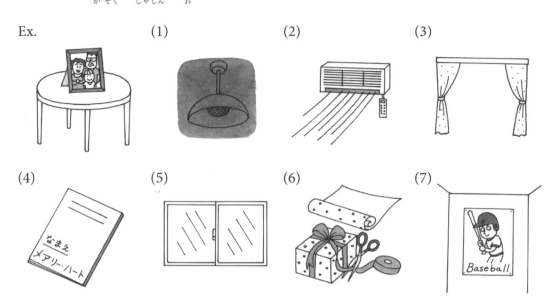

Ex.   (1)   (2)   (3)

(4)   (5)   (6)   (7)

B. Pair Work—You work as a house-sitter for a Japanese couple. They left you a list of the things you are expected to do before they come home. When they come home, you have finished only half of the things. First, choose three things you have done from the list and mark ✓. Then start the conversation as in the example.

Example:

(✓) Washing the car → A：車が洗ってありますか。
                           くるま あら
                                 B：はい、もう洗ってあります。
                                         あら
                                 A：どうもありがとう。

(   ) Washing the car → A：車が洗ってありますか。
                           くるま あら
                                   B：すみません、まだ洗ってありません。
                                                   あら
                                 すぐ、します。
                                 A：お願いします。
                                   ねが

```
< The things you are expected to do>
(      ) Cooking dinner
(      ) Giving the cat water
(      ) Doing laundry
(      ) Doing shopping
(      ) Putting the food in the refrigerator
(      ) Cleaning the room
```

C. Pair Work—You and your friend have been making preparations for a party. Using the dialogue below as a model, go down the list of things to do, finding out what your partner has already done and dividing the remaining tasks between the two. Add your own question. B's list is on p. 228.

Example:

Ａ：パーティーの準備をしなきゃいけませんね。カラオケが借りてありますか。

Ｂ：ええ、借りてあります。きのう、借りておきました。

Ａ：じゃ、私は借りなくてもいいですね。

Ｂ：部屋が掃除してありますか。

Ａ：いいえ、まだしてありません。今日忙しいから、してくれませんか。

Ｂ：えっ！ 私がするんですか。

A's List

	Decide who will do it:
カラオケを借りる	
部屋を掃除する	
飲み物を買う	(I have done it.)
ケーキを焼く	
料理を作る	(I have done it.)
友だちに連絡する	
冷蔵庫にビールを入れる	

Ⅲ 社長が寝ている間に起きます
しゃちょう　ね　　あいだ　お

A. You are a chauffeur, working for the president of a company. The following is the daily schedule of the president. Describe your day as a chauffeur. 🔊 K21-11

Example:　社長が寝ている間に起きます。
しゃちょう　ね　　あいだ　お

	the president			chauffeur
Ex.	still sleeping	7:00	←	gets up
1.	changing his clothes	9:00	←	puts the gas in the car
2.	eating breakfast at the cafe	11:00	←	buys a boxed lunch at a convenience store
3.	reading the newspaper	1:00	←	eats the boxed lunch
4.	attending a meeting	3:00	←	takes a nap
5.	going to see his factories	5:00	←	talks to his friends on the phone
6.	drinking at a party	7:00	←	drinks coffee in the car

B. Complete the following sentences.

1. 日本にいる間に＿＿＿＿＿＿＿＿＿＿＿＿＿＿＿たいです。
にほん　　　あいだ

2. 両親が出かけている間に＿＿＿＿＿＿＿＿＿＿＿＿＿＿＿＿。
りょうしん　で　　　　　あいだ

3. 赤ちゃんが寝ている間に＿＿＿＿＿＿＿＿＿＿＿＿＿＿＿＿。
あか　　　　　ね　　　あいだ

4. 休みの間に＿＿＿＿＿＿＿＿＿＿＿＿＿＿＿つもりです。
やす　　あいだ

5. 私が留守の間に＿＿＿＿＿＿＿＿＿＿＿＿＿＿＿＿ないでください。
わたし　る す　あいだ

6. ＿＿＿＿＿＿＿＿＿＿＿＿＿＿＿＿＿間にどろぼうに入られました。
あいだ　　　　　　　はい

7. ＿＿＿＿＿＿＿＿＿＿＿＿＿＿＿＿間に友だちから電話がありました。
あいだ　とも　　　　でんわ

Ⅳ 公園を多くします
こうえん　おお

A. There will be an election for mayor soon. You are one of the candidates. Say your pledges below using ～くします／～にします. 🔊 K21-12

Example:　increase parks　→　公園を多くします。
こうえん　おお

1. make the town cleaner
2. make the municipal hospital new
3. make the town safer
4. make the environment better
5. make the tax lower （安い）
やす
6. make school holidays longer
7. make the roads wider
8. make the town famous

B. Pair Work—Make a short dialogue in the following situations. Use 〜してください／〜ていただけませんか.

Example: Your teacher is so tough. He always gives you too much homework. Ask him to decrease homework.

→ A：先生、すみませんが、もっと宿題を少なくしていただけ
ませんか。多すぎて、ほかのクラスの勉強ができないん
です。

B：わからない時は手伝ってあげます。がんばってください。

1. Your teacher is so tough. Her tests are always difficult. Ask her to make exams easier.

2. Your host mother gave you too much rice. Ask her to give you less.

3. Someone who lives next door loves karaoke. He always sings very noisily. Ask him to be quiet.

4. Your boss always makes a long speech. He will make a speech at your wedding. Ask him to make it short.

5. You find a camera you want to buy, but it is a little expensive. Ask a shop clerk to make it cheaper.

Ⓥ たばこをやめてほしいです

A. Tell what you want the following people to do/not to do, using 〜てほしい.

🔊 K21-13

Example: お父さん／たばこをやめる
→ お父さんにたばこをやめてほしいです。

1. お母さん／仕事をする
2. おばあさん／若いころの話をする
3. 友だち／日本語の勉強を続ける
4. 友だち／遠い所に行かない
5. 同僚／夢をあきらめない
6. 先生／もっと学生をほめる
7. 昔の彼／私を忘れる
8. 昔の彼女／幸せになる

B. Tell what you want your friend to do/not to do, using 〜てほしい.

Example: Your friend likes cooking

→ 友だちは料理をするのが好きです。だから時々晩ご飯を作っ
てほしいです。

Your friend lies all the time

→ 友だちはいつもうそをつきます。だからうそをつかないでほし
いです。

Your friend . . .

1. has a car

2. is good at Japanese

3. has many friends

4. always complains

5. is rich

6. has been to various foreign countries

7. always comes late

C. Pair Work—Discuss what you and your partner want the following people or organizations to do/not to do. Give reasons.

Example: ルームメート

→ Ａ：私はルームメートに早く起きないでほしいです。
Ｂ：どうしてですか。
Ａ：私はもっと寝たいんですが、いつも早く起こされるから
です。

1. 友だち

2. 彼／彼女

3. 兄弟／親

4. 先生

5. あなたの学校／会社

6. あなたの国の政府

D. Pair Work—Ask a favor of your partner, explaining your situation. Then expand the conversation.

Example: You left your wallet at home

→　　A：あの、財布を忘れたから、少しお金を貸してほしいんだけど。
　　　　B：いくら？
　　　　A：二万円。
　　　　B：二万円も？
　　　　A：今日、新幹線の切符を買わなきゃいけないんだ。

1. The Japanese homework is difficult.

2. You want to take your boyfriend/girlfriend for a drive.

3. You are tired.

4. You are going to have a party at your house.

5. You have just lost your contact lens and can't find it.

6. You will arrive at the airport late at night.

Ⅵ まとめの練習

A. Tell about your bad experience using passive forms, e.g., when it happened/ what happened/how you felt about it.

Example:　先週、朝寝坊して、学校に行きました。急いでいたので、教室で
　　　　　ころんでしまいました。みんなに笑われました。とても恥ずかし
　　　　　かったです。

B. Role Play—One of you is a police officer. The other was involved in the following incidents and is calling the police to explain the situation. (Refer to the vocabulary list on the next page.)

Example:　　A burglar broke into your room and took your ring last night.

→　Police：はい。警察です。

Caller：もしもし。あのう、きのうの夜、どろぼうに入られて指輪を盗まれました。

Police：何時ごろですか。

Caller：アルバイトに行っている間に入られたので、八時から十一時までだと思います。

Police：取られたのはどんな指輪ですか。

Caller：ルビー (ruby) の指輪です。誕生日に彼からもらったんです。

1. You were punched by a man when you were walking on a street.

2. Your bicycle was stolen.

3. You were deceived by a sales person (セールスの人), and money was taken.

4. You were followed by a man from the station to your house.

5. Your wallet was taken while you were sleeping on a train.

Vocabulary ──犯罪・事件 (Crimes and Accidents)

ごうとう (強盗)	robber	おそう (襲う)	to attack
さぎ (詐欺)	fraud	ける	to kick
さぎし (詐欺師)	a con man/woman	ころす (殺す)	to murder; to kill
ストーカー	stalker	する	to pick one's pockets
すり	pickpocket	だます	to deceive
ちかん	sexual offender	つける	to follow
ひったくり	purse-snatching	なぐる (殴る)	to punch; to strike; to hit
まんびき (万引き)	shoplifting	ぬすむ (盗む)	to steal
ゆうかい (誘拐)	kidnapping	ひく	(a car) runs over
レイプ	rape	ゆする	to blackmail; to threaten

Pair Work Ⅱ C.

(→ p. 222)

Example:

Ａ：パーティーの準備をしなきゃいけませんね。カラオケが借りてありますか。

Ｂ：ええ、借りてあります。きのう、借りておきました。

Ａ：じゃ、私は借りなくてもいいですね。

Ｂ：部屋が掃除してありますか。

Ａ：いいえ、まだしてありません。今日忙しいから、してくれませんか。

Ｂ：えっ！私がするんですか。

B's List

	Decide who will do it:
カラオケを借りる	(I have done it.)
部屋を掃除する	
飲み物を買う	
ケーキを焼く	(I have done it.)
料理を作る	
友だちに連絡する	
冷蔵庫にビールを入れる	(I have done it.)

Culture Note

日本の宗教 Religion in Japan—Shinto and Buddhism
に　ほん　しゅうきょう

Japan's two major religions are Shinto (神道) and Buddhism (仏教). Native to Japan, Shinto is based on the belief that everything has a spirit. Instead of defining an explicit set of tenets, Shinto advises people to live and act in a way that does not incur the wrath of the deities. Buddhism originated in India and was introduced to Japan in the 6th century. Both Shinto shrines (神社) and Buddhist temples (お寺) can be found all over Japan.
きょう
じんじゃ　　　　　　　てら

神社（厳島神社・広島）
じんじゃ　いつくしまじんじゃ　ひろしま

お寺（清水寺・京都）
てら　きよみずでら　きょうと

According to a survey, about 85% of Japanese believe either Shinto or Buddhism, or both. Other religions, such as Christianity and Islam, have very few Japanese adherents.

Shinto and Buddhism have coexisted harmoniously in Japan for many years. It is common for most people to engage in the rituals of both religions; wedding ceremonies are often conducted by Shinto priests, while funeral rites are generally performed by Buddhist monks. On New Year's, many Japanese go to a temple or shrine, with the choice of either mattering little to most of them.

Tips for visiting temples and shrines
First, wash your hands and rinse your mouth at the purification fountain near the entrance. In front of the main hall, ring the bell (鈴), and throw offering coins (賽銭) into the offering box. Bow deeply (and if at a shrine, clap your hands twice), and pray with your palms clasped together. Finally, bow deeply again.
すず　　　　　　　　　　さいせん

おみくじ

At temples and shrines, you will likely see folded paper attached to trees and small wooden plaques hung on racks. The paper is called おみくじ, and tells one's fortune. Some people believe that bad fortunes will go away and good fortunes will come true if the おみくじ is tied around a tree branch. The plaques are called 絵馬. People write wishes or prayers on the plaques and hang them on racks with the hope that the wish or prayer will come true.
えま

絵馬
えま

日本の教育 Education in Japan
にほん　きょういく

会 話 D i a l o g u e
かい　わ

(I) Mary's host mother and host sister Yumi are talking. 🔊 K22-01/02

1 お母さん： ゆみ、勉強しなさい。来週は期末試験があるのにぜんぜん勉強して
かあ　　　　　　べんきょう　　らいしゅう　き まつ し けん　　　　　　　　　べんきょう
2 いないでしょ。

3 ゆ み： お母さん、私、もう十七なんだから、少しほっておいてよ。
かあ　わたし　　じゅうなな　　　　　すこ

4 お母さん： 今、がんばっておけば、いい大学に入れて、後で楽になるんだから。
かあ　　　いま　　　　　　　　　　　だいがく　はい　　　あと　らく

5 ゆ み： 私、別にいい大学に行けなくてもいい。
わたし　べつ　　だいがく　い

6 お母さん： お父さんとお母さんはあなたをいい大学に行かせてあげたいの。お
かあ　　　とう　　　　かあ　　　　　　　　だいがく　い
7 母さんのうちは貧乏だったから、大学に行かせてくれなかったのよ。
かあ　　　　　びんぼう　　　　　　だいがく　い

8 ゆ み： わかった、わかった。その話、もう何度も聞いた。
はなし　　なんど　き

(II) In Mary's room. 🔊 K22-03/04

1 ゆ み： メアリーも、高校の時、こんなふうだった？
こうこう　とき

2 メアリー： そうねえ、やっぱり親はうるさかったけ
おや
3 ど、もう少し自由があったかな。
すこ じゆう

4 ゆ み： うちの親、ちょっと変だと思うでしょ。
おや　　　へん　おも

5 メアリー： そんなことないよ。ちょっと厳しいかも
きび
6 しれないけど、ゆみちゃんのことを心配
しんぱい
7 しているんだよ。

(III) The next day Mary and Takeshi are on a date. 🔊 K22-05/06

1 メアリー： うちのゆみちゃん、高校生なのに忙しくて、ぜんぜん遊ぶ時間がな
こうこうせい　　いそが　　　　　　　　あそ　じかん
2 いみたい。

3 たけし：　子供も大変だけど、親も大変だと思うよ。塾に行かせたり、英会話
4 　　　　　を習わせたり、お金がかかるだろうなあ。
5 メアリー：　たけしくんも子供の時、ゆみちゃんのように塾に行ってた？
6 たけし：　ぼくはずっと遊んでた。自分の子供にも、自由に遊ばせてあげたい
7 　　　　　なあ。
8 メアリー：　でも、日本で子供を育てるのは大変そうだね。

Ⅰ

Host mother: Yumi, study! Even though you will have a final examination next week, you haven't studied at all, right?

Yumi: Mom, I am 17 years old. Leave me alone.

Host mother: If you do your best now, you will be able to enter a good university, and life will be easier later.

Yumi: It's okay not be able to go to a good university.

Host mother: Your father and I want to let you go to a good university. My parents didn't let me go to college because my family was poor.

Yumi: Okay, okay. I have heard that story many times.

Ⅱ

Yumi: Were you like me when you were in high school?

Mary: Let me think . . . My parents were strict, too, but I had a little more freedom, I guess.

Yumi: Don't you think that my parents are a bit strange?

Mary: I don't think so. They might be a little strict, but they are concerned about you.

Ⅲ

Mary: It seems that my host sister Yumi is too busy to have time to play at all even though she is a high school student.

Takeshi: Children are having a hard time, but I think that their parents are also suffering. They spend a lot letting their children go to cram schools, learn English conversation, and so on.

Mary: Did you go to a cram school like Yumi when you were a child?

Takeshi: I played all day. I want to let my children play freely.

Mary: But it seems that raising children in Japan is tough.

単語
たんご

 K22-07

Vocabulary

Nouns

あいて	相手	partner
うけつけ	受付	reception desk
* えいかいわ	英会話	English conversation
おじょうさん	お嬢さん	(someone's) daughter (polite)
かじ	家事	household matters
かぜ	風	wind
かみさま	神様	God
き	木	tree
こうはい	後輩	junior member of a group
さる	猿	monkey
* じゆう	自由	freedom
* じゅく	塾	cram school
しょるい	書類	document
せんぱい	先輩	senior member of a group
ひとりぐらし	一人暮らし	living alone
ぶか	部下	subordinate
ふくしゅう	復習	review of a lesson
プロジェクト		project
ボール		ball
むだづかい	無駄遣い	waste (money)
めんきょ	免許	license
ヨーロッパ		Europe
よしゅう	予習	preparation of lessons

い-adjective

* うるさい		noisy; annoying

な-adjectives

* しんぱい（な）	心配	worried about（〜が）
* びんぼう（な）	貧乏	poor
ぺらぺら（な）		fluent（*language* が）
* へん（な）	変	strange; unusual
* らく（な）	楽	easy; comfortable

* Words that appear in the dialogue

U-verbs

かぜがふく	風が吹く	the wind blows
かつ	勝つ	to win（〜に）
コピーをとる	コピーを取る	to make a photocopy
はこぶ	運ぶ	to carry（〜を）
はしる	走る	to run
ひろう	拾う	to pick up (something)（〜を）
* ほ（う）っておく	放っておく	to leave (someone/something) alone; to neglect（〜を）
まにあう	間に合う	to be in time（〜に）

Ru-verbs

けいかくをたてる	計画を立てる	to make a plan
* そだてる	育てる	to raise; to bring up（〜を）
たすける	助ける	to help; to rescue（〜を）
まける	負ける	to lose (a match)（〜に）

Irregular Verbs

おねがいする	お願いする	to pray for help（*person* に〜を）
さんせいする	賛成する	to agree（〜に）
しっぱいする	失敗する	to fail; to be unsuccessful
てつやする	徹夜する	to stay up all night
はんたいする	反対する	to oppose; to object to（〜に）
ほんやくする	翻訳する	to translate（〜を）

Adverbs and Other Expressions

* こんなふう		like this
* じゆうに	自由に	freely
* ずっと		for a long time; all the time
ぜったいに	絶対に	definitely
* そんなこと（は）ない		I don't think so.
〜とか		. . . for example
* なんども	何度も	many times
* もうすこし	もう少し	a little more

文 法 G r a m m a r

1 Causative Sentences

In this lesson, we learn yet another verb derivation called the "causative form." When you use the causative form of a verb, you can describe who *makes* someone do something, and who *lets* someone do something.

You can derive the causative form of a verb this way:

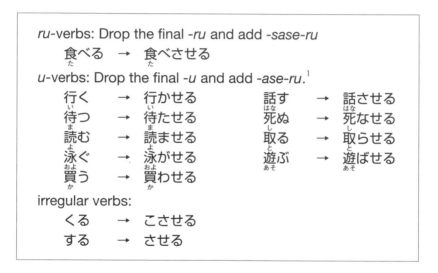

As you may have noticed already, the causative derivation is quite similar to the passive derivation, which we studied in the last lesson.

The basic structure of a causative sentence is like the following:

> 先生は   学生に   会話を覚えさせました。
> (director) は   (cast) に   (action)
> *The professor made the students memorize the dialogue.*
>
> The "director" decides what is allowed and what is to be done. Marked with は or が.
> The "cast" performs the action. Usually goes with に.[2]
> The "action" is described with a causative form of a verb.

Let us first be clear about the two meanings of the causative form. Any causative verb can be interpreted either with the "*make* somebody do" reading or with the "*let* somebody do" reading. Thus you cannot tell simply from the sentences below in isolation whether they describe an authoritarian parent (forcing the children to eat what they do not want) or a doting parent (allowing the children to have what they want). Only our general knowledge about the parents and the linguistic context of the sentence solve the issue.

お父さんは 子供に 野菜を食べさせました。
The father made/let his child eat vegetables.

お母さんは 子供に 本を読ませました。
The mother made/let her child read the book.

If the helping verb てあげる, てくれる, or てもらう follows a causative verb, you can assume in almost all cases that it is a "let" causative (see Lesson 16 for those helping verbs).

先生は 私に 英語を話させてくれませんでした。
The professor did not allow me to speak in English.

私は 自分の子供に 好きなことをさせてあげるつもりです。
I think I will let my children do what they love.

You can use the causative ＋ てください to ask for permission to do something and to volunteer to do something.

---

[1] With the verbs that end with the *hiragana* う, we see a "*w*" intervening, just as in the negative short forms and the passive forms.

[2] There are cases in which the cast gets を instead.

(1) When the caused action is a reflex, such as crying and laughing:
　　私は その子供を 泣かせてしまいました。
　　I accidentally made the child cry.
　　アレンさんは おもしろい映画を作って みんなを 笑わせました。
　　Mr. Allen made funny movies and made everyone laugh.

(2) When the verb that is turned into the causative originally did not call for を:
　　In the first two examples below, the verbs 行く and 座る do not take the particle を, and therefore を is up for grabs for marking the cast in the causative sentences. In the last example, in contrast, 読む already calls for を, and therefore を is not available for marking the cast in the causative.
　　先生は 私を トイレに 行かせました。　　*The professor made me go to the bathroom.*
　　その人は 私を そこに 座らせました。　　*That person made me sit there.*
　　× 両親は 私を 本を読ませました。　　*My parents made me read books.*

私にこの仕事をやらせてください。
Please let me do this job.

(director) は	(cast) に	causative verb	(director) *makes/lets* (cast) *do* . . .
(director) は	(cast) に	causative verb ＋ てあげる／てくれる	
			(director) *lets* (cast) *do* . . .
causative verb ＋ てください			*please let me do* . . .

2　verb stem ＋ なさい

The verb stem ＋ なさい is a command. なさい has a strong implication that you are "talking down" to somebody, or that you think you are more mature, know better, and should be obeyed. なさい, therefore, is appropriate for parents to use toward their children or for teachers toward their students. You also often see なさい in exam instructions.

うちに毎日電話しなさい。	*Call home every day.*
かっこの中に単語を入れなさい。	*Fill in the blanks with a word.*
文句を言うのをやめなさい。	*Stop complaining.*

You see in the last example above that you can express the idea of the negative "don't do . . ." using a verb followed by のを and やめなさい, which comes from the verb やめる.

3　〜ば

"Clause A ば clause B" is a conditional statement "if A, then B." We have already seen an instance of this construction in Lesson 18, namely, the ば-form in the pattern ばよかった (I wish I had done . . .).

Let us first review the conjugation rule of the verb ば-form.[3]

---

[3] We will focus on the verb ば-form in this lesson, but ば also goes with い-adjectives and negative predicates in general:

おもしろい	→	おもしろければ	元気じゃない	→	元気じゃなければ
おもしろくない	→	おもしろくなければ	学生じゃない	→	学生じゃなければ

With な-adjectives and nouns in the affirmative, だ either becomes なら (see Lesson 13) or であれば:

静かだ	→	静かなら or 静かであれば	先生だ	→	先生なら or 先生であれば

Verbs in the affirmative:

Drop the final -u and add -eba.

食べる → 食べれば

行く → 行けば   待つ → 待てば   買う → 買えば

する → すれば

くる → くれば

Verbs in the negative:

Drop the final い and add ければ.

行かない → 行かなければ

In an "A ば B" sentence, the "A" part describes the condition, *provided that* the consequence described in "B" will follow.

車があれば、いろいろな所に行けます。
If you have a car, you can go to various places.

かぎをかけておけば、どろぼうに入られません。
If you lock the doors and windows, you won't have your apartment broken into.

大家さんに言わなければ、わかりませんよ。
If you do not tell the landlord, he will never find that out.

You usually use the "A ば B" pattern when the condition "A" guarantees a *good result* in "B." Therefore, the sentence (i) below is natural, while the sentence (ii), though not impossible, sounds rather odd.[4]

(i)　　走れば、電車に間に合います。
　　　If I run, I will be able to catch the train.

(ii) ?? 歩けば、電車に遅れます。
　　　If I walk, I will be late for the train.

---

[4] You can express the idea in (ii) more appropriately with たら: 歩いたら、電車に遅れます. You may also note that (ii) is not totally ungrammatical. Embedded in a larger sentence that overtly cancels the "good result" implication, for example, (ii) improves significantly in acceptability:

歩けば電車に遅れるのはわかっていました。
I knew that I would be late for the train if I walked.

Because of this "good result" implication, "A ば B" is often used to advise "A." Sometimes the part "B" contains vacuous generic expressions like 大丈夫です or いいんです.

この薬を飲めば大丈夫です。
You will be okay, if you take this medicine.

先生に聞けばいいんです。
All you have to do is ask the teacher. (If you ask, everything will be fine.)

4　〜のに

のに connects two facts, A and B, which hold in spite of the expectation that if A is the case, B is not to be the case. "A のに B," therefore means "A, but contrary to expectations, B, too" or "B, despite the fact A."

この会社はお金があるのに、給料は安いです。
This company is rich, but its workers' salaries are low.

家にいるのに、電話に出ない。
She is home but does not answer the phone.

The predicate in the part A is in the short form. When A ends with a な-adjective or with a noun + です, it appears as な, just like in the explanatory んです construction.

田中さんは親切なのに、山田さんは田中さんがきらいです。
Ms. Tanaka is nice, but Ms. Yamada does not like her.

大きい問題なのに、あの人はだれにも相談しません。
It is a big issue, but he does not consult with anybody.

Because のに connects two facts, you cannot have non-factual sentences, like requests, and suggestions in the B clause:

　　　　×　日本語が少し難しいのに、これを読んでください。
Compare:　日本語が少し難しい<u>ですが</u>、これを読んでください。
　　　　　This Japanese is a little difficult, but please read it.

　　　　×　あまりおいしそうじゃないのに、ここで食べましょう。
Compare:　あまりおいしそうじゃない<u>けど</u>、ここで食べましょう。
　　　　　The food does not look very promising, but let's eat here.

5　〜のような/〜のように

"Noun A のような noun B" means "a B like/similar to A." When you say "A のような B," the "B" has the same quality or appearance as A, or A is an example of B.[5]

> 私は鎌倉のような町が好きです。
> わたし　かまくら　　　　　まち　す
> *I like towns like Kamakura.*

> 私はアウンサン・スーチーのような人になりたいです。
> わたし　　　　　　　　　　　　　　ひと
> *I want to be a person like Aung San Suu Kyi, the Burmese democracy leader.*

You use "noun A のように" when you want to describe an action which is "done in the same way as A" or a characteristic "which is comparable to A."

> メアリーさんは魚のように上手に泳げます。
> さかな　　　　じょうず　およ
> *Mary can swim very well, just like a fish.*

> アントニオさんは孫悟空のように強いです。
> そんごくう　　　　つよ
> *Antonio is strong like Son Goku.*

> この町は夜の墓場のように静かです。
> まち　よる　はかば　　　　　しず
> *This town is as quiet as a graveyard at night.*

---

[5] みたい, which we learned in Lesson 17, can be used in the same way as 〜のような + noun, and 〜のように + verb/adjective. Note that の does not come between the preceding noun and みたい.
　あの人はマザー・テレサみたいな人です。
　ひと　　　　　　　　　　　　　　ひと
She is a person just like Mother Teresa.
　あの人は壊れたレコードみたいに同じことを言います。
　ひと　こわ　　　　　　　　　　おな　　　　　い
She says the same thing over and over again, just like a broken vinyl record.

練 習 P r a c t i c e
れん しゅう

① 服を洗わせます
ふく あら

A. Change the following verbs into the causative forms. 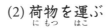 K22-08

Example: 食べる → 食べさせる
た   た

1. やめる   5. あきらめる   9. 取る   13. 持っていく
　　　　　　　　　　　　　　　　　　　　　 と　　　　　　　　 も

2. 働く   6. 来る   10. 拾う   14. 練習する
　 はたら   く   ひろ   れんしゅう

3. 飲む   7. 考える   11. 帰る
　 の   かんが   かえ

4. 持つ   8. 習う   12. 運ぶ
　 も   なら   はこ

B. Make sentences using the causative forms.

(a) You are on the tennis team and make junior students do these things. 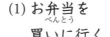 K22-09

Example: 後輩に服を洗わせます。
こうはい　ふく　あら

Ex. 服を洗う   (1) お弁当を   (2) 荷物を運ぶ   (3) 好きな人の電話
　 ふく　あら   べんとう   に もつ　はこ   す　 ひと　てん わ
                       買いに行く   番号を調べる
                       か　 い   ばんごう　しら

(4) 車を運転する   (5) ボールを拾う   (6) 宿題をする
　 くるま　 うんてん   　　　　　ひろ   しゅくだい

(b) You are the boss and make your subordinates do these things. 🔊 K22-10

Example: 部下に書類を翻訳させます。
ぶ か　　しょるい　ほんやく

Ex. 書類を翻訳する　(1) コピーを取る　(2) お茶をいれる　(3) 残業する
しょるい　ほんやく　　　　　　　　　と　　　　　ちゃ　　　　　　　ざんぎょう

(4) 空港に迎えに来る　(5) お客さんを案内する　(6) 安いホテルを探す
くうこう　むか　　く　　　　きゃく　　あんない　　　　　やす　　　　　さが

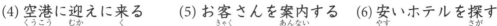

C. Group Work—Talk about the following topics with your classmates.

Example:　Ａ：あなたが先生だったら、学生に何をさせますか。
　　　　　　　　　　せんせい　　　　　　がくせい　　なに

　　　　　　Ｂ：私が先生だったら、学生に毎日テストをさせます。
　　　　　　　　わたし　せんせい　　　　がくせい　まいにち

　　　　　　Ｃ：どうしてですか。

　　　　　　Ｂ：毎日テストがあると、学生がたくさん勉強するからです。
　　　　　　　　まいにち　　　　　　　　がくせい　　　　　　　べんきょう
　　　　　　　　Ａさんはどう思いますか。
　　　　　　　　　　　　　　　　おも

1. あなたが日本語の先生だったら、学生に何をさせますか。
　　　　にほんご　せんせい　　　　　がくせい　なに

2. あなたが部長だったら、部下に何をさせますか。
　　　　ぶちょう　　　　　ぶ か　なに

3. あなたが先輩だったら、後輩に何をさせますか。
　　　　せんぱい　　　　　こうはい　なに

D. Pair Work—You are executives in a company who are preparing for a conference. Look at the profiles of your subordinates and discuss who would be the best person to do the tasks.

Example:　A：だれにコンピューターを使わせましょうか。

　　　　　　B：佐藤さんに使わせたらどうですか。コンピューターのことをよく知っていますから。

Ex. コンピューターを使う　　　　　　　　_____佐　藤_____

1. 町を案内する　　　　　　　　　　　　_____

2. 翻訳する　　　　　　　　　　　　　　_____

3. 受付に座る　　　　　　　　　　　　　_____

4. お客さんを空港に迎えに行く　　　　　_____

5. 部屋を掃除する　　　　　　　　　　　_____

6. 地図をかく　　　　　　　　　　　　　_____

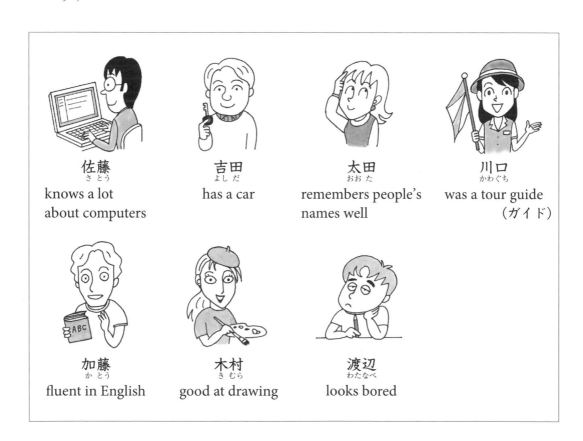

佐藤	吉田	太田	川口
knows a lot about computers	has a car	remembers people's names well	was a tour guide （ガイド）

加藤	木村	渡辺
fluent in English	good at drawing	looks bored

Ⅱ 大学に行かせてくれました
だい がく い

A. You wanted to do the following things. Your parents let you do some and didn't let you do others. Complete the sentences using 〜てくれる／〜てくれない. [🔊] K22-11

Example: 高校の時、一人暮らしをする （いいえ）
こうこう とき ひとり ぐ
　→　高校の時、両親は一人暮らしをさせてくれませんでした。
こうこう とき りょうしん ひとり ぐ

1. 子供の時、夜遅くテレビを見る （いいえ）
こども とき よるおそ み
2. 子供の時、友だちの家に泊まる （はい）
こども とき とも いえ と
3. 子供の時、ゲームをする （はい）
こども とき
4. 子供の時、お菓子をたくさん食べる （いいえ）
こども とき か し た
5. 子供の時、学校を休む （いいえ）
こども とき がっこう やす
6. 高校の時、車の免許を取る （はい）
こうこう とき くるま めんきょ と
7. 高校の時、友だちと旅行する （いいえ）
こうこう とき とも りょこう
8. 高校の時、アルバイトをする （はい）
こうこう とき
9. 自分が行きたい大学に行く （はい）
じ ぶん い だいがく い

B. Pair Work—Using the cues above, talk about the things your parents let you do/didn't let you do when you were a child and as a high school student.

Example: 高校の時、一人暮らしをする
こうこう とき ひとり ぐ
　→　Ａ：高校の時、両親は一人暮らしをさせてくれましたか。
こうこう とき りょうしん ひとり ぐ
　　　Ｂ：いいえ、一人暮らしをさせてくれませんでした。私は
ひとり ぐ わたし
　　　一人暮らしをしたかったんですけど。Ａさんは？
ひとり ぐ

C. Pair Work—Talk about the following topics.

Example: Ａ：親になったら、子供に何をさせてあげますか。
おや こども なに
　　　Ｂ：子供が楽器を習いたかったら、習わせてあげます。
こども がっき なら なら
　　　Ａ：どんな楽器ですか。
がっき
　　　Ｂ：バイオリンとか、ピアノとか。

1. 親になったら、子供に何をさせてあげますか。
2. 結婚したら、相手に何をさせてあげますか。
3. 社長になったら、部下に何をさせてあげますか。

D. You have been working for a company, but your boss underestimates you. Volunteer to do the following activities using the causative＋てください. 🔊 K22-12

Example:　コピーを取る　→　私にコピーを取らせてください。

1. 出張に行く
2. お客さんを案内する
3. 書類を翻訳する
4. その仕事をやる
5. 次のプロジェクトの計画を立てる
6. お嬢さんと結婚する

E. Pair Work—Make a short dialogue in the following situations. Use the causative＋てください.

Example:　　Today is the birthday of your child. You want to leave the office early. Ask the boss.

→　A：今日は早く帰らせてください。
　　B：どうしたの。
　　A：今日は子供の誕生日なので、一緒に晩ご飯を食べる約束をしたんです。
　　B：そうか。じゃあいいよ。

1. You want to go to Europe with your friend next month. You need a week off from the job. Ask the boss.
2. Your boss is looking for someone who can teach English to her/his child. You want the job.
3. You invited the boss out for dinner. After the meal, offer to pay for dinner.
4. Your boss is drunk, but he has to drive a car home.
5. You have been seeing someone for three months. He/she has just proposed marriage to you. You need time to think.

Ⅲ 掃除しなさい
そう じ

A. You are a parent. What would you say to your child in the following situations?

K22-13

Example:　　Your child's room is always messy.　　→　部屋を掃除しなさい。
へ や　　そう じ

1. Your child doesn't eat vegetables.

2. Your child doesn't study at all.

3. Your child stays up late.

4. Your child doesn't practice the piano.

5. Your child doesn't like to take a bath.

6. Your child always studies and doesn't play.

7. Your child doesn't come home right after school.

8. Your son has very long hair like a girl's.

B. Pair Work—Choose a situation below and make a short dialogue using 〜なさい.

1. Parent — Child　　　　　2. Teacher — Student

Example:　　Mother：ようこ、起きなさい。
お

　　　　　　　Child：　眠いよ。
ねむ

　　　　　　　Mother：早く起きなさい。もう八時よ。学校に行かなきゃ。
はや お　　　　　　 はち じ　　 がっこう　 い

　　　　　　　Child：　お母さん、今日は日曜日だよ。
かあ　　　 きょう　 にちよう び

Ⅳ 薬を飲めば、元気になります
くすり の　　　 げん き

A. Change phrases 1 through 6 into the ば-form and choose the correct phrase that follows from a through g. K22-14

Example:　　薬を飲む　　→　薬を飲めば、元気になります。
くすり の　　　　 くすり の　　　 げん き

Ex. 薬を飲む　　　　　　　・　　　・a. 涼しくなります。
くすり の　　　　　　　　　　　　　　　　すず

1. 風が吹く　　　　　　・　　　・b. ほしいものが買えます。
かぜ ふ　　　　　　　　　　　　　　　　　　　 か

2. 試験がない　　　　　・　　　・c. 迎えに来てくれます。
し けん　　　　　　　　　　　　　　　　 むか き

3. 走る　　　　　　　　・　　　・d. 元気になります。
はし　　　　　　　　　　　　　　　　　　　 げん き

4. 予習をする　　　　　・　　　・e. 授業に間に合います。
よ しゅう　　　　　　　　　　　　　 じゅぎょう ま あ

5. 友だちに電話する　　・　　　・f. 授業がよくわかります。
とも　　　　 でん わ　　　　　　　　　 じゅぎょう

6. 無駄遣いしない　　　・　　　・g. 遊びに行けます。
む だ づか　　　　　　　　　　　　　　 あそ い

B. Encourage the people below using 〜ば大丈夫ですよ。🔊 K22-15

Example: 復習すれば大丈夫ですよ。

Ex.

試験が心配なんです。

復習する

(1)

授業に間に合わないかもしれません。

走る

(2)

外国に行くけど、
言葉がわからないんです。

ジェスチャーを使う
(gesture)

(3)

レポートの締め切りに
間に合わないんです。

先生に頼む

(4)

服を汚したんです。

早く洗う

(5)

朝早く起きられないんです。

目覚まし時計をたくさん買っておく

(6) 仕事で失敗
したんです。
しごと　しっぱい

今度がんばる
こんど

(7) 絶対に
ぜったい
さくら大学に
だいがく
入りたいんです。
はい

神様にお願いする
かみさま　ねが

C. Pair Work—Ask your partner the following questions.

Example: A：どうすれば料理が上手になりますか。
　　　　　　　　りょうり　じょうず

　　　　　　B：料理をたくさん作れば、上手になりますよ。
　　　　　　　　りょうり　　　　つく　　じょうず

1. どうすれば日本語が上手になりますか。
　　　　　にほんご　じょうず

2. どうすれば日本人の友だちができますか。
　　　　　にほんじん　とも

3. どうすれば大学院に入れますか。
　　　　　だいがくいん　はい

4. どうすれば有名になれますか。
　　　　　ゆうめい

5. どうすればお金持ちになれますか。
　　　　　かね　も

6. どうすれば幸せになれますか。
　　　　　しあわ

ⓥ 早く寝たのに、眠いんです
　はや　ね　　　ねむ

A. Change the cues in 1 through 7 into のに clauses and choose the correct phrase that follows from the right column. 🔊 K22-16

Example: 日本に留学したことがないのに、日本語がぺらぺらです。
　　　　　にほん　りゅうがく　　　　　　　　にほんご

Ex. 日本に留学したことがありません・　　　・a. 眠くないです。
　　にほん　りゅうがく　　　　　　　　　　　　ねむ

1. かぎがかけてありました　　　　・　　・b. 人気がないです。
　　　　　　　　　　　　　　　　　　　にんき

2. 子供です　　　　　　　　　　　・　　・c. 仕事は大変です。
　　こども　　　　　　　　　　　　　　　しごと　たいへん

3. きのうの夜早く寝ました　　　　・　　・d. 日本語がぺらぺらです。
　　　　　よるはや　ね　　　　　　　　　にほんご

4. 彼女はとてもきれいです　　　　・　　・e. 試合に勝ちました。
　　かのじょ　　　　　　　　　　　　　　しあい　か

5. ぜんぜん練習しませんでした　　・　　・f. どろぼうに入られました。
　　　　　れんしゅう　　　　　　　　　　　はい

6. 給料が安いです　　　　　　　　・　　・g. 朝寝坊してしまいました。
　　きゅうりょう　やす　　　　　　　　　あさねぼう

7. 徹夜しました　　　　　　　　　・　　・h. 動物園がきらいです。
　　てつや　　　　　　　　　　　　　　　どうぶつえん

B. Pair Work—Complain about the following situations. When you hear the complaint, give advice or encouragement.

Example: You bought a camera last week. It has broken.

→   A：このカメラ、先週買ったのに、もう壊れてしまったんです。

B：店に持っていって、交換してもらったらどうですか。

1. You went to a baseball game. Your favorite team lost.

2. You studied a lot. You couldn't do well on the test.

3. You knitted a sweater for your boyfriend (girlfriend). He (She) never wears it.

4. Your relatives came to see you. You were busy and couldn't take them anywhere.

5. Today is your birthday. Your friend forgot it.

6. You want to live by yourself. Your parents don't let you do so.

7. You can do many things. Your boss makes you photocopy and serve tea (and do other simple things).

8. You tidied up the room yesterday, but your roommate made it messy.

Ⅵ 父のような人になりたいです

A. Pair Work—Ask your partner the following questions. When you answer, use ～のような as in the example.

Example: A：どんな人になりたいですか。

B：父のような人になりたいです。

A：どうしてですか。

B：父は強くて、やさしいからです。

1. どんな人になりたくないですか。

2. どんな人と結婚したいですか。

3. どんな町に住みたいですか。

B. Describe your classmates, friends, and family members, using ～のような.

Example: マイクさんはドラえもんのような人です。私が困った時、いつも助けてくれますから。

C. Pair Work—Talk about your classmates using 〜のように.

Example: ＿＿＿＿＿＿さん can climb up a tree like ＿＿＿＿＿＿.

→ A：ジョンさんはさるのように木に登れると思います。

B：そうですね。私もそう思います。

or 私はメアリーさんのほうが上手に木に登れると思います。

1. ＿＿＿＿＿＿さん can sing very well like ＿＿＿＿＿＿.

2. ＿＿＿＿＿＿さん can dance very well like ＿＿＿＿＿＿.

3. ＿＿＿＿＿＿さん eats a lot like ＿＿＿＿＿＿.

4. ＿＿＿＿＿＿さん is smart like ＿＿＿＿＿＿.

5. ＿＿＿＿＿＿さん is strong like ＿＿＿＿＿＿.

6. ＿＿＿＿＿＿さん is good-looking/beautiful like ＿＿＿＿＿＿.

7. ＿＿＿＿＿＿さん is fluent in Japanese like ＿＿＿＿＿＿.

Ⅶ まとめの練習

A. Group Work—In a group, choose one topic from below and discuss it.

Example: 親は子供に楽器を習わせたほうがいい

→ A：私は賛成です。子供の時に楽器を始めたら、上手になるから、習わせたほうがいいと思います。

B：私は反対です。習いたくないのに習わせたら、子供は音楽がきらいになるかもしれません。

C：私は賛成です。いろいろなことをさせるのはいいことだと思います。

Topics:

1. 子供を塾に行かせたほうがいい
2. アルバイトをさせたほうがいい
3. 家事を手伝わせたほうがいい
4. 外国語を勉強させたほうがいい
5. 大学に行かせたほうがいい

B. Talk about things that you wanted to do but were not allowed to do when you were a child. How did you feel about it? How did you react?

Example:　子供の時、ゲームをしたかったのに、両親はさせてくれませんでした。友だちはみんなゲームを持っていたから、すごく悲しかったです。それで、時々友だちのうちに行って、ゲームをしました。

C. Role Play—Using the first part of Dialogue I as a model, act the role of a mother/father or a child.

Father/Mother—Tell the child to do something using 〜なさい and try to convince him/her to do it.

Child—Take a defiant attitude toward the father/mother.

Example:

Father：ピアノの練習をしなさい。きのうもしなかっただろう。

Child：　うるさいなあ。少しほっておいてよ。

Father：毎日練習すれば、将来プロのピアニスト (professional pianist) になれるんだから。

Child：　私、別にピアニストになれなくてもいい。

Other cues:

go to bed / exercise / help cook / go to a cram school / eat vegetables / study English

Ｃulture Ｎote

日本の教育制度(2) にほん きょういくせいど Japan's Educational System (2)

University Entrance Exams （大学入試） だいがくにゅうし

In general, those seeking to enter a Japanese university or college need to pass an entrance exam (大学入試). Most entrance だいがくにゅうし exams are held sometime from January through March. There are also alternative admission methods, such as admission by recommendation. When applying, students have to choose the department they wish to enter. Since getting into good schools is highly competitive, many students supplement their

Celebration for passing an exam

regular class work by attending a special preparation school (塾 or 予備校) or getting private じゅく よびこう tutoring (家庭教師). Those who fail an entrance examination have to wait a year to take it かていきょうし again. These students are called 一浪, and those who fail the exam twice are called 二浪. いちろう にろう

College Life （大学生活） だいがくせいかつ

Here are some of the keywords that represent college life.

- サークル：サークル is a group of students devoted to a particular hobby, interest, sport, social activity, and so forth. Some examples are 映画サークル, アニメサークル, アウトドア えいが サークル, and 写真サークル. しゃしん

- ゼミ：ゼミ comes from the word "seminar." It is a class in which a small group of students studies an area of their major with a supervising professor. Students usually start taking ゼミ from their junior year.

- バイト （＝アルバイト）：Many students spend a lot of their time working at a part-time job, or バイト (see 読み書き編, Lesson 18). Common part-time jobs include tutoring, teach-よ か へん ing at preparation schools, and working at shops or restaurants.

- 就活：就活 is a short form of 就職活動, which means job hunting. Japa-しゅうかつ しゅうかつ しゅうしょくかつどう nese college students usually start to look for a job in their junior year. During 就活, most students wear a dark-colored business suit, and some しゅうかつ with dyed hair restore their hair to its natural black.

第23課 | L E S S O N 23

別れ Good-bye
わか

会 話 Dialogue
かい わ

Ⅰ Mary and her host family at their last dinner together. 🔊 K23-01/02

1 お母さん： メアリーがいなくなるとさびしくなるね。
かあ

2 メアリー： でも、来年大学を卒業したら、また日本に戻ってきますから。
らいねんだいがく そつぎょう にほん もど

3 お父さん、お母さん、本当にお世話になりました。
とう かあ ほんとう せ わ

4 お父さん： いや。私たちもメアリーがいて、とても楽しかったよ。
とう わたし たの

5 お母さん： 国に帰っても、私たちのことを忘れないでね。
かあ くに かえ わたし わす

6 メアリー： もちろん。アメリカにも遊びに来てください。
あそ き

7 お父さん： じゃあ、この夏はアメリカに行くことにしようか。
とう なつ い

8 お母さん： そうね。
かあ

Ⅱ On the way to the airport. 🔊 K23-03/04

1 たけし： この一年、いろいろなことがあったね。
いちねん

2 メアリー： そうそう。デートの時、よく待たされた。
とき ま

3 たけし： ぼくが約束の場所を間違えて、後で、ものすごく怒られたり。
やくそく ばしょ まちが あと おこ

4 メアリー： たけしくんが作った料理を食べさせられて、おなかをこわしたり。
つく りょうり た

5 たけし： 初めて一緒に踊った時、「盆踊りみたいだ」って笑われた。
はじ いっしょ おど とき ぼんおど わら

6 メアリー： あの時は足を踏まれて、痛かった。
とき あし ふ いた

7 たけし： 考え方が違うから、けんかもよくしたね。でもみんないい思い出だね。
かんが かた ちが おも で

Ⅲ At the airport. 🔊 K23-05/06

1 たけし： じゃあ、元気でね。
げんき

2 メアリー： うん。たけしくんも。たけしくんに会えて本当によかった。
あ ほんとう

₃ たけし：　　そんな悲_{かな}しそうな顔_{かお}しないで。

₄ メアリー：　わかってる。じゃあ、そろそろ行_いかなきゃ。

₅ たけし：　　メアリーが卒業_{そつぎょう}して日本_{にほん}に戻_{もど}ってくるまで、待_まっているから。

 I

Host mother: When you are gone, we will miss you.

Mary: But I will come back to Japan when I graduate

　　　　from college next year, so . . . Thank you for taking care of me, Father and Mother.

Host father: Don't mention it. We had a great time with you, Mary.

Host mother: Don't forget us even though you are going back to your country.

Mary: Of course I won't. Please come to see me in the U.S.

Host father: Then let's visit the U.S. this summer.

Host mother: That sounds good.

II

Takeshi: Many things happened in this one year.

Mary: You are right. You often made me wait when we had a date.

Takeshi: When I misunderstood where to meet, I was scolded badly later.

Mary: You made me eat that dish you cooked and I got a stomachache, and . . .

Takeshi: When we danced together for the first time, I was laughed at and you were saying "like a
　　　　Bon-odori."

Mary: You stepped on my foot then and it hurt.

Takeshi: Because we think differently, we also fought a lot. But they are all good memories . . .

III

Takeshi: Well, take care of yourself.

Mary: Okay. You, too. I'm really glad that I met you, Takeshi.

Takeshi: Don't look so sad.

Mary: I know, but . . . Well, I should go now.

Takeshi: I'll wait until you graduate and come back to Japan.

単語
たん　　ご
Vocabulary

 K23-07

Nouns

* おもいで	思い出	memory
かいがいりょこう	海外旅行	trip to a foreign country
からだ	体	body
くつした	靴下	socks
こくさいでんわ	国際電話	international call
しゃかい	社会	society
じゅぎょうりょう	授業料	tuition
しょうがっこう	小学校	elementary school
せんきょ	選挙	election
ソフト		software
タイヤ		tire
ただ		free of charge
* ばしょ	場所	place
べっそう	別荘	villa; vacation home
ボーナス		bonus
* ぼんおどり	盆踊り	*Bon* dance (Japanese traditional dance)
めんせつ	面接	interview
ゆうしょく	夕食	dinner
りそう	理想	ideal
るすばん	留守番	looking after a house during someone's absence

い-adjective

まずい		(food is) terrible

U-verbs

あめがやむ	雨がやむ	the rain stops
* いなくなる		(someone) is gone; to disappear （〜が）
* おせわになる	お世話になる	to be in someone's care （〜に）
* おなかをこわす		to have a stomachache
きにいる	気に入る	to find something agreeable （〜が/を）

* Words that appear in the dialogue

*	ちがう	違う	to be different; wrong（～と）
	なくなる		to be lost; to disappear（～が）
	わるぐちをいう	悪口を言う	to talk behind someone's back

Ru-verbs

	うける	受ける	to take (an examination, interview, etc.)（～を）
	かえる	換える	to change（～を）
	こたえる	答える	to answer（～に）
	はなれる	離れる	(something/someone) separates; parts from（～と）

Irregular Verbs

*	～かおをする	～顔をする	to look . . . (facial expression)
	がっかりする		to be disappointed（～に）
	がまんする	我慢する	to be tolerant/patient（～を）
	せわをする	世話をする	to take care of . . .（～の）
	どうじょうする	同情する	to sympathize（～に）
	パンクする		(tire) goes flat（～が）
*	もどってくる	戻ってくる	(something/someone) comes back
	ゆうしょうする	優勝する	to win a championship

Adverbs and Other Expressions

*	いや		no
*	げんきでね	元気でね	Take care of yourself.
	さいごに	最後に	finally
*	そうそう		You are right.
*	そろそろ		it is about time to . . .
*	そんな～		such . . . ; that kind of . . .
*	ものすごく		extremely

文法 G r a m m a r
ぶん ぽう

1 Causative-passive Sentences

"Causative-passive" sentences are the passive version of causative sentences. You can use causative-passive sentences when you want to say that you were made to do, or harassed or talked into doing, something that you did not want to.

（下手だから歌いたくなかったのに）歌を歌わされました。
　へ　た　　　　　　うた　　　　　　　　　　　　うた　　うた
(I didn't want to sing because I'm not a good singer, but) I was forced to sing.

（きらいだから食べたくないんですが、いつも）肉を食べさせられます。
　　　　　　　　た　　　　　　　　　　　　　　にく　　た
(I don't want to eat it because I don't like meat, but) I am (always) made to eat meat.

You make the causative-passive forms this way:

---

1. *ru*-verbs: Drop *-ru* and add *-sase-rare-ru*.
   食べる　→　　食べさせられる
   た　　　　　　　　た

2. *u*-verbs that end with す: Drop *-u* and add *-ase-rare-ru*.
   話す　→　　話させられる
   はな　　　　　　はな

3. all the other *u*-verbs: Drop *-u* and add *-asare-ru*.
   書く　→　書かされる　　　　立つ　→　立たされる
   か　　　　　か　　　　　　　た　　　　　た
   読む　→　読まされる　　　　撮る　→　撮らされる
   よ　　　　　よ　　　　　　　と　　　　　と
   泳ぐ　→　泳がされる　　　　遊ぶ　→　遊ばされる
   およ　　　　およ　　　　　　あそ　　　　あそ
   買う　→　買わされる
   か　　　　　か

4. irregular verbs:
   する　→　させられる
   くる　→　こさせられる

In the table above, you must have noticed that the causative-passive morphology in Groups 1, 2, and 4 is indeed the combination of the causative and the passive forms: *-(s)ase-rare*. In Group 3, however, the causative-passive suffix *-asare* is shorter than the sum of the causative (*-ase*) and the passive (*-rare*) suffixes.[1]

---

[1] The more transparently combinative *aserare* form, such as 書かせられる, are indeed grammatical, but causative-
か
passive verbs of the *asare* form, such as 書かされる, are much more common.
か

The basic makeup of a causative-passive sentence is like this:

> 私は 彼女に 車を洗わされました。
> わたし かのじょ くるま あら
> (puppet) は (puppet master) に (action)
>
> *I was tricked by my girlfriend into washing her car.*
>
> The "puppet" is forced into performing an action. Marked with は or が.
> The "puppet master" wields power over, and manipulates, the puppet.
> The particle is に.
> The "action" forced upon the puppet is described with a causative-
>   passive verb.

If you compare a causative-passive sentence with a causative sentence, you notice that the actors are switched between the two:

Causative-passive: 私は 友だちに 宿題を手伝わされました。
わたし とも しゅくだい て つだ

I was forced by my friend into helping him with his homework.

Causative: 友だちは 私に 宿題を手伝わせました。
とも わたし しゅくだい て つだ

My friend made me help him with his homework.

Compare a causative-passive sentence with a plain, noncausative nonpassive sentence. These two types of sentences have the same subject. You add the "puppet master" role to a plain sentence and make the verb longer, and you get a causative-passive sentence.

Causative-passive: ゆみは お母さんに 勉強させられました。
かあ べんきょう

Yumi was ordered by her mother to study.

Plain: ゆみは ———— 勉強しました。
べんきょう

Yumi studied.

2 ～ても

"A ても B" is "B, even if A." That is, B is still true in case of A (so is certainly true if A is not the case). Compare ても sentences with たら sentences, which have a more straightforward "if-then" meaning:

雨が降っても、ピクニックに行きます。
<small>あめ ふ い</small>
I will go on a picnic even if it rains.

雨が降ったら、ピクニックに行きません。
<small>あめ ふ い</small>
I will not go on a picnic if it rains.

暑くても、エアコンをつけません。
<small>あつ</small>
I will not turn on the air conditioner, even if it is hot.

暑かったら、エアコンをつけます。
<small>あつ</small>
I will turn on the air conditioner, if it is hot.

子供でも、わかります。
<small>こ ども</small>
Even a child will get it. (You will be able to understand it, even if you are a child.)

子供だったら、わかりません。
<small>こ ども</small>
If you are a child, you will not get it.

You can form a ても clause by adding も to the verb or adjective *te*-form. With な-adjectives and nouns, you have でも. Note that verb たら and ても forms look very much like each other, but adjective たら and ても forms look quite distinct.

				Compare:
verbs:	買う	→	買っても	買ったら
い-adjectives:	悲しい	→	悲しくても (× 悲しかっても)	悲しかったら
な-adjectives:	元気(な)	→	元気でも　(× 元気だっても)	元気だったら
nouns:	学生	→	学生でも　(× 学生だっても)	学生だったら

You can also form a negative ても clause, based on the short form negative.

				Compare:
verbs:	買わない	→	買わなくても	買わなかったら
い-adjectives:	悲しくない	→	悲しくなくても	悲しくなかったら
な-adjectives:	元気じゃない	→	元気じゃなくても	元気じゃなかったら
nouns:	学生じゃない	→	学生じゃなくても	学生じゃなかったら

The ても clause itself does not have tense. It can be followed either by a present tense clause (as in the above examples), or by a past tense clause.

私は、雨が降っていても、毎日、授業に行きました。
I went to class every day, even if it rained.

日本語の授業が難しくても、取ったでしょう。
I would have taken the Japanese class, even if it could have been difficult.

3 〜ことにする

ことにする means "decide to do . . . ." It follows the short form present tense of a verb. You can use a negated verb, too.

車を買うことにしました。
We have decided to buy a car.

あの人がかわいそうだから、あまり文句を言わないことにします。
I will not make too many complaints. I am feeling sorry for him already.

We sometimes use the volitional form of this construction, such as 行くことにしよう, instead of the simple volitional form of a verb, 行こう, in suggesting an activity. ことにしよう has the additional implication that the suggestion is being made after a deliberation.

今年の夏はベトナムに行くことにしよう。
Let's take the plunge. Let's go to Vietnam this summer.

ことにしている means "do something as a regular practice," that is, you have made up your mind that you should do something and have stuck to that determination.

毎日十一時に寝ることにしています。
I make it a rule to go to bed at eleven every night.

絶対にお酒を飲まないことにしています。
I have made this firm decision not to drink and have strictly followed it.

〜ことにする	*decide to do . . .*
〜ことにしている	*do . . . as a regular practice*

4 〜まで

A まで means "till A." The A in "A まで B" is the description of the change that coincides with or causes the end of B. The A, therefore, is usually a verb of the "change" kind (see Lesson 7). The verb in A is always in the present tense and in the affirmative.

晴れるまで、喫茶店でコーヒーを飲みながら、待ちます。
I will wait in the coffee shop, drinking coffee, till it clears up.

日本語が上手になるまで、国に帰りません。
I will not go back to my country, till I become fluent in Japanese.

When the subject of A is different from the subject of B, the former is marked with the particle が rather than は.

赤ちゃんが寝るまで、（私は）歌を歌ってあげます。
I will sing a lullaby till the baby falls asleep.

You can use "A まで B" in a sentence describing a situation in the past. Note that the verb in A is in the present tense nonetheless.

日本の生活に慣れるまで、大変でした。
It was tough until I got used to living in Japan.

5 〜方

The noun-forming suffix 方 follows the stem of a verb and means "the way in which the action is performed" or "how to do . . . ."

泳ぐ	→	泳ぎ方	*how to swim*
考える	→	考え方	*the way people think*

Nouns that are marked with other particles when they go with a verb are marked with の before 〜方.

漢字を読む	→ 漢字の読み方	*how to read the kanji; pronunciation*
はしを使う	→ はしの使い方	*how to use chopsticks*
空港に行く	→ 空港の行き方²	*how to go to the airport*
お風呂に入る	→ お風呂の入り方	*how to take a bath*

With compound する verbs, such as 勉強する, we have:

日本語を勉強する	→ 日本語の勉強のし方
ホテルを予約する	→ ホテルの予約のし方

〜方 is a noun and is followed by particles like は and を.

たけしさんのスパゲッティの食べ方はおもしろいです。

The way in which Takeshi eats spaghetti is interesting.

すみません。この漢字の書き方を教えていただけませんか。

Excuse me, can you tell me how to write this kanji?

---

² The goal of movement, normally marked with に, can be marked with the combination of particles への. Therefore we also say 空港への行き方 (how to get to the airport).

練習 P r a c t i c e
れん　しゅう

① 買い物に行かされました
か　もの　い

A. Change the following into the causative-passive forms. 🔊 K23-08

Example:　寝る　→　寝させられる
ね　　　　　　ね

1. 食べる
た
2. やめる
3. 受ける
う

4. 取る
と
5. 作る
つく
6. 待つ
ま

7. 習う
なら
8. 歌う
うた
9. 話す
はな

10. 迎えに行く
むか　い
11. 世話をする
せ　わ
12. 戻ってくる
もど

B. Hiroshi and Michiko are forced to do the following by each other. Describe the pictures using the causative-passive forms. 🔊 K23-09

Example:　ひろしさんはみちこさんに荷物を持たされます。
にもつ　も

Ex.

荷物を持つ
にもつ　も

(1)

買い物に付き合う
か　もの　つ　あ

(2)

駅に迎えに行く
えき　むか　い

(3)

高い服を買う
たか　ふく　か

(4)

パンクした時
とき
タイヤを換える
か

(5)

お弁当を作る
べんとう　つく

(6)

夕食をおごる
ゆうしょく

(7)

アイロンをかける

(8)　　　　　　　　　　(9)　　　　　　　　　　(10)

部屋を掃除する　　　　毎晩会社の文句を聞く　　　　靴を磨く
へ や そう じ　　　　まいばんかいしゃ　もん く　き　　　　　　　　くつ　みが

C. Pair Work—Ask your partner if, as a child, his/her parents made him/her do the following things using the causative-passive forms. (🔊) K23-10

Example:　買い物に行く
　　　　　か　もの　い
　　　→　Ａ：子供の時、買い物に行かされましたか。
　　　　　　　こども　とき　か　もの　い
　　　　　Ｂ：はい、行かされました。／いいえ、行かされませんでした。
　　　　　　　　　い　　　　　　　　　　　　　　　　い

1. 皿を洗う
　さら　あら
2. 自分の部屋を掃除する
　じ ぶん　へ や　そう じ
3. ピアノを習う
　　　　なら
4. 毎日勉強する
　まいにちべんきょう

5. ペットの世話をする
　　　　　せ わ
6. きらいな物を食べる
　　　　もの　た
7. 料理を手伝う
　りょう り　て つだ
8. 塾に行く
　じゅく　い

D. Pair work—First play *janken* (scissors-paper-rock) and decide who is in charge. Each time you win *janken*, you can give an order, such as dancing, singing a song, drawing a picture, and opening a window. The other person will act out the order. Repeat *janken* several times. You will then describe the actions, using the causative and causative-passive sentences.

Example:　open the window
　　　→　Ａ：窓を開けなさい。
　　　　　　　まど　あ
　　　　　Ｂ：はい、わかりました。　　(B will act out opening the window.)
　　　　　Ａ：Ｂさんに窓を開けさせました。
　　　　　　　　　　　まど　あ
　　　　　Ｂ：Ａさんに窓を開けさせられました。
　　　　　　　　　　　まど　あ

じゃんけん

じゃんけん (scissors-paper-rock) is a children's game. In じゃんけん, players call out "*Jan, ken, pon*" and make one of three forms with one hand: stone, scissors, or paper. "Stone" breaks "scissors," "scissors" cut "paper," and "paper" covers "stone." It is often played to determine who shall be "it" in games of tag or who shall go first in selecting teams.

E. Group Work—Talk with your classmates about what you were forced to do when you were children. Then discuss whether you would make your children do the same or not. You can use the cues in I-C (p. 263) as topics of your talk.

Example: 毎日勉強する
→ A：子供の時、毎日両親に勉強させられた？
B：うん、させられた。
A：じゃ、自分の子供にも毎日勉強させる？
B：うーん、宿題はさせるけど、もっといろいろなことをさせたい。スポーツとか旅行とか。

Ⅱ 学生がうるさくても、怒りません

A. Make sentences using 〜ても. 🔊 K23-11

Example: 学生がうるさい → 学生がうるさくても、絶対に怒りません。

絶対に怒りません。

山下先生

Ex. 学生がうるさい
1. 学生が授業中に寝ている
2. 学生が質問に答えられない
3. 学生に文句を言われる
4. 学生にばかにされる

けん

絶対に我慢します。
ぜったい　がまん

5. サークルの先輩に怒られる
　　せんぱい　おこ
6. サークルの練習が厳しい
　　れんしゅう　きび
7. 先輩に荷物を持たされる
　せんぱい　にもつ　も
8. 友だちと遊ぶ時間がない
　とも　あそ　じかん

たけし

絶対にメアリーと
ぜったい
結婚します。
けっこん

9. メアリーが料理が下手だ
　　　　　りょうり　へた
10. 親に反対される
　　おや　はんたい
11. 今は離れている
　　いま　はな
12. 言葉や文化が違う
　　ことば　ぶんか　ちが

B. Answer the following questions using 〜ても. 🔊 K23-12

Example:　Q：いじめられたら、学校を休みますか。
　　　　　　　　　　　　　　がっこう　やす
　　　　　　A：いいえ。いじめられても、学校を休みません。
　　　　　　　　　　　　　　　　　　　がっこう　やす

1. 朝寝坊したら、学校をサボりますか。
　あさねぼう　　　がっこう
2. 授業がつまらなかったら、先生に文句を言いますか。
　じゅぎょう　　　　　　　せんせい　もんく　い
3. 道に迷ったら、だれかに聞きますか。
　みち　まよ　　　　　　き
4. 電車の中で子供がうるさかったら、注意しますか。
　てんしゃ　なか　こども　　　　　　　　ちゅうい
5. 先生に怒られたら、泣きますか。
　せんせい　おこ　　　　な
6. 宝くじに当たったら、みんなにおごってあげますか。
　たから　あ
7. 友だちとけんかしたら、自分から謝りますか。
　とも　　　　　　じぶん　あやま
8. 自分が作った料理がまずかったら、食べませんか。
　じぶん　つく　りょうり　　　　　　た
9. 誕生日のプレゼントが靴下だったら、がっかりしますか。
　たんじょうび　　　　　　くつした

C. Pair Work—Ask your partner the questions in B above.

Example:　A：いじめられたら、学校を休みますか。
　　　　　　　　　　　　　　がっこう　やす
　　　　　　B：はい。いじめられたら、学校を休みます。／
　　　　　　　　　　　　　　　　　がっこう　やす
　　　　　　　いいえ。いじめられても、学校を休みません。
　　　　　　　　　　　　　　　　　　　がっこう　やす

D. Complete the following sentences.

1. ＿＿＿＿＿＿＿＿＿＿＿＿＿ても、怒りません。

2. ＿＿＿＿＿＿＿＿＿＿＿＿＿ても、仕事を続けます。

3. ＿＿＿＿＿＿＿＿＿＿＿＿＿ても、幸せです。

4. ＿＿＿＿＿＿＿＿＿＿＿＿＿ても、日本に住みたいです。

5. ＿＿＿＿＿＿＿＿＿＿＿＿＿ても、同情してあげません。

Ⅲ 日本語の勉強を続けることにしました

A. The semester is over and people are leaving. Tell what they have decided to do, using 〜ことにする. 🔊 K23-13

Example: メアリー：will go back to her country and continue the study of Japanese

→ メアリーさんは国に帰って、日本語の勉強を続けることにしました。

1. スー：will do research about Japanese society
2. ロバート：will have an interview at a Japanese company
3. ジョン：will not return to Australia because he will learn karate in Japan
4. たけし：will quit the company and look for a new job
5. みちこ：will study abroad
6. 山下先生：will teach Japanese in China
7. メアリーさんのホストファミリー：will go to the U.S. to see Mary
8. けん：will become an elementary school teacher

B. Pair Work—Make a dialogue as in the example.

Example: A：町をよくしたいから、選挙に出ることにしました。
B：選挙に勝ったら、何をするつもりですか。
A：学校の授業料をただにします。

A：＿＿＿＿＿＿＿＿から、＿＿＿＿＿＿＿＿。
B：＿＿＿＿＿＿＿＿＿＿＿＿＿＿＿＿＿。
A：＿＿＿＿＿＿＿＿＿＿＿＿＿＿＿＿＿。

C. Group Work—You are a family who has recently won a lottery. Discuss how you will spend your money.

Example:　　A：湖の近くに別荘を買うことにしようか。
　　　　　　B：別荘より店のほうがいいよ。店を始めることにしよう。
　　　　　　C：どんな店？……

Ⅳ 犬を散歩に連れていくことにしています

A. Tell what Mary and Takeshi make a habit/policy of doing or not doing, using 〜ことにしている。 ◀)) K23-14

Example:　　メアリーさんは一日に二回、犬を散歩に連れていくことにしています。

Ex. walk her dog
twice a day

(1) not talk behind
someone's back

(2) study in the library
on weekends

(3) read the newspaper
every day

(4) not watch TV and
study at the same time

(5) ask a person when she
doesn't understand

(6) not cry even if
he is sad

(7) buy flowers, cook, etc.,
on Mother's Day

(8) not drink coffee
before going to bed

B. Pair Work—Tell your partner what you make a practice of doing or not doing.

Example:　A：私は毎日日本語を練習することにしています。Bさんは？

　　　　　B：私はホストファミリーと日本語だけで話すことにしています。

Ⓥ 大学を卒業するまで、日本にいるつもりです

A. Describe how long they will stay in Japan or until when they will not get married, using 〜まで. 🔊 K23-15

Example:　ジョンさんは大学を卒業するまで、日本にいるつもりです。

(a) ＿＿＿＿＿＿＿＿＿＿まで、日本にいるつもりです。

　　Ex. ジョン　　　　till he graduates from college
　　 1. メアリー　　　till this semester ends
　　 2. スー　　　　 till she becomes fluent in Japanese
　　 3. ロバート　　　till money runs out
　　 4. ヤン　　　　 till he dies

(b) ＿＿＿＿＿＿＿＿＿＿まで結婚しません。

　　 5. ジョン　　　　till he finds an ideal partner
　　 6. けん　　　　 till his favorite team wins the championship
　　 7. スー　　　　 till she saves one million yen
　　 8. ロバート　　　till he becomes thirty years old

B. Complete the following sentences.

1. 日本語がぺらぺらになるまで、＿＿＿＿＿＿＿＿＿＿＿＿＿＿＿。

2. 死ぬまで、＿＿＿＿＿＿＿＿＿＿＿＿＿＿＿＿＿＿＿。

3. 雨がやむまで、＿＿＿＿＿＿＿＿＿＿＿＿＿＿＿＿＿。

4. ＿＿＿＿＿＿＿＿＿＿＿＿＿＿＿まで、仕事を続けます。

5. ＿＿＿＿＿＿＿＿＿＿＿まで、留守番をしなければいけません。

6. ＿＿＿＿＿＿＿＿＿＿＿＿＿＿まで、我慢しました。

C. Pair Work—Suggest the following plans to your partner. (The card for Student B is on p. 272.) When you respond, use 〜まで. Expand the conversation like the example.

Example:　Ａ：一緒に遊ぶ／Ｂ：You have a final exam pretty soon.
→　Ａ：一緒に遊ぼうよ。
Ｂ：もうすぐ期末試験だから、試験が終わるまで遊べないんだ。
Ａ：残念。じゃあ、試験が終わったら一緒に遊ぼうね。

Student A—Suggest 1, 3, and 5 to your partner.
Use 2, 4, and 6 to respond to your partner's suggestions.

1. 出かける
2. You are broke, but you will receive a bonus soon.
3. ケーキを食べる
4. You caught a cold and have a sore throat.
5. 海外旅行に行く
6. Your parents are strict and won't let you live away from home.

Ⅵ ソフトの使い方を教えてくれませんか

A. You want to know how to do the things below. Ask questions using 〜方. K23-16

Example:　how to use this software
→　すみませんが、このソフトの使い方を教えてくれませんか。

1. how to make delicious coffee
2. how to iron
3. how to ride a bicycle
4. how to drive a car
5. how to play the guitar
6. how to knit a sweater
7. how to make sushi
8. how to reserve a seat on the Shinkansen
9. how to bake a cake
10. how to wear kimono

B. Pair Work—Ask how to do the things below. Look at the pictures and explain as in the example.

Example: お金のおろし方
→ まず、カードを入れます。それから、暗証番号 (PIN) と金額 (amount) を押します。最後に、お金を取ります。(カードを取るのを忘れないでください!)

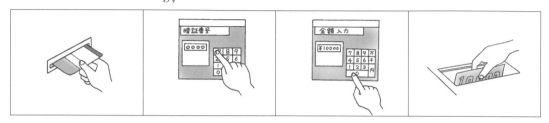

1. すきやきの作り方

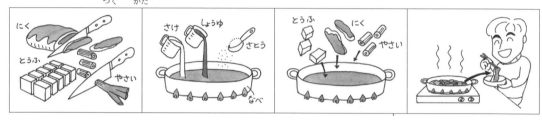

2. 切符の買い方

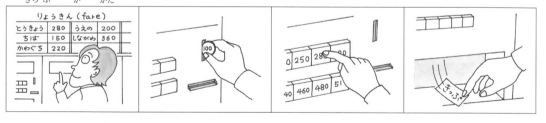

3. お茶のいれ方

C. Pair work—Ask your partner how to do the following. When you answer, explain it in detail.

Example: how to take a Japanese bath

→   Ａ：日本のお風呂の入り方を教えてくれませんか。

Ｂ：お風呂の入り方ですか。まず、お風呂に入る前に、体を洗います。それから、お風呂に入ってゆっくりします。

1. how to memorize kanji
2. how to take an inexpensive trip
3. how to find a part-time job
4. how to go to the airport
5. how to make an international call

Ⅶ まとめの練習

A. Tell your future plans. Have you decided to continue studying Japanese? What else have you decided to do? Tell the reasons, too.

Example: 私は日本語の勉強を続けることにしました。日本文化にとても興味があって、それについてもっと勉強したいからです。

B. Pair Work/Group Work—Using Dialogue Ⅱ as a model, talk about good and bad memories in Japan or in Japanese class in a pair/group.

C. Pair Work—Using Dialogue Ⅰ and Ⅲ as models, make short dialogues with your partner in the following situations.

1. You have lived with a host family in Japan for three months. You are leaving for your country tomorrow.

2. You and your friend had not seen each other for ten years. You have had a chance to meet the friend at a reunion. You have had a good time and now it is time to leave.

D. Do you agree with the following statements? Discuss with your classmates.

Example:

勉強が好きじゃなくても、大学に行ったほうがいい。

→　A：私は賛成です。大学を卒業しなかったら、いい会社に就職できません。がんばって勉強したほうがいいと思います。

　　B：私は反対です。自分が好きなことをしたほうがいいと思います。

1. ルームメートは彼／彼女を部屋に連れてきてはいけない。
2. 授業がつまらなかったら、先生に文句を言ったほうがいい。
3. 子供が生まれたら、仕事をやめたほうがいい。
4. もらったプレゼントが気に入らなくても、うれしそうな顔をしたほうがいい。
5. 結婚する前に一緒に住んだほうがいい。

Pair Work Ⓥ C.

(→ p. 269)

Example:　　A：一緒に遊ぶ／B：You have a final exam pretty soon.

→　A：一緒に遊ぼうよ。

　　B：もうすぐ期末試験だから、試験が終わるまで遊べないんだ。

　　A：残念。じゃあ、試験が終わったら一緒に遊ぼうね。

Student B—Suggest 2, 4 and 6 to your partner.
　　　　　　Use 1, 3, and 5 to respond to your partner's suggestions.

1. Your host family is out. You have to stay home.
2. 買い物に行く
3. You are on a diet and have determined to lose ten kilograms.
4. カラオケで歌う
5. You are working on a big project（大きい仕事）and can't take a vacation.
6. 一緒に住む

Culture Note

ことわざ Japanese Proverbs

Here are some Japanese proverbs and sayings. Do they represent a totally different culture from yours, or are there similar elements?

猫に小判
Giving gold coins to a cat.
(Casting pearls before swine.)

仏の顔も三度
Even Buddha would be upset
if his face were stroked three times.
(To try the patience of a saint.)

うそつきはどろぼうのはじまり
All thieves started
their careers with a lie.

郷に入れば郷に従え
When in a village,
follow their customs.
(When in Rome,
do as the Romans do.)

石の上にも三年
Even the coldest rock
becomes warm if you sit on it
for three years.
(Perseverance prevails.)

さるも木から落ちる
Even monkeys fall from trees.
(Nobody is perfect.)

善は急げ
Hasten to do good.

出る杭は打たれる
The stake that sticks out
gets hammered down.
(Don't be too conspicuous.)

花より団子
A rice dumpling is
better than a flower.
(Substance over show.)

読み書き編
よ　か　へん
Reading and Writing Section

第13課 LESSON 13

日本のおもしろい経験（けいけん） Interesting Experiences in Japan

	Kanji	Readings	Examples
146	物	▶ぶつ ▷もの (thing)	食べ物(たべもの) food　飲み物(のみもの) drink 物(もの) things　買い物(かいもの) shopping 動物(どうぶつ) animal (8) ノ 𠂉 牛 牛 牜 牞 物 物
147	鳥	▶ちょう ▷とり (bird)	鳥(とり) bird 焼き鳥(やきとり) grilled chicken　白鳥(はくちょう) swan (11) ′ 亻 户 户 白 皀 皀 鳥 鳥 鳥 鳥
148	料	▶りょう (ingredients; fare)	料理(りょうり) cooking 料金(りょうきん) charge　授業料(じゅぎょうりょう) tuition 給料(きゅうりょう) salary (10) 丶 丷 䒑 半 米 米 米 米 料 料
149	理	▶り (reason)	料理(りょうり) cooking 理由(りゆう) reason　地理(ちり) geography 無理な(むりな) impossible (11) 一 T 干 王 玑 玔 玾 玾 理 理 理
150	特	▶とく　とっ (special)	特に(とくに) especially 特別な(とくべつな) special　特徴(とくちょう) characteristic 特急(とっきゅう) super express (10) ノ 𠂉 牛 牛 牛 牛 牛 特 特 特
151	安	▶あん ▷やす (cheap; ease)	安い(やすい) cheap 安全な(あんぜんな) safe　安心(あんしん) relief 不安な(ふあんな) uneasy (6) ′ 丷 宀 安 安 安
152	飯	▶はん (food; cooked rice)	ご飯(ごはん) rice; meal　朝ご飯(あさごはん) breakfast 晩ご飯(ばんごはん) dinner (12) ノ 人 𠆢 今 今 今 食 食 食 飣 飯 飯
153	肉	▶にく (meat)	肉(にく) meat 牛肉(ぎゅうにく) beef　豚肉(ぶたにく) pork 肉屋(にくや) meat shop　筋肉(きんにく) muscle (6) 丨 冂 内 内 肉 肉

154 悪 (bad; wrong)	▶あく ▷わる	悪い（わるい）bad 気分が悪い（きぶんがわるい）to feel sick 最悪（さいあく）the worst　悪魔（あくま）devil (11) 一 厂 币 币 币 西 亜 亜 悪 悪 悪
155 体 (body)	▶たい ▷からだ	体（からだ）body 体重（たいじゅう）body weight 体操（たいそう）gymnastics; physical exercises (7) ノ イ 伫 什 休 休 体
156 空 (sky; empty)	▶くう ▷そら　あ 　から	空港（くうこう）airport　空気（くうき）air 空（そら）sky　空く（あく）to be vacant 空手（からて）karate (8) ' ' 宀 宀 灾 空 空 空
157 港 (port; harbor)	▶こう ▷みなと	空港（くうこう）airport 神戸港（こうべこう）Kobe Port　港（みなと）port 香港（ほんこん）Hong Kong (12) ` ⺀ ⺄ 氵 汁 洪 洪 洪 港 港
158 着 (to reach; to wear)	▶ちゃく ▷つ　き	着く（つく）to arrive　着る（きる）to wear 着物（きもの）kimono 大阪着（おおさかちゃく）arriving at Osaka (12) ` ⺍ 并 并 羊 羊 羊 着 着 着 着
159 同 (same)	▶どう ▷おな	同じ（おなじ）the same 同僚（どうりょう）coworker 同級生（どうきゅうせい）classmate　同時（どうじ）same time (6) 丨 冂 冋 同 同 同
160 海 (sea)	▶かい ▷うみ	海（うみ）sea 日本海（にほんかい）the Japan Sea　海外（かいがい）overseas 海岸（かいがん）coast (9) ` ⺀ 氵 氵 汇 汇 海 海 海
161 昼 (noon; daytime)	▶ちゅう ▷ひる	昼（ひる）noon; daytime　昼ご飯（ひるごはん）lunch 昼寝（ひるね）nap　昼休み（ひるやすみ）lunch break 昼食（ちゅうしょく）lunch (9) 一 フ コ 尸 尺 尺 昼 昼 昼

(▶ indicates the *on-yomi* [pronunciation originally borrowed from Chinese] and ▷ indicates the *kun-yomi* [native Japanese reading].)

Ⅰ 漢字の練習

A. 次の漢字の読み方 (reading) を覚えましょう。太字 (bold type) は新しい読み方です。

国 （くに）　　　　気分 （きぶん）　　　　一生 （いっしょう）

時 （とき）　　　　時々 （ときどき）

（☞　国 (058)　分 (052)　生 (054)　時 (015)　々 (133)）

B. 次の漢字を読みましょう。（答 (answer) は下にあります。）

1. 毎日　　　4. 午後　　　7. 住む　　　10. 話す

2. ある日　　5. 持つ　　　8. 電車の中　11. 聞く

3. 一度　　　6. 会社員　　9. 読む　　　12. 高校生

Ⅱ 日本のおもしろい経験

単　語

経験 （けいけん） experience
1 特に （とくに） especially
3 めずらしい　rare
6 なんでも　anything; everything
7 なべ　pot
10 ニヤニヤする　to grin [irr. verb]
11 不安な （ふあんな） uneasy; worried
13 すっぽん　snapping turtle; terrapin
14 かめ　turtle

14 気分が悪い （きぶんがわるい） to feel sick
15 体 （からだ） body
　　体にいい （からだにいい） good for
　　　health
16 一生に一度 （いっしょうにいちど） once in
　　a lifetime
18 やっぱり　after all
18 もう～ない　not any longer

[Ⅰ-B の答] 1. まいにち　　4. ごご　　　7. すむ　　　　10. はなす
　　　　　　2. あるひ　　　5. もつ　　　8. でんしゃのなか　11. きく
　　　　　　3. いちど　　　6. かいしゃいん　9. よむ　　　　12. こうこうせい

A. 質問に答えてください。(Answer the questions.)

1. (1)–(4) は日本の食べ物です。下の a–d のどの写真だと思いますか。

(1) (　　　　) うめぼし (pickled plums)

(2) (　　　　) のり (seaweed)

(3) (　　　　) すき焼き (beef and vegetable stewed in a large skillet)

(4) (　　　　) 焼き鳥 (grilled chicken)

a. 　　b. 　　c. 　　d.

2. 日本料理の中で何が一番好きですか。

B. 留学生のエイミーさんは日本の食べ物について書きました。読みましょう。　📢 Y13-1

1　　私は日本料理が大好きです。特にすき焼きや焼き鳥が好きです。国では日本料理は安くないから、あまり食べられませんでした。今、毎日食べられるので、とてもうれしいです。日本にはめずらしい食べ物がたくさんあります。国では、うめぼし、のりなどを見たことも聞いたこともありませんでした。私はめずらしい物に興味があるので、お

5　いしそうな食べ物は、なんでも食べてみます。

　　ある日、ホストファミリーと晩ご飯を食べに行きました。なべの中に野菜や肉がたくさんありました。私は「これは何の肉？鳥の肉？」と聞きました。お父さんは「食べてみて。おいしいから」と言いました。

10　「どう？おいしい？」「はい、とても。でも、何ですか？」みんなはニヤニヤして、何も言いません。私はちょっと不安になりました。でも、おなかがすいていたし、おいしかったので、たくさん食べました。「ごちそうさま」「エイミーさん、実は、これはすっぽんですよ」「すっぽん？」

「すっぽんはかめです」「えっ！……」私は気分が悪くなりました。お
15　父さんはすっぽんは体によくて、高い食べ物だと言っていました。

　これは一生に一度のとてもおもしろい経験でした。国に帰って、友
だちに「かめを食べたことがある」と言えます。かめはおいしかった
です。でも、やっぱり、もうかめを食べたくありません。

C.　文を読んで ○ (= true) か × (= false) を書いてください。

（　　）1. エイミーさんは日本料理は大好きだが、国ではあまり食べなかった。

（　　）2. エイミーさんは、国でうめぼしを食べたことがある。

（　　）3. エイミーさんは、めずらしい食べ物は何も食べられない。

（　　）4. エイミーさんは、ホストファミリーとなべ料理を食べた。

（　　）5. なべの中には鳥の肉があった。

（　　）6. なべ料理はとてもおいしかった。

（　　）7. エイミーさんは、すっぽんはめずらしいから、たくさん食べた。

（　　）8. エイミーさんは、またすっぽんを食べるつもりだ。

Ⅲ 満員電車
まん いん

単 語
たん ご

満員電車（まんいんでんしゃ）
  jam-packed train
第一印象（だいいちいんしょう）
  the first impression
込む（こむ）to get crowded [u-verb]
  込んでいる（こんでいる）to be
    crowded

1 空港（くうこう）airport
1 着く（つく）to arrive（〜に）[u-verb]
2 ラッシュ　the rush hour
2 スーツケース　suitcase
4 同じ（おなじ）same
7 考える（かんがえる）to think about ...
  （〜のことを）[ru-verb]

A. 質問に答えてください。
しつもん こた

  1. 日本に行ったことがありますか。日本の第一印象は下の a–e のどれでしたか。
だいいちいんしょう
    a. 小さい　　　b. 込んでいる　　　c. 高い　　　d. きれい　　　e. その他 (others)
こ た

  2. あなたは電車やバスによく乗りますか。
の
    電車やバスの中でたいてい何をしますか。

B. 会社員のネルソンさんは日本の電車について書きました。読みましょう。🔊 Y13-2

1　　日本に来て、満員電車にびっくりした。午後五時ごろ空港に着いた
まんいん
ので、ラッシュの時に電車に乗らなければいけなかった。大きいスー
の
ツケースを持って、電車に乗った。とても込んでいた。会社員や学生
こ
がたくさん電車に乗っていたが、みんな何も言わなかった。みんな同
5 じ顔だった。「ここには住めない。」これが私の日本の第一印象だった。
かお だいいちいんしょう
　　それから、私は電車がきらいになった。でも、毎日電車に乗らなけ
の
ればいけない。電車の中で、国の山や海のことを考えた。でも、やっ
かんが
ぱり電車がきらいだった。
　　ある日、仕事が休みになったので、昼ごろに電車に乗った。いつも
の
10 と同じ電車だが、同じではなかった。子供に本を読んでいるお母さん、
こども

話しているおばあさん、音楽を聞いている高校生、みんな楽しそうだ。それから、私は電車に乗るのが好きになった。いろいろな人がいておもしろい。時々、となりの人と話したりする。もう山や海のことを考えない。

C. 質問に答えてください。

1. ネルソンさんの日本の第一印象はどうでしたか。
   どうしてそう思いましたか。

2. 下の a–e はラッシュの電車で見ますか。昼の電車で見ますか。
   (　　) に a–e を書いてください。
   (1) ラッシュの電車で見る： (　　) (　　)
   (2) 昼の電車で見る：　　　 (　　) (　　) (　　)

> a. サラリーマンがたくさんいる。
> b. お母さんが子供に本を読んでいる。
> c. みんなとても静かだ。
> d. おばあさんが話している。
> e. みんなとても楽しそうだ。

Ⅳ 書く練習

あなたのおもしろい経験を書きましょう。

第14課 LESSON 14

悩み(なや)の相談(そうだん) Personal Advice Column

	Kanji	Readings	Examples / Stroke order
162	彼	▷かれ かの (he)	彼(かれ) he; boyfriend 彼女(かのじょ) she; girlfriend 彼ら(かれら) they (8) ノ ク 彳 彳 彳 彳 彼 彼
163	代	▶だい ▷か (age; replace)	時代(じだい) age; era 電気代(でんきだい) electricity fee 九十年代(きゅうじゅうねんだい) 90's 十代(じゅうだい) in one's teens 代わりに(かわりに) instead (5) ノ イ 仁 代 代
164	留	▶りゅう る (to stay; to keep)	留学生(りゅうがくせい) foreign students 留学する(りゅうがくする) to study abroad 留守(るす) absence from home (10) ′ ㇄ ㇄ 㓛 㓛 㓛 㓛 留 留 留
165	族	▶ぞく (family; tribe)	家族(かぞく) family 民族(みんぞく) race 水族館(すいぞくかん) aquarium 王族(おうぞく) member of royalty (11) ′ 亠 方 方 方 方 方 方 族 族 族
166	親	▶しん ▷おや した (parent; intimacy)	父親(ちちおや) father 親切な(しんせつな) kind 親友(しんゆう) best friend 両親(りょうしん) parents 親しい(したしい) intimate 母親(ははおや) mother (16) ′ 亠 亠 立 立 辛 辛 辛 亲 亲 新 新 親 親 親 親
167	切	▶せつ ▷き きっ (to cut)	親切な(しんせつな) kind 切る(きる) to cut 切符(きっぷ) ticket 切手(きって) postage stamp 大切な(たいせつな) precious (4) 一 七 切 切
168	英	▶えい (English; excellent)	英語(えいご) English 英国(えいこく) England 英会話(えいかいわ) English conversation 英雄(えいゆう) hero (8) 一 十 廾 廾 芇 芇 英 英
169	店	▶てん ▷みせ (shop)	店(みせ) shop 店員(てんいん) store attendant 売店(ばいてん) stall 書店(しょてん) book store (8) ′ 亠 广 广 庐 庐 店 店

170	去	▶きょ　こ ▷さ (past; to leave)	去年（きょねん）last year 過去（かこ）the past　去る（さる）to leave 消去する（しょうきょする）to erase (5) 一　十　土　去　去
171	急	▶きゅう ▷いそ (to hurry; 　emergency)	急に（きゅうに）suddenly　急ぐ（いそぐ）to hurry 急行（きゅうこう）express train 特急（とっきゅう）super express (9) ノ　ク　ワ　ヲ　刍　刍　急　急　急
172	乗	▶じょう ▷の (to ride)	乗る（のる）to ride 乗り物（のりもの）vehicle　乗車（じょうしゃ）riding a car 乗馬（じょうば）horseback riding (9) ￣　二　三　午　丐　乒　垂　乗　乗
173	当	▶とう ▷あ (to hit)	本当に（ほんとうに）really お弁当（おべんとう）lunch box　当時（とうじ）at that time 当たる（あたる）to hit (6) ｜　丷　丷　当　当　当
174	音	▶おん ▷おと　ね (sound)	音楽（おんがく）music 発音（はつおん）pronunciation　音（おと）sound 本音（ほんね）real intention (9) ｀　＾　十　立　产　音　音　音
175	楽	▶がく 　がっ　らく ▷たの (pleasure)	音楽（おんがく）music　楽しい（たのしい）fun 楽器（がっき）musical instrument 楽な（らくな）easy; comfortable (13) ｀　′　白　白　白　白　泊　泊　渖　渖　楽　楽　楽
176	医	▶い (doctor; medicine)	医者（いしゃ）doctor 歯医者（はいしゃ）dentist　医学（いがく）medical science 医院（いいん）clinic (7) 一　厂　厂　医　医　医　医
177	者	▶しゃ ▷もの (person)	医者（いしゃ）doctor 学者（がくしゃ）scholar　読者（どくしゃ）reader 若者（わかもの）young people (8) 一　十　土　耂　耂　者　者　者

(▶ indicates the *on-yomi* and ▷ indicates the *kun-yomi*.)

Ⅰ 漢字の練習
かんじ　れんしゅう

A. 次の漢字の読み方 (reading) を覚えましょう。太字 (bold type) は新しい読み方です。
かんじ　　かた　　　　　　　　　おぼ　　　　　　　ふとじ

彼女 （かのじょ）　　　年上 （としうえ）　　　六年間 （ろくねんかん）

上手 （じょうず）　　　家族 （かぞく）　　　北海道 （ほっかいどう）

三か月後 （さんかげつご）　　　（☞　女 (038)　上 (026)　手 (116)　家 (096)
　　　　　　　　　　　　　　　　　　　　 北 (047)　海 (160)　道 (109)）

B. 次の漢字を読みましょう。（答 (answer) は次のページの下にあります。）
かんじ　　　　　　　　　　こたえ

1. 仕事　　3. 思う　　5. 勉強　　7. 買い物　　9. 気分

2. 早く　　4. 東京　　6. 学校　　8. 病気　　10. 時間

Ⅱ 悩みの相談
なや　　そう だん

単　語
たん　ご

悩み （なやみ） worry
アドバイス　advice
2 年上 （としうえ） being older
3 時代 （じだい） age; era
3 先輩 （せんぱい） senior member of a group
4 ～年間 （～ねんかん） for ... years
4 付き合う （つきあう） to date [u-verb]

13 愛す （あいす） to love [u-verb]
36 父親 （ちちおや） father
36 急に （きゅうに） suddenly
40 出張 （しゅっちょう） business trip
48 本当に （ほんとうに） really
51 場合 （ばあい） case

A. 質問に答えてください。(Answer the questions.)
しつもん　こた

1. あなたは悩みがありますか。だれに相談しますか。
　　　　　なや　　　　　　　　　　　そうだん

2. あなたの友だちはどんな悩みがありますか。どんなアドバイスをしましたか。

B. 悩みの相談を読みましょう。
（なや）（そうだん）

■1 結婚と仕事
（けっこん）
🔊 Y14-1

26歳の会社員です。三歳年上の彼が
（さい）
います。彼は大学時代の先輩で、六
（せんぱい）
年間付き合っています。このごろ、
（つ）（あ）
彼は「早く結婚したい」と言ってい
（けっこん）
ます。彼はやさしいし、仕事もでき
るし、私も結婚したいと思っていま
す。でも、彼は東京に住んでいて、
私は大阪に住んでいます。彼は今の
仕事をやめられないと言っていま
す。私もやめたくありません。私が
仕事をやめて東京に行ったほうがい
いんでしょうか。彼を愛しています。
（あい）
（26歳・女）
（さい）

■2 日本語が上手にならない 🔊 Y14-2

カナダ人の留学生です。日本の大学
で勉強しています。私の悩みは日本
（なや）
語です。今、日本人のホストファミ
リーと住んでいます。家族は親切で
すが、みんなは私と英語を話した
がっています。だから、私は「英語
を話さなきゃ」と思って、英語を話
します。学校に日本人の友だちがた
くさんいますが、みんなの英語は私
の日本語より上手です。だから、たい
てい英語を使います。買い物の時も
「すみません。あの、これください」

と日本語で言いますが、お店の人は
「ツーハンドレッドエンね。サン
キュー！」と英語で言います。もう
六か月も日本にいますが、ぜんぜん
日本語が上手になりません。どうし
たらいいでしょうか。　（21歳・男）
（さい）

■3 飛行機がきらい
（ひこうき）
🔊 Y14-3

私は子供の時から飛行機がきらいで
（こども）（ひこうき）
す。去年、父親が急に病気になったの
で、飛行機で北海道に帰らなければ
いけませんでした。その時、気分が悪
くて大変でした。実は、三か月後に
（たいへん）（じつ）
会社の出張でブラジルに行くんです
（しゅっちょう）
が、日本からサンパウロまで27時
間ぐらい飛行機に乗っていなければ
いけません。どうしたらいいでしょ
うか。アドバイスをお願いします。
（ねが）
（32歳・男）
（さい）

アドバイス
🔊 Y14-4

私も飛行機に乗るのが好きじゃないの
（ひこうき）
で、あなたの悩みが本当によくわかり
（なや）
ます。私はよく飛行機の中で、大好き
なモーツァルトの音楽を聞きます。で
も、あなたの場合はもっと大変そうな
（ばあい）（たいへん）
ので、お医者さんに行って相談してみ
（そうだん）
たらどうですか。

[①-Bの答]　1. しごと　　3. おもう　　5. べんきょう　　7. かいもの　　9. きぶん
（こたえ）　　2. はやく　　4. とうきょう　　6. がっこう　　8. びょうき　　10. じかん

C. 質問に答えてください。
　　しつもん　こた

① 結婚と仕事
　　けっこん

　　1. この人の彼はどんな人ですか。

　　2. どうしてこの人はすぐ彼と結婚しないのですか。
　　　　　　　　　　　　　　　　けっこん

　　3. あなたはこの人が仕事をやめて結婚したほうがいいと思いますか。
　　　　どうしてですか。

　　4. あなたならどうすると思いますか。
　　　　(What would you do if you were in a similar situation?)

② 日本語が上手にならない

　　1. この人はホストファミリーと日本語で話しますか。どうしてですか。

　　2. 日本人の友だちと日本語で話しますか。どうしてですか。

　　3. お店の人はどうですか。

　　4. あなたも同じ悩みがありますか。
　　　　　　　　　　なや

③ 飛行機がきらい
　　ひこうき

　　1. この人はいつ飛行機に乗りましたか。飛行機はどうでしたか。
　　　　　　　　　　ひこうき

　　2. どうしてブラジルに行きたくないのですか。

　　3. あなたはこの人がブラジルに行くと思いますか。

Ⅲ 書く練習
　　れんしゅう

A. Ⅱ-B の **1** と **2** の人にアドバイスを書きましょう。

B. Imagine that you are one of the characters in the list below, and write about their problems.

　　留学生　　お父さん／お母さん　　日本語の先生　　ねこ　　その他 (others)
　　　　　　　　　　　　　　　　　　　　　　　　　　　　　　　　　　た

第15課 | L E S S O N 15

私が好きな所 My Favorite Place

178	死 (death; to die)	▶し ▷し	死ぬ(しぬ) to die 死(し) death　必死(ひっし) desperate 死者(ししゃ) the dead
		(6)	一 ア ダ ヲ 歹 死
179	意 (mind; meaning)	▶い	意味(いみ) meaning 注意する(ちゅういする) to watch out 意見(いけん) opinion　用意する(よういする) to prepare
		(13)	丶 亠 立 立 产 产 产 音 音 音 音 意 意 意
180	味 (flavor; taste)	▶み ▷あじ	意味(いみ) meaning 趣味(しゅみ) hobby　興味(きょうみ) interest 味噌(みそ) soybean paste　味(あじ) taste
		(8)	丨 口 口 口 吽 叶 味 味
181	注 (to pour; to shed)	▶ちゅう ▷そそ	注意する(ちゅういする) to watch out 注文する(ちゅうもんする) to order 注ぐ(そそぐ) to pour
		(8)	丶 丶 氵 汁 汁 汁 注 注
182	夏 (summer)	▶か ▷なつ	夏(なつ) summer 夏休み(なつやすみ) summer vacation 初夏(しょか) early summer
		(10)	一 一 ァ 百 百 百 百 夏 夏 夏
183	魚 (fish)	▶ぎょ ▷さかな うお	魚(さかな) fish 魚市場(うおいちば) fish market　金魚(きんぎょ) goldfish 人魚(にんぎょ) mermaid
		(11)	⺈ ⺈ ⺈ 刍 刍 角 角 角 魚 魚 魚
184	寺 (temple)	▶じ ▷てら　でら	お寺(おてら) temple 東寺(とうじ) Toji (the name of a temple) 寺院(じいん) sacred building　禅寺(ぜんでら) zen temple
		(6)	一 十 土 土 寺 寺
185	広 (spacious; wide)	▶こう ▷ひろ	広い(ひろい) wide; spacious 広場(ひろば) square; open space 広島(ひろしま) Hiroshima　広告(こうこく) advertisement
		(5)	丶 亠 广 広 広

186	転	▶てん ▷ころ (to roll over)	自転車（じてんしゃ）bicycle 運転する（うんてんする）to drive　回転ずし（かいてんずし） rotating sushi　転ぶ（ころぶ）to tumble; to fall down
			⑾ 一 二 三 亖 亘 車 軒 軒 転 転
187	借	▶しゃく 　しゃっ ▷か (to borrow)	借りる（かりる）to borrow 借地（しゃくち）rented land　借金（しゃっきん）debt 借家（しゃくや）rented house
			⑽ ノ イ 仁 仁 仕 仕 供 借 借 借
188	走	▶そう ▷はし (to run)	走る（はしる）to run 走り書き（はしりがき）hasty writing 脱走（だっそう）escape from a prison
			⑺ 一 十 土 キ キ 走 走
189	建	▶けん ▷たて　た (to build)	建物（たてもの）building 建てる（たてる）to build　建つ（たつ）to be built 建国（けんこく）founding a nation
			⑼ フ ョ ヨ ヨ 聿 聿 建 建 建
190	地	▶ち　じ (ground)	地下（ちか）underground 地下鉄（ちかてつ）subway　地図（ちず）map 地球（ちきゅう）earth; globe　地震（じしん）earthquake
			⑹ 一 十 土 扚 坩 地
191	場	▶じょう ▷ば (place)	広場（ひろば）square; open space 場所（ばしょ）place　場合（ばあい）case 駐車場（ちゅうしゃじょう）parking garage
			⑿ 一 十 土 圹 坍 坍 坍 坍 坍 塌 場 場
192	足	▶そく ▷あし　た (foot; leg)	足（あし）foot; leg　足りる（たりる）to be sufficient 一足（いっそく）one pair of shoes 水不足（みずぶそく）lack of water
			⑺ 丶 口 口 甲 甲 尺 足
193	通	▶つう ▷とお　かよ (to pass; to commute)	通る（とおる）to go through; to pass 通う（かよう）to commute　通学（つうがく）going to school 通勤（つうきん）going to work
			⑽ マ マ マ 冈 甬 甬 甬 涌 通 通

（▶ indicates the *on-yomi* and ▷ indicates the *kun-yomi*.）

Ⅰ 漢字の練習

A. 次の漢字の読み方 (reading) を覚えましょう。太字 (bold type) は新しい読み方です。

生まれる（うまれる）　　　二十万人（にじゅうまんにん）

一年中（いちねんじゅう）　　楽しむ（たのしむ）

人気（にんき）　　　　　　地下（ちか）

お金（おかね）　　　　　　（☞　生 (054)　中 (028)　下 (027)　金 (023)）

B. 次の漢字を読みましょう。（答 (answer) は下にあります。）

1. 町	4. 神社	7. 赤い	10. 今度
2. 近く	5. 青い	8. 南	11. 古い
3. 有名	6. 色	9. 今年	12. 手

Ⅱ 私が好きな所

単　語

1

1 生まれる（うまれる）to be born [ru-verb]

1 原爆（げんばく）atomic bomb

3 落とされる（おとされる）to be dropped

6 残す（のこす）to leave; to preserve [u-verb]

6 平和記念資料館（へいわきねんしりょうかん）Peace Memorial Museum

8 平和（へいわ）peace

11 島（しま）island

13 緑（みどり）green

13 鹿（しか）deer

15 注意する（ちゅういする）to watch out [irr. verb]

2

5 南（みなみ）south

6 一年中（いちねんじゅう）all year

[Ⅰ-B の答]

1. まち	4. じんじゃ	7. あかい	10. こんど
2. ちかく	5. あおい	8. みなみ	11. ふるい
3. ゆうめい	6. いろ	9. ことし	12. て

6 楽しむ（たのしむ）to enjoy [*u*-verb]
9 くじら　whale

3
3 自然（しぜん）nature
4 紅葉（こうよう）red leaves; autumn tints
6 竹（たけ）bamboo
8 トロッコ列車（トロッコれっしゃ）small train usually for tourists
8 走る（はしる）to run [*u*-verb]
9 景色（けしき）scenery

4
2 建物（たてもの）building
3 昔（むかし）old days
4 地下（ちか）underground
4 広場（ひろば）square; open space
6 戦争（せんそう）war
6 手（て）hand; arm
6 通る（とおる）to pass; to go through [*u*-verb]
10 ホームレス　homeless

A. 質問に答えてください。(Answer the questions.)

1. あなたはどんな所に行ってみたいですか。どうしてですか。

2. (1)–(4) はどんな所ですか。行ったことがありますか。

 (1) 広島・宮島　　(2) 沖縄　　(3) 京都　　(4) 東京

3. 上の (1)–(4) は右の地図の a–d のどこですか。

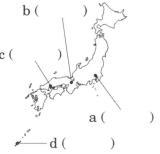

b (　　　)

c (　　　)

a (　　　)

d (　　　)

B. 四人の日本人が好きな所を紹介しています。読みましょう。

1 広島と宮島　 Y15-1

1　広島は私が生まれた町です。広島には原爆ドームがあります。1945 年 8 月 6 日、広島に世界で初めて原爆が落とされました。この原爆で二十万人の人が死にました。広
5 島の人は原爆を忘れてはいけないと思い、*原爆ドームを残しました。近くには平和記念資料館があり、原爆につ

原爆ドーム
（げんばく）

---

l. 5　忘れてはいけないと思い

In the written language, sentences can be connected by using either the stem or *te*-form of the verb.

　原爆を忘れてはいけないと思い、原爆ドームを残しました。
　＝原爆を忘れてはいけないと思って、原爆ドームを残しました。

いて読んだり、写真を見たりできます。こ
こに来た人は、平和の意味について考えま
す。

10　広島の近くには宮島があります。宮島は
小さい島で、有名な神社があります。この

宮島

神社は海の近くにあるので、天気がいい日は、海の青い色と神社の赤
い色、そして山の緑がとてもきれいです。この島には鹿がたくさんい
ます。鹿はたいていおなかがすいているので、食べ物を持っている人
15　は注意したほうがいいでしょう。

② 沖縄　🔊 Y15-2

1　　私は今まで日本のいろいろな所に行きまし
たが、その中で沖縄が一番好きです。沖縄は
エメラルドグリーンの海と白いビーチで有名
です。世界のビーチの中で一番きれいだと思
5　います。沖縄は日本の一番南にあって、冬も
暖かいです。だから、ゴルフなどのスポーツが一年中楽しめます。

　　今年の夏、私は沖縄で初めてダイビングをしてみました。海の中に
はいろいろな色の魚がたくさん泳いでいて、本当に感動しました。
十二月から四月まではくじらが見られるので、今度は冬に行こうと
10　思っています。

③ 京都（嵐山・嵯峨野）　🔊 Y15-3

1　　京都には古いお寺がたくさんあります
が、私がよく行く所は嵐山です。嵐山には
お寺も自然もあります。嵐山は人気があっ
て、紅葉の時は特に込んでいます。

5　　嵐山の近くに嵯峨野があります。嵯峨野

嵐山

は広いので、自転車を借りたほうがいいでしょう。嵯峨野には竹がた
くさんあり、竹で作ったおみやげを売っています。

　嵯峨野からトロッコ列車が走っています。列車から見える山と川の
景色はとてもきれいです。

④ 東京・新宿  Y15-4

1　私は子供の時、新宿駅の近くに住んでいま
した。今は、新宿には高い建物がたくさんあ
りますが、昔はまだあまりありませんでした。
1970年ごろ、新宿駅西口の地下広場では、学
5 生がギターを弾いたり歌を歌ったりしていま
した。そのとなりでは、戦争で手や足をなくした人が通る人にお金を
もらっていました。

　今、新宿にはたくさんの会社や店があって、仕事に行く人や買い物を
する人でとてもにぎやかです。でも、駅から少し歩いてみてください。
10 近くの公園には、ホームレスの人がたくさんいます。寝ているホーム
レスの人の前を、会社員たちが急いで通ります。

　「見える日本」と「見えない日本」。どちらも今の新宿です。

C. 質問に答えてください。

1. ①を読んで、次の質問に答えましょう。

　a. 原爆が世界で初めて落とされた所はどこですか。それはいつでしたか。
　　何人の人が死にましたか。

　b. 平和記念資料館で何ができますか。

　c. 宮島はどんな所ですか。

　d. 宮島で食べ物を持っている人は、どうして気をつけなければいけないの
　　ですか。

2. ② – ④ について質問を考えて、となりの人に聞きましょう。

3. あなたは広島・宮島、沖縄、京都、東京の中でどこに一番行ってみたいですか。そこで何がしてみたいですか。

D. 次の人たちは旅行に行きたがっています。広島・宮島、沖縄、京都、東京の中でどこがいいと思いますか。どうしてですか。

ジョンさん

自然や動物 (animal) が好きで、人がたくさんいる所がきらいです。

ハワイで生まれたので、海とスポーツが大好きです。

ケリーさん

トムさん

日本の社会 (society) についてレポートを書いています。

インドネシアから来たので紅葉を見たことがありません。

ユンさん

Ⅲ 書く練習

あなたが好きな所を紹介しましょう。

第16課 LESSON 16
まんが「ドラえもん」 The Manga *Doraemon*

194	供	▶きょう ▷ども　そな (companion; offer)	子供(こども) child 供える(そなえる) to offer something to the spirit 提供(ていきょう) offer
			(8) ノ　イ　仁　什　卅　世　供　供
195	世	▶せ　せい ▷よ (world; generation)	世界(せかい) the world　世話(せわ) care 世代(せだい) generation　三世(さんせい) the third generation 世の中(よのなか) the society
			(5) 一　十　卅　世　世
196	界	▶かい (world)	世界(せかい) the world 視界(しかい) visibility　政界(せいかい) political world 限界(げんかい) limit
			(9) 丶　口　m　m　田　田　尹　界　界
197	全	▶ぜん ▷まった　すべ (all)	全部(ぜんぶ) all 安全(あんぜん) safety　全国(ぜんこく) whole country 全く(まったく) entirely　全て(すべて) all
			(6) ノ　人　△　今　全　全
198	部	▶ぶ　へ (part; section)	全部(ぜんぶ) all　部屋(へや) room テニス部(テニスぶ) tennis club 部長(ぶちょう) department manager
			(11) 丶　亠　立　立　咅　咅　音　音　部　部　部
199	始	▶し ▷はじ (to begin)	始まる(はじまる) (something) begins 始める(はじめる) to begin (something) 始発(しはつ) first train　開始(かいし) start
			(8) く　女　女　女　如　始　始　始
200	週	▶しゅう (week)	毎週(まいしゅう) every week　先週(せんしゅう) last week 一週間(いっしゅうかん) one week 二週目(にしゅうめ) second week　週末(しゅうまつ) weekend
			(11) 丿　刀　月　冃　用　用　周　周　凋　调　週
201	以	▶い (by means of; compared with)	〜以外(〜いがい) other than . . . 〜以上(〜いじょう) . . . or more　〜以下(〜いか) . . . or less 〜以内(〜いない) within . . .　以前(いぜん) before; formerly
			(5) 丨　レ　レ　以　以

202	考	▶こう ▷かんが (to think; idea)	考える（かんがえる）to think 考え（かんがえ）idea　考古学（こうこがく）archeology 参考（さんこう）reference (6) 一　十　土　耂　耂　考
203	開	▶かい ▷あ　ひら (to open)	開ける（あける）to open (something) 開く（あく）(something) opens　開く（ひらく）to open 開店（かいてん）opening of a store (12) 丨　冂　冂　門　門　門　門　門　門　閂　閉　開
204	屋	▶おく ▷や (shop; house)	部屋（へや）room　本屋（ほんや）bookstore 魚屋（さかなや）fish shop　屋上（おくじょう）rooftop 屋内（おくない）indoor (9) 一　コ　尸　尸　尸　居　居　屋　屋
205	方	▶ほう ▷かた　がた (direction; person)	味方（みかた）person on one's side 読み方（よみかた）way of reading　夕方（ゆうがた）evening 両方（りょうほう）both　方法（ほうほう）method (4) 丶　亠　方　方
206	運	▶うん ▷はこ (transport; luck)	運動（うんどう）exercise　運転（うんてん）driving 運がいい（うんがいい）lucky　運命（うんめい）fate 運ぶ（はこぶ）to carry (12) 丶　冖　冖　𠃊　宣　宣　軍　軍　運　運
207	動	▶どう ▷うご (to move)	運動（うんどう）exercise 動く（うごく）to move　自動車（じどうしゃ）automobile 動物（どうぶつ）animal　動詞（どうし）verb (11) 一　二　千　千　千　自　重　重　重　動　動
208	教	▶きょう ▷おし (to teach)	教える（おしえる）to teach　教室（きょうしつ）classroom 教会（きょうかい）church　キリスト教（キリストきょう） Christianity　教科書（きょうかしょ）textbook (11) 一　十　土　耂　耂　考　孝　孝　教　教　教
209	室	▶しつ (room)	教室（きょうしつ）classroom 研究室（けんきゅうしつ）professor's office　地下室（ちかしつ） basement　待合室（まちあいしつ）waiting room (9) 丶　丷　宀　宀　宎　宎　宮　室　室

(▶ indicates the *on-yomi* and ▷ indicates the *kun-yomi*.)

Ⅰ 漢字の練習

A. 次の漢字の読み方を覚えましょう。太字は新しい読み方です。

空（そら）　　　　小学生（しょうがくせい）　　出す（だす）

場所（ばしょ）　　　　　　　（☞ 空 (156)　小 (061)　出 (049)　所 (127)）

B. 次の漢字を読みましょう。（答は下にあります。）

1. 国　　　　　4. 次　　　　　7. 食べる

2. 来た　　　　5. 自分　　　　8. テストの前

3. 使う　　　　6. 書く

Ⅱ まんが「ドラえもん」

単 語

1　空（そら）　sky
1　飛ぶ（とぶ）　to fly [*u*-verb]
1　違う（ちがう）　to be different [*u*-verb]
3　そんな〜　such . . .
4　未来（みらい）　future
4　ロボット　robot
5　ひみつ　secret
5　道具（どうぐ）　tool
5　ポケット　pocket
6　小学生（しょうがくせい）　elementary
　　school students
7　助ける（たすける）　to help; to rescue [*ru*-verb]
11　〜のようなもの　something like . . .

12　写す（うつす）　to copy [*u*-verb]
17　続く（つづく）　to continue [*u*-verb]
19　例えば（たとえば）　for example
19　どこでも　anywhere
20　すると　. . . Then . . .
21　場所（ばしょ）　place
24　また　in addition
24　弱い（よわい）　weak
24　味方（みかた）　person on one's side
29　戻る（もどる）　to return; to go back
　　[*u*-verb]
29　教室（きょうしつ）　classroom
34　〜以外（〜いがい）　other than . . .

[Ⅰ-B の答]　1. くに　　　4. つぎ　　　7. たべる
　　　　　　2. きた　　　5. じぶん　　8. テストのまえ
　　　　　　3. つかう　　6. かく

A. 質問に答えてください。

1. あなたはどんなまんがを見たことがありますか。
日本のまんがを知っていますか。

2. 右の絵は「ドラえもん」です。何だと思いますか。
「ドラえもん」を見たことがありますか。
あなたの国でも「ドラえもん」が見られますか。

© 藤子プロ

B. まんが「ドラえもん」について読みましょう。 🔊 Y16

は人気があるのでしょうか。

それは、ドラえもんが夢をたくさんくれるからです。例えば、「ど
こでもドア」。行きたい所を考えて、このドアを開けます。すると、
ドアの向こうにはその場所があるのです。このドアであなたの部屋か
らどこでも行きたい所に行けます。あなたもこんな「ひみつ道具」が
あるといいと思いませんか。

また、ドラえもんは弱い子供の味方です。のび太くんは勉強もあま
りできないし、けんかも弱いし、運動もできません。でも、ドラえも
んはいつものび太くんを助けてくれます。子供たちはそんなやさしい
ドラえもんが大好きなのです。

そして、ドラえもんはのび太くんにいろいろなことを教えてくれま
す。「アンキパン」の話に戻りましょう。……教室ではテストが始ま
りました。でものび太くんは何も覚えていません。のび太くんはテス
トの前に、おなかが痛くなって、トイレに行ったのです。やっぱり自
分で勉強しなければいけないのです。

ドラえもんのテレビ番組は、シンガポールやインドネシアなど、日
本以外の国でも見られます。あなたの国にもドラえもんが来るかもし
れません。

C. 質問に答えてください。

1. ドラえもんはどこから来ましたか。

2. ドラえもんはポケットの中に何を持っていますか。

3. 「アンキパン」はどんな道具ですか。

4. 「どこでもドア」はどんな道具ですか。

5. のび太くんのテストはどうでしたか。

6. どうして「ドラえもん」は人気がありますか。三つ書いてください。

7. 「ドラえもん」のテレビ番組はどの国で見られますか。

15　　　　　10　　　　　5　　　　　1

「ドラえもん」

子供の時、「空を飛んでみたい」「違う世界に行ってみたい」と思いませんでしたか。まんが「ドラえもん」の中でそんな夢がかないます。ドラえもんは未来から来たロボットです。未来のいろいろな便利な「ひみつ道具」をポケットの中に持っていて、小学生ののび太くんが困った時、その道具を使って助けてくれます。

ある日、のび太くんはテストがあるのを忘れて、ぜんぜん勉強しませんでした。困ったのび太くんはドラえもんに言いました。「ドラえもん、助けてよ。次のテストは自分で勉強するから。」ドラえもんはポケットからパンのようなものを出して、のび太くんにあげました。「これは『アンキパン』だよ。覚えたいことをこのパンに写して、食べてみて。覚えられるから。」のび太くんはパンに写して、全部食べました。もうテストは大丈夫です。のび太くんはうれしそうに学校に行きました……。

まんが「ドラえもん」は一九七〇年に雑誌で始まりました。七三年にはテレビ番組になり、今も毎週続いています。どうしてドラえもん

© 藤子プロ

D. In what order did the following events take place? Write the number in each
    (   ).

(   ) のび太くんはおなかが痛くなったので、トイレに行った。

(   ) のび太くんはテストがぜんぜんできなかった。

(   ) のび太くんは「アンキパン」に覚えたいことを写して、全部食べた。

(   ) のび太くんはテストがあるのを忘れていた。

(   ) ドラえもんはポケットから「アンキパン」を出した。

(   ) のび太くんは困って、ドラえもんに相談した。

E. 次の質問に答えましょう。

   1. あなたは「アンキパン」で何を覚えたいですか。

   2. あなたはどんな時「どこでもドア」を使いたいですか。

Ⅲ 書く練習

あなたはドラえもんにどんな道具を出してもらいたいですか。それで何をしたいですか。
ほしい道具について書きましょう。

第17課 | LESSON 17

オノ・ヨーコ Yoko Ono

210	歳 (year; age)	▶さい せい	二十五歳 (にじゅうごさい) twenty-five years old お歳暮 (おせいぼ) year-end gift 二十歳 (はたち) twenty years old
			(13) 丿 ト 屵 屵 产 产 岸 岸 岸 岸 歳 歳 歳
211	習 (to learn)	▶しゅう ▷なら	習う (ならう) to learn 習字 (しゅうじ) calligraphy　練習 (れんしゅう) practice 習慣 (しゅうかん) habit; custom
			(11) 𠃌 刁 刁 羽 羽 羽 羽 羿 習 習 習
212	主 (main; lord)	▶しゅ ▷おも ぬし	主に (おもに) mainly　ご主人 (ごしゅじん) husband 主婦 (しゅふ) housewife　主語 (しゅご) subject of a sentence 持ち主 (もちぬし) owner
			(5) 丶 二 十 主 主
213	結 (to tie; to join)	▶けっ けつ ▷むす	結婚する (けっこんする) to get married 結果 (けっか) result　結論 (けつろん) conclusion 結ぶ (むすぶ) to tie a knot
			(12) 乚 纟 纟 纟 纟 糸 糸 紶 結 結 結 結
214	婚 (marriage)	▶こん	結婚する (けっこんする) to marry 離婚 (りこん) divorce　婚約者 (こんやくしゃ) fiancée 新婚 (しんこん) newlywed　未婚 (みこん) unmarried
			(11) 乚 𡛔 女 𡛸 妒 妒 娇 婚 婚 婚 婚
215	集 (to gather)	▶しゅう ▷あつ	集める (あつめる) to collect 特集 (とくしゅう) (magazine) feature 集中する (しゅうちゅうする) to concentrate
			(12) 丿 亻 亻 什 什 仹 隹 隹 隹 集 集
216	発 (to start; to reveal)	▶はっ はつ ぱつ	発表する (はっぴょうする) to make public; to give a presentation 発音 (はつおん) pronunciation　出発 (しゅっぱつ) departure 発明 (はつめい) invention
			(9) フ ヌ ヌ 癶 癶 癶 癶 発 発
217	表 (to express; surface)	▶ぴょう ひょう ▷あらわ おもて	発表する (はっぴょうする) to make public; to give a presentation 表紙 (ひょうし) cover page　表現 (ひょうげん) expression 表す (あらわす) to express　表 (おもて) the front
			(8) 一 十 キ 主 丰 表 表 表

218	品	▶ひん ▷しな　じな (goods; refinement)	作品（さくひん）piece of work 上品な（じょうひんな）elegant　手品（てじな）magic 品物（しなもの）merchandise article
			(9) ⼃ 口 ⼝ 口 吕 品 品 品 品
219	字	▶じ (character; letter)	文字（もじ）character 赤字（あかじ）deficit　名字（みょうじ）family name 大文字（おおもじ）uppercase letters　漢字（かんじ）kanji
			(6) ⼂ ⼍ 宀 字 宁 字
220	活	▶かつ　かっ (lively)	活動（かつどう）activity　生活（せいかつ）life; living 活発な（かっぱつな）active　活用（かつよう）conjugation 活気（かっき）liveliness
			(9) ⼀ ⼆ ⼵ ⼵ ⼵ 汗 汗 活 活
221	写	▶しゃ ▷うつ (to copy)	写真（しゃしん）photograph　写す（うつす）to copy 写生（しゃせい）sketch 描写する（びょうしゃする）to describe
			(5) ⼂ ⼍ ⼌ 写 写
222	真	▶しん ▷ま (true; reality)	写真（しゃしん）photograph　真ん中（まんなか）center 〜の真上（〜のまうえ）right above... 真夜中（まよなか）midnight
			(10) 一 十 广 市 市 肖 盲 直 真 真
223	歩	▶ほ　ぽ ▷ある (to walk)	歩く（あるく）to walk 歩道（ほどう）sidewalk　散歩する（さんぽする）to stroll 一歩（いっぽ）one step　進歩（しんぽ）progress
			(8) ⼁ ⼂ 止 止 ⺊ 步 赤 歩
224	野	▶や ▷の (field)	分野（ぶんや）realm; field　小野さん（おのさん）Mr./Ms. Ono 長野（ながの）Nagano 野球（やきゅう）baseball　野菜（やさい）vegetable
			(11) ⼃ 口 日 日 甲 甲 里 野 野 野 野

（▶ indicates the *on-yomi* and ▷ indicates the *kun-yomi*.）

Ⅰ 漢字の練習

A. 次の漢字の読み方を覚えましょう。太字は新しい読み方です。

作品（さくひん）　　文字（もじ）　　その後（そのご）

二人（ふたり）　　年代（ねんだい）　　何度も（なんども）

（☞　作 (076)　文 (070)　二 (002)　人 (018)）

B. 次の漢字を読みましょう。（答は次のページの下にあります。）

1. 生まれる　　4. 音楽　　7. 始める　　10. この年
2. 父親　　5. 名前　　8. 三年後　　11. 歌
3. 仕事　　6. 見る　　9. 作る

Ⅱ オノ・ヨーコ

単　語

2 芸術（げいじゅつ）　art

4 主に（おもに）　mainly

4 詩（し）　poem

6 発表する（はっぴょうする）　to make public; to publish [irr. verb]

6 俳句（はいく）　*haiku* (Japanese poetry)

7 数える（かぞえる）　to count [*ru*-verb]

8 雲（くも）　cloud

9 名前をつける（なまえをつける）　to name [*ru*-verb]

10 完成する（かんせいする）　to be completed [irr. verb]

11 展覧会（てんらんかい）　art exhibition

11 作品（さくひん）　artistic piece

12 天井（てんじょう）　ceiling

12 はしご　ladders

12 虫めがね（むしめがね）　magnifying glass

16 文字（もじ）　letter; character

19 その後（そのご）　after that

20 活動（かつどう）　activities

22 1960 年代（せんきゅうひゃくろくじゅうねんだい）　1960's

23 ～のための　for the sake of . . .

26 何度も（なんども）　many times

27 影響を受ける（えいきょうをうける）　to be affected（～に）[*ru*-verb]

29 主夫（しゅふ）　"house husband"

31 大ヒット（だいヒット）　big hit

32 しかし　however

33 銃で撃たれる（じゅうでうたれる）　to be shot

35 分野（ぶんや）　field; realm

A. 質問に答えてください。
   しつもん　こた

1. 左の英語は右のカタカナのどれですか。

   a. Vietnam　　・　　　　　・(1) メンバー

   b. member　　・　　　　　・(2) ニューヨーク

   c. grapefruit　・　　　　　・(3) イギリス

   d. rock band　・　　　　　・(4) ベトナム

   e. Britain　　・　　　　　・(5) アルバム

   f. album　　　・　　　　　・(6) グレープフルーツ

   g. New York　・　　　　　・(7) ロックバンド

2. ビートルズを知っていますか。どんなビートルズの歌を知っていますか。

3. この人はオノ・ヨーコ（小野洋子）です。
   どんな人だと思いますか。
     ようこ

写真提供：共同通信社

[①-B の答]　1. うまれる　　4. おんがく　　7. はじめる　　10. このとし
    こたえ　　2. ちちおや　　5. なまえ　　　8. さんねんご　11. うた
         　　3. しごと　　　6. みる　　　　9. つくる

B. オノ・ヨーコ（小野洋子）の伝記 (biography) を読みましょう。 🔊 Y17

1　　オノ・ヨーコ（小野洋子）は 1933 年に東京で生まれました。ヨーコの両親は芸術が好きで、ヨーコも子供の時、ピアノを習っていました。ヨーコは 1953 年、父親の仕事で家族とアメリカに行き、ニューヨークの大学に入りました。大学では主に音楽と詩を勉強しました。

5　　1964 年、31 歳の時、ヨーコは自分の詩を集めて『グレープフルーツ』を発表します。ヨーコの詩は短くて、俳句みたいです。

数えなさい*

雲を数えて

名前をつけなさい

10　　この詩は、読んだ人が雲を数えて名前をつけた時に完成します。

　　1966 年、イギリスでヨーコの展覧会がありました。その中の作品の一つが「天井の絵」（写真）でした。見に来た人は、はしごの上で虫めがねを使って天井にある絵を見るのです。ある日、一人の髪が長い男が来て、虫めがねで天15　井の絵を見てみました。そこには小さい "yes" の文字がありました。"yes" ——この言葉に、男はとても感動しました。彼の名前はジョン・レノン。有名なロックバンド、ビートルズのメンバーでした。その後、二人はいっしょに音楽20　活動や芸術活動を始めます。そして、三年後、二人は結婚しました。

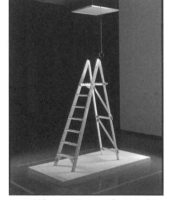

© Yoko Ono/Lenono Photo Archive

---

l. 7 数えなさい　　*l. 9*　名前をつけなさい

The verb stem ＋なさい is a command that has a strong implication. More detail is in Lesson 22.

　　勉強しなさい。　*Study.*　　起きなさい。　*Get up.*

1960 年代、世界はベトナム戦争の中にありました。ヨーコとジョンはいろいろな平和活動をしました。1971 年に、二人は平和のための歌、「ハッピー・クリスマス（戦争は終わった)」を作りました。同
25 じ年、ジョンは「イマジン」を発表しました。ヨーコは『グレープフルーツ』の中である言葉を何度も使っています。それが "imagine" です。ジョンはヨーコの詩に影響を受けて、この歌を作ったそうです。1975 年、ヨーコとジョンの間には男の子ショーンが生まれ、ジョンは音楽活動をやめて、「主夫」になります。

30 1980 年、ジョンはまた音楽活動を始め、ヨーコと一枚のアルバムを発表しました。この中の歌、「スターティング・オーバー」は大ヒットになりました。しかし、この年の 12 月 8 日、ヨーコとジョンがニューヨークの家の前で車を降りて歩いていた時、ジョンは銃で撃たれました。

35 ジョンが死んでからも、オノ・ヨーコは芸術の分野でいろいろな作品を発表し、平和のための活動をしています。

C. オノ・ヨーコ（小野洋子）の年表 (chronology) を作りましょう。

1933 年	オノ・ヨーコ（小野洋子)＿＿＿＿＿＿＿
＿＿＿年	アメリカに行く
1964 年	＿＿＿＿＿＿＿＿＿＿＿＿＿＿＿
＿＿＿年	イギリスで展覧会をする
＿＿＿年	ジョン・レノンと結婚する
1971 年	＿＿＿＿＿＿＿＿＿＿＿＿＿＿＿
1975 年	＿＿＿＿＿＿＿＿＿＿＿＿＿＿＿
＿＿＿年	ジョンとアルバムを発表する
	＿＿＿＿＿＿＿＿＿＿＿＿＿＿＿

Ⅲ 書く練習

A. 下は「イマジン」の歌詞 (lyrics) です。日本語に訳してみましょう。

```
              Imagine
           by John Lennon

     Imagine there's no heaven
        It's easy if you try
         No hell below us
        Above us only sky
      Imagine all the people
         Living for today
```

B. あなたが知っている人について書きましょう。

第18課 | L E S S O N 18
大学生活 College Life

225	目 (eye)	▶もく ▷め	目的 (もくてき) purpose 目 (め) eyes 目薬 (めぐすり) eye drops 二番目 (にばんめ) the second 目上の人 (めうえのひと) one's superiors
			(5) 丨 冂 冃 月 目
226	的 (target; -ish)	▶てき ▷まと	目的 (もくてき) purpose 現代的 (げんだいてき) modern 社会的 (しゃかいてき) social 的 (まと) target
			(8) 丶 亻 竒 甶 白 白 的 的
227	力 (power)	▶りょく りき ▷ちから	力仕事 (ちからしごと) physical labor such as construction 協力 (きょうりょく) cooperation 努力 (どりょく) endeavor 力士 (りきし) sumo wrestler
			(2) フ 力
228	洋 (ocean; overseas)	▶よう	洋服 (ようふく) clothes 東洋 (とうよう) the East 洋食 (ようしょく) Western food 大西洋 (たいせいよう) the Atlantic
			(9) 丶 冫 氵 汀 汫 洋 洋 洋 洋
229	服 (clothes)	▶ふく	服 (ふく) clothes 洋服 (ようふく) Western clothes 制服 (せいふく) uniform 和服 (わふく) Japanese clothes
			(8) 丿 刀 月 月 肝 肥 服 服
230	堂 (hall)	▶どう	食堂 (しょくどう) dining room 公会堂 (こうかいどう) public hall 堂々とした (どうどうとした) dignified; imposing
			(11) 丶 丷 丷 冖 学 学 常 営 営 堂 堂
231	授 (to instruct)	▶じゅ ▷さず	授業 (じゅぎょう) class 教授 (きょうじゅ) professor 授かる (さずかる) to be given
			(11) 一 十 扌 扌 扩 扩 护 护 护 授 授
232	業 (business; vocation)	▶ぎょう	授業 (じゅぎょう) class 職業 (しょくぎょう) occupation 産業 (さんぎょう) industry サービス業 (サービスぎょう) service industry
			(13) 丶 丷 丷 丷 丱 业 业 业 堂 堂 業 業 業

233	試	▶し ▷こころ (test; to try)	試験（しけん）exam 試合（しあい）game; match　入試（にゅうし）entrance exam 試みる（こころみる）to try
			(13) ⟋ ⟍ ⟍ ⟍ ⟍ ⟍ 言 言 計 試 試 試 試
234	験	▶けん (to examine)	試験（しけん）exam 実験（じっけん）experiment　経験（けいけん）experience 受験（じゅけん）taking examination
			(18) ⼁ ⼁ ⻢ ⻢ ⻢ ⻢ 馬 馬 馬 馬 馬 馬 駅 駅 験 験 験 験
235	貸	▶たい ▷か (to lend; loan)	貸す（かす）to lend 貸し出し（かしだし）lending 賃貸マンション（ちんたいマンション）apartment for rent
			(12) ⟋ ⼈ 亻 代 代 代 伐 伐 貸 貸 貸 貸
236	図	▶と　ず ▷はか (drawing; to devise)	図書館（としょかん）library　地図（ちず）map 図（ず）figure　合図（あいず）signal　図る（はかる）to attempt
			(7) ⼁ 冂 冂 円 図 図 図
237	館	▶かん (building; hall)	図書館（としょかん）library　映画館（えいがかん）movie theater　旅館（りょかん）Japanese inn 大使館（たいしかん）embassy
			(16) ⟋ ⼈ 亼 今 今 会 食 食 食' 食' 飠 飠 飠 飠 館 館
238	終	▶しゅう ▷お (end)	終わる（おわる）to come to an end 終わり（おわり）end　終点（しゅうてん）last stop 最終〜（さいしゅう〜）the last …
			(11) ⼂ ⼂ ⼂ ⼂ ⼂ 糸 糸 約 終 終 終
239	宿	▶しゅく ▷やど (inn; to lodge in)	宿題（しゅくだい）homework 下宿（げしゅく）boardinghouse　宿泊（しゅくはく）lodging 宿（やど）inn
			(11) ⼂ ⼂ 宀 宀 宀 宀 宿 宿 宿 宿 宿
240	題	▶だい (title; topic)	宿題（しゅくだい）homework 問題（もんだい）problem; question 話題（わだい）topic of conversation　題（だい）title
			(18) ⼁ 冂 日 日 旦 早 早 昇 是 是 是 匙 題 題 題 題 題 題

（▶ indicates the *on-yomi* and ▷ indicates the *kun-yomi*.）

Ⅰ 漢字の練習

A. 次の漢字の読み方を覚えましょう。太字は新しい読み方です。

女子 （じょし）　　男子 （だんし）　　以上 （いじょう）

電気代 （でんきだい） 入れる （いれる）　毎月 （まいつき）

食堂 （しょくどう）　三日 （みっか）　　空手 （からて）

親しい （したしい）　来週 （らいしゅう） 図書館 （としょかん）

（☞　子 (060)　男 (039)　入 (072)　月 (019)　食 (042)
三 (003)　日 (016)　空 (156)　親 (166)　書 (093)）

B. 次の漢字を読みましょう。（答は下にあります。）

1. 学生　　3. 旅行　　5. 生活　　7. 楽しみ

2. 店　　　4. 一か月　6. 飲む

Ⅱ 大学生のアルバイト

単　語

目的 （もくてき）　object; purpose
時給 （じきゅう）　an hourly wage
女子学生 （じょしがくせい）　female
　　student
男子学生 （だんしがくせい）　male student

生活のゆとり （せいかつのゆとり）　extra
　　money to spare for the cost of living
洋服 （ようふく）　clothes
生活費 （せいかつひ）　the cost of living
貯金 （ちょきん）　savings
〜以上 （いじょう）　. . . or more

[Ⅰ-B の答] 1. がくせい　　3. りょこう　　5. せいかつ　　7. たのしみ
　　　　　 2. みせ　　　　4. いっかげつ　6. のむ

A. 質問に答えてください。

1. あなたはアルバイトをしたことがありますか。
   どんなアルバイトをしましたか／していますか。

2. あなたのアルバイトの目的は何ですか。

3. あなたの国で人気があるアルバイトは何ですか。

B. 日本の大学生のアルバイトについて調べました。下のグラフ (graph) を見て、質問に答えてください。

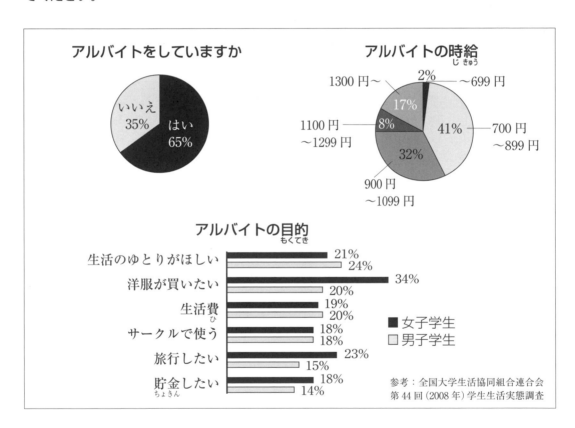

参考：全国大学生活協同組合連合会
第44回（2008年）学生生活実態調査

1. アルバイトをしている人としていない人と、どちらのほうが多いですか。

2. 時給 1300 円以上もらっている人は何パーセントですか。

3. 女子学生のアルバイトの目的で一番多いのは何ですか。

4. 男子学生のアルバイトの目的で一番多いのは何ですか。

Ⅲ 橋本くんの大学生活
はしもと

単　語
たんご

2 ワンルームマンション　one-room
　　apartment; a studio
4 食費（しょくひ）food cost
5 〜代（〜だい）charge; fee
　　電気代（でんきだい）charge for electricity
7 毎月（まいつき）every month

9 家庭教師（かていきょうし）tutor
13 引っ越し（ひっこし）moving
13 力仕事（ちからしごと）physical labor such
　　as construction
23 初めは（はじめは）at first
26 親しい（したしい）close; intimate

A.　ある新聞が大学生の橋本くんの生活を紹介しています。* 📶 Y18
　　　　　　　　しんぶん　　　はしもと　　　　しょうかい

橋本くんは大学三年生だ。大学の近くのワンルームマンションに住んでいる。家賃は一か月五万円だ。食費、電気代などを入れて、一か月の生活費は、十万円ぐらいだ。毎月、両親が八万円送ってくれる。

今、家庭教師をしたり、大学の食堂でアルバイトをしたりしている。家庭教師は一週間に一回、食堂は三日だ。時々、引っ越しなどの力仕事もする。アルバイトをしながら勉強するのは大変だ。よく遅刻したり、授業をサボったりしてしまう。

橋本くんは空手のサークルに入っている。一週間に三日、練習をする。また、時々サークルのみんなと飲みに行く。「大きらいなお酒を飲まなきゃいけないから、初めはあまり行きたくなかったんです。でも、そのおかげで、先輩たちと親しくなれたし、今の彼女にも会えたんですよ。」

来週から試験が始まる。同じクラスの友だちにノートを貸してもらって、図書館で勉強するつもりだ。「もっと早く勉強を始めればよかった」と思っている。橋本くんは今、試験が終わってから、サークルのみんなと旅行に行くのを楽しみにしている。

B. 質問に答えてください。
   しつもん こた

1. 橋本くんはどんな所に住んでいますか。
   はしもと

2. 橋本くんはどんなアルバイトをしていますか。

3. 橋本くんはアルバイトをしなかったら、家賃が払えませんか。
   や ちん はら

4. 橋本くんはいい学生だと思いますか。どうしてですか。

5. 橋本くんはサークルの友だちと飲みに行って、どんないいことがありましたか。

6. 橋本くんは、今、何をしなければいけませんか。

C. 下は一人で生活している大学生の生活費です。あなたはいくらぐらい使いますか。
   ひ
   生活費を書きましょう。

	日本の大学生の生活費 ひ	あなたの生活費
食費 しょく ひ	24,430 円	円
家賃・電気代など や ちん	54,720 円	円
本代	2,410 円	円
電車・バス代など	3,450 円	円
電話代	5,090 円	円
その他 (others) た	33,820 円	円
計 (total) けい	123,920 円	円

参考：全国大学生活協同組合連合会
第 44 回 (2008 年) 学生生活実態調査

---

* Note that this passage is written in short form, which expresses formality rather than casualness, as expected in journalistic and scholarly articles.

D. 次の文を読んで、あなたがすること／そう思うことに○、しないこと／そう思わないことに×を書いてください。

（　　）1. 授業を聞きながら、時々寝てしまう。
（　　）2. 今年、五回以上授業をサボってしまった。
（　　）3. よく朝寝坊をする。
（　　）4. よく友だちに宿題を見せてもらう。
（　　）5. よく宿題を忘れる。
（　　）6. よく授業に遅刻する。
（　　）7. やさしい先生のほうがきびしい先生より好きだ。
（　　）8. 試験の後、「もっと勉強すればよかった」とよく思う。

いくつ○がありましたか。

```
7〜8     ……とても悪い学生
5〜6     ……悪い学生
3〜4     ……普通の (average) 学生
1〜2     ……いい学生
 0       ……とてもいい学生
```

Ⅳ 書く練習

A. あなたの友だちの生活について書きましょう。

B. 興味があることについてアンケートを作って聞きましょう。
アンケートの後で、わかったことを書きましょう。

第19課 | L E S S O N 19

手紙とメール Letters and E-mails

241	春 (spring)	▶しゅん ▷はる	春(はる) spring 春巻(はるまき) spring roll　春分(しゅんぶん) vernal equinox 青春(せいしゅん) youth
			(9) 一 二 三 声 夫 表 耒 春 春
242	秋 (autumn)	▶しゅう ▷あき	秋(あき) autumn 秋学期(あきがっき) fall semester 秋分(しゅうぶん) autumnal equinox
			(9) 一 二 千 千 禾 禾 利 秒 秋
243	冬 (winter)	▶とう ▷ふゆ	冬(ふゆ) winter　冬休み(ふゆやすみ) winter vacation 暖冬(だんとう) warm winter 春夏秋冬(しゅんかしゅうとう) four seasons
			(5) ノ ク 久 冬 冬
244	花 (flower)	▶か ▷はな　ばな	花(はな) flower　花見(はなみ) flower viewing 花火(はなび) fireworks　花粉症(かふんしょう) hay fever 生け花(いけばな) flower arrangement
			(7) 一 十 サ サ 苧 花 花
245	様 (Mr.; Ms.; condition)	▶よう ▷さま	〜様(〜さま) Mr./Ms. . . . お客様(おきゃくさま) dear customer 皆様(みなさま) everyone　様子(ようす) manner
			(14) 一 十 オ 材 材 ザ 栏 样 样 様 様 様 様
246	不 (negative; non-)	▶ふ　ぶ	不安な(ふあんな) uneasy; worried 不景気(ふけいき) recession　不便(ふべん) inconvenience 水不足(みずぶそく) water shortage
			(4) 一 ア 不 不
247	姉 (older sister)	▶し ▷あね　ねえ	姉(あね) older sister　お姉さん(おねえさん) older sister 姉妹(しまい) sisters　姉妹都市(しまいとし) sister city
			(8) く 夕 女 女' 妒 妒 姊 姉
248	兄 (older brother)	▶きょう　けい ▷あに　にい	兄(あに) older brother お兄さん(おにいさん) older brother 兄弟(きょうだい) brothers
			(5) 丨 ロ ロ 尸 兄

249	漢	▶かん		漢字(かんじ) Chinese character
				漢方薬(かんぽうやく) Chinese herbal medicine
				漢和辞典(かんわじてん) Kanji dictionary
		(China)		(13) ` 冫 氵 氵 汁 汁 泸 芦 芦 茳 淳 漢 漢
250	卒	▶そつ		卒業する(そつぎょうする) to graduate
				卒業式(そつぎょうしき) graduation ceremony
				大卒(だいそつ) university graduate
		(to graduate)		(8) ` 亠 宀 𣥂 卆 卒 卆 卒
251	工	▶こう く		工学(こうがく) engineering
				工事(こうじ) construction　工場(こうじょう) factory
				大工(だいく) carpenter
		(craft; construction)		(3) 一 丁 工
252	研	▶けん ▷と		研究(けんきゅう) research
				研究者(けんきゅうしゃ) researcher　研修(けんしゅう) training
				研ぐ(とぐ) to sharpen
		(to polish; study)		(9) 一 ァ 石 石 石 石 研 研
253	究	▶きゅう ▷きわ		研究(けんきゅう) research
				探究(たんきゅう) inquiry
				究める(きわめる) to investigate thoroughly
		(research)		(7) ` ` 宀 宀 究 究 究
254	質	▶しつ しち		質問(しつもん) question
				質がいい(しつがいい) good quality　素質(そしつ) aptitude
				質屋(しちや) pawn shop
		(quality; matter)		(15) ` ⺇ ⺮ 斤 斦 斦 斦 所 斦 斦 筲 筲 質 質 質
255	問	▶もん ▷と		質問(しつもん) question
				問題(もんだい) problem　訪問(ほうもん) visit
				問う(とう) to question
		(question)		(11) l ｢ ｢ ｢ ｢ ｢ 門 門 門 問 問
256	多	▶た ▷おお		多い(おおい) many
				多分(たぶん) probably　〜の多く(〜のおおく) many of ...
				多数決(たすうけつ) decision by majority
		(many; much)		(6) ノ ク タ タ 多 多

(▶ indicates the *on-yomi* and ▷ indicates the *kun-yomi*.)

① 漢字の練習

A. 次の漢字の読み方を覚えましょう。太字は新しい読み方です。

世話 (せわ)　　不安 (ふあん)　　思い出す (おもいだす)

大切 (たいせつ)　　友人 (ゆうじん)　　大学院 (だいがくいん)

(☞　安 (151)　大 (055)　友 (094))

B. 次の漢字を読みましょう。(答は下にあります。)

1. 手紙　　　4. 上手　　　7. 来年　　　10. 特に

2. さむい日　5. 教える　　8. その時

3. 出る　　　6. 本当に　　9. 十日

[①-B の答]　1. てがみ　　　4. じょうず　　7. らいねん　　10. とくに
　　　　　　2. さむいひ　　5. おしえる　　8. そのとき
　　　　　　3. でる　　　　6. ほんとうに　9. とおか

Ⅱ お礼の手紙
れい

単 語
たん ご

2 いかが　how (polite expression of どう)

4 たつ　(time) pass [*u*-verb]

5 〜中（〜ちゅう）　while . . .

5 たいへん　greatly

5 お世話になる（おせわになる）　to be in
someone's care（〜に）[*u*-verb]

9 しょうぎ　Japanese chess

10 思い出す（おもいだす）　to recall [*u*-verb]

12 なつかしい　to miss; to long for

17 それでは　well then

17 みな様（みなさま）　everyone (polite
expression of みなさん)

18 大切にする（たいせつにする）　to take
good care of [irr. verb]

A. 質問に答えてください。
こた

1. あなたはよく手紙を書きますか。どんな時に手紙を書きますか。

2. 日本語の手紙はたいてい季節のあいさつ (greeting) で始まります。次の文は
き せつ
どの季節ですか。

春　夏　秋　冬

a. 暑い日が続きます。　　　　　　　　　　　　　　（　　　）
あつ　　つづ
b. 桜 (cherry tree) の花がきれいな季節になりました。（　　　）
さくら　　　　　　　　　　　　　き せつ
c. 今年初めて雪が降りました。　　　　　　　　　　（　　　）
はじ　　ゆき ふ
d. 山の紅葉がとてもきれいです。　　　　　　　　　（　　　）
こうよう

B. ジェイソンさんはホームステイの家族へお礼の手紙を書きました。次のページの手紙を読
れい
みましょう。 🔊 Y19-1

C. 質問に答えてください。
こた

1. ジェイソンさんはどうしてもっと早く手紙を書かなかったのですか。

2. ジェイソンさんは何を思い出しますか。

3. ジェイソンさんは冬休みに何をしますか。

4. ジェイソンさんはいつ日本にもどるつもりですか。

小野様

ロンドンでは、さむい日がつづいていますが、東京はいかがですか。

もっと早く手紙を書こうと思っていたのですが、大学の授業でいそがしくて、日本を出てから三か月もたってしまいました。

留学中はたいへんお世話になりました。はじめは日本語がわからなくて、不安でした。でもお母さんとお父さんのおかげで、日本語が上手になりました。日本語や日本の生活についていろいろ教えてくださってどうもありがとうございました。

お姉さんといっしょにテニスをしたり、お兄さんとしょうぎをしたりしたことを今も思い出します。日本に行って、本当に、よかったと思います。あまり好きじゃなかった日本のおふろやまんいん電車も今はなつかしいです。

私はこの冬休みは自分で漢字を勉強しようと思っています。来年大学を卒業したら、もう一度日本にもどるつもりです。

その時、会えるのを楽しみにしています。

それでは、みな様によろしくおつたえください。

お体を大切になさってください。

十二月十日

ジェイソン・グリーンバーグ

Ⅲ マリアさんのメール

単 語
たん　ご

2 突然（とつぜん）suddenly	11 〜のために for ...
3 友人（ゆうじん）friend	13 申し込み（もうしこみ）application
3 〜の紹介で（〜のしょうかいで）through the introduction of	15 もし〜たら if ...
5 国際（こくさい）international	17 質問（しつもん）question
7 電気工学（でんきこうがく）electric engineering	17 申し訳ありません（もうしわけありません）You have my apologies.
10 受ける（うける）to take (an examination) [ru-verb]	18 どうぞよろしくお願いします（どうぞよろしくおねがいします）Thank you in advance.

A. マリアさんは日本に留学しているパクさんにメールを書きました。次のページのメールを読みましょう。　🔊Y19-2

B. 下の文を完成してください。
かんせい

マリアさんは今カリフォルニア大学で＿＿＿＿＿＿＿＿を勉強しています。

卒業したら、＿＿＿＿＿＿＿＿＿＿＿＿＿＿＿＿＿たいと思っています。

パクさんは＿＿＿＿＿＿＿＿＿＿＿＿＿＿＿ています。マリアさんは日

本の大学院について聞きたいので、パクさんにメールを書きました。メールで

質問を三つしました。

1) ＿＿＿＿＿＿＿＿＿＿＿＿＿＿＿＿＿＿＿＿＿＿＿＿＿＿＿＿＿＿＿＿

2) ＿＿＿＿＿＿＿＿＿＿＿＿＿＿＿＿＿＿＿＿＿＿＿＿＿＿＿＿＿＿＿＿

3) ＿＿＿＿＿＿＿＿＿＿＿＿＿＿＿＿＿＿＿＿＿＿＿＿＿＿＿＿＿＿＿＿

From:	Maria Evans <mariae@cali-u.ac.jp>
To:	parks@sakura-u.ac.jp
Subject:	はじめまして

1　パク・スーマン様

突然のメールで失礼します。私はマリア・エバンスと言います。
友人のモハメッドさんの紹介でメールを書いています。

私は今、カリフォルニア大学の四年生です。
5　卒業したら、日本の大学院で国際政治を勉強しようと思っています。
私の専攻は政治で、大学では特にアメリカと日本の関係について
勉強しました。パクさんは日本の大学院で電気工学を研究して
いらっしゃると聞きました。
日本の大学院について教えていただけないでしょうか。

10　大学院に入る前に、日本語の試験を受けなければいけないと
聞きましたが、パクさんは試験のためにどんな勉強を
なさいましたか。

また、日本は生活費が高いそうなので、奨学金の申し込みを
したいのですが、どうしたらいいでしょうか。
15　もし奨学金がもらえなかったら、アルバイトを探そうと思っています。
留学生がアルバイトを見つけるのはむずかしいでしょうか。

質問が多くなってしまって、申し訳ありません。
お忙しいと思いますが、どうぞよろしくお願いします。

マリア・エバンス
20　mariae@cali-u.ac.jp

Ⅳ 書く練習

A. お世話になった人にお礼の手紙を書きましょう。

B. 質問の手紙を書きましょう。

カード／はがきの表現
Useful Expressions for Greeting Cards

1. New Year's Greetings

   あけましておめでとうございます。
   (Happy New Year)

   謹賀新年 (Happy New Year)

   昨年は大変お世話になりました。
   (Thank you for all your kind help
   during the past year.)

   本年もどうぞよろしくお願いいたします。
   (I hope for your continued good
   will this year.)

2. Summer Greetings

   暑中お見舞い申し上げます。 (I hope you are keeping well during the hot weather.)

3. Sending Congratulations

   ご卒業おめでとうございます。 (Congratulations on your graduation.)

   ご結婚おめでとうございます。 (Congratulations on your marriage.)

   誕生日おめでとう。 (Happy Birthday)

4. Sending Get-well Cards

   早くよくなってください。 (Get well soon.)

第20課 LESSON 20

猫の皿 A Cat's Plate
ねこ

257	皿 (plate)	▷さら ざら	皿(さら) plate; dish 紙皿(かみざら) paper plate　灰皿(はいざら) ashtray
			(5) 丶 冂 冊 皿 皿
258	声 (voice)	▶せい ▷こえ	声(こえ) voice 音声学(おんせいがく) phonetics 擬声語(ぎせいご) onomatopoeia　声優(せいゆう) voice actor
			(7) 一 十 士 声 吉 吉 声
259	茶 (tea)	▶ちゃ さ	お茶(おちゃ) Japanese tea　茶店(ちゃみせ) teahouse 紅茶(こうちゃ) black tea　茶色(ちゃいろ) brown 喫茶店(きっさてん) cafe
			(9) 一 十 サ ヌ 艾 芝 苂 茶 茶
260	止 (to stop)	▶し ▷と	止まる(とまる) (something) stops 中止する(ちゅうしする) to cancel 禁止する(きんしする) to prohibit
			(4) 丨 ト 止 止
261	枚 (sheet of . . .)	▶まい	一枚(いちまい) one sheet 枚数(まいすう) number of flat things
			(8) 一 十 オ 木 朾 朾 枚 枚
262	両 (both)	▶りょう	三両(さんりょう) three ryoo　両親(りょうしん) parents 両手(りょうて) both hands　両替(りょうがえ) exchange 両方(りょうほう) both sides
			(6) 一 厂 冂 两 両 両
263	無 (none)	▶む ぶ ▷な	無理な(むりな) impossible 無駄な(むだな) wasteful　無料(むりょう) free of charge 無礼な(ぶれいな) rude　無い(ない) there is no . . .
			(12) 丿 丿 乍 乍 午 午 無 無 無 無 無 無
264	払 (to pay)	▷はら ばら	払う(はらう) to pay 支払い(しはらい) payment　払い戻し(はらいもどし) refund 分割払い(ぶんかつばらい) payment in installments
			(5) 一 十 扌 払 払

265	心	▶ しん ▷ こころ (heart; mind)	心(こころ) heart; mind 心配する(しんぱいする) to worry 熱心な(ねっしんな) enthusiastic 安心な(あんしんな) safe 好奇心(こうきしん) curiosity
			(4) 丶 心 心 心
266	笑	▶ しょう ▷ わら え (to laugh)	笑う(わらう) to laugh 笑顔(えがお) smile 微笑む(ほほえむ) to smile 爆笑する(ばくしょうする) to burst into laughter
			(10) ノ ヒ ド ドト ヤケ ヤヤ ヤヤ 竺 笑 笑
267	絶	▶ ぜっ ぜつ ▷ た (to discontinue)	絶対に(ぜったいに) definitely 絶える(たえる) to die out 絶滅(ぜつめつ) extinction 気絶する(きぜつする) to faint 絶望(ぜつぼう) despair
			(12) 乙 幺 幺 幺 糸 糸 糸' 糸フ 紹 絶 絶 絶
268	対	▶ たい つい (opposite)	絶対に(ぜったいに) definitely 反対する(はんたいする) to oppose 日本対中国(にほんたいちゅうごく) Japan versus China 一対(いっつい) a pair
			(7) 丶 二 ナ 文 文 対 対
269	痛	▶ つう ▷ いた (pain)	痛い(いたい) painful 痛み止め(いたみどめ) painkiller 頭痛(ずつう) headache 腹痛(ふくつう) stomachache 腰痛(ようつう) lower back pain
			(12) 丶 二 广 广 广 疒 疒 疒 疔 痄 痛 痛
270	最	▶ さい ▷ もっと (utmost)	最悪(さいあく) the worst 最近(さいきん) recently 最高(さいこう) the best 最新(さいしん) the latest 最後に(さいごに) lastly 最も(もっとも) most
			(12) 丨 冂 日 日 旦 旦 早 早 昌 昌 最 最
271	続	▶ ぞく ▷ つづ (to continue)	続ける(つづける) to continue 手続き(てつづき) procedure 相続する(そうぞくする) to inherit 連続ドラマ(れんぞくドラマ) serial TV drama
			(13) 乙 幺 幺 幺 糸 糸 糸 紗 紗 紣 綒 続 続

(▶ indicates the *on-yomi* and ▷ indicates the *kun-yomi*.)

Ⅰ 漢字の練習
れん

A. 次の漢字の読み方を覚えましょう。太字は新しい読み方です。
おぼ　　　　　　　　　　ふと

外（そと）　　　　　最悪（さいあく）　　　（☞　外 (057)　悪 (154)）

B. 次の漢字を読みましょう。（答は下にあります。）
こたえ

1. 時代　　　4. 人気　　　7. 買う　　　10. 知らない

2. 始まる　　5. 所　　　　8. 歩く　　　11. 家族

3. 話　　　　6. 物　　　　9. 入る　　　12. 売れる

Ⅱ 猫の皿
ねこ

単　語
たん　ご

落語（らくご） comic monologue

1 江戸時代（えどじだい） Edo period
　　（1603−1867）

3 落語家（らくごか） comic storyteller

4 身ぶり（みぶり） gesture

7 いなか　countryside

8 江戸（えど） former name of Tokyo

8 値段（ねだん） price

9 茶店（ちゃみせ） teahouse

10 えさ　feed

11 止まる（とまる） to stop [u-verb]

12 両（りょう） a unit of currency used in the
　　Edo period

12 する　to cost [irr. verb]

14 主人（しゅじん） owner

14 あんなに　so; such

15 そうだ！　I have an idea!

15 だます　to deceive [u-verb]

17 抱く（だく） to hold something in one's
　　arm [u-verb]

17 にこにこする　to smile [irr. verb]

20 無理な（むりな） impossible

28 やった！　I did it!

29 心（こころ） mind; heart

33 絶対に（ぜったいに） definitely; no matter what

33 渡す（わたす） to give; to hand [u-verb]

34 がっかりする　to be disappointed [irr. verb]

34 ひっかく　to scratch [u-verb]

36 最悪（さいあく） the worst

42 売れる（うれる） to be sold [ru-verb]

[Ⅰ-B の答] 1. じだい　　4. にんき　　7. かう　　　10. しらない
こたえ　　2. はじまる　5. ところ　　8. あるく　　11. かぞく
　　　　　3. はなし　　6. もの　　　9. はいる　　12. うれる

A. 質問に答えてください。

1. これは日本です。何年ぐらい前だと思いますか。

広重／東都大伝馬街繁栄之図（東京都立中央図書館東京誌料文庫所蔵）

2. この人は何をしていると思いますか。

写真：アフロ

B. 落語「猫の皿」を読みましょう。 🔊Y20

1 落語は今から三百年以上前の江戸時代に始まりました。この時代に
たくさんの人の前でおもしろい話をして、お金をもらう人がいました。
このおもしろい話を落語と言い、落語をする人を落語家と言います。
落語家は一人でいろいろな声や身ぶりを使って、おもしろい話をしま
5 す。今でも落語はとても人気があります。

　　江戸時代の落語の一つ、「猫の皿」を読んでみましょう。

　　ある所に、一人の男がいました。男はいなかに行って古い物を買い、
江戸でそれを高い値段で売っていました。

　　ある日、男は川の近くにある茶店に入りました。男は茶店でお茶を
10 飲みながら、外を見ていました。その時、猫が歩いてきて、えさが入っ
た皿の前で止まりました。男はびっくりしました。その皿はとてもめ
ずらしい物で、一枚三百両もする皿だったのです。

　　男は思いました。

　　「茶店の主人はあの皿がいくらか知らないんだ。だからあんなに高い
15 物を猫の皿に使っているんだ。そうだ！ 主人をだまして、あの皿を
いただこう！」

　　男は猫を抱き、にこにこしながら主人に言いました。

　　「かわいい猫だね。私は猫が大好きなんだ。前に猫を飼っていたけど、
どこかに行っちゃって……。ご主人、この猫くれないか。」

20 「無理でございます。この猫は私の家
族みたいで、とてもかわいいんです。」
と主人は言いました。

　　「じゃあ、三両払うから、どうだ？」

　　三両というお金はとても大きいお
25 金です。

「わかりました。猫をさしあげましょう。」茶店の主人はうれしそうに言いました。

「やった！」

男は心の中で笑いました。そして主人に三両払って、言いました。

30　「この猫の皿もいっしょに持っていくよ。」

「それはさしあげられません。」主人は言いました。

「どうして。こんなきたない皿。いいだろう。」

男は何度も頼みましたが、主人は絶対に皿を渡しませんでした。

男はがっかりしました。その時、猫が男をひっかきました。

35　「痛い！　何だ、この猫！　こんな猫、いらないよ！」

皿はもらえないし、猫はひっかくし、最悪です。男は主人に聞いてみました。

「どうしてその皿を渡したくないんだ。」

「これはとてもめずらしい皿で、一枚三百両もいたします。家に置く

40　とあぶないので、こちらに持ってきたんです。」

主人は話を続けました。

「それに、ここに皿を置いておくと、時々猫が三両で売れるんですよ。」

C. 質問に答えてください。

1. 男はどんな仕事をしていましたか。

2. 茶店にあった皿の値段はいくらですか。

3. どうして男は猫をほしがったのですか。

4. 男はいくらで猫を買いましたか。

5. 男は皿を持って帰りましたか。

6. どうして主人は皿を茶店に置いておくのですか。

7. 茶店の主人と、男と、どちらがかしこい (clever) ですか。

Ⅲ 書く練習

A. 下のまんがを見て、話を考えて書きましょう。

(1)

根本進『クリちゃん＜みどりの本＞』
p. 4「あ　わすれちゃった」
（さ・え・ら書房、1978 年）

(2)

根本進『クリちゃん＜そらいろの本＞』
p. 18「きっとおかあさんがくるよ」
（さ・え・ら書房、1978 年）

B. あなたが知っているおもしろい話や楽しい話を書きましょう。

第21課 | L E S S O N 21

厄年 Unlucky Ages
やく　どし

発信（はっしん）=send email

272	信	▶しん (to trust; to believe)	信じる（しんじる）to believe
			自信（じしん）confidence　信号（しんごう）traffic signal
			迷信（めいしん）superstition
			(9) ノ イ イ 伫 伫 信 信 信 信
273	経	▶けい たつ (to pass through)	経験（けいけん）experience　経済（けいざい）economy
			神経質（しんけいしつ）over sensitive　経営学（けいえいがく）
			management studies　パリ経由（パリけいゆ）via Paris
			(11) く ⼅ ⼅ ⼅ ⼅ 糸 糸 紀 紀 経 経 経
274	台	▶たい　だい (stand)	台風（たいふう）typhoon
			二台（にだい）two vehicles/machines/etc.
			舞台（ぶたい）stage　台所（だいどころ）kitchen
			(5) ⼃ ム ⼺ 台 台
275	風	▶ふう　ふ ▷かぜ (wind)	台風（たいふう）typhoon
			お風呂（おふろ）bath　和風（わふう）Japanese style
			風（かぜ）wind　風邪をひく（かぜをひく）to catch a cold
			(9) ⼃ 几 几 凡 凡 凡 風 風 風
276	犬	▶けん ▷いぬ (dog)	犬（いぬ）dog
			子犬（こいぬ）puppy　番犬（ばんけん）watch dog
			盲導犬（もうどうけん）seeing-eye dog
			(4) 一 ナ 大 犬
277	重	▶じゅう ちょう ▷おも　かさ (heavy; to pile up)	重い（おもい）heavy; serious (illness)
			重ねる（かさねる）to pile up　体重（たいじゅう）body weight
			貴重品（きちょうひん）valuables
			(9) ⼀ ⼆ 亡 亡 宁 盲 重 重 重
278	初	▶しょ ▷はじ　はつ (first)	初めは（はじめは）at first　初めて（はじめて）first time
			最初（さいしょ）first　初雪（はつゆき）first snow
			初恋（はつこい）first love
			(7) ` ⼀ ⼆ ⼆ ネ 初 初
279	若	▷わか (young)	若い（わかい）young
			若者（わかもの）young people
			若々しい（わかわかしい）youthful
			(8) 一 ⼗ サ サ 芊 芋 若 若

洋風=ようふう=western style

和風=わふう Japanese style

和食=わしょく

秋田犬=あきたけん Akita breed of dog

初日の出=first sunrise of the year

初めは=at first

280	送 (to send)	▶そう ▷おく	送る（おくる）to send　送金（そうきん）sending money 送料（そうりょう）postage　放送（ほうそう）broadcast 回送電車（かいそうでんしゃ）out-of-service train　*送信*
			(9) 丶 ⺍ ⺌ ⺌ 关 关 关 送 送
281	幸 (happiness)	▶こう ▷しあわ 　さいわ	*不運＝bad luck* 幸せな（しあわせな）happy 幸福な（こうふくな）happy　幸運（こううん）good fortune 不幸（ふこう）misfortune　幸い（さいわい）fortunately
			(8) 一 十 土 圭 幸 幸 幸 幸
282	計 (to measure)	▶けい ▷はか	時計（とけい）a watch 計画（けいかく）plan　合計（ごうけい）sum 計る（はかる）to measure
			(9) 丶 二 ニ 言 言 言 言 計 計
283	遅 (late)	▶ち ▷おく　おそ	遅れる（おくれる）to be late　乗り遅れる（のりおくれる） to miss (transportation)　遅い（おそい）late 遅刻する（ちこくする）to be late
			(12) ⁻ ⁼ 尸 尸 尸 尸 屖 屖 犀 犀 遅 遅
284	配 (to deliver)	▶ぱい　はい ▷くば	心配な（しんぱいな）worried about 配る（くばる）to distribute　配達（はいたつ）delivery 宅配便（たくはいびん）home delivery service
			(10) 一 ⺀ 冂 卉 西 酉 酉 酉 配 配
285	弟 (younger brother)	▶だい　で ▷おとうと	弟（おとうと）younger brother　兄弟（きょうだい）brothers 弟子（でし）apprentice
			(7) 丶 丷 ⺍ 肖 弟 弟 弟
286	妹 (younger sister)	▶まい ▷いもうと	妹（いもうと）younger sister 姉妹（しまい）sisters　姉妹校（しまいこう）sister school
			(8) ⺅ 女 女 女 妹 妹 妹 妹

（▶ indicates the *on-yomi* and ▷ indicates the *kun-yomi*.)

Ⅰ 漢字の練習

A. 次の漢字の読み方を覚えましょう。太字は新しい読み方です。

入院 （にゅういん）　　食事 （しょくじ）　　時計 （とけい）

通う （かよう）　　心配 （しんぱい）

（☞　入 (072)　事 (078)　時 (015)　通 (193)　心 (265)）

B. 次の漢字を読みましょう。（答は次のページの下にあります。）

1. 起こる　　4. 病気　　7. 親　　10. 自転車

2. 昔　　5. 長い間　　8. 乗る　　11. 写真

3. 二十五歳　　6. 去年　　9. 部屋　　12. 悪い

Ⅱ 厄年

単語

迷信 （めいしん）　superstition	16 ぜいたくをする　to indulge in luxury [irr. verb]
起こる （おこる）　to occur; to happen [u-verb]	17 めったに〜ない　seldom
1 多くの〜 （おおくの〜）　many . . .	17 食事 （しょくじ）　meal
2 信じる （しんじる）　to believe [ru-verb]	21 ところが　however; on the contrary
4 ただの〜　nothing more than . . .	27 楽しみ （たのしみ）　pleasure
7 入院する （にゅういんする）　to be hospitalized [irr. verb]	28 通う （かよう）　to commute to （〜に） [u-verb]
9 占い （うらない）　fortunetelling	30 不便な （ふべんな）　inconvenient
9 気にする （きにする）　to worry [irr. verb]	35 心配な （しんぱいな）　worried about
11 長い間 （ながいあいだ）　long time	36 お守り （おまもり）　charm (against evils); amulet
12 一生懸命 （いっしょうけんめい）　very hard	

A. 質問に答えてください。

1. あなたの国にはどんな迷信がありますか。

例 (example)：黒い猫を見ると、悪いことが起こります。

2. 今までに悪いことがたくさん起こった時がありましたか。

その時どうしましたか。

B. 厄年の話を読みましょう。　🔊 Y21

> 厄年 (やくどし)　Critical or unlucky ages. According to Japanese folk belief, at certain ages an individual is most likely to experience calamities or misfortunes. It is customary in these unlucky years to visit temples and shrines.

1　　「厄年」という言葉を聞いたことがありますか。昔から多くの日本
人は、厄年に悪いことがよく起こると信じています。男の人の厄年は
二十五歳と四十二歳、女の人の厄年は十九歳と三十三歳です。これは
ただの迷信だと言う人もいますが、厄年に大変なことを経験する人も
5　多いそうです。ある友だちは台風で家が壊れてしまいました。ある友
だちは飼っていた犬に死なれました。また、ある友だちは急に重い病
気になって入院しなければいけませんでした。

　　私は今年が厄年です。友だちは気をつけたほうがいいと言いました
が、私は占いや迷信が大きらいなので、初めはぜんぜん気にしていま
10　せんでした。でも……

　　私は今、オーストラリアで勉強しています。外国で勉強するのは長
い間の夢でした。日本で大学を卒業してから、ずっと一生懸命仕事を
してお金をためました。そして、去年ここに来ました。

[I-B の答] 1. おこる　　　　4. びょうき　　　7. おや　　　　10. じてんしゃ
　　　　　　2. むかし　　　　5. ながいあいだ　8. のる　　　　11. しゃしん
　　　　　　3. にじゅうごさい　6. きょねん　　　9. へや　　　　12. わるい

15 ここには若い日本人の留学生がたくさんいます。みんな親にお金を送ってもらって、いいアパートに住んで、いい車に乗っています。休みには、いろいろな所に旅行に行ったりしています。私はそんなぜいたくができません。安いアパートに住んで、めったに外で食事をしたり、旅行に行ったりしません。でも、夢がかなったので、毎日がとても幸せでした。ほかの日本人をうらやましいと思ったことはありませ

20 んでした。

ところが、きのう大変なことがありました。アパートに帰った時、ドアのかぎが壊され、部屋がめちゃくちゃになっていたのです。びっくりして何が起こったのかわかりませんでした。でも、すぐ「どろぼうに入られた。」と気がつきました。

25 いろいろな物を取られました。パソコン、テレビ、カメラ、時計、そして自転車も。インターネットをしたり、テレビを見たりするのは、私の楽しみでした。カメラにはオーストラリアで初めて行った旅行の写真が入っていました。自転車は、学校に通う時使っていました。今日からバスで通わなければいけません。バスはよく遅れるし、一時間

30 に一台しか来ないから、とても不便です。

「どうしてどろぼうは私のアパートに入ったんだろう。どうしてお金持ちの日本人のアパートに入らなかったんだろう。」と思ってしまいました。日本人の友だちに話したら、「厄年だから、やっぱり悪いことが起こったんだよ。」と言われました。

35 今、とても心配です。また悪いことが起こるかもしれません。今度、弟か妹にお守りを送ってもらおうと思います。みなさんは厄年を信じますか。

C. 質問に答えてください。

1. 厄年にこの人の友だちはどんなことを経験しましたか。

   (1) _____

   (2) _____

   (3) _____

2. この人はオーストラリアに行く前、厄年を信じていましたか。

3. この人の夢は何でしたか。

4. この人と若い日本人の留学生は、どんなところが違いますか。

5. きのう何がありましたか。

6. 何を取られましたか。

7. 今日からどうやって学校に通いますか。

8. 友だちはどうして悪いことが起こったと思っていますか。

9. この人は今、厄年を信じていますか。

Ⅲ 書く練習

あなたの悪い経験について書きましょう。

第22課 | L E S S O N ·························22
友美さんの日記 Tomomi's Diary
ともみ

287 記 (to write down)	▶き	日記(にっき) diary 記入する(きにゅうする) to fill in　記事(きじ) an article; news 暗記する(あんきする) to memorize
		(10) ` ⸍ ⸾ 亖 言 言 言 訂 訂 記
288 銀 (silver)	▶ぎん	銀行(ぎんこう) bank 銀メダル(ぎんメダル) silver medal 銀世界(ぎんせかい) land covered with snow
		(14) ⼃ 𠂉 ⼂ 冬 年 缶 舎 金 釒 釘 釘 鈤 鈤 銀
289 回 (. . . times; to turn)	▶かい ▷まわ	一回(いっかい) one time 回送バス(かいそうバス) out-of-service bus　最終回(さいしゅうかい) last inning; last episode　回す(まわす) to turn
		(6) ⼁ 冂 冋 叵 回 回
290 夕 (evening)	▷ゆう	夕方(ゆうがた) evening 夕食(ゆうしょく) dinner　七夕(たなばた) *Tanabata* 夕日(ゆうひ) setting sun　夕刊(ゆうかん) evening newspaper
		(3) ⼃ ク 夕
291 黒 (black)	▶こく ▷くろ	黒木さん(くろきさん) Mr./Ms. Kuroki　黒い(くろい) black 白黒写真(しろくろしゃしん) black and white photograph 黒板(こくばん) blackboard
		(11) ⼃ 冂 甲 日 甲 甲 里 昗 黒 黒 黒
292 用 (task; to use)	▶よう	用事(ようじ) a thing to take care of 用意する(よういする) to prepare 子供用(こどもよう) for children　費用(ひよう) cost
		(5) ⼃ 刀 月 月 用
293 守 (to keep; to protect)	▶す しゅ ▷まも	留守(るす) absence; not at home 留守番電話(るすばんでんわ) answering machine お守り(おまもり) charm　守衛(しゅえい) security guard
		(6) ⼂ ⼍ 宀 宁 守 守
294 末 (the end of)	▶まつ ▷すえ	週末(しゅうまつ) weekend 月末(げつまつ) end of the month　年末(ねんまつ) year-end 期末試験(きまつしけん) final examination　末(すえ) the end
		(5) ⼀ 二 十 才 末

295 待 (to wait)	▶たい ▷ま　まち	待つ (まつ) to wait 待合室 (まちあいしつ) waiting room 期待する (きたいする) to expect　招待 (しょうたい) invitation
		(9) ノ　ク　イ　彳　彳　往　往　待　待
296 残 (to remain)	▶ざん ▷のこ	残業 (ざんぎょう) over-time work　残す (のこす) to leave 残念 (ざんねん) regrettable　心残り (こころのこり) regret 残高 (ざんだか) account balance
		(10) 一　ア　ヲ　歹　歹　歹　歼　残　残　残
297 番 (order; number)	▶ばん	留守番電話 (るすばんでんわ) answering machine 一番 (いちばん) the first 番号 (ばんごう) number　番組 (ばんぐみ) TV program
		(12) ノ　ハ　ハ　平　平　平　来　来　乑　番　番　番
298 駅 (station)	▶えき	駅 (えき) station　東京駅 (とうきょうえき) Tokyo Station 駅員 (えきいん) station attendant 駅前 (えきまえ) vicinity; in front of the station
		(14) l　厂　F　F　E　馬　馬　馬　馬　馬　駅　駅　駅
299 説 (theory; to explain)	▶せつ　せっ	説明する (せつめいする) to explain　小説 (しょうせつ) novel 小説家 (しょうせつか) novelist 説教する (せっきょうする) to preach
		(14) 、　ヒ　ヒ　言　言　言　言　訪　訪　訪　訪　説
300 案 (idea; proposal)	▶あん	案内する (あんないする) to guide 案内所 (あんないじょ) information desk 案 (あん) idea; proposal　提案 (ていあん) proposal
		(10) 、　宀　宀　安　安　安　宰　案　案
301 内 (inside; inner)	▶ない ▷うち	案内する (あんないする) to guide 家内 (かない) my wife　国内 (こくない) domestic 内科 (ないか) internal medicine　内側 (うちがわ) inside
		(4) l　冂　内　内
302 忘 (to forget)	▶ぼう ▷わす	忘れる (わすれる) to forget 忘れ物 (わすれもの) lost article 忘年会 (ぼうねんかい) year-end party
		(7) 、　亠　亡　忘　忘　忘

(▶ indicates the *on-yomi* and ▷ indicates the *kun-yomi*.)

① 漢字の練習

A. 次の漢字の読み方を覚えましょう。太字は新しい読み方です。

日記（にっき）　　夕方（ゆうがた）　　親友（しんゆう）

説明（せつめい）　　代わりに（かわりに）

二日間（ふつかかん）　　留守番電話（るすばんでんわ）

（☞　日 (016)　方 (205)　明 (120)　代 (163)　二 (002)　留 (164)）

B. 次の漢字を読みましょう。（答は下にあります。）

1. 東京　　3. 彼女　　5. 後は　　7. 何度も　　9. 本当に

2. 一か月　　4. 急に　　6. 夜　　8. 先週

② 友美さんの日記

単語

5 うらやましがる　(somebody is) envious	23 なんだか　somehow
6 帰ってくる（かえってくる）to come back home [irr. verb]	24 しかたがない　cannot be helped
8 相変わらず（あいかわらず）as usual	25 ホーム　platform
11 タイプ　type	25 楽しそうに（たのしそうに）joyfully
13 うまく　well; successfully; skillfully　うまくいく　to go well [u-verb]	27 親友（しんゆう）best friend
20 待ち遠しい（まちどおしい）to wait eagerly for . . .（〜が）	33 勇気（ゆうき）courage
	33 逃げる（にげる）to run away; to escape [ru-verb]
23 伝言（でんごん）message	35 代わりに（かわりに）instead
	36 二日間（ふつかかん）for two days

[①-B の答] 1. とうきょう　3. かのじょ　5. あとは　7. なんども　9. ほんとうに　　2. いっかげつ　4. きゅうに　6. よる　8. せんしゅう

A. 質問に答えてください。

1. あなたは日記を書きますか。日記にどんなことを書きますか。

2. 彼や彼女がいない時、友だちにだれか紹介してもらったことがありますか。

B. 友美さんの日記を読みましょう。 [♨)]Y22

1 三月二十一日（日）

　　研一に会いに東京に行った。彼が東京の銀行に就職してからもう二
年がたつ。大学の時は毎日会っていたのに、今は私が東京に行ったり、
彼が大阪に来たりして一か月に一回ぐらいしか会えない。夏子はいつ
5 も私たちのことをうらやましがっているけど、東京まで会いに行くの
は大変。早く大阪に帰ってきてほしい。

四月二十三日（金）

　　今日は研一が大阪に来て、夕方お酒を飲みに行った。研一は相変わ
らず仕事が忙しそうだ。研一の同僚の黒木さんが彼女を探していると
10 聞いた。東京に行った時、研一に紹介してもらったけど、すごくおも
しろくていい人だ。黒木さんは夏子のように静かな人がタイプかもし
れない。今度二人を会わせようと思う。夏子が東京に行った時、研一
が黒木さんを紹介する予定。うまくいくといいけど。

五月十二日（水）

15 　　今日の夏子はちょっと変だった。東京のことを聞いてみたが、あま
り話してくれなかった。黒木さんに急に用事ができて、会えなかった
と言っただけで、後は話したくなさそうだった。夜、研一に何度も電
話したけど、出なかった。研一ならいろいろ教えてくれると思ったの
に、残念。仕事が忙しいんだろう。でも、週末は大阪で会える。今か
20 ら待ち遠しい。

五月十四日（金）

今日も残業で疲れた。それに「急に出張が入って大阪に行けなくなった」という研一の伝言が留守番電話に残されていた。なんだか落ち込んでしまった。仕事だからしかたがないけど。

帰る時、駅のホームで夏子を見た。男の人と一緒に楽しそうに話していた。顔は見えなかったけど、背が高い男の人だった。彼ができたのかな。どうして私に言ってくれないんだろう。親友なのに。

五月二十二日（土）

今日研一から手紙が来た。……

友美へ

　友美に手紙を書くのは本当にひさしぶりだね。ぼくは友美にうそをついていた。ずっと言わなきゃいけないと思っていたんだけど、勇気がなくて今まで逃げていた。うまく説明できるといいんだが……。夏子さんが東京に来た時、黒木は急に用事ができて、来られなくなってしまった。それで、ぼくが代わりに二日間東京を案内してあげたんだ。美術館に行ったり、東京ディズニーランドに行ったりして、楽しかった。彼女が大阪に帰った後も、彼女のことが忘れられなかった。先週の週末、「出張で大阪に行けない」と言ったけど、本当は大阪で夏子さんに会っていたんだ。

C. 正しいものに○をつけてください。

(　　) 1. 研一は今東京に住んでいる。

(　　) 2. いつも研一と友美は大阪で会っていた。

(　　) 3. 研一と黒木は同じ銀行で働いている。

(　　) 4. 夏子は東京で黒木に会った。

(　　) 5. 研一は出張に行っていたから、友美に会えなかった。

D. 質問に答えてください。

1. 友美が夏子に東京のことを聞いた時、夏子はどうしてあまり話したがらなかったのですか。

2. 研一は友美にどんなうそをつきましたか。どうしてうそをついたのですか。

3. あなたが研一／友美／夏子だったら、どうしますか。

Ⅲ 書く練習

A. 二か月後の友美の日記を書きましょう。

B. 自分の日記を書きましょう。

第23課 | L E S S O N ⋯⋯⋯⋯ 23
これはどんな顔? What Does This Face Mean?

303	顔 (face)	▶がん ▷かお　がお	顔(かお) face
			顔色(かおいろ) complexion　笑顔(えがお) smiling face 洗顔(せんがん) washing one's face
			⑱ ` 亠 ナ ヰ 立 产 产 彦 彦 彦 彦 產 節 顏 顏 顏 顏 顏

304	情 (emotion; condition)	▶じょう ▷なさ	表情(ひょうじょう) expression
			友情(ゆうじょう) friendship　情報(じょうほう) information 情け(なさけ) mercy
			⑪ ` ｀ 忄 忄 忄 忭 忭 情 情 情 情

305	怒 (to get angry)	▶ど ▷おこ　いか	怒る(おこる) to get angry
			怒り(いかり) anger; rage 喜怒哀楽(きどあいらく) human emotions
			⑨ く 夕 夕 如 奴 奴 怒 怒 怒

306	変 (change; abnormal)	▶へん ▷か	変な(へんな) strange　大変な(たいへんな) tough; hectic
			変化(へんか) change　変人(へんじん) eccentric person 変える(かえる) to change (something)
			⑨ ` 亠 ナ 亣 亣 亦 亦 変 変

307	相 (mutual)	▶しょう　そう ▷あい	相手(あいて) partner
			首相(しゅしょう) prime minister　相談(そうだん) consultation 相互の(そうごの) mutual
			⑨ 一 十 オ 木 朾 相 相 相 相

308	横 (sideways)	▶おう ▷よこ	横(よこ) side　横書き(よこがき) horizontal writing
			横綱(よこづな) grand champion of sumo 横断する(おうだんする) to traverse
			⑮ 一 十 オ 木 朾 栏 栏 栏 栏 栫 横 横 横 横

よこ　ばい　= cutting in line
横入り

309	比 (to compare)	▶ひ ▷くら	比べる(くらべる) to compare
			比較(ひかく) comparison　比例(ひれい) proportion 対比(たいひ) contrast　比喩(ひゆ) figure of speech
			④ 一 ヒ ヒ 比

310	化 (to change into)	▶か　け ▷ば	文化(ぶんか) culture
			化学(かがく) chemistry　同化(どうか) assimilation お化け(おばけ) goblin; ghost　化粧(けしょう) makeup
			④ ノ イ 仁 化

311	違 (to differ)	▶い ▷ちが	違う（ちがう）different 間違える（まちがえる）to make a mistake 違法（いほう）illegal　違反（いはん）violation
		(13)	⼀ ⼗ ⼟ ⼟ ⼟ ⼟ ⼟ ⼟ ⾱ ⾱ ⾱ 違 違

312	悲 (sad)	▶ひ ▷かな	悲しい（かなしい）sad 悲劇（ひげき）tragedy　悲惨な（ひさんな）miserable 悲しむ（かなしむ）to grieve
		(12)	） ⼅ ⼅ ⼅ ⼅ 非 非 非 非 悲 悲 悲

313	調 (to investigate)	▶ちょう ▷しら	調査（ちょうさ）survey; research　調べる（しらべる）to look into 調子（ちょうし）condition 強調する（きょうちょうする）to emphasize
		(15)	` ⼆ ⼆ ⼆ ⼊ 言 言 言 訂 訂 訂 調 調 調 調

314	査 (to inspect)	▶さ	調査（ちょうさ）survey; research 検査（けんさ）inspection　審査（しんさ）screening 捜査（そうさ）criminal investigation
		(9)	⼀ ⼗ ⼤ ⽊ ⽊ 杏 杏 查 查

315	果 (fruit; result)	▶か ▷は	結果（けっか）result 果汁（かじゅう）fruit juice　効果（こうか）effect 使い果たす（つかいはたす）to use up　果物（くだもの）fruit
		(8)	） ⼝ ⼞ ⽇ ⽇ 甲 果 果

316	感 (to sense; to feel)	▶かん	感情（かんじょう）emotion　感動する（かんどうする）to be moved 感じる（かんじる）to feel　感謝（かんしゃ）gratitude 感想（かんそう）impression　第六感 ＝ 6th sense
		(13)	） ⼚ ⼚ ⼚ ⼚ ⼚ 咸 咸 咸 感 感 感 感

317	答 (answer)	▶とう ▷こた　こたえ	答える（こたえる）to answer　答え/答（こたえ）answer 回答（かいとう）reply; answer 答案（とうあん）examination paper
		(12)	） ⼂ ⽵ ⽵ 竹 竹 竹 答 答 答 答 答

（▶ indicates the *on-yomi* and ▷ indicates the *kun-yomi*.）

Ⅰ 漢字の練習

A. 次の漢字の読み方を覚えましょう。太字は新しい読み方です。

最初（さいしょ）　最後（さいご）　口（くち）　人間（にんげん）

社会（しゃかい）　表す（あらわす）　全員（ぜんいん）

（☞　初 (278)　口 (048)　間 (095)　表 (217)）

B. 次の漢字を読みましょう。（答は下にあります。）

1. 二つ　　4. 気持ち　　7. 同じ　　10. 留学生

2. 笑う　　5. 文字　　6. 使う

3. 自分　　6. 使う　　8. 最近　　9. 研究

3. 自分　　　　　　9. 研究

Ⅱ これはどんな顔?

単　語

表情（ひょうじょう）facial expression
1 マーク　mark
3 最初の〜（さいしょの〜）first . . .
3 最後の〜（さいごの〜）last . . .
5 気持ち（きもち）feeling
6 冗談（じょうだん）joke
8 簡単に（かんたんに）easily
10 バンザイをする　to raise hands and shout "Banzai!"
12 横（よこ）side; horizontal
13 比べる（くらべる）to compare [ru-verb]
15 縦（たて）vertical

17 このように　like this; this way
17 〜によって　depending on . . .
17 人間（にんげん）human being
21 ほとんど　almost
21 同じような（おなじような）similar
24 調査（ちょうさ）survey
24 結果（けっか）result
26 感情（かんじょう）feeling; emotion
26 表す（あらわす）to express; to show [u-verb]
27 全員（ぜんいん）all members
29 答え（こたえ）answer

[Ⅰ-B の答] 1. ふたつ　4. きもち　7. おなじ　10. りゅうがくせい
2. わらう　5. もじ　8. さいきん
3. じぶん　6. つかう　9. けんきゅう

A. 質問に答えてください。

1. 次の顔はどんな表情だと思いますか。

a. 　　　　b.

2. あなたは、びっくりした時／うれしい時／怒った時、どんな顔をしますか。
やってみましょう。

B. 次の話を読みましょう。Y23

1　　友だちからメールをもらうと、時々変なマークが書いてあります。
アメリカやオーストラリアの友だちから来るメールでは :-D や :-)、:-(
などのマークを見ます。最初の二つはうれしくて笑っている顔、最後
のマークはあまりうれしくない時の顔です。このようなマークを「顔
5　文字」といいます。文字だけでは自分の気持ちが相手にわかってもら
えないと思った時、「これは冗談ですよ、私がにこにこしながらこれ
を書いているのがわかりますか」と説明するのは大変ですが、顔文字
を使えば、同じことがとても簡単に伝えられます。
　　日本人もメールでよく顔文字を使います。うれしい時の顔は (^_^)
10　や (^^) です。もっとうれしい時は、「バンザイ」をさせて、\(^o^)/ と
書きます。(^^)v もうれしい時の顔です。日本人が写真を撮っている
のを見たことがある*人は、顔の横の v が何かわかるでしょう。

---

l. 11　日本人が写真を撮っているのを見たことがある (have seen Japanese people taking pictures)
〜ているの is used with verbs like 見る, 見える, and 聞こえる to describe an ongoing situation which is seen
or heard.
　　メアリーさんが図書館で勉強しているのを見ました。　　*I saw Mary studying in the library.*
　　スーさんが歌っているのが聞こえる。　　*We can hear Sue singing.*

英語の顔文字と日本語の顔文字を比べると、おもしろいことに気が
つきます。まず、英語の顔文字は顔が横になっていますが、日本語の

15　顔文字は縦になっています。また、英語では口が笑っていますが、日
本語では目が笑っています。

　このように、言葉や文化によって顔文字は違いますが、人間の表情
はどうでしょうか。みなさんは、ほかの国から来た人の表情を見た時、
その人がどんな気持ちかわかりますか。

20　最近の研究によると、うれしい時の顔とびっくりした時の顔は、言
葉や文化が違っても、ほとんど同じようです。ところが、悲しい時や
怒っている時の表情は、国や社会によってずいぶん違うことがわかり
ました。

　ある調査の結果を見てみましょう。この調査では、日本人の大学生

25　とアメリカから日本に来ている留学生に写真を見せて、それがどんな
感情を表している写真か答えてもらいました。

(1) 　　(2)

　(1)の写真を見た時は、日本人もアメリカ人も、ほとんど全員が、
これは「うれしい」表情だと答えました。ところが、(2)の写真を見
た時は、国によって答えが少し違いました。日本人はこの写真を見て、

30　ほとんど全員が「怒っている」と答えましたが、アメリカ人は66%

---

l. 22　**ずいぶん違うことがわかりました**

ずいぶん違うこと means "the fact that (expressions) differ significantly." Verbs like わかる and 知っている
are used with a clause ＋ こと to describe the fact that is known.

　考え方が違うことがわかる。　　*We can conclude that they think differently.*

　メアリーさんがスペイン語が話せることを知っています。　　*I know that Mary speaks Spanish.*

しかそう考えませんでした。ほかの調査では、ある写真を見て、アメ
リカ人の十人に九人が「こわい」という気持ちを表している表情だと
考えましたが、日本人は十人に六人が「悲しい」表情だと答えました。

35 みなさんは、日本語を勉強している時や日本人と話している時、「日
本人はずいぶん私と違う」と思ったり、「ああ、やっぱり日本人も、
私と同じ人間なんだ」と思ったりしませんか。表情や身ぶりについて
も、同じようなことが言えるかもしれません。

C. 質問に答えてください。

1. :-D や :-) はどんな気持ちを表していますか。

2. どうしてメールで顔文字を使うのですか。

3. (^_^)、(^^)、\(^o^)/ の中で、どれが一番うれしそうですか。
   どうしてですか。

4. (^^)v は何を表していますか。

5. 英語と日本語の顔文字は、何が違いますか。

6. (1) の写真を見て、日本人はどう思いましたか。アメリカ人はどうですか。

7. (2) の写真を見て、日本人はどう思いましたか。アメリカ人はどうですか。

D. 次の顔文字はどんな意味か考えましょう。

1. m(_ _)m   4. (>_<)   7. (-_-〆)

2. (^o^)/   5. (^_-)   8. (@_@)

3. φ(^o^)   6. (-_-;)   9. (-_-)zzz

Ⅲ 書く練習

A. 日本人の友だちに、顔文字を使ってメールを書きましょう。

B. 日本語を勉強している時や日本人と話している時、自分と日本人はどんなところが違うと思いますか。書きましょう。

巻末
<ruby>かん<rt></rt></ruby> <ruby>まつ<rt></rt></ruby>
Appendix

さくいん 1 J a p a n e s e - E n g l i s h

いつか　五日　five days　会L13

いつか　五日　the fifth day of a month 会L4(e)

いっさい　一歳　one year old　会L1(e)

いっしょうけんめい　一生懸命　very hard　読L21-II

いっしょうにいちど　一生に一度　once in a lifetime　読L13-II

いっしょに　一緒に　together　会L5

いつつ　五つ　five　会L9

いってきます　I'll go and come back.　会G

いってらっしゃい　Please go and come back.　会G

いっぱくにしょくつき　一泊二食付 one night with two meals　会L15(e)

いっぷん　一分　one minute　会L1(e)

いつも　always　読L6-III, 会L8

いなか　countryside　読L20-II

いなくなる　(someone) is gone; to disappear [u]　会L23

いぬ　犬　dog　会L4

いま　今　now　会L1

いますぐ　今すぐ　right away　会L18

いみ　意味　meaning　会L11(e), 会L12

いもうと（さん）　妹（さん）　younger sister　会L1, 会L7

いや　no　会L23

いらっしゃいます　(someone honorable) is present/home　会L13

いらっしゃいませ　Welcome (to our store).　会L2

いらっしゃる　honorific expression for いく, くる, and いる [u]　会L19

いりぐち　入口　entrance　会L10(e)

いる　(a person) is in . . . ; stays at . . . [ru]　会L4

いる　to need [u]　会L8

いれる　to make tea, coffee, etc. [ru]　会L17

いれる　入れる　to put (something) in [ru]　会L16

いろ　色　color　会L9

いろいろ（な）　various; different kinds of 読L9-II, 会L13

インターネット　Internet　会L15

ううん　uh-uh; no　会L8

うえ　上　on　会L4

ウエイター　waiter　会L13

うかがう　伺う　to humbly visit; to humbly ask [u]　会L20

うけつけ　受付　reception desk　会L22

うける　受ける　to take (an examination, interview, etc.) [ru]　読L19-III, 会L23

うし　牛　cow　読L12-II

うしろ　後ろ　back　会L4

うそをつく　to tell a lie [u]　会L11

うた　歌　song　会L7

うたう　歌う　to sing [u]　会L7

うち　home; house; my place　会L3

うちゅうじん　宇宙人　space alien　会L20

うちゅうひこうし　宇宙飛行士 astronaut　会L11

うつす　写す　to copy [u]　読L16-II

うまく　well; successfully; skillfully 読L22-II

うまくいく　to go well [u]　読L22-II

うまれる　生まれる　to be born [ru] 読L15-II, 会L17

うみ　海　sea　会L5

うらない　占い　fortunetelling　読L21-II

うらやましい　envious　会L17

うらやましがる　(somebody is) envious 読L22-II

うる　売る　to sell [u]　読L10-II, 会L15

うるさい　noisy; annoying　会L22

うれしい　glad　会L13

うれる　売れる　to be sold [ru]　読L20-II

うん　uh-huh; yes　会L8

うんてんする　運転する　to drive [irr.] 会L8

うんどうする　運動する　to do physical exercises [irr.]　会L9

え　絵　painting; picture; drawing　会L15

エアコン　air conditioner　会L18

えいが　映画　movie　会L3

えいかいわ　英会話　English conversation　会L22

えいがかん　映画館　movie theater　会L15

えいきょうをうける　影響を受ける　to be affected [ru]　読L17-II

えいご　英語　English language　会L1

ええ　yes　会L1

ええと　well . . . ; let me see . . .　会L16

えき　駅　station　読L6-I, 会L10

えきいん（さん）　駅員（さん）　station attendant　会L16

えさ　feed　読L20-II

えど　江戸　former name of Tokyo 読L20-II

えどじだい　江戸時代　Edo period 読L20-II

えらぶ　選ぶ　to choose; to select [u] 会L17

～えん　～円　. . . yen　会L2

えんぴつ　鉛筆　pencil　会L2, 会L2(e)

えんりょする　遠慮する　to hold back for the time being; to refrain from [irr.] 会L19

おあずけいれ　お預け入れ　deposit 会L13(e)

おいしい　delicious　会L2

おいのりする　お祈りする　to pray [irr.] 会L17

おうふく　往復　round trip　会L10(e)

おおい　多い　there are many . . .　会L12

おおきい　大きい　large　会L5

おおきさ　大きさ　size　会L16

おおくの～　多くの～　many . . . 読L21-II

オーストラリア　Australia　会L1, 会L11

おおやさん　大家さん　landlord; landlady　会L14

おかあさん　お母さん　mother 会L1, 会L2

おかえし　お返し　return (as a token gratitude)　会L14

おかえり（なさい）　Welcome home.　会G

おかげで　thanks to . . .　会L18

おかし　お菓子　snack; sweets　会L11

おかね　お金　money　会L6

おかねもち　お金持ち　rich person　会L10

おきゃくさん　お客さん　guest; visitor; client; customer　会L17

おきる　起きる　to get up [ru]　会L3

おく　置く　to put; to lay; to place [u] 会L21

おくさま　奥様　(your/his) wife (polite) 会L19

おくさん　奥さん　(your/his) wife　会L14

おくる　送る　to send [u]　会L14

おくる　送る　to walk/drive (someone) [u] 会L19

おくれる　遅れる　to become late [ru] 会L19

おこさん　お子さん　(your/their) child (polite)　会L19

おこす　起こす　to wake (someone) up [u] 会L16

おこる　怒る　to get angry [u] 読L12-II, 会L19

おこる　起こる　to occur; to happen [u] 読L21-II

おごる　to treat (someone) to a meal [u] 会L16

おさきにしつれいします　お先に失礼します　See you. (lit., I'm leaving ahead of you.)　会L18

おさけ　お酒　sake; alcohol　会L3

おじいさん　grandfather; old man　会L7

おしえる　教える　to teach; to instruct [ru]　会L6

おじさん　uncle; middle-aged man　会L14

おじぞうさん　guardian deity of children
　　　　　　　読L10-II

おしょうがつ　お正月　New Year's
　　　　　　　読L10-II, 会L11

おじょうさん　お嬢さん　(someone's)
　daughter (polite)　会L22

おしり　buttocks　会L7(e)

おしろ　お城　castle　読L5-II

おす　押す　to press; to push [u]　会L18

おせわになる　お世話になる　to be in
　someone's care [u]　読L19-II, 会L23

おそい　遅い　slow; late　会L10

おそく　遅く　(do something) late
　　　　　　　読L4-III, 会L6

おそくなる　遅くなる　to be late [u]
　　　　　　　会L8

おだいじに　お大事に　Get well soon.
　　　　　　　会L12

おたく　お宅　(someone's) house/home
　　　　　　　会L13

おちこむ　落ち込む　to get depressed [u]
　　　　　　　会L16

おちゃ　お茶　green tea　会L3

おちる　落ちる　(something) drops [ru]
　　　　　　　会L18

おつかれさま(でした)　お疲れ様(でし
　た)　You must be tired after working so
　hard. (ritualistic expression)　会L18

おっしゃる　honorific expression for いう
　[u]　会L19

おてあらい　お手洗い　restroom　会L12

おてら　お寺　temple　会L4

おと　音　sound　会L20

おとうさん　お父さん　father
　　　　　　　会L1, 会L2

おとうと(さん)　弟(さん)　younger
　brother　会L1, 会L7

おとこ　男　man　読L11-II, 会L17

おとこのこ　男の子　boy　会L11

おとこのひと　男の人　man　会L7

おとされる　落とされる　to be dropped
　　　　　　　読L15-II

おとす　落とす　to drop (something) [u]
　　　　　　　会L18

おととい　the day before yesterday
　　　　　　　会L4(e), 会L19

おととし　the year before last　会L4(e)

おとな　大人　adult　読L12-II, 会L13

おどる　踊る　to dance [u]　会L9

おなか　stomach　会L7(e), 会L12

おなかがすく　to become hungry [u]
　　　　　　　会L11

おなかをこわす　to have a stomachache
　[u]　会L23

おなじ　同じ　same　読L13-III, 会L14

おなじような　同じような　similar
　　　　　　　読L23-II

おにいさん　お兄さん　older brother
　　　　　　　会L1, 会L7

おにぎり　rice ball　会L20

おねえさん　お姉さん　older sister
　　　　　　　会L1, 会L7

おねがいします(〜を)　. . ., please.　会L2

おねがいする　お願いする　to pray for
　help [irr.]　会L22

おばあさん　grandmother; old woman
　　　　　　　会L7

おばさん　aunt; middle-aged woman
　　　　　　　会L14

おはよう　Good morning.　会G

おはようございます　Good morning.
　(polite)　会G

おひきだし　お引き出し　withdrawal
　　　　　　　会L13(e)

おふりこみ　お振込　bank transfer
　　　　　　　会L13(e)

おふろ　お風呂　bath　会L6

おふろにはいる　お風呂に入る　to take
　a bath [u]　会L6

おへんじ　お返事　reply　読L11-II

おべんとう　お弁当　boxed lunch　会L9

おぼえる　覚える　to memorize [ru]
　　　　　　　会L9

おまつり　お祭り　festival　会L11

おまもり　お守り　charm (against evils);
　amulet　読L21-II

おまんじゅう　sweet bun　読L4-III

おみやげ　お土産　souvenir　会L4

おめでとうございます　Congratulations!
　　　　　　　会L17

おもい　重い　heavy; serious (illness)
　　　　　　　会L20

おもいだす　思い出す　to recall [u]
　　　　　　　読L19-II

おもいで　思い出　memory　会L23

おもう　思う　to think [u]　会L8

おもしろい　面白い　interesting; funny
　　　　　　　会L5

おもち　rice cake　読L10-II

おもちゃ　toy　会L11

おもに　主に　mainly　読L17-II

おや　親　parent　会L16

おや?　Oh!　会L20

おやすみ(なさい)　Good night.　会G

おやすみになる　お休みになる
　honorific expression for ねる [u]　会L19

おゆ　お湯　hot water　会L17

おゆがわく　お湯が沸く　water boils [u]
　　　　　　　会L18

おゆをわかす　お湯を沸かす　to boil
　water [u]　会L17

およぐ　泳ぐ　to swim [u]　会L5

おりる　降りる　to get off [ru]　会L6

おる　extra-modest expression for いる [u]
　　　　　　　会L20

おれい　お礼　expression of gratitude
　　　　　　　会L19

おろす　下ろす　to withdraw (money) [u]
　　　　　　　会L15

おわる　終わる　(something) ends [u]
　　　　　　　会L9

おんがく　音楽　music　会L3

おんせん　温泉　spa; hot spring　会L11

おんな　女　woman　読L11-II, 会L17

おんなのこ　女の子　girl　会L11

おんなのひと　女の人　woman　会L7

━━━━━ **か** ━━━━━

か　蚊　mosquito　会L21

〜か〜　or　会L10

〜が　. . ., but　読L5-II, 会L7

カーテン　curtain　会L2(e), 会L18

〜かい　〜階　. . .th floor　会L20

〜かい　〜回　. . . times　会L13

かいがいりょこう　海外旅行　trip to a
　foreign country　会L23

かいぎ　会議　business meeting;
　conference　会L21

がいこく　外国　foreign country　会L11

がいこくご　外国語　foreign language
　　　　　　　会L13

がいこくじん　外国人　foreigner　会L15

かいさつ　改札　gate　会L10(e)

かいしゃ　会社　company　会L7

かいしゃいん　会社員　office worker
　　　　　　　会L1, 会L8

かいすうけん　回数券　coupons
　　　　　　　会L10(e)

かいだん　階段　stairs　会L10(e)

かいもの　買い物　shopping　会L4

かう　買う　to buy [u]　会L4

かう　飼う　to own (a pet) [u]　会L11

かえす　返す　to return (a thing) [u]　会L6

かえってくる　帰ってくる　to come
　back home [irr.]　読L22-II

かえる　換える　to change [ru]　会L23

かえる　帰る　to go back; to return [u]
　　　　　　　会L3

かお　顔　face　会L7(e), 会L10

かおがあおい　顔が青い　to look pale
　　　　　　　会L9(e)

〜かおをする　〜顔をする　to look . . .
　(facial expression) [irr.]　会L23

かがく　科学　science　会L1

かかりのもの　係の者　our person in charge　会L20

かかる　to take (amount of time/money) [u]　会L10

かぎ　lock; key　会L17

かきとめ　書留　registered mail　会L5(e)

かぎをかける　to lock [ru]　会L17

かく　描く　to draw; to paint [u]　会L15

かく　書く　to write [u]　会L4

かぐ　家具　furniture　会L15

がくせい　学生　student　会L1

がくわり　学割　student discount　会L10(e)

〜かげつ　〜か月　for . . . months　会L10

かける　to sit down [ru]　会L19

かける（めがねを）　to put on (glasses) [ru]　会L7

かさ　bamboo hat　読L10-II

かさ　傘　umbrella　会L2

かし　菓子　snack; sweets　会L11

かじ　火事　fire　会L17

かじ　家事　household matters　会L22

かしこまりました　Certainly.　会L20

かしゅ　歌手　singer　会L11

かす　貸す　to lend; to rent [u]　会L13

かぜ　風邪　cold　会L12

かぜ　風　wind　会L22

かぜがふく　風が吹く　the wind blows [u]　会L22

かぜをひく　風邪をひく　to catch a cold [u]　会L12

かぞえる　数える　to count [ru]　読L17-II

かぞく　家族　family　会L7

ガソリン　gasoline　会L21

かた　肩　shoulder　会L7(e)

かたいいいかた　かたい言い方　bookish expression　会L11(e)

かたづける　片付ける　to tidy up [ru]　会L18

かたみち　片道　one way　会L10(e)

かつ　勝つ　to win [u]　会L22

がっかりする　to be disappointed [irr.]　読L20-II, 会L23

がっき　楽器　musical instrument　会L13

かっこ　parenthesis　会L11(e)

かっこいい　good-looking　会L5

がっこう　学校　school　会L3

カット　cut　会L17(e)

かつどう　活動　activities　読L17-II

かていきょうし　家庭教師　tutor　読L18-III

かど　角　corner　会L6(e), 会L20

〜かな（あ）　I wonder . . . (casual)　会L17

かなう　to be realized [u]　読L12-II

かなしい　悲しい　sad　読L10-II, 会L13

かね　金　money　会L6

かねもち　金持ち　rich person　会L10

かのじょ　彼女　girlfriend　読L11-II, 会L12

かばん　bag　会L2, 会L2(e)

かぶき　歌舞伎　Kabuki; traditional Japanese theatrical art　会L9

かぶせる　to put (a hat) on a person's head [ru]　読L10-II

かぶる　to put on (a hat) [u]　会L7

がまんする　我慢する　to be tolerant/patient [irr.]　会L23

かみ　髪　hair　会L7, 会L7(e)

かみ　紙　paper　会L17

かみがた　髪形　hair style　会L17(e)

かみさま　神様　God　読L12-II, 会L22

かみをとかす　髪をとかす　to comb one's hair [u]　会L17

かめ　turtle　読L13-II

カメラ　camera　会L8

かよう　通う　to commute to [u]　読L21-II

かようび　火曜日　Tuesday　会L4, 会L4(e)

〜から　because . . .　会L6

〜から　from . . .　読L7-II, 会L9

からい　辛い　hot and spicy; salty　会L13

カラオケ　karaoke　会L8

からだ　体　body　読L13-II, 会L23

からだにいい　体にいい　good for health　読L13-II

からだにきをつける　体に気をつける　to take care of oneself [ru]　読L7-II

からて　空手　karate　会L13

かりる　借りる　to borrow [ru]　会L6

かる　刈る　to crop [u]　会L17(e)

かるい　軽い　light　会L20

かれ　彼　boyfriend　会L12

カレー　curry　会L13

かわ　川　river　会L11

かわいい　cute　会L7

かわいそう（な）　pitiful　読L12-II

かわりに　代わりに　instead　読L22-II

がんか　眼科　ophthalmologist　会L12(e)

かんがえる　考える　to think (about); to consider [ru]　読L13-III, 会L18

かんきょう　環境　environment　会L21

かんこうする　観光する　to do sightseeing [irr.]　会L15

かんこく　韓国　Korea　会L1, 会L2

かんごし　看護師　nurse　会L11

かんじ　漢字　kanji; Chinese character　会L6

かんじょう　感情　feeling; emotion　読L23-II

かんせいする　完成する　to be completed [irr.]　読L17-II

かんたん（な）　簡単　easy; simple　会L10

かんたんに　簡単に　easily　読L23-II

かんどうする　感動する　to be moved/touched (by . . .) [irr.]　会L13

かんぱい　乾杯　Cheers! (a toast)　会L8

がんばる　頑張る　to do one's best; to try hard [u]　会L13

き　木　tree　会L22

きいろい　黄色い　yellow　会L9(e)

きえる　消える　(something) goes off [ru]　会L18

きおん　気温　temperature (weather)　会L12

きがえる　着替える　to change clothes [ru]　会L21

きがつく　気が付く　to notice [u]　会L21

きく　聞く　to ask [u]　会L5

きく　聞く　to listen; to hear [u]　会L3

きこえる　聞こえる　to be audible [ru]　会L20

きせつ　季節　season　会L10

きた　北　north　会L6(e)

ギター　guitar　会L9

きたない　汚い　dirty　会L16

きつえんルーム　喫煙ルーム　smoking room　会L15(e)

きっさてん　喫茶店　cafe　会L2

きって　切手　postal stamps　会L5, 会L5(e)

きっぷ　切符　ticket　会L5

きっぷうりば　切符売り場　ticket vending area　会L10(e)

きにいる　気に入る　to find something agreeable [u]　会L23

きにする　気にする　to worry [irr.]　読L21-II

きのう　昨日　yesterday　会L4, 会L4(e)

きびしい　厳しい　strict　会L13

きぶんがわるい　気分が悪い　to feel sick　読L13-II, 会L18

きまつしけん　期末試験　final examination　会L16

きまる　決まる　to be decided [u]　会L19

きめる　決める　to decide [ru]　会L10

きもち　気持ち　feeling　読L23-II

きもの　着物　kimono; Japanese traditional dress　読L9-II, 会L13

キャッシュカード　bank card　会L13(e)

キャンプ　camp　会L11

きゅうこう　急行　express　会L10(e)

きゅうさい　九歳　nine years old　会L1(e)

きゅうに　急に　suddenly　読L14-II
ぎゅうにゅう　牛乳　milk　会L10
きゅうふん　九分　nine minutes　会L1(e)
きゅうりょう　給料　salary　会L17
きょう　今日　today　会L3, 会L4(e)
きょうかしょ　教科書　textbook　会L6
きょうしつ　教室　classroom　読L16-II
きょうじゅうに　今日中に　by the end of today　会L16
きょうだい　兄弟　brothers and sisters　会L7
きょうみがある　興味がある　to be interested (in) [u]　会L12
〜ぎょうめ　〜行目　line number . . .　会L11(e)
きょねん　去年　last year　会L4(e), 会L9
きらい（な）　嫌い　disgusted with; to dislike　会L5
きる　切る　to cut [u]　会L8, 会L17(e)
きる　着る　to put on (clothes above your waist) [ru]　会L7
きれい（な）　beautiful; clean　会L5
〜キロ　. . . kilometers; . . . kilograms　会L13
きをつける　気をつける　to be cautious/careful [ru]　会L15
きんいろ　金色　gold　会L9(e)
ぎんいろ　銀色　silver　会L9(e)
きんえんしゃ　禁煙車　nonsmoking car　会L10(e)
きんえんルーム　禁煙ルーム　nonsmoking room　会L15(e)
きんがく　金額　amount　会L13(e)
ぎんこう　銀行　bank　会L2
きんじょ　近所　neighborhood　読L11-II
きんちょうする　緊張する　to get nervous [irr.]　会L12
きんぱつ　金髪　blonde hair　会L9(e)
きんようび　金曜日　Friday　会L4, 会L4(e)

くうき　空気　air　会L8
くうこう　空港　airport　読L13-III, 会L20
くがつ　九月　September　会L4(e)
くじ　九時　nine o'clock　会L1(e)
くじら　whale　読L15-II
くすり　薬　medicine　会L9
くすりをのむ　薬を飲む　to take medicine [u]　会L9
くだけたいいかた　くだけた言い方　colloquial expression　会L11(e)
ください（〜を）　Please give me . . .　会L2
くださる　下さる　honorific expression for くれる [u]　会L19

くち　口　mouth　会L7, 会L7(e)
くつ　靴　shoes　会L2
くつした　靴下　socks　会L23
クッション　cushion　会L18
くに　国　country; place of origin　会L7
くび　首　neck　会L7(e)
くも　雲　cloud　読L17-II
くもり　曇り　cloudy weather　会L12
くらい　暗い　dark　会L18
〜ぐらい　about (approximate measurement)　会L4
クラス　class　会L4
グラス　tumbler; glass　会L14
クラブ　night club　会L15
くらべる　比べる　to compare [ru]　読L23-II
グリーン　green　会L9(e)
クリスマス　Christmas　会L14
くる　来る　to come [irr.]　会L3
くるま　車　car　会L7
グレー　gray　会L9(e)
クレジットカード　credit card　会L10, 会L13(e)
くれる　to give (me) [ru]　会L14
くろい　黒い　black　会L9, 会L9(e)
〜くん　〜君　Mr./Ms. . . . (casual)　会L14

けいかくをたてる　計画を立てる　to make a plan [ru]　会L22
けいけん　経験　experience　読L13-II, 会L15
けいご　敬語　honorific language　会L19
けいざい　経済　economics　会L1, 会L2
けいさつ　警察　police; police station　会L21
けいさつかん　警察官　police officer　会L11
げいじゅつ　芸術　art　読L17-II
ケーキ　cake　会L10
ゲーム　game　会L7
けが　injury　会L12(e)
げか　外科　surgeon　会L12(e)
けさ　今朝　this morning　会L8
けしき　景色　scenery　読L15-II
けしゴム　消しゴム　eraser　会L2(e)
けしょうする　化粧する　to put makeup on [irr.]　会L17
けす　消す　to turn off; to erase [u]　会L6
けち（な）　stingy; cheap　会L14
けっか　結果　result　読L23-II
けっこうです　結構です　That would be fine.; That wouldn't be necessary.　会L6
けっこんしき　結婚式　wedding　会L15

けっこんする　結婚する　to get married [irr.]　会L7
げつようび　月曜日　Monday　会L4, 会L4(e)
〜けど　. . ., but; . . ., so　会L15
ける　to kick [u]　会L21
けんかする　to have a fight; to quarrel [irr.]　会L11
げんき（な）　元気　healthy; energetic　会L5
げんきがない　元気がない　don't look well　会L12
げんきでね　元気でね　Take care of yourself.　会L23
けんきゅう　研究　research　会L16
げんばく　原爆　atomic bomb　読L15-II

〜こ　〜個　[counter for smaller items]　会L14, 会L14(e)
〜ご　〜後　in . . . time; after . . .　会L10
〜ご　〜語　. . . language　会L1
こうえん　公園　park　会L4
こうかんする　交換する　to exchange [irr.]　会L20
こうくうびん　航空便　airmail　会L5(e)
こうこう　高校　high school　会L1
こうこうせい　高校生　high school student　会L1
こうこく　広告　advertisement　会L13
こうざ　口座　account　会L13(e)
こうじょう　工場　factory　会L21
こうせいぶっしつ　抗生物質　antibiotic　会L12(e)
こうちゃ　紅茶　tea (black tea)　会L13
こうはい　後輩　junior member of a group　会L22
こうよう　紅葉　red leaves; autumn tints　読L15-II
こえ　声　voice　読L10-II
コーヒー　coffee　会L3
ゴールド　gold　会L9(e)
ごがつ　五月　May　会L4(e)
こくさい　国際　international　読L19-III
こくさいかんけい　国際関係　international relations　会L1
こくさいでんわ　国際電話　international call　会L23
こくばん　黒板　blackboard　会L2(e), 会L8
ここ　here　会L2
ごご　午後　P.M.　会L1
ここのか　九日　nine days　会L13
ここのか　九日　the ninth day of a month　会L4(e)

ここのつ　九つ　nine　会L9
こころ　心　mind; heart　読L20-II
ごさい　五歳　five years old　会L1(e)
ござる　extra-modest expression for ある [u]　会L20
ごじ　五時　five o'clock　会L1(e)
ごしゅじん　ご主人　(your/her) husband　会L14
ごぜん　午前　A.M.　会L1
ごぜんちゅう　午前中　in the morning　読L9-II
こたえ　答/答え　answer　会L11(e), 読L23-II
こたえる　答える　to answer [ru]　読L8-II, 会L23
ごちそう　excellent food　読L9-II
ごちそうさま（でした）　Thank you for the meal. (after eating)　会G
ごちそうする　to treat/invite (someone) to a meal [irr.]　会L19
こちら　this person (polite)　会L11
こちら　this way (polite)　会L19
こづつみ　小包　parcel　会L5(e)
こと　事　things; matters　読L11-II, 会L21
ことし　今年　this year　会L4(e), 会L10
ことば　言葉　language　会L13
こども　子供　child　会L4
この　this ...　会L2
このあいだ　この間　the other day　会L16
このぐらい　about this much　会L16
このごろ　these days　会L10
このように　like this; this way　読L23-II
ごはん　ご飯　rice; meal　会L4
コピーをとる　コピーを取る　to make a photocopy [u]　会L22
ごふん　五分　five minutes　会L1(e)
こまる　困る　to have difficulty [u]　会L16
ごみ　garbage　会L16
こむ　込む　to get crowded [u]　読L13-III, 会L17
ごめん　I'm sorry. (casual)　会L16
ごめんなさい　I'm sorry.　会L4
ごらんになる　ご覧になる　honorific expression for みる [u]　会L19
ゴルフ　golf　会L13
これ　this one　会L2
これから　from now on　読L11-II, 会L16
ころ　time of ...; when ...　会L21
～ごろ　at about ...　会L3
ころぶ　転ぶ　to fall down [u]　会L18
こわい　怖い　frightening　会L5
こわす　壊す　to break (something) [u]　会L18
こわれる　壊れる　(something) breaks [ru]　会L18

こんがっき　今学期　this semester　会L11
こんげつ　今月　this month　会L4(e), 会L8
コンサート　concert　会L9
こんしゅう　今週　this week　会L4(e), 会L6
コンタクト　contact lenses　会L17
こんでいる　込んでいる　to be crowded　読L13-III
こんど　今度　near future　会L9
こんな～　... like this; this kind of ...　会L14
こんなふう　like this　会L22
こんにちは　Good afternoon.　会G
こんばん　今晩　tonight　会L3
こんばんは　Good evening.　会G
コンビニ　convenience store　会L7
コンピューター　computer　会L1, 会L2

さあ　I am not sure, ...　会L20
サークル　club activity　会L7
サーフィン　surfing　会L5
～さい　～歳　... years old　会L1, 会L1(e)
さいあく　最悪　the worst　読L20-II
さいきん　最近　recently　会L15
さいごに　最後に　finally; lastly　読L8-II, 会L23
さいごの～　最後の～　last ...　読L23-II
さいしょの～　最初の～　first ...　読L23-II
さいてい　最低　the lowest; the worst　会L17
さいふ　財布　wallet　会L2
さがす　探す　to look for [u]　会L15
さかな　魚　fish　会L2
さく　咲く　to bloom [u]　会L18
さくひん　作品　artistic piece　読L17-II
さくぶん　作文　essay; composition　会L9
さけ　酒　sake; alcohol　会L3
さしあげる　差し上げる　humble expression for あげる [ru]　会L20
さす　刺す　to bite [u]　会L21
さそう　誘う　to invite [u]　会L15
～さつ　～冊　[counter for bound volumes]　会L14, 会L14(e)
さっか　作家　writer　会L11
サッカー　soccer　会L10
ざっし　雑誌　magazine　会L3
さとう　砂糖　sugar　会L16
さびしい　寂しい　lonely　会L9
サボる　to cut (classes) [u]　会L11
～さま　～様　Mr./Ms. ...　読L5-II
さむい　寒い　cold (weather)　会L5
さようなら　Good-bye.　会G

さら　皿　plate; dish　会L14
さらいげつ　再来月　the month after next　会L4(e)
さらいしゅう　再来週　the week after next　会L4(e)
さらいねん　再来年　the year after next　会L4(e)
サラリーマン　salaryman; company employee　会L17
さる　猿　monkey　会L22
さわる　触る　to touch [u]　会L21
～さん　Mr./Ms....　会L1
さんがつ　三月　March　会L4(e)
ざんぎょう　残業　overtime work　読L8-II, 会L17
さんさい　三歳　three years old　会L1(e)
さんじ　三時　three o'clock　会L1(e)
さんじっぷん/さんじゅっぷん　三十分　thirty minutes　会L1(e)
さんせいする　賛成する　to agree [irr.]　会L22
ざんだかしょうかい　残高照会　balance inquiry　会L13(e)
ざんねん（ですね）　残念（ですね）　That's too bad.　会L8
さんふじんか　産婦人科　obstetrician and gynecologist　会L12(e)
さんぶん　三分　three minutes　会L1(e)
さんぽする　散歩する　to take a walk [irr.]　会L9

し　詩　poem　読L17-II
じ　字　letter; character　会L20
～じ　～時　o'clock　会L1
しあい　試合　match; game　会L12
しあわせ（な）　幸せ　happy (lasting happiness)　読L10-II, 会L13
CD（シーディー）　CD　会L6
ジーンズ　jeans　会L2
シェフ　chef　読L6-III
しか　鹿　deer　読L15-II
しか　歯科　dentist　会L12(e)
しかし　however　読L17-II
しかたがない　cannot be helped　読L22-II
しがつ　四月　April　会L4(e)
じかん　時間　time　会L14
～じかん　～時間　... hours　会L4
じきゅう　時給　an hourly wage　読L18-II
しけん　試験　exam　会L9
しごと　仕事　job; work; occupation　会L1, 会L8
じしょ　辞書　dictionary　会L2, 会L2(e)
じしん　地震　earthquake　会L15
しずか（な）　静か　quiet　会L5

しぜん　自然　nature　読L15-II

じぞう　guardian deity of children
　　　　読L10-II

した　下　under　会L4

じだい　時代　age; era　読L14-II

したしい　親しい　close; intimate
　　　　読L18-III

しちがつ　七月　July　会L4(e)

しちじ　七時　seven o'clock　会L1(e)

じっさい　十歳　ten years old　会L1(e)

しっています　知っています　I know
　　　　会L7

じつは　実は　as a matter of fact, . . .
　　　　会L13

しっぱいする　失敗する　to fail; to be
　unsuccessful [irr.]　会L22

じっぷん　十分　ten minutes　会L1(e)

しつもん　質問　question
　　　　会L11(e), 読L19-III

しつれいしました　失礼しました　I'm
　very sorry.　会L20

しつれいします　失礼します　Excuse
　me.; Sorry to interrupt you.　会L16

していせき　指定席　reserved seat
　　　　会L10(e)

してん　支店　branch office　会L20

じてんしゃ　自転車　bicycle　会L2

しぬ　死ぬ　to die [u]　会L6

じはつ　次発　departing second　会L10(e)

じびか　耳鼻科　otorhinolaryngologist;
　ENT doctor　会L12(e)

じぶん　自分　oneself　読L10-II, 会L17

じぶんで　自分で　(do something) by
　oneself　会L16

しま　島　island　読L15-II

しまる　閉まる　(something) closes [u]
　　　　会L18

しみんびょういん　市民病院　municipal
　hospital　会L6

しめきり　締め切り　deadline
　　　　会L11(e), 会L15

しめる　閉める　to close (something) [ru]
　　　　会L6

じゃあ　then . . . ; if that is the case, . . .
　　　　会L2

ジャーナリスト　journalist　会L11

しゃかい　社会　society　会L23

ジャケット　jacket　会L15

しゃしん　写真　picture; photograph
　　　　会L4

しゃちょう　社長　president of a company
　　　　会L11

シャツ　shirt　会L10

しゃべる　to chat [u]　会L15

シャワー　shower　会L6

シャワーをあびる　シャワーを浴びる
　to take a shower [ru]　会L6

シャンプー　shampoo　会L17(e), 会L18

じゆう　自由　freedom　会L22

じゅういちがつ　十一月　November
　　　　会L4(e)

じゅういちじ　十一時　eleven o'clock
　　　　会L1(e)

じゅういちにち　十一日　the eleventh
　day of a month　会L4(e)

じゅういっさい　十一歳　eleven years
　old　会L1(e)

じゅういっぷん　十一分　eleven minutes
　　　　会L1(e)

じゅうがつ　十月　October　会L4(e)

しゅうかん　習慣　custom　会L15

～しゅうかん　～週間　for . . . weeks
　　　　会L10

じゅうきゅうふん　十九分　nineteen
　minutes　会L1(e)

じゅうごふん　十五分　fifteen minutes
　　　　会L1(e)

じゅうさんぷん　十三分　thirteen
　minutes　会L1(e)

じゅうじ　十時　ten o'clock　会L1(e)

しゅうしょくする　就職する　to get a
　full-time job (at . . .) [irr.]　会L17

ジュース　juice　会L12

じゆうせき　自由席　general admission
　seat　会L10(e)

じゅうでうたれる　銃で撃たれる　to be
　shot　読L17-II

しゅうでん　終電　last train
　　　　会L10(e), 会L21

じゅうななふん　十七分　seventeen
　minutes　会L1(e)

じゆうに　自由に　freely　会L22

じゅうにがつ　十二月　December
　　　　会L4(e)

じゅうにじ　十二時　twelve o'clock
　　　　会L1(e)

じゅうにふん　十二分　twelve minutes
　　　　会L1(e)

じゅうはちふん / じゅうはっぷん
　十八分　eighteen minutes　会L1(e)

しゅうまつ　週末　weekend　会L3

じゅうよっか　十四日　the fourteenth
　day of a month　会L4(e)

じゅうよんぷん　十四分　fourteen
　minutes　会L1(e)

じゅうろっぷん　十六分　sixteen
　minutes　会L1(e)

じゅぎょう　授業　class　会L11

じゅぎょうちゅうに　授業中に　in class;
　during the class　会L16

じゅぎょうりょう　授業料　tuition
　　　　会L23

じゅく　塾　cram school　読L7-II, 会L22

しゅくだい　宿題　homework
　　　　会L5, 会L11(e)

しゅじゅつ　手術　operation　会L12(e)

しゅしょう　首相　prime minister　会L17

しゅじん　主人　owner　読L20-II

じゅっさい　十歳　ten years old　会L1(e)

しゅっしん　出身　coming from　会L11

しゅっちょう　出張　business trip
　　　　読L14-II, 会L19

じゅっぷん　十分　ten minutes　会L1(e)

しゅふ　主夫　"house husband"
　　　　読L17-II

しゅふ　主婦　housewife　会L1

しゅみ　趣味　hobby; pastime
　　　　読L11-II, 会L20

しゅるい　種類　a kind; a sort　会L19

じゅんび　準備　preparation　会L21

しょうかいする　紹介する　to introduce
　[irr.]　会L11

しょうがくきん　奨学金　scholarship
　　　　会L16

しょうがくせい　小学生　elementary
　school students　読L16-II

しょうがつ　正月　New Year's
　　　　読L10-II, 会L11

しょうがっこう　小学校　elementary
　school　会L23

しょうぎ　Japanese chess　読L19-II

じょうしゃけん　乗車券　(boarding)
　ticket　会L10(e)

しょうしょう　少々　a few seconds
　　　　会L20

じょうず(な)　上手　skillful; good at . . .
　　　　会L8

しょうせつ　小説　novel　会L20

しょうたいする　招待する　to invite
　someone (to an event/a place) [irr.]　会L19

じょうだん　冗談　joke　読L23-II

しょうぼうし　消防士　firefighter　会L11

しょうゆ　しょう油　soy sauce　会L18

しょうらい　将来　future　会L11

しょくじ　食事　meal　読L21-II

しょくじつき　食事付　with meals
　　　　会L15(e)

しょくどう　食堂　cafeteria; dining
　commons　会L7

しょくひ　食費　food cost　読L18-III

じょしがくせい　女子学生　female
　student　読L18-II

ショッピングモール　shopping mall
　　　　会L17

じょゆう　女優　actress　会L11

しょるい　書類　document　会L22

しらべる　調べる　to look into (a matter) [ru]　会L15

しり　buttocks　会L7(e)

しりあう　知り合う　to get acquainted with [u]　会L19

しりません　知りません　I do not know　会L7

しる　知る　to get to know [u]　会L7

シルバー　silver　会L9(e)

しろ　城　castle　読L5-II

しろい　白い　white　会L9, 会L9(e)

しろくろ　白黒　black and white　会L9(e)

じろじろみる　じろじろ見る　to stare (at) [ru]　会L8

〜じん　〜人　...people　会L1

しんかんせん　新幹線　Shinkansen; "Bullet Train"　会L10

シングル　single room　会L15(e)

しんごう　信号　traffic light　会L6(e), 会L20

じんじゃ　神社　shrine　会L11

しんじる　信じる　to believe [ru]　読L21-II

しんせき　親せき　relatives　会L16

しんせつ（な）　親切　kind　会L7

しんぱい（な）　心配　worried about　読L21-II, 会L22

しんぱいする　心配する　to worry [irr.]　会L12

しんぶん　新聞　newspaper　会L2

しんゆう　親友　best friend　読L22-II

じんるいがく　人類学　anthropology　会L1

すいせんじょう　推薦状　letter of recommendation　会L16

スイッチ　switch　会L18

ずいぶん　very　会L17

すいようび　水曜日　Wednesday　会L4, 会L4(e)

スウェーデン　Sweden　会L1

スーツケース　suitcase　読L13-III

スーパー　supermarket　会L4

スープ　soup　会L18

スカート　skirt　会L18

すき（な）　好き　fond of; to like　会L5

スキー　ski　会L9

すぐ　right away　会L6

すくない　少ない　a little; a few　会L17

すごい　すごい　incredible; awesome　会L13

すごく　extremely　会L5

すこし　少し　a little　読L7-II, 会L21

すし　sushi　会L10

すずしい　涼しい　cool (weather)　会L10

ずっと　for a long time; all the time　会L22

すっぽん　snapping turtle; terrapin　読L13-II

すてき（な）　素敵　nice　会L12

すてる　捨てる　to throw away [ru]　会L8

ストレス　stress　読L8-II

スニーカー　sneakers　会L20

スピーチ　speech　会L21

スプーン　spoon　会L17

スポーツ　sports　会L3

すみません　Excuse me.; I'm sorry.　会G

すむ　住む　to live [u]　会L7

する　to cost [irr.]　読L20-II

する　to decide on (an item) [irr.]　会L15

する　to do [irr.]　会L3

する　to wear small items (necktie, watch, etc.) [irr.]　会L17

すると　...Then, ...　読L16-II

すわる　座る　to sit down [u]　会L6

せいかく　性格　personality　会L19

せいかつ　生活　life; living　会L10

せいかつする　生活する　to lead a life [irr.]　会L20

せいかつのゆとり　生活のゆとり　extra money to spare for the cost of living　読L18-II

せいかつひ　生活費　the cost of living　読L18-II

ぜいきん　税金　tax　会L15

せいけいげか　整形外科　orthopedic surgeon　会L12(e)

せいじ　政治　politics　会L1, 会L12

せいせき　成績　grade (on a test, etc.)　会L12

ぜいたくをする　to indulge in luxury [irr.]　読L21-II

せいふ　政府　government　会L21

セーター　sweater　会L13

せかい　世界　world　会L10

せがたかい　背が高い　tall (stature)　会L7

せがひくい　背が低い　short (stature)　会L7

せき　cough　会L12

せきがでる　せきが出る　to cough [ru]　会L12

ぜったいに　絶対に　definitely; no matter what　読L20-II, 会L22

セット　set　会L17(e)

せつめいする　説明する　to explain [irr.]　会L16

せなか　背中　back (body)　会L7(e)

ぜひ　是非　by all means　会L9

せまい　狭い　narrow; not spacious　会L12

せわをする　世話をする　to take care of ... [irr.]　会L23

ぜんいん　全員　all members　読L23-II

せんきゅうひゃくろくじゅうねんだい　1960年代　1960's　読L17-II

せんきょ　選挙　election　会L23

せんげつ　先月　last month　会L4(e), 会L9

せんこう　専攻　major　会L1

せんしゅう　先週　last week　会L4, 会L4(e)

せんす　扇子　fan　会L20

せんせい　先生　teacher; Professor ...　会L1

ぜんぜん ＋ negative　全然　not at all　会L3

せんそう　戦争　war　読L15-II

せんたくする　洗濯する　to do laundry [irr.]　会L8

せんぱい　先輩　senior member of a group　読L14-II, 会L22

せんぱつ　先発　departing first　会L10(e)

ぜんぶ　全部　all　会L13

ぞう　象　elephant　会L13

そうか　I see. (casual)　会L17

そうじする　掃除する　to clean [irr.]　会L8

そうそう　You are right.　会L23

そうだ！　I have an idea!　読L20-II

そうだんする　相談する　to consult [irr.]　会L14

そうです　That's right.　会L1

そうですか　I see.; Is that so?　会L1

そうですね　That's right.; Let me see.　会L3

そくたつ　速達　special delivery　会L5(e)

そこ　there　会L2

そして　and then　読L9-II, 会L11

そだてる　育てる　to raise; to bring up [ru]　会L22

そつぎょうしき　卒業式　graduation ceremony　会L15

そつぎょうする　卒業する　to graduate (from ...) [irr.]　会L15

そと　外　outside　会L18

その　that ...　会L2

そのご　その後　after that　読L17-II

そば　soba; Japanese buckwheat noodle　会L15

ソファ　sofa　会L18

ソフト　software　会L23

そめる　to dye [ru]　会L17(e)

そら　空　sky　読L16-II

ばいてん　売店　shop; stand　会L10(e)

バイト　abbreviation of アルバイト　会L21

ハイヒール　high heels　会L20

はいゆう　俳優　actor; actress　会L11

はいる　入る　to enter [u]　会L6

はがき　葉書　postcard　会L5, 会L5(e)

ばかにする　to insult; to make a fool of . . .
[irr.]　会L21

はく　to put on (items below your waist) [u]
会L7

～はく　～泊　. . . nights　会L15(e)

はこぶ　運ぶ　to carry [u]　会L22

はし　chopsticks　会L8

はしご　ladders　読L17-II

はじまる　始まる　(something) begins [u]
会L9

はじめて　初めて　for the first time　会L12

はじめは　初めは　at first　読L18-III

はじめまして　How do you do？　会G

はじめる　始める　to begin [ru]　会L8

ばしょ　場所　place　読L16-II, 会L23

はしる　走る　to run [u]　読L15-II, 会L22

バス　bus　会L5

はずかしい　恥ずかしい　embarrassing;
to feel embarrassed　会L18

はずかしがりや　恥ずかしがり屋　shy
person　会L19

バスてい　バス停　bus stop　会L4

パソコン　personal computer　会L6

はたけ　畑　farm　読L12-II

はたち　二十歳　twenty years old　会L1(e)

はたらく　働く　to work [u]　会L11

はたをおる　はたを織る　to weave [u]
読L12-II

はちがつ　八月　August　会L4(e)

はちじ　八時　eight o'clock　会L1(e)

はちふん　八分　eight minutes　会L1(e)

ばつ　×（wrong）　会L11(e)

はつおん　発音　pronunciation　会L11(e)

はつか　二十日　the twentieth day of a
month　会L4(e)

はっさい　八歳　eight years old　会L1(e)

はっぴょう　発表　presentation　会L15

はっぴょうする　発表する　to make
public; to publish [irr.]　読L17-II

はっぷん　八分　eight minutes　会L1(e)

はな　花　flower　会L12

はな　鼻　nose　会L7(e)

はなし　話　chat; talk　会L19

はなしをする　話をする　to have a talk
[irr.]　読L9-II, 会L19

はなす　話す　to speak; to talk [u]　会L3

バナナ　banana　会L18

はなれる　離れる　(something/someone)
separates; parts from [ru]　会L23

はは　母　(my) mother　会L7

はやい　早い　early　会L3

はやい　速い　fast　会L7

はやく　早く／速く　(do something)
early; fast　会L10

はらう　払う　to pay [u]　会L10

はる　春　spring　会L10

はる　貼る　to post; to stick [u]　会L21

はれ　晴れ　sunny weather　会L12

はれる　晴れる　to become sunny [ru]
会L19

バレンタインデー　St. Valentine's Day
会L14

はん　半　half　会L1

～ばん　～番　number . . .
会L11(e), 会L15

パン　bread　会L4

パンクする　(tire) goes flat [irr.]　会L23

ばんぐみ　番組　broadcast program
会L15

ばんごう　番号　number　会L1

ばんごはん　晩ご飯　dinner　会L3

バンザイをする　to raise hands and shout
"Banzai!"　読L23-II

～ばんせん　～番線　track number . . .
会L10(e)

パンダ　panda　会L17

はんたいする　反対する　to oppose; to
object to [irr.]　会L22

パンツ　pants　会L10

バンド　band　読L11-II

はんにん　犯人　criminal　会L21

ハンバーガー　hamburger　会L3

ひ　日　day　会L16

ピアノ　piano　会L9

ヒーター　heater　会L17

ビール　beer　会L11

ひがし　東　east　会L6(e)

～ひき　～匹　[counter for smaller
animals]　会L14, 会L14(e)

ひく　弾く　to play (a string instrument or
piano) [u]　会L9

ひげ　beard　会L17

ひげをそる　to shave one's beard [u]　会L17

ひこうき　飛行機　airplane　会L5

ピザ　pizza　読L6-III, 会L9

ひさしぶり　久しぶり　it has been a long
time　会L11

ビジネス　business　会L1, 会L2

びじゅつかん　美術館　art museum
会L11

ひだり　左　left　会L4

ひだりがわ　左側　left side　会L6(e)

ひっかく　to scratch [u]　読L20-II

びっくりする　to be surprised [irr.]
読L10-II, 会L21

ひっこし　引っ越し　moving　読L18-III

ひっこす　引っ越す　to move (to another
place to live) [u]　会L19

ビデオカメラ　camcorder　会L14

ひと　人　person　会L4

ひどい　awful　会L21

ひとつ　一つ　one　会L9

ひとつめ　一つ目　first　会L6(e)

ひとびと　人々　people　読L12-II

ひとり　一人　one person　会L7

ひとりぐらし　一人暮らし　living alone
会L22

ひとりで　一人で　alone　会L4

ひふか　皮膚科　dermatologist　会L12(e)

ひま（な）　暇　not busy; have a lot of
free time　会L5

ひみつ　秘密　secret　読L16-II, 会L17

ひゃくえんだま　百円玉　100-yen coin
会L13(e)

びよういん　美容院　beauty parlor　会L10

びょういん　病院　hospital　会L4

びょうき　病気　illness; sickness
会L9, 会L12(e)

ひょうじゅんご　標準語　standard
Japanese　会L11(e)

ひょうじょう　表情　facial expression
読L23-II

ひる　昼　noon　読L9-II

ひるごはん　昼ご飯　lunch　会L3

ひるねをする　昼寝をする　to take a nap
[irr.]　会L21

ひろい　広い　spacious; wide　会L15

ひろう　拾う　to pick up (something) [u]
会L22

ひろば　広場　square; open space
読L15-II

びん　便　flight　会L10

ピンク　pink　会L9(e)

びんぼう（な）　貧乏　poor　会L22

ファイル　file; portfolio　会L16

ふあんな　不安な　uneasy; worried
読L13-II

ブーツ　boots　会L17

ふうふ　夫婦　married couple; husband
and wife　会L14

プール　swimming pool　会L15

ぶか　部下　subordinate　会L22

ふく　服　clothes　会L12

ふくしゅう　復習　review of a lesson
会L22

まる　○ (correct)　会L11(e)

まんいんでんしゃ　満員電車　jam-packed train　読L13-III

まんが　漫画　comic book　会L14

まんがか　漫画家　cartoonist　会L11

まんじゅう　sweet bun　読L4-III

マンション　multistory apartment building; condominium　会L14

みえる　見える　to be visible [ru]　会L15

みがく　磨く　to brush (teeth); to polish [u]　会L13

みかた　味方　person on one's side　読L16-II

みかん　mandarin orange　会L14

みぎ　右　right　会L4

みぎがわ　右側　right side　会L6(e)

みじかい　短い　short (length)　会L7

みず　水　water　会L3

みずいろ　水色　light blue　会L9(e)

みずうみ　湖　lake　会L11

みせ　店　shop; store　読L4-III, 会L13

みせる　見せる　to show [ru]　会L16

～みたいなX　X such as . . .　会L20

みち　道　way; road; directions　会L16

みちにまよう　道に迷う　to become lost; to lose one's way [u]　会L16

みっか　三日　the third day of a month　会L4(e)

みっか　三日　three days　会L13

みつかる　見つかる　to be found [u]　会L16

みつける　見つける　to find [ru]　読L12-II, 会L21

みっつ　三つ　three　会L9

みどり　緑　green　会L9(e), 読L15-II

みなさま　みな様　everyone (polite expression of みなさん)　読L19-II

みなさん　皆さん　everyone; all of you　読L6-III, 会L14

みなみ　南　south　会L6(e), 読L15-II

みぶり　身ぶり　gesture　読L20-II

みみ　耳　ear　会L7(e)

みやげ　土産　souvenir　会L4

みらい　未来　future　読L16-II

みる　見る　to see; to look at; to watch [ru]　会L3

みんな　all　読L7-II, 会L9

みんなで　all (of the people) together　会L8

むいか　六日　six days　会L13

むいか　六日　the sixth day of a month　会L4(e)

むかえにいく　迎えに行く　to go to pick up [u]　会L16

むかえにくる　迎えに来る　to come to pick up [irr.]　会L16

むかし　昔　old days; past　読L15-II, 会L21

むかしむかし　昔々　once upon a time　読L10-II

むこう　向こう　the other side; over there　読L12-II

むし　虫　insect　会L18

むしめがね　虫めがね　magnifying glass　読L17-II

むずかしい　難しい　difficult　会L5

むすめ　娘　daughter　読L12-II

むだづかい　無駄遣い　waste (money)　会L22

むっつ　六つ　six　会L9

むね　胸　breast　会L7(e)

むらさき　紫　purple　会L9(e)

むりな　無理な　impossible　読L20-II

め　目　eye　会L7, 会L7(e)

～め　～目　-th　会L15

～めい　～名　. . . person(s)　会L15(e)

～めいさま　～名様　party of . . . people　会L19

めいしん　迷信　superstition　読L21-II

メール　e-mail　会L4

めがね　眼鏡　glasses　会L7

メキシコ　Mexico　読L5-II

めざましどけい　目覚まし時計　alarm clock　会L16

めしあがる　召し上がる　honorific expression for たべる and のむ [u]　会L19

めずらしい　rare　読L13-II

めちゃくちゃ(な)　messy; disorganized　会L21

めったに～ない　seldom　読L21-II

メニュー　menu　会L2

めんきょ　免許　license　会L22

めんせつ　面接　interview　会L23

もう　already　会L9

もういちど　もう一度　one more time　会L15

もうしこみ　申し込み　application　読L19-III

もうしわけありません　申し訳ありません　You have my apologies.　読L19-III, 会L20

もうす　申す　extra-modest expression for いう [u]　会L20

もうすぐ　very soon; in a few moments/ days　会L12

もうすこし　もう少し　a little more　会L22

もう～ない　not any longer　読L13-II

もくてき　目的　object; purpose　読L18-II

もくようび　木曜日　Thursday　会L4, 会L4(e)

もじ　文字　letter; character　読L17-II

もし～たら　if . . .　読L19-III

もしもし　Hello? (used on the phone)　会L7

もち　rice cake　読L10-II

もちろん　of course　会L7

もつ　持つ　to carry; to hold [u]　会L6

もっていく　持っていく　to take (a thing) [u]　会L8

もってくる　持ってくる　to bring (a thing) [irr.]　会L6

もっと　more　会L11

もてる　もてる　to be popular (in terms of romantic interest) [ru]　会L19

もどってくる　戻ってくる　(something/ someone) comes back [irr.]　会L23

もどる　戻る　to return; to come/go back [u]　読L16-II, 会L20

もの　物　thing (concrete object)　会L12

ものすごく　extremely　会L23

もみあげ　sideburns　会L17(e)

もらう　to get (from somebody) [u]　会L9

もんく　文句　complaint　会L21

もんくをいう　文句を言う　to complain [u]　会L21

～や　～屋　. . . shop　会L20

やきゅう　野球　baseball　会L10

やきゅうせんしゅ　野球選手　baseball player　会L11

やく　焼く　to bake; to burn; to grill [u]　会L21

やくざ　yakuza; gangster　会L13

やくす　訳す　to translate [u]　会L16

やくそく　約束　promise; appointment　会L13

やくそくをまもる　約束を守る　to keep a promise [u]　会L13

やさい　野菜　vegetable　会L2

やさしい　easy (problem); kind (person)　会L5

やすい　安い　inexpensive; cheap (thing)　会L5

やすみ　休み　holiday; day off; absence　会L5

やすむ　休む　to be absent (from); to rest [u]　会L6

やせています　to be thin　会L7

やせる　to lose weight [ru]　会L7

やちん　家賃　rent　会L18

あいうえお　かきくけこ　さしすせそ　たちつてと　なにぬねの　はひふへほ　まみむめも　**やゆよ　らりるれろ　わをん**

やった！　I did it!　読L20-II
やっつ　八つ　eight　会L9
やっぱり　after all　読L13-II, 会L17
やま　山　mountain　読L5-II, 会L11
やまみち　山道　mountain road　読L10-II
やめる　to quit [ru]　会L11
やる　to do; to perform [u]　会L5
やる　to give (to pets, plants, younger siblings, etc.) [u]　会L21

ゆうがた　夕方　evening　会L18
ゆうき　勇気　courage　読L22-II
ゆうしょうする　優勝する　to win a championship [irr.]　会L23
ゆうしょく　夕食　dinner　会L23
ゆうじん　友人　friend　読L19-III
ゆうびんきょく　郵便局　post office　会L2
ゆうめい（な）　有名　famous　会L8
ゆうめいじん　有名人　celebrity　会L10
ゆき　雪　snow　読L10-II, 会L12
ゆっくり　slowly; leisurely; unhurriedly　会L6
ゆび　指　finger　会L7(e)
ゆびわ　指輪　ring　会L14
ゆめ　夢　dream　会L11

ようか　八日　eight days　会L13
ようか　八日　the eighth day of a month　会L4(e)
ようこそ　Welcome.　会L19
ようじ　用事　business to take care of　会L12
ようふく　洋服　clothes　読L18-II
ヨーロッパ　Europe　会L22
よかったら　if you like　会L7
よきん　預金　savings　会L13(e)
よく　often; much　会L3
よく　well　会L14
よこ　横　side; horizontal　読L23-II
よごす　汚す　to make dirty [u]　会L18
よごれる　汚れる　to become dirty [ru]　会L18
よじ　四時　four o'clock　会L1(e)
よしゅう　予習　preparation of lessons　会L22
よっか　四日　four days　会L13
よっか　四日　the fourth day of a month　会L4(e)
よっつ　四つ　four　会L9
よてい　予定　schedule; plan　会L15
よぶ　呼ぶ　to call (one's name); to invite [u]　会L19
よむ　読む　to read [u]　会L3
よやく　予約　reservation　会L10

よやくする　予約する　to reserve [irr.]　会L15
よる　夜　night　読L5-II, 会L6
よる　寄る　to stop by [u]　会L19
よろしかったら　if it is okay (polite)　会L20
よろしくおつたえください　よろしくお伝えください　Please give my best regards (to . . .)　会L19
よろしくおねがいします　よろしくお願いします　Nice to meet you.　会G
よわい　弱い　weak　読L16-II
よんさい　四歳　four years old　会L1(e)
よんぷん　四分　four minutes　会L1(e)

らいがっき　来学期　next semester　会L10
らいげつ　来月　next month　会L4(e), 会L8
らいしゅう　来週　next week　会L4(e), 会L6
らいねん　来年　next year　会L4(e), 会L6
らく（な）　楽　easy; comfortable　会L22
らくご　落語　comic monologue　読L20-II
らくごか　落語家　comic storyteller　読L20-II
ラジオ　radio　会L14
ラッシュ　the rush hour　読L13-III

りこんする　離婚する　to get a divorce [irr.]　会L17
りそう　理想　ideal　会L23
りゅうがくする　留学する　to study abroad [irr.]　会L11
りゅうがくせい　留学生　international student　会L1
りょう　両　a unit of currency used in the Edo period　読L20-II
りょう　寮　dormitory　読L9-II, 会L17
りょうしん　両親　parents　会L14
りょうり　料理　cooking　読L6-III
りょうりする　料理する　to cook [irr.]　会L8
りょかん　旅館　Japanese inn　会L15
りょこう　旅行　travel　会L5
りょこうがいしゃ　旅行会社　travel agency　会L17
りょこうする　旅行する　to travel [irr.]　会L10
りれきしょ　履歴書　résumé　会L14
りんご　apple　会L10

ルームメート　roommate　会L11
るす　留守　absence; not at home　会L21

るすばん　留守番　looking after a house during someone's absence　会L23
るすばんでんわ　留守番電話　answering machine　会L18

れい　例　example　会L11(e)
れいぞうこ　冷蔵庫　refrigerator　会L18
れきし　歴史　history　会L1, 会L2
レストラン　restaurant　会L4
レポート　(term) paper　会L13
れんしゅう　練習　exercise　会L11(e)
れんしゅうする　練習する　to practice [irr.]　会L10
レントゲン　X-ray　会L12(e)
れんらくする　連絡する　to contact [irr.]　会L21

ろうそく　candle　会L18
ろくがつ　六月　June　会L4(e)
ろくさい　六歳　six years old　会L1(e)
ろくじ　六時　six o'clock　会L1(e)
ろっぷん　六分　six minutes　会L1(e)
ロボット　robot　読L16-II

ワイン　wine　読L6-III
わかい　若い　young　会L9
わかる　to understand [u]　会L4
わかれる　別れる　to break up; to separate [ru]　会L12
わすれる　忘れる　to forget; to leave behind [ru]　会L6
わたくし　私　I (formal)　会L13
わたし　私　I　会L1
わたしたち　私たち　we　読L12-II, 会L14
わたす　渡す　to give; to hand [u]　読L20-II
わたる　渡る　to cross [u]　会L6(e)
わらう　笑う　to laugh [u]　会L16
わりびきけん　割引券　discount coupon　会L15
わるい　悪い　bad　会L12
わるぐちをいう　悪口を言う　to talk behind someone's back [u]　会L23
ワンルームマンション　one-room apartment; a studio　読L18-III

さくいん2 English-Japanese

会……会話・文法編
(Conversation and Grammar section)
読……読み書き編
(Reading and Writing section)
G……あいさつ (Greetings)
(e)……Useful Expressions
I・II・III……問題番号（読み書き編）
(number of exercise in the
Reading and Writing section)
[u] u-verb　[ru] ru-verb　[irr.] irregular verb

A

abbreviation of アルバイト　バイト　会L21
about . . . 　〜について　会L8
about (approximate measurement)
　〜ぐらい　会L4
about this much　このぐらい　会L16
absence　やすみ　休み　会L5
absence　るす　留守　会L21
absent (from)　やすむ　休む [u]　会L6
according to . . . 　〜によると　会L17
account　こうざ　口座　会L13(e)
activities　かつどう　活動　読L17-II
actor　はいゆう　俳優　会L11
actress　はいゆう/じょゆう　俳優/女優
　会L11
adult　おとな　大人　読L12-II, 会L13
advertisement　こうこく　広告　会L13
advice　アドバイス　読L14-II
(be) affected　えいきょうをうける　影響
　を受ける [ru]　読L17-II
after . . . 　〜ご　〜後　会L10
after (an event)　（〜の）あと　（〜の）後
　読L8-II, 会L11
after all　やっぱり　読L13-II, 会L17
after that　そのご　その後　読L17-II
again　また　読L5-II, 会L20
age　じだい　時代　読L14-II
agree　さんせいする　賛成する [irr.]
　会L22
air　くうき　空気　会L8
air conditioner　エアコン　会L18
airmail　こうくうびん　航空便　会L5(e)
airplane　ひこうき　飛行機　会L5
airport　くうこう　空港　読L13-III, 会L20
alarm clock　めざましどけい　目覚まし
　時計　会L16
alcohol　（お）さけ　（お）酒　会L3
all　ぜんぶ　全部　会L13
all　みんな　読L7-II, 会L9
all (of the people) together　みんなで
　会L8
all day long　いちにちじゅう　一日中
　会L15

all members　ぜんいん　全員　読L23-II
all of you　みなさん　皆さん　会L14
all the time　ずっと　会L22
all year　いちねんじゅう　一年中
　読L15-II
almost　ほとんど　読L23-II
alone　ひとりで　一人で　会L4
already　もう　会L9
always　いつも　読L6-III, 会L8
A.M.　ごぜん　午前　会L1
amount　きんがく　金額　会L13(e)
amulet　おまもり　お守り　読L21-II
an hourly wage　じきゅう　時給
　読L18-II
and so forth　〜など　読L12-II
and then　そして　読L9-II, 会L11
and then　それから　会L5
(get) angry　おこる　怒る [u]　読L12-II
animation　アニメ　会L20
annoying　うるさい　会L22
answer　こたえ　答/答え
　会L11(e), 読L23-II
answer　こたえる　答える [ru]
　読L8-II, 会L23
answering machine　るすばんでんわ
　留守番電話　会L18
anthropology　じんるいがく　人類学
　会L1
antibiotic　こうせいぶっしつ　抗生物質
　会L12(e)
anyhow　とにかく　会L21
anything　なんでも　読L13-II
anything else　ほかに　会L11(e)
anyway　とにかく　会L21
anywhere　どこでも　読L16-II
apartment　アパート　会L7
apologize　あやまる　謝る [u]　会L18
appear　でる　出る [ru]　会L9
apple　りんご　会L10
application　もうしこみ　申し込み
　読L19-III
appointment　やくそく　約束　会L13
April　しがつ　四月　会L4(e)
arm　て　手　会L7(e), 読L15-II
(be) arrested　つかまる　捕まる [u]
　会L21
arrive　つく　着く [u]　読L13-III, 会L15
art　げいじゅつ　芸術　読L17-II
art exhibition　てんらんかい　展覧会
　読L17-II
art museum　びじゅつかん　美術館
　会L11
artistic piece　さくひん　作品　読L17-II
as a matter of fact, . . . 　じつは　実は
　会L13
as far as (a place)　〜まで　会L5

as much as possible　できるだけ
　会L12
as usual　あいかわらず　相変わらず
　読L22-II
Asian studies　アジアけんきゅう　アジ
　ア研究　会L1
ask　きく　聞く [u]　会L5
ask (a favor)　たのむ　頼む [u]　会L18
astronaut　うちゅうひこうし　宇宙飛行
　士　会L11
at about . . . 　〜ごろ　会L3
at first　はじめは　初めは　読L18-III
at the time of . . . 　とき　時　会L4
atomic bomb　げんばく　原爆　読L15-II
attend　でる　出る [ru]　会L9
audible　きこえる　聞こえる [ru]　会L20
August　はちがつ　八月　会L4(e)
aunt　おばさん　会L14
Australia　オーストラリア　会L1, 会L11
autumn tints　こうよう　紅葉　読L15-II
awesome　すごい　会L13
awful　ひどい　会L21

B

baby　あかちゃん　赤ちゃん　会L21
back　うしろ　後ろ　会L4
back (body)　せなか　背中　会L7(e)
bad　わるい　悪い　会L12
bag　かばん　会L2, 会L2(e)
baggage　にもつ　荷物　会L6
bake　やく　焼く [u]　会L21
balance inquiry　ざんだかしょうかい
　残高照会　会L13(e)
ball　ボール　会L22
bamboo　たけ　竹　読L15-II
bamboo hat　かさ　読L10-II
banana　バナナ　会L18
band　バンド　読L11-II
bank　ぎんこう　銀行　会L2
bank card　キャッシュカード　会L13(e)
bank transfer　おふりこみ　お振込
　会L13(e)
barbecue　バーベキュー　会L8
barber's　とこや　床屋　会L10
baseball　やきゅう　野球　会L10
baseball player　やきゅうせんしゅ
　野球選手　会L11
bath　（お）ふろ　（お）風呂　会L6
battery　でんち　電池　会L15
beard　ひげ　会L17
beautiful　きれい（な）　会L5
beauty parlor　びよういん　美容院
　会L10
because . . . 　〜から　会L6
because . . . 　〜ので　会L12
become　なる [u]　会L10

become dirty よごれる 汚れる [ru] 会L18

become late おくれる 遅れる [ru] 会L19

become lost みちにまよう 道に迷う [u] 会L16

become sunny はれる 晴れる [ru] 会L19

beer ビール 会L11

before . . . まえ 前 会L17

begin はじめる 始める [ru] 会L8

(something) begins はじまる 始まる [u] 会L9

being older としうえ 年上 読L14-II

believe しんじる 信じる [ru] 読L21-II

best いちばん 一番 会L10

best friend しんゆう 親友 読L22-II

between あいだ 間 会L4

bicycle じてんしゃ 自転車 会L2

big hit だいヒット 大ヒット 読L17-II

birthday たんじょうび 誕生日 会L5

bite さす 刺す [u] 会L21

black くろい 黒い 会L9, 会L9(e)

black and white しろくろ 白黒 会L9(e)

blackboard こくばん 黒板 会L2(e), 会L8

blonde hair きんぱつ 金髪 会L9(e)

bloom さく 咲く [u] 会L18

blow-dry ブロー 会L17(e)

blue あおい 青い 会L9, 会L9(e)

board のる 乗る [u] 会L5

boarding ticket じょうしゃけん 乗車券 会L10(e)

boat ふね 船 会L10

body からだ 体 読L13-II, 会L23

boil water おゆをわかす お湯を沸かす [u] 会L17

Bon dance (Japanese traditional dance) ぼんおどり 盆踊り 会L23

bonus ボーナス 会L23

book ほん 本 会L2, 会L2(e)

bookish expression かたいいいかた かたい言い方 会L11(e)

bookstore ほんや 本屋 会L4

boots ブーツ 会L17

boring つまらない 会L5

(be) born うまれる 生まれる [ru] 読L15-II, 会L17

borrow かりる 借りる [ru] 会L6

bound for . . . ～いき ～行き 会L10(e)

boxed lunch （お）べんとう （お）弁当 会L9

boy おとこのこ 男の子 会L11

boyfriend かれ 彼 会L12

branch office してん 支店 会L20

bread パン 会L4

break (something) こわす 壊す [u] 会L18

break up わかれる 別れる [ru] 会L12

breakfast あさごはん 朝ご飯 会L3

(something) breaks こわれる 壊れる [ru] 会L18

breast むね 胸 会L7(e)

bright あかるい 明るい 会L18

bright あたまがいい 頭がいい 会L7

bring (a person) つれてくる 連れてくる [irr.] 会L6

bring (a person) back つれてかえる 連れて帰る [u] 読L12-II

bring (a thing) もってくる 持ってくる [irr.] 会L6

bring up そだてる 育てる [ru] 会L22

Britain イギリス 会L1, 会L2

broadcast program ばんぐみ 番組 会L15

brothers and sisters きょうだい 兄弟 会L7

brown ちゃいろい 茶色い 会L9(e)

brush (teeth) みがく 磨く [u] 会L13

building たてもの 建物 読L15-II

Bullet Train しんかんせん 新幹線 会L10

bully いじめる [ru] 会L21

burglar どろぼう 泥棒 会L21

burn やく 焼く [u] 会L21

bus バス 会L5

bus stop バスてい バス停 会L4

business ビジネス 会L1, 会L2

business meeting かいぎ 会議 会L21

business to take care of ようじ 用事 会L12

business trip しゅっちょう 出張 読L14-II, 会L19

busy (people/days) いそがしい 忙しい 会L5

but でも 会L3

. . . , but ～が 読L5-II, 会L7

. . . , but ～けど 会L15

buttocks （お）しり 会L7(e)

buy かう 買う [u] 会L4

buy insurance ほけんにはいる 保険に入る [u] 会L15

by (means of transportation) ～で 会L10

by (time/date) ～までに 読L12-II, 会L18

by all means ぜひ 是非 会L9

(do something) by oneself じぶんで 自分で 会L16

by the end of today きょうじゅうに 今日中に 会L16

by the way ところで 会L9

by what means どうやって 会L10

═════ Ⓒ ═════

cafe きっさてん 喫茶店 会L2

cafeteria しょくどう 食堂 会L7

cake ケーキ 会L10

call でんわする 電話する [irr.] 会L8

call (one's name) よぶ 呼ぶ [u] 会L19

camcorder ビデオカメラ 会L14

camera カメラ 会L8

camp キャンプ 会L11

candle ろうそく 会L18

cannot be helped しかたがない 読L22-II

cap ぼうし 帽子 会L2

car くるま 車 会L7

Car No. 1 いちごうしゃ 一号車 会L10(e)

careful きをつける 気をつける [ru] 会L15

carry はこぶ 運ぶ [u] 会L22

carry もつ 持つ [u] 会L6

cartoonist まんがか 漫画家 会L11

case ばあい 場合 会L14-II

castle （お）しろ （お）城 読L5-II

cat ねこ 猫 会L4

catch a cold かぜをひく 風邪をひく [u] 会L12

(be) caught つかまる 捕まる [u] 会L21

cautious きをつける 気をつける [ru] 会L15

CD シーディー CD 会L6

ceiling てんじょう 天井 読L17-II

celebrity ゆうめいじん 有名人 会L10

Certainly. かしこまりました 会L20

chair いす 会L2(e), 会L4

change かえる 換える [ru] 会L23

change clothes きがえる 着替える [ru] 会L21

character じ 字 会L20

character もじ 文字 読L17-II

charge ～だい ～代 読L18-III

charge for electricity でんきだい 電気代 読L18-III

charm (against evils) おまもり お守り 読L21-II

chat しゃべる [u] 会L15

chat はなし 話 会L19

cheap けち（な） 会L14

cheap (thing) やすい 安い 会L5

checking in チェックイン（する） [irr.] 会L15(e)

checking out チェックアウト（する） [irr.] 会L15(e)

cheerful あかるい 明るい 読L11-II

Cheers! (a toast) かんぱい 乾杯 会L8

chef シェフ 読L6-III

child こども 子供 会L4

(your/their) child (polite) おこさん お子さん 会L19

China ちゅうごく 中国 会L1, 会L2

Chinese character かんじ 漢字 会L6

chocolate チョコレート 会L14

choose えらぶ 選ぶ [u] 会L17

chopsticks はし 会L8

Christmas クリスマス 会L14

A B **C** **D** E F G H I J K L M N O P Q R S T U V W X Y Z

departing first　せんぱつ　先発　会L10(e)
departing second　じはつ　次発
　　　　　　　　　　　　　　　会L10(e)
department manager　ぶちょう　部長
　　　　　　　　　　　　　　　会L19
department store　デパート　会L4
depending on . . .　～によって　読L23-II
deposit　おあずけいれ　お預け入れ
　　　　　　　　　　　　　　　会L13(e)
dermatologist　ひふか　皮膚科　会L12(e)
desk　つくえ　机　会L2(e), 会L4
dialect　ほうげん　方言　会L11(e)
diary　にっき　日記　読L9-II, 会L18
dictionary　じしょ　辞書　会L2, 会L2(e)
die　しぬ　死ぬ [u]　会L6
difference　ちがい　違い　会L17
different　ちがう　違う [u]
　　　　　　　　　　　読L16-II, 会L23
different kinds of　いろいろ（な）　会L13
difficult　むずかしい　難しい　会L5
diligent　まじめ（な）　読L12-II, 会L19
dining commons　しょくどう　食堂
　　　　　　　　　　　　　　　会L7
dinner　ばんごはん　晩ご飯　会L3
dinner　ゆうしょく　夕食　会L23
directions　みち　道　会L16
dirty　きたない　汚い　会L16
disappear　いなくなる [u]　会L23
disappear　なくなる [u]　会L23
(be) disappointed　がっかりする [irr.]
　　　　　　　　　読L20-II, 会L23
discount coupon　わりびきけん　割引
　券　会L15
disgusted with　きらい（な）　嫌い　会L5
dish　さら　皿　会L14
dislike　きらい（な）　嫌い　会L5
disorganized　めちゃくちゃ（な）　会L21
do　する [irr.]　会L3
do　やる [u]　会L5
do laundry　せんたくする　洗濯する [irr.]
　　　　　　　　　　　　　　　会L8
do one's best　がんばる　頑張る [u]
　　　　　　　　　　　　　　　会L13
do physical exercises　うんどうする
　運動する [irr.]　会L9
do sightseeing　かんこうする　観光す
　る [irr.]　会L15
doctor　いしゃ　医者　会L1, 会L10
document　しょるい　書類　会L22
dog　いぬ　犬　会L4
don't look well　げんきがない　元気が
　ない　会L12
door　と　戸　読L10-II
door　ドア　会L2(e)
dormitory　りょう　寮　読L9-II, 会L17
double room　ダブル　会L15(e)
draw　かく　描く [u]　会L15
drawing　え　絵　会L15
dream　ゆめ　夢　会L11

drink　のみもの　飲み物　会L5
drink　のむ　飲む [u]　会L3
drive　うんてんする　運転する [irr.]　会L8
drive　ドライブ　会L11
drive (someone)　おくる　送る [u]　会L19
drop (something)　おとす　落とす [u]
　　　　　　　　　　　　　　　会L18
(be) dropped　おとされる　落とされる
　　　　　　　　　　　　　　　読L15-II
(something) drops　おちる　落ちる [ru]
　　　　　　　　　　　　　　　会L18
during the class　じゅぎょうちゅうに
　授業中に　会L16
DVD　ディーブイディー　DVD　会L7
dye　そめる [ru]　会L17(e)

=============== **E** ===============

e-mail　メール　会L4
ear　みみ　耳　会L7(e)
early　はやい　早い　会L3
(do something) early　はやく　早く/
　速く　会L10
earthquake　じしん　地震　会L15
easily　かんたんに　簡単に　読L23-II
east　ひがし　東　会L6(e)
easy　かんたん（な）　簡単　会L10
easy　らく（な）　楽　会L22
easy (problem)　やさしい　会L5
eat　たべる　食べる [ru]　会L3
economics　けいざい　経済　会L1, 会L2
Edo period　えどじだい　江戸時代
　　　　　　　　　　　　　　　読L20-II
eight　やっつ　八つ　会L9
eight days　ようか　八日　会L13
eight minutes　はっぷん/はちふん
　八分　会L1(e)
eight o'clock　はちじ　八時　会L1(e)
eight years old　はっさい　八歳　会L1(e)
eighteen minutes　じゅうはっぷん/じゅ
　うはちふん　十八分　会L1(e)
eighth day of a month, the　ようか
　八日　会L4(e)
election　せんきょ　選挙　会L23
electric engineering　でんきこうがく
　電気工学　読L19-III
electricity　でんき　電気　会L2(e), 会L6
electronic dictionary　でんしじしょ
　電子辞書　会L20
elementary school　しょうがっこう
　小学校　会L23
elementary school students　しょう
　がくせい　小学生　読L16-II
elephant　ぞう　象　会L13
eleven minutes　じゅういっぷん　十一
　分　会L1(e)
eleven o'clock　じゅういちじ　十一時
　　　　　　　　　　　　　　　会L1(e)
eleven years old　じゅういっさい　十一
　歳　会L1(e)

eleventh day of a month, the　じゅう
　いちにち　十一日　会L4(e)
embarrassing　はずかしい　恥ずかしい
　　　　　　　　　　　　　　　会L18
emotion　かんじょう　感情　読L23-II
(something) ends　おわる　終わる [u]
　　　　　　　　　　　　　　　会L9
energetic　げんき（な）　元気　会L5
English (language)　えいご　英語　会L1
English conversation　えいかいわ
　英会話　会L22
enjoy　たのしむ　楽しむ [u]　読L15-II
enough　たりる　足りる [ru]　会L17
ENT doctor　じびか　耳鼻科　会L12(e)
enter　はいる　入る [u]　会L6
entrance　いりぐち　入口　会L10(e)
envious　うらやましい　会L17
(somebody is) envious　うらやましが
　る　読L22-II
environment　かんきょう　環境　会L21
era　じだい　時代　読L14-II
erase　けす　消す [u]　会L6
eraser　けしゴム　消しゴム　会L2(e)
escape　にげる　逃げる [ru]　読L22-II
especially　とくに　特に　読L13-II
essay　さくぶん　作文　会L9
Europe　ヨーロッパ　会L22
evening　ゆうがた　夕方　会L18
every day　まいにち　毎日　会L3
every month　まいつき　毎月　読L18-III
every morning　まいあさ　毎朝　会L19
every night　まいばん　毎晩　会L3
every week　まいしゅう　毎週　会L8
everyone　みなさん　皆さん
　　　　　　　　　　読L6-III, 会L14
everyone (polite expression of みなさ
　ん)　みなさま　みな様　読L19-II
everything　なんでも　読L13-II
Everything is under control.　だいじょ
　うぶ　大丈夫　会L5
exactly　ちょうど　会L14
exam　しけん　試験　会L9
example　れい　例　会L11(e)
excellent food　ごちそう　読L9-II
exchange　こうかんする　交換する [irr.]
　　　　　　　　　　　　　　　会L20
Excuse me.　しつれいします　失礼しま
　す　会L16
Excuse me.　すみません　会G
exercise　れんしゅう　練習　会L11(e)
exit　でぐち　出口　会L10(e)
exit　でる　出る [ru]　読L6-I, 会L9
expensive　たかい　高い　会L2
experience　けいけん　経験
　　　　　　　　　　読L13-II, 会L15
explain　せつめいする　説明する [irr.]
　　　　　　　　　　　　　　　会L16
express　あらわす　表す [u]　読L23-II
express　きゅうこう　急行　会L10(e)

expression of gratitude　おれい　お礼
　　　会L19
extra money to spare for the cost of
　living　せいかつのゆとり　生活のゆとり
　　　読L18-II
extra-modest expression for ある
　ござる [u]　会L20
extra-modest expression for いう
　もうす　申す [u]　会L20
extra-modest expression for いく
　and くる　まいる　参る [u]　会L20
extra-modest expression for いる
　おる [u]　会L20
extra-modest expression for する
　いたす　致す [u]　会L20
extra-modest expression for たべる
　and のむ　いただく　頂く [u]　会L20
extra-modest expression for ～ている
　～ておる [u]　会L20
extra-modest expression for です
　～でござる [u]　会L20
extremely　すごく　会L5
extremely　ものすごく　会L23
eye　め　目　会L7, 会L7(e)

F

face　かお　顔　会L7(e), 会L10
facial expression　ひょうじょう　表情
　　　読L23-II
factory　こうじょう　工場　会L21
fail　しっぱいする　失敗する [irr.]　会L22
fall　あき　秋　会L10
fall down　ころぶ　転ぶ [u]　会L18
family　かぞく　家族　会L7
famous　ゆうめい（な）　有名　会L8
fan　せんす　扇子　会L20
far (away)　とおい　遠い　会L21
farm　はたけ　畑　読L12-II
fast　はやい　速い　会L7
(do something) fast　はやく　早く／
　速く　会L10
father　おとうさん　お父さん　会L1, 会L2
father　ちちおや　父親　読L14-II
(my) father　ちち　父　会L7
February　にがつ　二月　会L4(e)
fee　～だい　～代　読L18-III
feed　えさ　読L20-II
feel embarrassed　はずかしい　恥ずか
　しい　会L18
feel sick　きぶんがわるい　気分が悪い
　　　読L13-II, 会L18
feeling　かんじょう　感情　読L23-II
feeling　きもち　気持ち　読L23-II
female student　じょしがくせい　女子
　学生　読L18-II
festival　（お）まつり　（お）祭り　会L11
few, a　すくない　少ない　会L17
few seconds, a　しょうしょう　少々
　　　会L20

field　ぶんや　分野　読L17-II
fifteen minutes　じゅうごふん　十五分
　　　会L1(e)
fifth day of a month, the　いつか
　五日　会L4(e)
file　ファイル　会L16
final examination　きまつしけん　期末
　試験　会L16
finally　さいごに　最後に　会L23
find　みつける　見つける [ru]
　　　読L12-II, 会L21
find something agreeable　きにいる
　気に入る [u]　会L23
finger　ゆび　指　会L7(e)
fire　かじ　火事　会L17
firefighter　しょうぼうし　消防士　会L11
first　ひとつめ　一つ目　会L6(e)
first . . .　さいしょの～　最初の～
　　　読L23-II
first car　いちばんまえ　一番前　会L10(e)
first day of a month, the　ついたち
　一日　会L4(e)
first impression, the　だいいちいんしょ
　う　第一印象　読L13-III
first of all　まず　読L8-II, 会L18
first-year student　いちねんせい　一年
　生　会L1
fish　さかな　魚　会L2
fishing　つり　会L11
five　いつつ　五つ　会L9
five days　いつか　五日　会L13
five minutes　ごふん　五分　会L1(e)
five o'clock　ごじ　五時　会L1(e)
five years old　ごさい　五歳　会L1(e)
fix　なおす　直す [u]　会L16
flight　びん　便　会L10
flower　はな　花　会L12
fluent　べらべら（な）　会L22
fly　とぶ　飛ぶ [u]　読L16-II
fond of　すき（な）　好き　会L5
food　たべもの　食べ物　会L5
food cost　しょくひ　食費　読L18-III
foot　あし　足　会L7(e), 会L12
for . . .　～のために　読L19-III
for . . . months　～かげつ　～か月
　　　会L10
for . . . weeks　～しゅうかん　～週間
　　　会L10
for . . . years　～ねんかん　～年間
　　　読L14-II
for a long time　ずっと　会L22
for example　たとえば　例えば
　　　会L11(e), 読L16-II, 会L17
. . . for example　～とか　会L22
for the first time　はじめて　初めて
　　　会L12
for the sake of . . .　～のための　読L17-II
for two days　ふつかかん　二日間
　　　読L22-II

for two to three days　にさんにち
　二三日　会L12
foreign country　がいこく　外国　会L11
foreign language　がいこくご　外国語
　　　会L13
foreigner　がいこくじん　外国人　会L15
forget　わすれる　忘れる [ru]　会L6
former name of Tokyo　えど　江戸
　　　読L20-II
(be) found　みつかる　見つかる [u]　会L16
four　よっつ　四つ　会L9
four days　よっか　四日　会L13
four minutes　よんぷん　四分　会L1(e)
four o'clock　よじ　四時　会L1(e)
four years old　よんさい　四歳　会L1(e)
fourteen minutes　じゅうよんぷん
　十四分　会L1(e)
fourteenth day of a month, the　じゅ
　うよっか　十四日　会L4(e)
fourth day of a month, the　よっか
　四日　会L4(e)
free of charge　ただ　会L23
freedom　じゆう　自由　会L22
freely　じゆうに　自由に　会L22
Friday　きんようび　金曜日　会L4, 会L4(e)
friend　ともだち　友だち　会L1
friend　ゆうじん　友人　読L19-III
frightening　こわい　怖い　会L5
from . . .　～から　読L7-II, 会L9
from now on　これから　読L11-II, 会L16
front　まえ　前　会L4
front desk　フロント　会L15(e)
front end　いちばんまえ　一番前　会L10(e)
fun　たのしい　楽しい　会L5
funny　おもしろい　面白い　会L5
furniture　かぐ　家具　会L15
future　しょうらい　将来　会L11
future　みらい　未来　読L16-II

G

gain weight　ふとる　太る [u]　会L7
game　ゲーム　会L7
game　しあい　試合　会L12
gangster　やくざ　会L13
garbage　ごみ　会L16
garden　にわ　庭　会L15
gasoline　ガソリン　会L21
gate　かいさつ　改札　会L10(e)
general admission seat　じゆうせき
　自由席　会L10(e)
(generic counter for smaller items)
　～こ　～個　会L14
Germany　ドイツ　会L20
gesture　みぶり　身ぶり　読L20-II
get (a grade)　とる　取る [u]　会L11
get (from somebody)　もらう [u]　会L9
get a divorce　りこんする　離婚する
　[irr.]　会L17

get a full-time job (at . . .)　しゅうしょ
くする　就職する [irr.]　会L17
get acquainted with　しりあう　知り合
う [u]　会L19
get along well　なかがいい　仲がいい
会L19
get angry　おこる　怒る [u]
読L12-II, 会L19
get crowded　こむ　込む [u]
読L13-III, 会L17
get depressed　おちこむ　落ち込む [u]
会L16
get off　おりる　降りる [ru]　会L6
get to know　しる　知る [u]　会L7
get up　おきる　起きる [ru]　会L3
get used to . . .　なれる　慣れる [ru]
会L17
Get well soon.　おだいじに　お大事に
会L12
girl　おんなのこ　女の子　会L11
girlfriend　かのじょ　彼女
読L11-II, 会L12
give　わたす　渡す [u]　読L20-II
give (me)　くれる [ru]　会L14
give (to others)　あげる [ru]　会L14
give (to pets, plants, younger
siblings, etc.)　やる [u]　会L21
give up　あきらめる [ru]　会L14
give warning　ちゅういする　注意する
[irr.]　会L19
glad　うれしい　会L13
glass　グラス　会L14
glasses　めがね　眼鏡　会L7
gloves　てぶくろ　手袋　会L10
go　いく　行く [u]　会L3
go back　かえる　帰る [u]　会L3
go back　もどる　戻る [u]　読L16-II
go on a diet　ダイエットする [irr.]　会L11
go out　でかける　出かける [ru]　会L5
go through　とおる　通る [u]　読L15-II
go to pick up　むかえにいく　迎えに行
く [u]　会L16
go to sleep　ねる　寝る [ru]　会L3
go well　うまくいく [u]　読L22-II
God　かみさま　神様　読L12-II, 会L22
(tire) goes flat　パンクする [irr.]　会L23
(something) goes off　きえる　消える
[ru]　会L18
gold　きんいろ　金色　会L9(e)
gold　ゴールド　会L9(e)
golf　ゴルフ　会L13
good　いい　会L3
Good afternoon.　こんにちは　会G
good at . . .　じょうず(な)　上手　会L8
good child　いいこ　いい子　会L9
good deed　いいこと　読L10-II
Good evening.　こんばんは　会G
good for health　からだにいい　体に
いい　読L13-II

Good morning.　おはよう / おはようご
ざいます　会G
Good night.　おやすみ(なさい)　会G
Good-bye.　さようなら　会G
good-looking　かっこいい　会L5
government　せいふ　政府　会L21
grade (on a test, etc.)　せいせき　成績
会L12
graduate (from . . .)　そつぎょうする
卒業する [irr.]　会L15
graduate school　だいがくいん　大学院
会L16
graduate student　だいがくいんせい
大学院生　会L1
graduation ceremony　そつぎょうしき
卒業式　会L15
grammar　ぶんぽう　文法　会L11(e), 会L13
grandfather　おじいさん　会L7
grandmother　おばあさん　会L7
gray　グレー　会L9(e)
gray　はいいろ　灰色　会L9(e)
greatly　たいへん　読L19-II
green　グリーン　会L9(e)
green　みどり　緑　会L9(e), 読L15-II
green tea　(お)ちゃ　(お)茶　会L3
grill　やく　焼く [u]　会L21
grin　ニヤニヤする [irr.]　読L13-II
guardian deity of children　じぞう /
おじぞうさん　読L10-II
guest　おきゃくさん　お客さん　会L17
guitar　ギター　会L9

Ⓗ

haiku (Japanese poetry)　はいく
俳句　読L17-II
hair　かみ　髪　会L7, 会L7(e)
hair style　かみがた　髪形　会L17(e)
half　はん　半　会L1
half past two　にじはん　二時半　会L1
hamburger　ハンバーガー　会L3
hand　て　手　会L7(e), 読L15-II
hand　わたす　渡す [u]　読L20-II
hand in (something)　だす　出す [u]
会L16
hangover　ふつかよい　二日酔い　会L12
happen　おこる　起こる [u]　読L21-II
happy (lasting happiness)　しあわせ
(な)　幸せ　読L10-II, 会L13
hat　ぼうし　帽子　会L2
hate　だいきらい(な)　大嫌い　会L5
have a fever　ねつがある　熱がある [u]
会L12
have a fight　けんかする [irr.]　会L11
have a lot of free time　ひま(な)　暇
会L5
have a scheduling conflict　つごうが
わるい　都合が悪い　会L12
have a stomachache　おなかをこわす
[u]　会L23

have a talk　はなしをする　話をする [irr.]
読L9-II, 会L19
have difficulty　こまる　困る [u]　会L16
have one's hair permed　パーマをかけ
る [ru]　会L17(e)
head　あたま　頭　会L7(e)
healthy　げんき(な)　元気　会L5
hear　きく　聞く [u]　会L3
heart　こころ　心　読L20-II
heater　ヒーター　会L17
heavens, the　てん　天　読L12-II
heavy　おもい　重い　会L20
Hello? (used on the phone)　もしもし
会L7
help　たすける　助ける [ru]
読L16-II, 会L22
help　てつだう　手伝う [u]　会L6
(be) helped　たすかる　助かる [u]　会L18
here　ここ　会L2
Here it is.　どうぞ　会L2
high　たかい　高い　会L2
high heels　ハイヒール　会L20
high school　こうこう　高校　会L1
high school student　こうこうせい
高校生　会L1
history　れきし　歴史　会L1, 会L2
hit　なぐる　殴る [u]　会L21
hobby　しゅみ　趣味　読L11-II, 会L20
hold　もつ　持つ [u]　会L6
hold back for the time being　えん
りょする　遠慮する [irr.]　会L19
hold something in one's arm　だく
抱く [u]　読L20-II
holiday　やすみ　休み　会L5
home　いえ　家　会L3
home　うち　会L3
(someone's) home　おたく　お宅　会L13
homeless　ホームレス　読L15-II
homesickness　ホームシック　会L12
homestay　ホームステイ　会L8
homework　しゅくだい　宿題
会L5, 会L11(e)
honorific expression for いう　おっ
しゃる [u]　会L19
honorific expression for いく, くる,
and いる　いらっしゃる [u]　会L19
honorific expression for くれる　くだ
さる　下さる [u]　会L19
honorific expression for する　なさる
[u]　会L19
honorific expression for たべる and の
む　めしあがる　召し上がる [u]　会L19
honorific expression for 〜ている
〜ていらっしゃる [u]　会L19
honorific expression for ねる　おやす
みになる　お休みになる [u]　会L19
honorific expression for みる　ごらん
になる　ご覧になる [u]　会L19
honorific language　けいご　敬語　会L19

(K)

Kabuki　かぶき　歌舞伎　会L9

kanji　かんじ　漢字　会L6

karaoke　カラオケ　会L8

karate　からて　空手　会L13

keep a promise　やくそくをまもる　約束を守る [u]　会L13

keep company　つきあう　付き合う [u]　会L15

keep (someone) waiting　またせる　待たせる [ru]　会L20

key　かぎ　会L17

kick　ける [u]　会L21

. . . kilograms　～キロ　会L13

. . . kilometers　～キロ　会L13

kimono　きもの　着物　読L9-II, 会L13

kind　しんせつ（な）　親切　会L7

kind (person)　やさしい　会L5

kind, a　しゅるい　種類　会L19

knit　あむ　編む [u]　会L13

(get to) know　しる　知る [u]　会L7

Korea　かんこく　韓国　会L1, 会L2

(L)

ladders　はしご　読L17-II

lake　みずうみ　湖　会L11

landlady　おおやさん　大家さん　会L14

landlord　おおやさん　大家さん　会L14

language　ことば　言葉　会L13

. . . language　～ご　～語　会L1

large　おおきい　大きい　会L5

last . . .　さいごの～　最後の～　読L23-II

last car　いちばんうしろ　一番後ろ　会L10(e)

last month　せんげつ　先月　会L4(e), 会L9

last train　しゅうでん　終電　会L10(e), 会L21

last week　せんしゅう　先週　会L4, 会L4(e)

last year　きょねん　去年　会L4(e), 会L9

lastly　さいごに　最後に　読L8-II

late　おそい　遅い　会L10

late (for)　おそくなる　遅くなる [u]　会L8

late (for an appointment)　ちこくする　遅刻する [irr.]　会L11

(do something) late　おそく　遅く　読L4-III, 会L6

later on　あとで　後で　会L6

laugh　わらう　笑う [u]　会L16

lawyer　べんごし　弁護士　会L1, 会L13

lay　おく　置く [u]　会L21

lazy person　なまけもの　怠け者　会L19

lead a life　せいかつする　生活する [irr.]　会L20

learn　ならう　習う [u]　会L11

leave　のこす　残す [u]　読L15-II

leave (someone/something) alone　ほ（う）っておく　放っておく [u]　会L22

leave behind　わすれる　忘れる [ru]　会L6

left　ひだり　左　会L4

left side　ひだりがわ　左側　会L6(e)

leg　あし　足　会L7(e), 会L12

leisurely　ゆっくり　会L6

lend　かす　貸す [u]　会L13

let me see . . .　ええと　会L16

Let me see.　そうですね　会L3

letter　じ　字　会L20

letter　てがみ　手紙　会L4

letter　もじ　文字　読L17-II

letter of recommendation　すいせんじょう　推薦状　会L16

library　としょかん　図書館　会L2

license　めんきょ　免許　会L22

life　せいかつ　生活　会L10

light　かるい　軽い　会L20

light blue　みずいろ　水色　会L9(e)

like　すき（な）　好き　会L5

like this　このように　読L23-II

like this　こんなふう　会L22

. . . like this　こんな～　会L14

line number . . .　～ぎょうめ　～行目　会L11(e)

listen　きく　聞く [u]　会L3

literature　ぶんがく　文学　会L1, 読L7-II

little, a　すくない　少ない　会L17

little, a　すこし　少し　読L7-II, 会L21

little, a　ちょっと　会L3

little more, a　もうすこし　もう少し　会L22

live　すむ　住む [u]　会L7

lively　にぎやか（な）　会L5

living　せいかつ　生活　会L10

living alone　ひとりぐらし　一人暮らし　会L22

living with a local family　ホームステイ　会L8

local (train)　ふつう　普通　会L10(e)

lock　かぎ　会L17

lock　かぎをかける [ru]　会L17

lonely　さびしい　寂しい　会L9

long　ながい　長い　会L7

long for　なつかしい　読L19-II

long time　ながいあいだ　長い間　読L21-II

look . . . (facial expression)　～かおをする　～顔をする [irr.]　会L23

look at　みる　見る [ru]　会L3

look for　さがす　探す [u]　会L15

look forward (to)　（～を）たのしみにする　楽しみにする [irr.]　読L7-II

look good (on somebody)　にあう　似合う [u]　会L14

look into (a matter)　しらべる　調べる [ru]　会L15

look pale　かおがあおい　顔が青い　会L9(e)

looking after a house during someone's absence　るすばん　留守番　会L23

looking for . . .　～ぼしゅう　～募集　読L11-II

lose　なくす [u]　会L12

lose (a match)　まける　負ける [ru]　会L22

lose one's way　みちにまよう　道に迷う [u]　会L16

lose weight　やせる [ru]　会L7

(be) lost　なくなる [u]　会L23

lot, a　たくさん　会L4

lottery　たからくじ　宝くじ　会L17

love　あいす　愛す [u]　読L14-II

love　だいすき（な）　大好き　会L5

lowest, the　さいてい　最低　会L17

lunch　ひるごはん　昼ご飯　会L3

(M)

(be) made　できる [ru]　会L14

magazine　ざっし　雑誌　会L3

magnifying glass　むしめがね　虫めがね　読L17-II

mainly　おもに　主に　読L17-II

major　せんこう　専攻　会L1

make　つくる　作る [u]　会L8

make a fool of . . .　ばかにする [irr.]　会L21

make a mistake　まちがえる　間違える [ru]　会L21

make a phone call　でんわをかける　電話をかける [ru]　会L6

make a photocopy　コピーをとる　コピーを取る [u]　会L22

make a plan　けいかくをたてる　計画を立てる [ru]　会L22

make dirty　よごす　汚す [u]　会L18

make hair even　そろえる [ru]　会L17(e)

make public　はっぴょうする　発表する [irr.]　読L17-II

make tea, coffee, etc.　いれる [ru]　会L17

(makes a noun plural)　～たち　会L14

male student　だんしがくせい　男子学生　読L18-II

man　おとこ　男　読L11-II, 会L17

man　おとこのひと　男の人　会L7

mandarin orange　みかん　会L14

many　たくさん　会L4

many . . .　おおくの～　多くの～　読L21-II

many times　なんども　何度も　読L17-II, 会L22

map　ちず　地図　会L15

March　さんがつ　三月　会L4(e)

mark　マーク　読L23-II

(get) married　けっこんする　結婚する [irr.]　会L7

married couple　ふうふ　夫婦　会L14

match　しあい　試合　会L12

matters　こと　事　読L11-II, 会L21

May　ごがつ　五月　会L4(e)

maybe　たぶん　多分　会L12

meal　ごはん　ご飯　会L4

meal　しょくじ　食事　読L21-II

mean-spirited　いじわる（な）　意地悪　会L9

meaning　いみ　意味　会L11(e), 会L12

meat　にく　肉　会L2

medicine　くすり　薬　会L9

meet　あう　会う　覚える [u]　会L4

memorize　おぼえる　覚える [ru]　会L9

memory　おもいで　思い出　会L23

menu　メニュー　会L2

message　でんごん　伝言　読L22-II

messy　めちゃくちゃ（な）　会L21

Mexico　メキシコ　読L5-II

middle-aged man　おじさん　会L14

middle-aged woman　おばさん　会L14

milk　ぎゅうにゅう　牛乳　会L10

Milky Way, the　あまのがわ　天の川　読L12-II

mind　こころ　心　読L20-II

minus　マイナス　会L12

miss　なつかしい　読L19-II

miss (a train, bus, etc.)　のりおくれる　乗り遅れる [ru]　会L16

mistake　まちがい　間違い　会L19

Monday　げつようび　月曜日　会L4, 会L4(e)

money　（お）かね　（お）金　会L6

monkey　さる　猿　会L22

month after next, the　さらいげつ　再来月　会L4(e)

moon　つき　月　会L20

more　もっと　会L11

moreover, . . .　それに　会L17

morning　あさ　朝　会L3

mosquito　か　蚊　会L21

mother　おかあさん　お母さん　会L1, 会L2

(my) mother　はは　母　会L7

motorcycle　バイク　会L13

mountain　やま　山　読L5-II, 会L11

mountain road　やまみち　山道　読L10-II

mouth　くち　口　会L7, 会L7(e)

move (to another place to live)　ひっこす　引っ越す [u]　会L19

(be) moved (by . . .)　かんどうする　感動する [irr.]　会L13

movie　えいが　映画　会L3

movie theater　えいがかん　映画館　会L15

moving　ひっこし　引っ越し　読L18-III

Mr./Ms. . . .　〜さま　〜様　読L5-II

Mr./Ms. . . .　〜さん　会L1

Mr./Ms. . . . (casual)　〜くん　〜君　会L14

much　よく　会L3

multistory apartment building　マンション　会L14

municipal hospital　しみんびょういん　市民病院　会L6

music　おんがく　音楽　会L3

musical instrument　がっき　楽器　会L13

my name is . . .　〜ともうします　〜と申します　会L13

my place　うち　会L3

name　なまえ　名前　会L1

name　なまえをつける　名前をつける [ru]　読L17-II

narrow　せまい　狭い　会L12

nature　しぜん　自然　読L15-II

near　ちかい　近い　会L13

near　ちかく　近く　会L4

near future　こんど　今度　会L9

nearby　ちかく　近く　会L4

neck　くび　首　会L7(e)

necktie　ネクタイ　会L14

need　いる [u]　会L8

neglect　ほ（う）っておく　放っておく [u]　会L22

neighborhood　きんじょ　近所　読L11-II

(get) nervous　きんちょうする　緊張する [irr.]　会L12

new　あたらしい　新しい　会L5

New Year's　（お）しょうがつ　（お）正月　読L10-II, 会L11

news　ニュース　会L17

newspaper　しんぶん　新聞　会L2

next　つぎ　次　会L6

next　となり　隣　会L4

next (stop), . . .　つぎは〜　次は〜　会L10(e)

next month　らいげつ　来月　会L4(e), 会L8

next semester　らいがっき　来学期　会L10

next week　らいしゅう　来週　会L4(e), 会L6

next year　らいねん　来年　会L4(e), 会L6

nice　すてき（な）　素敵　会L12

Nice to meet you.　よろしくおねがいします　よろしくお願いします　会G

night　よる　夜　読L5-II, 会L6

night club　クラブ　会L15

. . . nights　〜はく　〜泊　会L15(e)

nine　ここのつ　九つ　会L9

nine days　ここのか　九日　会L13

nine minutes　きゅうふん　九分　会L1(e)

nine o'clock　くじ　九時　会L1(e)

nine years old　きゅうさい　九歳　会L1(e)

nineteen minutes　じゅうきゅうふん　十九分　会L1(e)

1960's　せんきゅうひゃくろくじゅうねんだい　1960年代　読L17-II

ninth day of a month, the　ここのか　九日　会L4(e)

no　いや　会L23

no　ううん　会L8

No.　いいえ　会G

no good　だめ（な）　会L13

no matter what　ぜったいに　絶対に　読L20-II

noisy　うるさい　会L22

nonsmoking car　きんえんしゃ　禁煙車　会L10(e)

nonsmoking room　きんえんルーム　禁煙ルーム　会L15(e)

noon　ひる　昼　読L9-II

north　きた　北　会L6(e)

nose　はな　鼻　会L7(e)

not . . . anything　なにも + negative　何も　会L7

not . . . yet　まだ + negative　会L8

not any longer　もう〜ない　読L13-II

not at all　ぜんぜん + negative　全然　会L3

Not at all.　いいえ　会G

not at home　るす　留守　会L21

not busy　ひま（な）　暇　会L5

not much　あまり + negative　会L3

not spacious　せまい　狭い　会L12

Not to worry.　だいじょうぶ　大丈夫　会L5

notebook　ノート　会L2

nothing in particular　べつに + negative　別に　会L7

nothing more than . . .　ただの〜　読L21-II

notice　きがつく　気が付く [u]　会L21

novel　しょうせつ　小説　会L20

November　じゅういちがつ　十一月　会L4(e)

now　いま　今　会L1

number　ばんごう　番号　会L1

number . . .　〜ばん　〜番　会L11(e), 会L15

nurse　かんごし　看護師　会L11

object　もくてき　目的　読L18-II

object to　はんたいする　反対する [irr.]　会L22

obstetrician and gynecologist　さんふじんか　産婦人科　会L12(e)

occupation　しごと　仕事　会L1, 会L8

occur　おこる　起こる [u]　読L21-II

o'clock　〜じ　〜時　会L1

October　じゅうがつ　十月　会L4(e)

of course　もちろん　会L7

office worker　かいしゃいん　会社員
　　会L1, 会L8
often　よく　会L3
Oh!　おや?　会L20
okay　まあまあ　会L11
old (thing)　ふるい　古い　会L5
old days　むかし　昔　読L15-II, 会L21
old man　おじいさん　会L7
old woman　おばあさん　会L7
older brother　おにいさん　お兄さん
　　会L1, 会L7
(my) older brother　あに　兄　会L14
older sister　おねえさん　お姉さん
　　会L1, 会L7
(my) older sister　あね　姉　会L7
on　うえ　上　会L4
(be) on close terms　なかがいい　仲が
　　いい　会L19
on foot　あるいて　歩いて　会L10
(be) on good terms　なかがいい　仲が
　　いい　会L19
on the contrary　ところが　読L21-II
(be) on the heavy side　ふとっています
　　太っています　会L7
once a year　いちねんにいちど　一年に
　　一度　読L12-II
once in a lifetime　いっしょうにいちど
　　一生に一度　読L13-II
once upon a time　むかしむかし　昔々
　　読L10-II
one　ひとつ　一つ　会L9
one . . .　ある〜　読L12-II
one day　いちにち　一日　会L13
one hour　いちじかん　一時間　会L4
100-yen coin　ひゃくえんだま　百円玉
　　会L13(e)
one minute　いっぷん　一分　会L1(e)
one more time　もういちど　もう一度
　　会L15
one night with two meals　いっぱくに
　　しょくつき　一泊二食付　会L15(e)
one o'clock　いちじ　一時　会L1, 会L1(e)
one person　ひとり　一人　会L7
one way　かたみち　片道　会L10(e)
one year old　いっさい　一歳　会L1(e)
one-room apartment　ワンルームマン
　　ション　読L18-III
oneself　じぶん　自分　読L10-II, 会L17
only . . .　〜だけ　会L11
open (something)　あける　開ける [ru]
　　会L6
open space　ひろば　広場　読L15-II
(something) opens　あく　開く [u]
　　会L18
operation　しゅじゅつ　手術　会L12(e)
ophthalmologist　がんか　眼科　会L12(e)
oppose　はんたいする　反対する [irr.]
　　会L22
or　〜か〜　会L10

. . . or more　〜いじょう　〜以上　読L18-II
originally　ほんとうは　本当は　会L19
orthopedic surgeon　せいけいげか
　　整形外科　会L12(e)
other　ほかの　会L16
other day, the　このあいだ　この間
　　会L16
other side, the　むこう　向こう　読L12-II
other than . . .　〜いがい　〜以外
　　読L16-II
otorhinolaryngologist　じびか　耳鼻科
　　会L12(e)
our person in charge　かかりのもの
　　係の者　会L20
outdoor activities　アウトドア　読L11-II
outside　そと　外　会L18
over there　あそこ　会L2
over there　むこう　向こう　読L12-II
oversleep　あさねぼうする　朝寝坊する
　　[irr.]　会L16
overtime work　ざんぎょう　残業
　　読L8-II, 会L17
own (a pet)　かう　飼う [u]　会L11
owner　しゅじん　主人　読L20-II

Ⓟ

page　ページ　会L6
page number . . .　〜ページ　会L11(e)
painful　いたい　痛い　会L12
paint　かく　描く [u]　会L15
painting　え　絵　会L15
panda　パンダ　会L17
pants　パンツ　会L10
paper　かみ　紙　会L17
(term) paper　レポート　会L13
parcel　こづつみ　小包　会L5(e)
parent　おや　親　会L16
parenthesis　かっこ　会L11(e)
parents　りょうしん　両親　会L14
park　こうえん　公園　会L4
part-time job　アルバイト　会L4
partner　あいて　相手　会L22
parts from　はなれる　離れる [ru]　会L23
party　パーティー　会L8
party of . . . people　〜めいさま　〜名
　　様　会L19
pass　とおる　通る [u]　読L15-II
(time) pass　たつ [u]　読L19-II
passbook　つうちょう　通帳　会L13(e)
passbook update　つうちょうきにゅう
　　通帳記入　会L13(e)
past　むかし　昔　会L21
pastime　しゅみ　趣味　会L20
patient　がまんする　我慢する [irr.]
　　会L23
pay　はらう　払う [u]　会L10
peace　へいわ　平和　読L15-II
Peace Memorial Museum　へいわきねん
　　しりょうかん　平和記念資料館　読L15-II

pen　ペン　会L2, 会L2(e)
pencil　えんぴつ　鉛筆　会L2, 会L2(e)
people　ひとびと　人々　読L12-II
. . . people　〜じん　〜人　会L1
perform　やる [u]　会L5
permanent　パーマ　会L17(e)
person　ひと　人　会L4
. . . person(s)　〜めい　〜名　会L15(e)
person on one's side　みかた　味方
　　読L16-II
personal computer　パソコン　会L6
personal identification number　あん
　　しょうばんごう　暗証番号　会L13(e)
personality　せいかく　性格　会L19
pervert　ちかん　会L21
pet　ペット　会L15
photograph　しゃしん　写真　会L4
physical labor such as construction
　　ちからしごと　力仕事　読L18-III
physician　ないか　内科　会L12(e)
piano　ピアノ　会L9
pick up (something)　ひろう　拾う [u]
　　会L22
picture　え　絵　会L15
picture　しゃしん　写真　会L4
pink　ピンク　会L9(e)
pitiful　かわいそう(な)　読L12-II
pizza　ピザ　読L6-III, 会L9
place　おく　置く [u]　会L21
place　ところ　所　会L8
place　ばしょ　場所　読L16-II, 会L23
place an order　ちゅうもんする　注文す
　　る [irr.]　会L18
place of origin　くに　国　会L7
plan　よてい　予定　会L15
plate　さら　皿　会L14
platform　ホーム　会L10(e), 読L22-II
play　あそぶ　遊ぶ [u]　会L6
play (a string instrument or piano)
　　ひく　弾く [u]　会L9
Please.　どうぞ　会L2
. . ., please.　(〜を)おねがいします
　　会L2
Please give me . . .　(〜を)ください
　　会L2
Please give my best regards (to . . .)
　　よろしくおつたえください　よろしくお
　　伝えください　会L19
Please go and come back.　いって
　　らっしゃい　会G
pleasure　たのしみ　楽しみ　読L21-II
P.M.　ごご　午後　会L1
pocket　ポケット　読L16-II
poem　し　詩　読L17-II
. . . points　〜てん　〜点　会L11
police　けいさつ　警察　会L21
police officer　けいさつかん　警察官
　　会L11
police station　けいさつ　警察　会L21

A B C D E F G H I J K L M N O P Q R **S** T U V W X Y Z

say nice things　ほめる [ru]　会L21

scenery　けしき　景色　読L15-II

schedule　よてい　予定　会L15

scholarship　しょうがくきん　奨学金　会L16

school　がっこう　学校　会L3

science　かがく　科学　会L1

scratch　ひっかく [u]　読L20-II

sea　うみ　海　会L5

season　きせつ　季節　会L10

second　ふたつめ　二つ目　会L6(e)

second day of a month, the　ふつか　二日　会L4(e)

secondly　つぎに　次に　読L8-II

secret　ひみつ　秘密　読L16-II, 会L17

see　みる　見る [ru]　会L3

see (a person)　あう　会う [u]　会L4

See you. (lit., I'm leaving ahead of you.)　おさきにしつれいします　お先に失礼します　会L18

seldom　めったに～ない　読L21-II

select　えらぶ　選ぶ [u]　会L17

sell　うる　売る [u]　読L10-II, 会L15

send　おくる　送る [u]　会L14

senior member of a group　せんぱい　先輩　読L14-II, 会L22

separate　わかれる　別れる [ru]　会L12

(something/someone) separates　はなれる　離れる [ru]　会L23

September　くがつ　九月　会L4(e)

serious　まじめ（な）　読L12-II, 会L19

serious (illness)　おもい　重い　会L20

serving . . . areas　～ほうめん　～方面　会L10(e)

set　セット　会L17(e)

seven　ななつ　七つ　会L9

seven days　なのか　七日　会L13

seven minutes　ななふん　七分　会L1(e)

seven o'clock　しちじ　七時　会L1(e)

seven years old　ななさい　七歳　会L1(e)

seventeen minutes　じゅうななふん　十七分　会L1(e)

seventh day of a month, the　なのか　七日　会L4(e)

sexual offender　ちかん　会L21

shampoo　シャンプー　会L17(e), 会L18

shave　そる [u]　会L17(e)

shave one's beard　ひげをそる [u]　会L17

Shinkansen　しんかんせん　新幹線　会L10

ship　ふね　船　会L10

shirt　シャツ　会L10

shoes　くつ　靴　会L2

shop　ばいてん　売店　会L10(e)

shop　みせ　店　読L4-III, 会L13

. . . shop　～や　～屋　会L20

shopping　かいもの　買い物　会L4

shopping mall　ショッピングモール　会L17

short (length)　みじかい　短い　会L7

short (stature)　せがひくい　背が低い　会L7

short form of ～（ん）でしょう　～（ん）だろう　会L18

(be) shot　じゅうでうたれる　銃で撃たれる　読L17-II

shoulder　かた　肩　会L7(e)

show　あらわす　表す [u]　読L23-II

show　みせる　見せる [ru]　会L16

show (someone) around　あんないする　案内する [irr.]　読L9-II, 会L16

shower　シャワー　会L6

shrine　じんじゃ　神社　会L11

shy person　はずかしがりや　恥ずかしがり屋　会L19

sickness　びょうき　病気　会L9, 会L12(e)

side　よこ　横　読L23-II

sideburns　もみあげ　会L17(e)

silver　ぎんいろ　銀色　会L9(e)

silver　シルバー　会L9(e)

similar　おなじような　同じような　読L23-II

simple　かんたん（な）　簡単　会L10

sing　うたう　歌う [u]　会L7

singer　かしゅ　歌手　会L11

single room　シングル　会L15(e)

sit down　かける [ru]　会L19

sit down　すわる　座る [u]　会L6

six　むっつ　六つ　会L9

six days　むいか　六日　会L13

six minutes　ろっぷん　六分　会L1(e)

six o'clock　ろくじ　六時　会L1(e)

six years old　ろくさい　六歳　会L1(e)

sixteen minutes　じゅうろっぷん　十六分　会L1(e)

sixth day of a month, the　むいか　六日　会L4(e)

size　おおきさ　大きさ　会L16

ski　スキー　会L9

skillful　じょうず（な）　上手　会L8

skillfully　うまく　読L22-II

skirt　スカート　会L18

sky　そら　空　読L16-II

sky, the　てん　天　読L12-II

sleep　ねる　寝る [ru]　会L3

sleepy　ねむい　眠い　会L10

slow　おそい　遅い　会L10

slowly　ゆっくり　会L6

small　ちいさい　小さい　会L5

small train usually for tourists　トロッコれっしゃ　トロッコ列車　読L15-II

smart　あたまがいい　頭がいい　会L7

smile　にこにこする [irr.]　読L20-II

smoke　たばこをすう　たばこを吸う [u]　会L6

smoking room　きつえんルーム　喫煙ルーム　会L15(e)

snack　（お）かし　（お）菓子　会L11

snapping turtle　すっぽん　読L13-II

sneakers　スニーカー　会L20

snow　ゆき　雪　読L10-II, 会L12

so　あんなに　会L20-II

so　だから　会L4

. . ., so　～けど　会L15

soba　そば　会L15

sober　まじめ（な）　読L12-II, 会L19

soccer　サッカー　会L23

society　しゃかい　社会　会L23

socks　くつした　靴下　会L23

sofa　ソファ　会L18

software　ソフト　会L23

(be) sold　うれる　売れる [ru]　読L20-II

somehow　なんだか　読L22-II

something　なにか　何か　会L8

something like . . .　～のようなもの　読L16-II

sometimes　ときどき　時々　会L3

song　うた　歌　会L7

Sorry to interrupt you.　しつれいします　失礼します　会L16

sort, a　しゅるい　種類　会L19

so-so　まあまあ　会L11

sound　おと　音　会L20

soup　スープ　会L18

south　みなみ　南　会L6(e), 読L15-II

souvenir　（お）みやげ　（お）土産　会L4

soy sauce　しょうゆ　しょう油　会L18

spa　おんせん　温泉　会L11

space alien　うちゅうじん　宇宙人　会L20

spacious　ひろい　広い　会L15

speak　はなす　話す [u]　会L3

special delivery　そくたつ　速達　会L5(e)

speech　スピーチ　会L21

spend time pleasantly　あそぶ　遊ぶ [u]　会L6

spoon　スプーン　会L17

sports　スポーツ　会L3

spring　はる　春　会L10

square　ひろば　広場　読L15-II

St. Valentine's Day　バレンタインデー　会L14

stairs　かいだん　階段　会L10(e)

stand　ばいてん　売店　会L10(e)

stand up　たつ　立つ [u]　会L6

standard Japanese　ひょうじゅんご　標準語　会L11(e)

stare (at)　じろじろみる　じろじろ見る [ru]　会L8

station　えき　駅　読L6-I, 会L10

station attendant　えきいん（さん）　駅員（さん）　会L16

stay (at a hotel, etc.)　とまる　泊まる [u]　会L10

日本地図 Map of Japan
にほんちず

広島（原爆ドーム）
ひろしま　げんばく

京都（東寺）
きょうと　とうじ

日本アルプス
にほん

姫路（姫路城）
ひめじ　ひめじじょう

伊万里（伊万里焼）
いまり　いまりやき

金沢
かなざわ

琵琶湖
びわこ

神戸
こうべ

長崎（平和の像）
ながさき　へいわ　ぞう

名古屋
なごや

大阪
おおさか

桜島
さくらじま

沖縄（琉球舞踊）
おきなわ　りゅうきゅうぶよう

奈良（大仏）
なら　だいぶつ

白川郷
しらかわごう

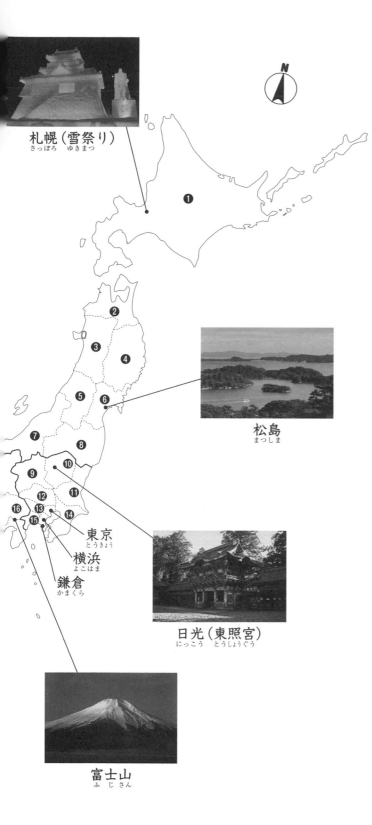

札幌（雪祭り）
さっぽろ　ゆきまつり

松島
まつしま

日光（東照宮）
にっこう　とうしょうぐう

富士山
ふじさん

東京
とうきょう

横浜
よこはま

鎌倉
かまくら

北海道地方
ほっかいどうちほう
❶ 北海道
　ほっかいどう

東北地方
とうほくちほう
❷ 青森県
　あおもりけん
❸ 秋田県
　あきたけん
❹ 岩手県
　いわてけん
❺ 山形県
　やまがたけん
❻ 宮城県
　みやぎけん
❼ 新潟県
　にいがたけん
❽ 福島県
　ふくしまけん

関東地方
かんとうちほう
❾ 群馬県
　ぐんまけん
❿ 栃木県
　とちぎけん
⓫ 茨城県
　いばらきけん
⓬ 埼玉県
　さいたまけん
⓭ 東京都
　とうきょうと
⓮ 千葉県
　ちばけん
⓯ 神奈川県
　かながわけん

中部地方
ちゅうぶちほう
⓰ 山梨県
　やまなしけん
⓱ 長野県
　ながのけん
⓲ 静岡県
　しずおかけん
⓳ 富山県
　とやまけん
⓴ 石川県
　いしかわけん
㉑ 福井県
　ふくいけん
㉒ 岐阜県
　ぎふけん
㉓ 愛知県
　あいちけん

近畿地方
きんきちほう
㉔ 滋賀県
　しがけん
㉕ 三重県
　みえけん
㉖ 京都府
　きょうとふ
㉗ 大阪府
　おおさかふ
㉘ 奈良県
　ならけん
㉙ 和歌山県
　わかやまけん
㉚ 兵庫県
　ひょうごけん

中国地方
ちゅうごくちほう
㉛ 鳥取県
　とっとりけん
㉜ 島根県
　しまねけん
㉝ 岡山県
　おかやまけん
㉞ 広島県
　ひろしまけん
㉟ 山口県
　やまぐちけん

四国地方
しこくちほう
㊱ 香川県
　かがわけん
㊲ 徳島県
　とくしまけん
㊳ 愛媛県
　えひめけん
㊴ 高知県
　こうちけん

九州地方
きゅうしゅうちほう
㊵ 福岡県
　ふくおかけん
㊶ 佐賀県
　さがけん
㊷ 長崎県
　ながさきけん
㊸ 大分県
　おおいたけん
㊹ 熊本県
　くまもとけん
㊺ 宮崎県
　みやざきけん
㊻ 鹿児島県
　かごしまけん
㊼ 沖縄県
　おきなわけん

写真提供・協力：東寺／東大寺(撮影：矢野建彦)／奈良市観光協会／伊万里市観光課

数 Numbers
かず

	regular				h→p	h→p/b	p	k
1	いち				いっp	いっp	（いっ）	いっ
2	に							
3	さん				p	b		
4	よん	し	よ	よ	p			
5	ご							
6	ろく				ろっp	ろっp	（ろっ）	ろっ
7	なな	しち	しち					
8	はち				（はっp）	はっp	（はっ）	はっ
9	きゅう	く	く					
10	じゅう				じゅっp じっp	じゅっp じっp	じゅっ じっ	じゅっ じっ
how many	なん				p	b		
	〜ドル dollars 〜円 yen 〜枚 sheets 〜度 degrees 〜十 ten 〜万 ten thousand	〜月 month	〜時 o'clock 〜時間 hours	〜年 year 〜年間 years 〜人 people	〜分 minute 〜分間 minutes	〜本 sticks 〜杯 cups 〜匹 animals 〜百 hundred	〜ページ page 〜ポンド pounds	〜か月 months 〜課 lesson 〜回 times 〜個 small items

This chart shows how sounds in numbers (1-10) and counters change according to their combination.

1. *Hiragana* indicate the sound changes in numbers, and alphabets show the changes in the initial consonant of counters.
2. ( ) means that the change is optional.
3. An empty box means no sound change occurs.

k→g	s	s→z	t	special vocabulary for numbers			
いっ	いっ	いっ	いっ	ひとつ	ついたち	ひとり	1
				ふたつ	ふつか	ふたり	2
g		z		みっつ	みっか		3
				よっつ	よっか		4
				いつつ	いつか		5
ろっ				むっつ	むいか		6
				ななつ	なのか		7
はっ	はっ	はっ	はっ	やっつ	ようか		8
				ここのつ	ここのか		9
じゅっ じっ	じゅっ じっ	じゅっ じっ	じゅっ じっ	とお	とおか		10
g		z		いくつ			how many
～階 *floor* ～軒 *houses*	～セント *cents* ～週間 *weeks* ～冊 *books* ～歳 *years of age*	～足 *shoes* ～千 *thousand*	～通 *letters* ～丁目 *street address*	*small items* *years of age* cf. はたち (20 years old)	*date* cf. じゅうよっか (14) はつか (20) にじゅうよっか (24) なんにち (how many)	*people* cf. ～人 (three or more people)	

活用表 Conjugation Chart
かつ よう ひょう

verb types	dictionary forms	long forms (*masu*) (L.3)	*te*-forms (L.6)	short past (L.9)	short present neg. (L.8)	short past neg. (L.9)
irr.	する	します	して	した	しない	しなかった
irr.	くる	きます	きて	きた	こない	こなかった
ru	たべる	〜ます	〜て	〜た	〜ない	〜なかった
u	かう	〜います	〜って	〜った	〜わない	〜わなかった
u	まつ	〜ちます	〜って	〜った	〜たない	〜たなかった
u	とる	〜ります	〜って	〜った	〜らない	〜らなかった
u	ある	〜ります	〜って	〜った	*ない	*なかった
u	よむ	〜みます	〜んで	〜んだ	〜まない	〜まなかった
u	あそぶ	〜びます	〜んで	〜んだ	〜ばない	〜ばなかった
u	しぬ	〜にます	〜んで	〜んだ	〜なない	〜ななかった
u	かく	〜きます	〜いて	〜いた	〜かない	〜かなかった
u	いく	〜きます	*〜って	*〜った	〜かない	〜かなかった
u	いそぐ	〜ぎます	〜いで	〜いだ	〜がない	〜がなかった
u	はなす	〜します	〜して	〜した	〜さない	〜さなかった

The forms with * are exceptions.

potential (L.13)	volitional (L.15)	ば-forms (L.18)	passive (L.21)	causative (L.22)	causative-passive (L.23)
できる	しよう	すれば	される	させる	させられる
こられる	こよう	くれば	こられる	こさせる	こさせられる
〜られる	〜よう	〜れば	〜られる	〜させる	〜させられる
〜える	〜おう	〜えば	〜われる	〜わせる	〜わされる
〜てる	〜とう	〜てば	〜たれる	〜たせる	〜たされる
〜れる	〜ろう	〜れば	〜られる	〜らせる	〜らされる
		〜れば			
〜める	〜もう	〜めば	〜まれる	〜ませる	〜まされる
〜べる	〜ぼう	〜べば	〜ばれる	〜ばせる	〜ばされる
〜ねる	〜のう	〜ねば	〜なれる	〜なせる	〜なされる
〜ける	〜こう	〜けば	〜かれる	〜かせる	〜かされる
〜ける	〜こう	〜けば	〜かれる	〜かせる	〜かされる
〜げる	〜ごう	〜げば	〜がれる	〜がせる	〜がされる
〜せる	〜そう	〜せば	〜される	〜させる	〜させられる